the persistence of
POLYGAMY

JOSEPH SMITH and the origins of MORMON POLYGAMY

the persistence of POLYGAMY

JOSEPH SMITH and the origins of MORMON POLYGAMY

edited by NEWELL G. BRINGHURST and CRAIG L. FOSTER

JOHN WHITMER BOOKS
Independence, Missouri

© 2010 BY THE JOHN WHITMER HISTORICAL ASSOCIATION

Published by John Whitmer Books
John Whitmer Books is a trademark of the John Whitmer Historical Association

ISBN: 1-934901-13-x
ISBN13: 978-1-934901-13-7

Second printing with corrections

View our complete catalog online at www.JohnWhitmerBooks.com
Learn more about the John Whitmer Historical Association at www.JWHA.info

Cover and interior design and typesetting by John Hamer

PRINTED IN THE UNITED STATES OF AMERICA

To the women in our families who sacrificed so much for their belief in "the Principle"

Newell G. Bringhurst's two great-great-grandmothers

JESSIE EDDENS TRIPP
(1839–1923)
4th wife of Enoch Bartlett Tripp

MARY ELLEN MAYNE
(1847–1897)
2nd wife of Frederick Albert Cooper

And Craig L. Foster's great-grandmother

SARAH BENNETT
(1862–1934)
5th wife of William George Butler

Table of Contents

Foreword *by Linda King Newell* ix

Introduction *by Newell G. Bringhurst and Craig L. Foster* 1

Mormon Polygamy before Nauvoo? The Relationship of Joseph Smith and Fanny Alger *by Don Bradley* 14

Section 132 of the LDS Doctrine and Covenants: Its Complex Contents and Controversial Legacy *by Newell G. Bringhurst* 59

Doctrine and Covenants Section 132 and Joseph Smith's Expanding Concept of Family *by Craig L. Foster* 87

Joseph Smith and the Puzzlement of "Polyandry" *by Brian C. Hales* 99

The Age of Joseph Smith's Plural Wives in Social and Demographic Context *by Craig L. Foster, David Keller, and Gregory L. Smith* 152

Early Marriage in the New England and Northeastern States, and in Mormon Polygamy: What Was the Norm? *by Todd M. Compton* 184

Joseph Smith, the Question of Polygamous Offspring, and DNA Analysis *by Ugo A. Perego* 233

RLDS Church Reaction to the LDS Doctrine and Covenants' Section 132: Conflicting Responses and Changing Perceptions *by Newell G. Bringhurst* 257

Afterword *by Jessie L. Embry* 284

Appendix: Joseph Smith's Plural Wives: Total Number, Reasons for, and Methods of Selection 290

About the Contributors 299

Foreword

by Linda King Newell

Given the plethora of books, articles and essays dealing with Mormon polygamy, one could ask, "What more is there to say?" Newell G. Bringhurst and Craig L. Foster, the editors of *The Persistence of Polygamy: Joseph Smith and the Origins of Mormon Polygamy*, confidently answer, "A lot." The essays in this, the first in a three-volume history on Mormon polygamy, prove them right. Projecting their own scholarly research over the groundwork of others, each of the authors of the eight essays herein present new details and insights to some of the persistent questions that revolve around the beginnings of the doctrine of plural marriage as practiced in the Church of Jesus Christ of Latter-day Saints. From the multitude of historical documents available to researchers, they all have gleaned facts that help answer many of these questions.

This volume represents an impersonal treatment. What the authors do not do is wring the human reaction from the body of evidence—the emotional responses left behind in diaries, journals and letters—and bring it to bear on these issues. From the earliest hints of its presence in Mormonism, plural marriage evoked feelings of anger, caution, hostility, anxiety, sorrow, joy, rejection, and acceptance. Some of the participants in this ongoing drama—both men and women—experienced all of these feelings. Plural marriage was difficult, even in the early Utah pioneer period when there were rules that protected women in certain cases, and it was practiced openly as doctrine within the larger church membership. In contrast, Nauvoo polygamy was difficult at best and wrenching at its worst. Woman who married in secret ceremonies to already married men lived in secret. They could not celebrate or even acknowledge their union. If they became pregnant, they remained secreted in attics away from the probing public eye. It became a divisive issue between husband and wife, and in the Women's Relief Society, where Joseph Smith himself had charged the women to look after the morals of the community. Polygamy affected women most profoundly and their voices are nearly absent in this anthology.

That said, the essays herein provide important insights into the nature of the practice and help us sort out the various claims and interpretations of the historical record. The book progresses in a more-or-less chronological approach, beginning with the earliest rumors of Joseph Smith Jr.'s involvement with women other than his legal wife, Emma Hale, and ending with a study of the view taken by members of the Reorganized Church of Jesus Christ of Latter Day Saints (now Community of Christ) from the 1860s to the present.

Don Bradley in "Mormon Polygamy Before Nauvoo? The Relationship of Joseph Smith and Fanny Alger" examines the various accounts pertaining to Joseph Smith's involvement with Alger, and analyzes them thoroughly and insightfully. In pursuing the Fanny Alger story, he asks three questions: "*Did* it occur? If so, *when* did it occur? And, most importantly, was it a *marriage* or an *affair*?" Bradley then proceeds to look at every aspect of the stories that have been handed down, what other writers have concluded about these accounts, and whether or not their conclusions stand up under his close scrutiny. His research in both primary and secondary sources is extensive and his analysis deft.

The two essays that follow look in detail at the written revelation commanding the introduction of "celestial marriage," "the new and everlasting covenant," or, the more commonly understood term, polygamy. Newell G. Bringhurst's title, "Section 132 of the LDS Doctrine and Covenants: Its Complex Contents and Controversial Legacy," is an apt capsulation and analysis of the document that launched the heretofore private teachings of plural marriage into a canonized form that is still part of LDS scripture. He breaks the revelation into its basic admonitions and instructions, and examines those parts individually, both through related historical sources and through the interpretations of other historians and writers. Bringhurst not only dissects the text of Section 132 of the Doctrine and Covenants, but carries the discussion through Church President Wilford Woodruff's 1890 Manifesto, to an "Official Statement," written in 1933 by J. Reuben Clark of the LDS First Presidency, and known as the Final Manifesto. He ends by looking at the revelation's impact on today's Mormon Fundamentalist groups that still hold the doctrine as an active tenet of their core beliefs.

Craig L. Foster takes a different route with his essay "Doctrine and Covenants Section 132 and Joseph Smith's Expanding Concept of Family," by discussing the "kinship-based covenant system" embedded in the revelation. He lays a foundation by exploring the importance of kinship in British and early American cultures, then shows how Joseph Smith's revelations in both Kirtland and Nauvoo provided an increasingly complex doctrinal basis for those family ties to continue after death and into the eternities. Church members were assured that their loved ones who had died before accepting being baptized by immersion could have that saving ordinance done for them by proxy here on earth. The final step is to tie families together throughout eternity through the "new and everlasting covenant" of marriage as contained in Section 132 of the Doctrine and Covenants. Only through obedience to that covenant could Latter-day Saints come forth on the morning of the first resurrection, receive "the glory of all things," and be sealed to their families for eternity. Foster skillfully leads the reader through this doctrinal progression.

The actual practice of celestial marriage took some unsettling turns with Joseph Smith's marriages to eleven women who already had husbands. These marriages where women have more than one husband are called polyandry. Brian C. Hales delves into this issue in his essay, "Joseph Smith and the Puzzlement of 'Polyandry.'" He explores the marital circumstances of each of these women, asking similar questions about their ties to Joseph Smith: What kind of marriages were these? Were they "ceremonial polyandry?" Were the women sealed to Joseph for eternity only, or did they include "sexual polyandry," wherein there was a physical relationship? What were the reactions of the women's legal husbands to their wives' marriages to Joseph Smith? And how does sexual polyandry fit into LDS theology? These are probing questions and Hales examines them with a non-judgmental probing of their implications.

Two essays deal with polygamous marriages that involve teenage brides as young as fourteen. The first, "The Age of Joseph Smith's Plural Wives in Social and Demographic Context," by Craig L. Foster, David Keller, and Gregory L. Smith, a broad and in-depth statistical examination of marriage ages throughout frontier America, goes on to compare that data with early Mormon polygamous marriages in general, and with those of Joseph Smith Jr. specifically. The authors begin with establishing what they determined to be the most accurate list of Joseph Smith's plural wives, their ages, and time of marriage to him. The discussion then moves to an overview of the more sensational modern-day reactions to marital unions involving teenage girls. From there they look at long-term marriage trends, legal traditions for marriage ages, cultural and economic factors, and regional marriage patterns in various areas of nineteenth century America.

The second essay on this topic is Todd M. Compton's, "Early Marriage in the New England and Northeastern States, and in Mormon Polygamy: What Was the Norm?" Compton addresses some of the same issues as Foster, Keller, and Smith, but in a more analytic narrative. He also looks more closely at nineteenth-century demographics of polygamy in Utah, Arizona, Idaho, and Canada. An often used reason for the establishment of plural marriage is that there were more women than men and plural marriage provided an opportunity for these "extra" women to fulfill their desire for marriage and children. In fact, the female-male ratio in the early LDS Church was very nearly equal. In the Mormon colonies on the western frontier, polygamy had cut into the pool of the population of unmarried women so drastically that in the town of Manti in 1860, "there were three unmarried males for every unmarried female." This imbalance was not unusual—and it is not just specific to that area or era. Today's Fundamentalist Church of Jesus Christ of Latter Day Saints (FLDS) struggles with the same issue and has tried to solve it by forcing scores of teenage boys out of the community, leaving them to fend for themselves in a modern society that they are ill-equipped to negotiate. Some of Compton's conclusions are similar to those of Foster, Smith, and Keller. But he also differs with them on others, and makes the case that there are factors beyond statistics that can sway an argument.

One of the most controversial topics having to do with Joseph Smith's plural wives is whether they involved sexual relationships and did they have children born to him as a result of these marriages. Ugo A. Perego examines this quagmire of opinion that prevailed from early LDS history to the modern-day science of DNA testing. At the outset, the reader assumes the method to be straightforward and conclusive. Not so. Perego not only demonstrates how extremely complicated the science of establishing blood relationships through DNA can be, but how important it is to recognize both the limitations and strengths of such a study. First, he establishes fourteen possible offspring of Joseph Smith by his plural wives, and gives a brief history of each of them and what historical information exists to tie them to Smith. Of the fourteen, eight were male, four were female, and two he identifies as "alleged son or daughter." Perego is able to draw some indisputable conclusions as to the paternity of some of these children, but not all of them. Either way, his work provides an important landmark in the study of plural marriage.

The last essay of this volume is by Newell G. Bringhurst: "RLDS Church Reaction to the LDS Doctrine and Covenants' Section 132: Conflicting Responses and Changing Perceptions." None of Joseph Smith's children with his legal wife Emma Hale Smith ended up with the main body of the LDS Church in Utah. Of those who lived to adulthood, Julia Murdock (the adopted twin daughter) became a Catholic, Frederick Granger Williams Smith died before his brothers became affiliated with the Reorganization, and the other three sons, Joseph Smith III, Alexander Hale Smith, and David Hyrum Smith, assumed leadership positions within the Reorganization. Raised on the belief that Brigham Young was the author of Mormon polygamy, the three Smiths refused to believe that their father had taken plural wives. Bringhurst tells the story of the Smith family's attempts to keep that belief intact, with their mother's own denial of their father's involvement stoking the coals of contradiction, not only in their own minds but among rank-and-file members of the RLDS Church. He then follows the trail of approach-avoidance to the issue from the sons' early missions to Utah—the indisputable information they encountered from and about women their father had taken as plural wives—to the attitudes and beliefs of modern Community of Christ members. Bringhurst brings together a number of sources that will be unfamiliar to many LDS readers and adds his insightful interpretations of the dilemma and sometimes crises of faith amongst the RLDS membership over this issue.

As the reader moves forward through this volume, he/she will develop an increased understanding of the complexity of the doctrine of plural marriage, as well as a healthy skepticism for glibly drawn conclusions. These essays are certainly not the last word on the study of this thorny practice—as the next two volumes will surely attest.

Introduction[1]

BY NEWELL G. BRINGHURST AND CRAIG L. FOSTER

POLYGAMY HAS BEEN a persistent theme within Mormonism from the founding of what became known as the Church of Jesus Christ of Latter-day Saints in 1830 down to the present.[2] Over the years Mormon involvement with plural marriage evolved through three distinct phases. The first, lasting from 1830 to 1844, focused on Joseph Smith, who inaugurated and promoted the practice through his role as Mormon prophet, seer, and revelator. The second phase, lasting from 1844 until 1890, involved the continuation of plural marriage among a number of the Latter Day Saint factions that emerged following Joseph Smith's death—the most prominent being the Utah-based LDS Church under the leadership of Brigham Young. The third phase, which commenced

---

1. The editors gratefully acknowledge the assistance of Jessie Embry, Lawrence Foster, Brian Hales, and Steven Bringhurst with the composition of this introduction.
2. When first founded in April 1830, this organization was known as the "Church of Christ." In 1835, it was renamed "Church of the Latter Day Saints" and then in 1838, it adopted the name "Church of Jesus Christ of Latter Day Saints." Standardized as "The Church of Jesus Christ of Latter-day Saints," this final version continues to be the name of the largest organization tracing its origin to Joseph Smith, the Utah-based LDS Church.

with the 1890 Manifesto and ended with the two subsequent manifestos, called for the suspension of new polygamous marriages, leading to the emergence of Mormon Fundamentalism.

Throughout this period, literally hundreds of books, both fiction and non-fiction, have been written on the topic of Mormon polygamy. In recent years, moreover, a number of studies written by scholars well-versed in primary and secondary literature have appeared in print.[3] Four important books focus on the polygamous activities of Mormonism's founder, Joseph Smith, namely: Lawrence Foster's *Religion and Sexuality*; Linda King Newell's and Valeen Tippetts Avery's *Mormon Enigma: Emma Hale Smith, Prophet's Wife, "Elect Lady," Polygamy's Foe*; Todd Compton's *In Sacred Loneliness: The Plural Wives of Joseph Smith*; and most recently, George D. Smith's *Nauvoo Polygamy: "…but we call it celestial marriage."*[4] Also considering Smith's involvement with plural marriage from contrasting biographical perspectives are: Fawn M. Brodie's *No Man Knows My History: The Life of Joseph Smith*; Donna Hill's *Joseph Smith: The First Mormon*; and Richard Lyman Bushman's *Joseph Smith: Rough Stone Rolling*.[5]

---

3. On the general topic of plural marriage, the most important scholarly works include: Richard S. Van Wagoner, *Mormon Polygamy: A History* (Salt Lake City: Signature Books, 1986); Jessie L. Embry, *Mormon Polygamous Families, Life in the Principle* (Salt Lake City: University of Utah Press, 1987) ; B. Carmon Hardy, *Solemn Covenant: The Mormon Polygamous Passage* (Urbana, Illinois: University of Illinois Press, 1992); Kathryn M. Daynes, *More Wives than One: Transformation of the Mormon Marriage System, 1840–1910* (Urbana, Illinois: University of Illinois Press, 2001); Sarah Barringer Gordon, *The Mormon Question: Polygamy and Constitutional Conflict in Nineteenth Century America* (Chapel Hill, North Carolina: University of North Carolina Press, 2002); B. Carmon Hardy, *Doing the Works of Abraham : Mormon Polygamy, Its origins, practice, and decline* (Norman Oklahoma: The Arthur H. Clark Co.,2007); and Jessie L. Embry, *Mormons & Polygamy: Setting the Record Straight* (Orem, UT: Millennial Press, 2007).

4. Lawrence Foster, *Religion and Sexuality: Three American Communal Experiments of the Nineteenth Century* (New York: Oxford University Press, 1981); Linda King Newell and Valeen Tippetts Avery, *Mormon Enigma: Emma Hale Smith, Prophet's Wife, "Elect Lady," Polygamy's Foe* (New York: Doubleday & Co., 1985); Todd Compton, *In Sacred Loneliness: The Plural Wives of Joseph Smith* (Salt Lake City: Signature Books, 1997); George D. Smith, *Nauvoo Polygamy:… but we call it celestial marriage* (Salt Lake City: Signature Books, 2008). Also worth noting is a significant unpublished work, Danel W. Bachman, "A Study of the Mormon Practice of Plural Marriage Before the Death of Joseph Smith," (Master's Thesis, Purdue University, 1976). And forthcoming in 2011 is a two volume work by Brian C. Hales, *Joseph Smith's Polygamy: History*; and *Joseph Smith's Polygamy: Theology*, both volumes to be published by Greg Kofford Books.

5. Fawn M. Brodie, *No Man Knows My History: The Life of Joseph Smith, The Mormon Prophet* (New York: Alfred A. Knopf, 1945); Donna Hill, *Joseph Smith: The First Mormon* (Garden City,

Given these many studies, the obvious question is: why another book dealing with Mormon polygamy? First, this anthology, focusing on Joseph Smith, provides fresh insights on a number of aspects of this practice heretofore neglected and/or inadequately examined. Second, the volume's eight essays provide a different perspective in that each is an original, never-before-published work, written by a scholar with expertise and/or deep interest in the particular topic under consideration. Third, the book utilizes a point/counterpoint format in evaluating differing, often conflicting viewpoints on various controversial topics. And finally, the essays in this volume utilize a variety of methodologies. In addition to a traditional historical narrative, this interdisciplinary study includes quantitative statistical analysis and data drawn from the field of physical science.

Joseph Smith's interest in, and ultimate involvement with, plural marriage manifested itself throughout the fourteen-year period that he led the Mormon movement. Such concern, in fact, predated the formal organization of the church in April 1830, as reflected through those pages of the Book of Mormon that condemned the practice. As dictated by Smith, specific verses of this scriptural work excoriated polygamy, linking it with "fornication," "whoredoms," and "problems of family disorganization."[6] According to the Book of Mormon:

> Behold, David and Solomon truly had many wives and concubines, which thing was abominable before me, saith the Lord...Wherefore, I the Lord God, will not suffer that this people shall do like unto them of old...for there shall not any man among you have save it be one wife: and concubines he shall have none.[7]

Yet just three verses later this same work suggests the possibility that plural marriage might be introduced in the future, declaring "For if I will, saith the Lord of Hosts, raise up seed unto me, I will command my people; otherwise they shall hearken unto these things."[8]

New York: Doubleday & Co., 1977); Richard L. Bushman, *Joseph Smith: Rough Stone Rolling* (New York: Alfred A. Knopf, 2005).

6. Specific Book of Mormon anti-polygamous passages include Jacob 1:15; Jacob 2:31–34, 35–37, 41, 45–47; 2:23, 24, 26, 27, 28, 32, 35; 2:54–55; Mosiah 7:2, 7, 20; and Ether 4:48.

7. Book of Mormon, Jacob 2:27

8. Ibid., Jacob 2:30

In the wake of the Book of Mormon's publication, Smith's views shifted to a more favorable position regarding plural marriage. He "first became convinced that polygamy should be reintroduced" in early 1831 while working on his inspired revision of the Old Testament.[9] Specifically, "it was the translation of Genesis, the Abrahamic passages" that, according to one scholar, "caused Joseph to pray about polygamy in February 1831 and receive his first revelations on the topic."[10] Some six months later, a July 1831 revelation advocated the actual practice of plural marriage by married Mormon elders preaching amongst the American Indians along the western frontier. It proclaimed "that in time, ye should take unto you wives of the Lamanites and Nephites that their posterity may become white, delightsome and just…"[11]

During this period, moreover, it was rumored that Joseph Smith himself was involved with women other than his wife, Emma Hale. As early as 1830, an unsympathetic contemporary account spoke of Smith's "attempt to seduce Elizabeth Winters, a friend of Emma's in Harmony, Pennsylvania."[12] And the following year, after Smith had moved to Kirtland, Ohio, critics of the church suggested that the Mormon leader had engaged in an "improper association" with Nancy Marinda Johnson.[13]

More controversial was Joseph Smith's relationship with Fanny Alger, a nineteen-year-old servant, who resided with the Smith family during the mid-1830s. In the first essay in this volume, entitled "Mormon Polygamy before Nauvoo? The Relationship of Joseph Smith and Fanny Alger," Don Bradley examines the controversy surrounding their clandestine relationship, focusing on three central questions: factuality, timing, and the nature of the relationship. Specifically, did it occur? If so,

---

9. As asserted by Foster in *Religion and Sexuality*, 134.

10. Compton, *In Sacred Loneliness*, 10. Providing further insight into this development is Danel Bachman, "A Study of the Mormon Practice of Plural Marriage Before the Death of Joseph Smith," 47–103.

11. Joseph Smith's July 17, 1831, Revelation, in William Wines Phelps to Brigham Young, August 12, 1861, Revelation Collection, LDS Archives. "This revelation is not found in the LDS Church's official canon of revelations. It is known from two manuscript copies prepared by William Wines Phelps (1792–1872) who was present when it was given on July 17, 1831, and recalled the event in this letter to Brigham Young." This according to Hardy, *Doing the Works of Abraham*, 36, ff. 13.

12. As described in Bushman, *Joseph Smith*, 323.

13. As noted in Newell and Tippets Avery, *Mormon Enigma*, 65. Some scholars, like Brian Hales, have questioned the reliability of these accusations. See: Brian C. Hales, "Fanny Alger and Joseph Smith's Pre-Nauvoo Reputation," *Journal of Mormon History* 35 (Fall 2009): 90–112.

when did it occur? And most importantly, was it a marriage or an affair? Bradley considers both the pros and cons of these three questions in exploring the complex nature of the interaction between Joseph Smith and Fanny Alger.

It has also been debated whether Joseph Smith may have taken a second plural wife during the 1830s, Lucinda Pendleton Morgan Harris. According to at least two scholars, Smith married Harris, the widow of the famous anti-Mason martyr, William Morgan, and later the wife of George Washington Harris, a Latter Day Saint leader and close friend of Joseph Smith. This marriage allegedly took place in 1838, following the Mormon leader's migration from Kirtland, Ohio, to Far West, Missouri.[14]

Joseph Smith's involvement in polygamy intensified following the Mormon expulsion from Missouri in 1839–40 and the founding of Nauvoo, Illinois, as the church's principal gathering place. Commencing in April 1841 with Smith's marriage to Louisa Beaman, in his first plural marriage ceremony attested to by witnesses, and continuing over the next three years, the Mormon leader persuaded an estimated "thirty additional women" to enter into plural marriage with him, although the precise number is open to debate.[15] And under Smith's direction, "some thirty" of the Mormon leader's most trusted, loyal male followers took plural wives of their own.[16]

Also in dispute are Joseph Smith's precise motives for implementing plural marriage. On a basic level, it has been argued that Smith was "an oversexed individual—a lusty, good-natured libertine, perhaps—who

---

14. Compton, *In Sacred Loneliness*, 43–54; Brodie, *No Man Knows My History*, 449–50. George D. Smith in his *Nauvoo Polygamy*, 621, while agreeing with both Compton and Brodie that Lucinda Pendleton Morgan Harris entered into polygamy with Joseph Smith, asserts they did not marry until January 17, 1842.

15. This number of plural wives cited by Bushman, *Joseph Smith*, 437. As for actual number of Smith's wives, the "numbers vary widely. The totals range from 27 as reported by Andrew Jenson, an Assistant LDS Church Historian, to a grand total of 84 reported by independent historian Stanley S. Ivins. In between are 48 reported by controversial Joseph Smith biographer, Fawn M. Brodie, and 36 by historian D. Michael Quinn, as reported by Jessie Embry, *Mormons & Polygamy*, 33. Questions surrounding the debate over the precise number of women married to Joseph Smith are discussed in an essay presented in Appendix I at the end of this volume.

16. Smith, *Nauvoo Polygamy*, 50–51. Daynes, *More Wives Than One*, 32, reports the number as twenty nine.

was trying rationalize his libertine propensities."[17] Or in the words of controversial Joseph Smith biographer Fawn M. Brodie:

> Monogamy seemed to [Smith]—as it has seemed to many men who have not stopped loving their wives, but who have grown weary of connubial exclusiveness—an intolerably circumscribed way of life… But Joseph was no careless libertine, who could be content with clandestine mistresses. There was too much of the Puritan in him, and he could not rest until he had redefined the nature of sin and erected a stupendous theological edifice to support his new theories on marriage.[18]

Yet historian Lawrence Foster counters that such an explanation "is too simple," even though he concedes that "Smith was unquestionably a handsome, dynamic leader with great physical and intellectual vitality" whose "many statements reveal a basically positive attitude toward sexual expression, as well as the difficulty he had in sometimes keeping his impulses in check."[19]

It has also been suggested that Smith's introduction of polygamy was the product of "psychological problems" brought on by behavior as "a deeply disturbed individual with paranoid obsessions."[20] William Morain has argued that Smith's "perverse behavior…[which] compelled him to degrade women into sexual objects and that prevented him from enjoying the true intimacy of one-and-one relationship that most adults ultimately enjoy" was rooted in childhood trauma, specifically a major operation on his leg when he was just seven.[21] Also assessing Smith's behavior from a psycho-biographical perspective is Robert D. Anderson, who argues that the Mormon leader's introduction of polygamy was the product of his "narcissistic personality" manifested in an "emotional life" that was "shallow," with his polygamous activities reflective of minimal "empathy for the feelings of others."[22] And Lawrence Foster has suggested, elaborating on the reflection of Mormon psychiatrist Jess Groesbeck,

---

17. Foster, *Religion and Sexuality*, 126..
18. Brodie, *No Man Knows My History*, 297.
19. Foster, *Religion and Sexuality*, 126.
20. Embry, *Mormons & Polygamy*, 32–33; Foster, *Religion and Sexuality*, 127.
21. William D. Morain, *The Sword of Laban: Joseph Smith and the Dissociated Mind* (Washington D.C.: The American Psychiatric Press, 1998), 193–207.
22. Robert D. Anderson, *Inside the Mind of Joseph Smith: Psychobiography and the Book of Mormon* (Salt Lake City: Signature Books, 1999), 127–31.

that Smith's embrace of plural marriage appeared to be associated with activity that seemed "strikingly similar to behavior that psychiatrists associate with manic-depressive syndromes."[23] Yet as Foster himself admits "psychological reductionist approaches are not fully satisfactory."[24] Indeed, the hazards of trying to get into a dead person's psyche are obvious.

Moving beyond theories concerned with personal behavior, there are indications that Smith was influenced as much, if not more, by outside factors; among the most important was social ferment in the larger antebellum American society of his time. Plural marriage has been characterized as "an attempt to restore earlier patriarchal patterns in marriage" then believed to be under attack. In the words of Lawrence Foster, the practice "at the deepest level" represented "fundamental protest against the careless individualism of romantic love, which seemed to threaten the very roots of family life and social solidarity."[25] On another level, it appears that the introduction of Mormon polygamy, with its emphasis on male dominance, represented a counter-reaction against the contemporary women's rights movement then sweeping the nation, which ultimately culminated in the Seneca Falls Conference of 1848.[26] Mormon concern over such developments was reflected in an 1842 pamphlet entitled *The Peace Maker, or The Doctrines of the Millennium*, authored by Udney Hay Jacob, who was identified as "An Israelite, and a Shepherd of Israel" and published by "J. Smith, Printer." Specifically *The Peace Maker* argued that "a shift in the locus of [patriarchal] authority had led to a decline of the status of the father to the benefit of his inner-directed children" and insisted that "patriarchal order in the home must be restored 'if social chaos is to be avoided.'"[27]

---

23. Lawrence Foster, "The Psychology of Religious Genius: Joseph Smith and the Origins of New Religious Movements," 190 as reprinted in Bryan Waterman, ed., *The Prophet Puzzle: Interpretative Essays on Joseph Smith* (Salt Lake City: Signature Books, 1999.)
24. Foster, *Religion and Sexuality*, 127.
25. Ibid., 139.
26. For two discussions of the emerging women's rights movement see: Nancy F. Cott, *The Grounding of Modern Feminism* (1987); and William L. O'Neill, *Feminism in America* (1969: 2nd ed., 1989).
27. As quoted in Klaus J. Hansen, *Mormonism and the American Experience* (Chicago: University of Chicago Press, 1981) 164, who erroneously attributes such ideas directly to Joseph Smith, himself. The actual author of *The Peace Maker* was Udney Hay Jacob identified in the pamphlet in the following enigmatic terms: "The author of this work is not a Mormon, although it

Yet another related factor may have also affected Smith: the prevalence of various forms of marital experimentation in America at large during this period, particularly in the upstate New York environment where he had grown up. Among the more controversial of such groups were the celibate Shakers, founded by Ann Lee, in which men and women were strictly separated from each other but lived in the same dwelling houses; and the Oneida Community, founded by John Humphrey Noyes, which practiced a form of "complex marriage" in which all adult members of the community were considered heterosexually married to each other in what was viewed as "an enlarged family."[28]

Within Mormonism itself it has been theorized that plural marriage served as a supreme test of loyalty to Joseph Smith. Kathryn M. Daynes argues that such loyalty became a "vital issue to members of the church" particularly in the wake of pervasive dissent and division within Mormonism during the late 1830s, first in Kirtland, Ohio, and then at Far West, Missouri.[29] Accepting Joseph Smith's directive to enter polygamy "caused considerable anguish" because "it was secret and because it countered the monogamous tradition in the Western world and within the church in its earliest days." Thus acceptance of the principle "was a dramatic sign of loyalty to the community's leaders," particularly Joseph Smith.[30] In this regard, Klaus J. Hansen points out that plural marriage "irrevocably tied its practitioners to Mormonism. For polygamists it was virtually impossible to defect from the kingdom."[31]

Yet another related factor apparently prompted Joseph Smith's advocacy of plural marriage—specifically, it served "as a means of strengthening kinship relations" among his followers while affirming "social solidar-

---

is printed by their press. It was most convenient. But the public will soon find out what he is, by his work." For a full discussion of this work see: Lawrence Foster, "A Little-known Defense of Polygamy from the Mormon Press in 1842," *Dialogue: A Journal of Mormon Thought* 9 (Winter 1974): 26

28. As with his discussion of the Mormons, Lawrence Foster's, *Religion and Sexuality*, 21–122, represents the most complete discussion of the marital practices of these two groups. For a somewhat different perspective on the Shakers and Oneida Community as well as the Mormons see: Louis J. Kern, *An Ordered Love: Sex Roles and Sexuality in Victorian Utopias—the Shakers, the Mormons, and the Oneida Community* (Chapel Hill, North Carolina: The University of North Carolina Press, 1981).

29. Daynes, *More Wives Than One*, 24.

30. Ibid., 26.

31. Hansen, *Mormonism and the American Experience*, 157–58.

ity" within the larger Mormon movement.³² The practice, in the words of Klaus J. Hansen, "was part of a larger effort to reestablish social cohesion and kinship ties in a socially and intellectually disordered environment."³³ Or as John L. Brooke has stated, "Just as baptism for the dead and eternal marriage reinforced a sacred kinship, plural marriage worked to weld the Mormon elite into a familial, organic whole, irreconcilably setting them apart for their separate purpose."³⁴ At least eight of the Mormon leader's plural marriages have been classified as "dynastic," that is, establishing kinship through family relationships between Smith and other important Mormon leaders and/or close associates.³⁵

Even more important in inspiring Joseph Smith's introduction of polygamy was the evolution of Mormon theology, which reached a critical stage of development by the early 1840s. Smith introduced a number of important doctrinal concepts, including sacred, secret temple ceremonies as essential for complete Mormon salvation, along with several revolutionary concepts concerning the nature of God and humankind's own relationship with the supernatural. Accordingly, Mormons viewed God as not only anthropomorphic (humanlike in basic form and substance) but as a plurality of distinct persons in a divine community. In other words, while advocating the worship of this single, solitary anthropomorphic God, Smith also promoted the existence of a plurality of gods, specifically the existence of numerous divine beings throughout the total expanse of the universe. He, moreover, preached an even more radical concept that humans currently living on the earth had the potential to become like God, ultimately assuming dominion over worlds of their own through a process known as "eternal progression."³⁶ This concept was succinctly summed up in poetic fashion by important Mormon leader and future LDS Church president Lorenzo Snow as follows: "As

---

32. Foster, *Religion and Sexuality*, 139–40.
33. Hansen, *Mormonism and the American Experience*, 161.
34. John L. Brooke, *The Refiner's Fire: The Making of Mormon Cosmology, 1644–1844* (New York City: Cambridge University Press, 1994), 266.
35. As asserted by Todd Compton, *In Sacred Loneliness: The Plural Wives of Joseph Smith*, 12. Two other discussions of Mormon dynastic marriages are: D. Michael Quinn, *The Mormon Hierarchy: Extensions of Power* (Salt Lake City: Signature Books, 1997); 178–90; Brooke, *The Refiner's Fire*. 265–66. For an extensive discussion of the dynastic implications of Joseph Smith's plural marriages see Appendix A at the end of this volume.
36. Foster, *Religion and Sexuality*, 143–44, 179.

man is, God once was. As God is, man may become."³⁷ Ultimate godhood, however, could be secured only through the strict adherence to various Mormon ordinances and practices, particularly at this time, plural marriage. It was believed by many that the practice of plural marriage, moreover, would enable faithful Mormon males to produce the largest possible number of offspring subject to their authority in the hereafter, thereby further enhancing their godlike status.³⁸

Further legitimizing such theological motives was the fact that Joseph Smith both "in public and private…spoke as if guided by God," an assertion made by Richard L. Bushman, who further states that the Mormon leader viewed God "as both kind and terrible." Such a perspective is reflected in the divine mandate ordering Smith to practice polygamy. According to the recollections of a number of individuals close to the Mormon leader, Smith was visited by an angel of the Lord who approached him on three different occasions with "drawn sword" in hand commanding him to "obey the principle" or suffer divine retribution.³⁹

This array of crucial theological developments, culminating in Mormon polygamy, was most succinctly expressed in Joseph Smith's July 1843 revelation pertaining to the "New and Everlasting Covenant," ultimately canonized as Section 132 in the LDS Doctrine and Covenants. This, among the most seminal of Smith's revelations, is discussed in a series of three different essays in this volume. In the first, "Section 132 of the LDS Doctrine and Covenants: Its Complex Contents and Controversial Legacy," Newell G. Bringhurst describes the revelation's origins, its various provisions, and the changing ways in which it has been interpreted by various leaders and spokesmen within the LDS Church from the time of its initial public disclosure in 1852 down to the present. In the second, "Doctrine and Covenants Section 132 and Joseph Smith's Expanding Concept of Family," Craig L. Foster asserts the central importance of family as a prime motivating factor and reason for the revelation. In es-

---

37. Lorenzo Snow, as quoted in Thomas C. Romney, *The Life of Lorenzo Snow* (Salt Lake City: Deseret News Press, 1955), 46.

38. Lawrence Foster's *Religion and Sexuality*, 143–44, 179, provides a brief, effective overview of such theological developments. Richard L. Bushman, in his *Joseph Smith*, 417–58, provides a more extensive discussion of Joseph Smith's active role in this process.

39. Bushman, *Joseph Smith*, 437–38. Brian Hales has identified twenty retrospective accounts describing an angel with a drawn sword commanding Joseph Smith to practice plural marriage. See Hales, "The Angel with a Sword," *Mormon Historical Studies* (forthcoming).

sence, the revelation, as stated in a key verse, operated as divine "law" or "commandment" given by God "before the foundation of the world."⁴⁰ In turn, it facilitated Joseph Smith's "control over the marriage of church members, in the interest of their salvation" while serving as an "essential prerequisite to achievement of the kingdom of God."⁴¹

By contrast, in a third essay, "RLDS Church Reaction to the LDS Doctrine and Covenants, Section 132: Conflicting Responses and Changing Perceptions," Newell G. Bringhurst traces varying reactions to the revelation by leaders and spokesmen within the Midwestern-based Reorganized Church of Jesus Christ of Latter Day Saints (now known as the Community of Christ), who dismissed the revelation as not produced by Joseph Smith but as a "spurious document" concocted following Smith's death by Utah Mormon leaders under the direction of Brigham Young.

A group of four essays explores three controversial topics surrounding Joseph Smith's involvement with polygamy. Among the most potentially problematic was Joseph Smith's marriage to women who were already married to other men, a total of twelve or thirteen—one-third of his wives.⁴² In "Joseph Smith and the Puzzlement of 'Polyandry,'" Brian C. Hales explores the extent of conjugal relations involving Smith and the women in question.

Equally controversial is the issue of Joseph Smith's marriages to teenagers, significant in that eleven young women, or an additional one-third of the Mormon leader's plural wives, ranged in age from 14 to 20.⁴³ Two essays, "The Age of Joseph Smith's Plural Wives in Social and Demographic Context" by Craig L. Foster, David Keller, and Gregory L. Smith, and "Early Marriage in the New Englad and Northeastern States, and in Mormon Polygamy: What was the Norm?" by Todd M. Compton, explore this topic in relationship to prevailing practices and customs involving the age at first marriage of females in both the larger American society and in other cultures during various periods of history.

A final controversial issue involves speculation about whether Joseph Smith fathered any offspring from his polygamous unions. Claims about

---

40. Doctrine and Covenants 132: 63.
41. These the words of Sarah Barringer Gordon in *The Mormon Question*, 22.
42. This total according to Todd Compton, *In Sacred Loneliness*, 15.
43. This total, again drawn from Todd Compton, *In Sacred Loneliness*, 11.

his alleged offspring have been made by various individuals within the LDS Church since the late nineteenth century and continuing well into the twentieth. By contrast, the Community of Christ has traditionally contended that the lack of definitive proof for such offspring supports their fundamental assertion that Joseph Smith neither practiced nor promoted polygamy. In "Joseph Smith, the Question of Polygamous Offspring, and DNA Analysis," Ugo A. Perego utilizes scientific analysis in an attempt to answer the fundamental question: did the Mormon leader, in fact, produce any progeny through any of his polygamous wives?

The varied controversies inherent to plural marriage generated intense opposition within the Mormon movement, culminating in outright schism by the spring of 1844, with a number of important Latter Day Saints, most notably William Law, a special counselor in the LDS Church First Presidency, declaring Joseph Smith a "fallen prophet." Presenting themselves as reformers, these dissidents set up a rival church organization, the True Church of Jesus Christ of Latter Day Saints, and began publication of their own newspaper, the *Nauvoo Expositor*, which revealed details of the still-secret practice of plural marriage. Smith reacted swiftly in his capacity as Nauvoo mayor, proclaiming the *Expositor* a "public nuisance" and ordering its destruction. Smith's summary action set the stage for his arrest, imprisonment, and assassination at the hands of a well-organized mob at Carthage, Illinois, on June 27, 1844.[44]

In summary, this volume seeks to provide fresh insights concerning Joseph Smith's involvement with plural marriage, but it does not purport to be the definitive study on this topic. Instead, its purpose is to stimulate discussion and debate, and more importantly encourage further scholarly research into Smith's polygamous activities as part of a larger effort to better understand the ever-elusive founder and first leader of the Latter Day Saint movement.

---

44. For three differing accounts of the causes, circumstances, and consequences of the assassination of Joseph Smith see: Dallin H. Oakes and Marvin S. Hill, *Carthage Conspiracy: The Trial of the Accused Assassins of Joseph Smith* (Urbana, Illinois: University of Illinois Press, 1975); Robert S. Wicks and Fred R. Foister, *Janius & Joseph: Presidential Politics and the Assassination of the First Mormon Prophet* (Logan, UT: Utah State University Press, 2005); LeGrand Baker, *Murder of the Mormon Prophet: Political Prelude to the Death of Joseph Smith* (Salt Lake City, UT: Eborn Books, 2006).

This volume is the first of a three-part anthology under the general title *The Persistence of Polygamy*, exploring varied aspects of Mormon plural marriage as it evolved from the time of Joseph Smith down to the present. Forthcoming is Volume II which will consider Mormon polygamy as practiced by various Latter Day Saint factions that emerged following the death of Joseph Smith, especially the Church of Jesus Christ of Latter-day Saints led by Brigham Young, which ultimately suspended the practice with the 1890 Manifesto. Volume III will trace the emergence of Mormon Fundamentalism, which developed when the mainstream LDS Church abandoned the practice of polygamy but others insisted that the practice must be continued. This has led to the proliferation of a large number of independent Fundamentalists as well as a variety of organized groups, most notably the Fundamentalist Church of Jesus Christ of Latter Day Saints (FLDS) and the Apostolic United Brethren.

Mormon Polygamy before Nauvoo? The Relationship of Joseph Smith and Fanny Alger

BY DON BRADLEY

ON APRIL 3, 1836, the Mormon prophet Joseph Smith and his assistant church president, Oliver Cowdery, closed the curtain by the Kirtland temple pulpit, isolating themselves from the congregation, and prayed. As later recorded, the two shared a heavenly visitation of Jesus and the biblical prophets Moses, Elijah, and "Elias," likely John the Revelator, a spiritual crescendo for both and an event that gathered "keys" from across sacred history and across the testaments into a single movement of restoration. Yet despite this shared experience of the holy, Cowdery, within a matter of months, was painting a public picture of Smith as somewhat less than sanctified, spreading the rumor that he had engaged in an illicit relationship with a teenage girl living in his home. Still affirming the truth of these accusations against Smith in early 1838, he wrote to his brother, Warren, of "a dirty, nasty, filthy affair of his and

Fanny Alger's."[1] Cowdery soon faced accusations of his own in an ecclesiastical trial, including the charge of defaming Smith by "falsely insinuating that he was guilty of adultery." The assistant president was ultimately excommunicated.[2]

Of all Joseph Smith's reported non-monogamous relationships, this, perhaps the earliest, has engendered the most controversy. Fanny Alger, as accounts go, had lived happily in the Smith home for some time when Smith's first wife Emma unceremoniously decanted her from the house in the night, after finding her on a hay loft with Joseph. Joseph reportedly sent for Cowdery to keep the peace between himself and Emma. One of the two men arranged for Alger to temporarily stay with Chauncey and Eliza Webb.[3] Alger, reportedly pregnant, soon headed west toward Missouri with family. She stopped in Indiana, where she lost no time in marrying non-Mormon Solomon Custer on November 16, 1836, and laid down roots where they raised a large family.[4]

By 1837, many Latter Day Saints had heard whispers of a close, and reportedly immoral, connection between Smith and Alger. When the main source of these rumors, Oliver Cowdery, was excommunicated, the story should have been largely discredited within the church. But it was not. The Alger family in later years consistently affirmed the occurrence of the relationship—and its identity as a marriage. And in 1886 future LDS Assistant Church Historian, Andrew Jenson, published Fanny Alger's name as of one of Smith's earliest plural wives.[5]

---

1. Oliver Cowdery to Warren Cowdery, January 21, 1838, Oliver Cowdery Letterbook, Henry E. Huntington Library, San Marino, California.

2. Donald Q. Cannon and Lyndon W. Cook, eds., *Far West Record: Minutes of The Church of Jesus Christ of Latter-day Saints, 1830-1844* (Salt Lake City: Deseret Book, 1983), April 12, 1838, 162–169.

3. For considerable background on Alger's life and relationship with Joseph Smith, see Todd Compton, *In Sacred Loneliness: The Plural Wives of Joseph Smith* (Salt Lake City: Signature Books, 1997), 25–42; and, "Fanny Alger Smith Custer: Mormonism's First Plural Wife?" *Journal of Mormon History* 22 (Spring 1996):174–207; and Brian C. Hales, "Fanny Alger and Joseph Smith's Pre-Nauvoo Reputation," *Dialogue: A Journal of Mormon Thought* 35 (Fall 2009):112–190.

4. Alger's pregnancy is reported by Chauncey Webb, to whose home she turned when evicted from the Smiths': "In Kirtland, he was sealed there secretly to Fanny Alger. Emma was furious, and drove the girl, who was unable to conceal the consequences of her celestial relation with the prophet, out of her house." Wilhelm Wyl [Wilhelm Ritter von Wymetal], *Mormon Portraits: Joseph Smith the Prophet, His Family, and His Friends* (Salt Lake City: Tribune Printing and Publishing Company, 1886), 57.

5. Andrew Jenson, "Plural Marriage," *Historical Record* 6 (May–August 1887): 232.

The controversy over the relationship then, as now, involves three central questions: the factuality, timing, and nature of the relationship. *Did it occur? If so, when did it occur? And, most importantly, was it a marriage or an affair?*

The question of Mormon polygamy's beginnings may have implications for understanding its purposes and justification. If it began in 1841, when Smith was married to Louisa Beaman in Nauvoo, Illinois, by her brother-in-law, Joseph B. Noble, who alleged this was the first Mormon plural marriage, then its purposes must be understood in the light of the Nauvoo theology of progression toward exaltation, or deification. Similarly if it began in either the early or mid-1830s with a solemnized relationship between Smith and Fanny Alger, then it must be set in the context of Kirtland theology, and Kirtland theology must reciprocally be understood in light of it. And, if it began with an extramarital affair that Smith had with Alger, a relationship driven by sexual, and perhaps romantic, motivations, devoid of theological justification and religious motive, an affair *rationalized* years later as polygamy, then Mormon polygamy's theological underpinning should be seen as a conscious or unconscious overlay on Smith's private passions.

Though some sources place Smith in other non-monogamous relationships before the institution of plainly recognizable polygamy in Nauvoo in 1841 (such as one with Lucinda Pendleton Morgan Harris in 1838 Missouri[6]), the reported Fanny Alger relationship is the only one for which there is substantial documentation, and therefore, the only one on which confident conclusions about timing, nature, and even occurrence might be drawn. It is the best test case for whether Smith had any such relationships before Nauvoo, and whether they were marital or extramarital; in short, for whether *polygamy* as such existed at the highest levels of the LDS Church prior to Nauvoo.

When Oliver Cowdery spread stories of Joseph Smith and Fanny Alger in 1837–1838, there appears to have been considerable dissension over *whether* an intimate relationship had occurred. At present, such dispute is minimal or nonexistent.

---

6. Compton, *In Sacred Loneliness*, 43–54; Hales, "Fanny Alger and Joseph Smith's Pre-Nauvoo Reputation," 129–135.

There are two reasons to suppose Joseph Smith may not have had a sexual relationship with Fanny Alger. First, at Cowdery's trial Smith denied having committed adultery with Alger, and the high council judging the case became convinced he was not guilty of this crime. Second, the earliest case of polygamy for which there is a definite officiator is that of Louisa Beaman in 1841, and the officiator, her brother-in-law Joseph B. Noble, asserted in succeeding decades that this was the first of Smith's plural marriages.[7] These reasons, however, are problematic. Cowdery's conviction on the charge of "falsely insinuating that [Smith] was guilty of *adultery*" need not indicate the high council was convinced *no* relationship occurred. And the testimony of Joseph B. Noble provides weak evidence, at best, that no relationship occurred between Smith and Alger. Noble, the source for the idea that polygamy began with the 1841 Beaman marriage, neither stated that he understood this from Smith, nor spoke without bias. Believing this was the first of Smith's polygamous unions conferred on Noble the special status of having *performed* the first plural marriage. Yet Noble's report, assumed true, would show only that Smith and Alger were not *married*, not that they had no relationship.

Given the weakness of these objections and the volume and reliability of the sources reporting the relationship (which will be reviewed in discussing its nature and timing), few deny a relationship occurred. Indeed, *no* scholar of Joseph Smith's polygamy has taken the position in print that there was no intimacy between the pair.

Timing

The beginnings of the relationship between Joseph Smith and Fanny Alger are cloudy. Although there is one source that purports to narrate how Smith approached Alger for a plural marriage and pinpoint a time for the marriage, this late source has fully persuaded only one major scholar and the relationship's beginnings remain an open question. Mystery also surrounds the relationship's demise. Although some have inferred that Emma Smith discovered the intimacy between her husband

---

7. Joseph B. Noble offered this testimony a number of times. See, for instance, Franklin D. Richards Journal, January 22, 1869, Historical Department of the Church of Jesus Christ of Latter-day Saints. Noble also claimed to have sired the first child by polygamy within the LDS Church.

and Fanny around the summer or fall of 1835, no unambiguous evidence for this has been adduced.

The sole detailed account of when and how the relationship began comes from Fanny Alger's first cousin Mosiah Hancock (1834–1907). Hancock, who was a toddler at the time the relationship was discovered and not yet been conceived at the time it supposedly started, wrote his account in 1896 as an addendum to the autobiography of his father, Levi Hancock.[8] Although Levi Hancock had written about his own life at the time in question, he had omitted any direct reference to Joseph Smith's relationship with his niece Fanny (daughter to his sister Clarissa Hancock Alger).[9] Mosiah, believing he had accurate information to fill this lacuna, did so.

On the younger Hancock's account, the marriage of Joseph Smith to Levi's niece came about through a kind of swap. In 1833, Mosiah reports, his father fell in love with Clarissa Reed, but it was presumed that she, then living in the Smith home, was intended as a polygamous wife for Smith. Mosiah's father nonetheless approached the prophet to see if he would relinquish her. Smith, apparently uninterested in Reed, offered Levi a deal: "Brother Levi I want to make a bargain with you—If you will get Fanny Alger for me for a wife you may have Clarissa Reed. I love Fanny."[10] Levi then reportedly sought the permission of both sets of parents, who promptly gave their approval. Smith then had Levi Hancock perform the marriage for them, and gave his blessing for Levi to marry Clarissa Reed.

This account has the following strengths: It provides an explanation for an otherwise mysterious event. It comes from a relatively close family source who may have had access to inside information on a Smith-Alger marriage, particularly if his father were the officiator. And, finally, there is an inherent plausibility in the account of Levi Hancock's niece moving into the Smith home when his new wife moved out.[11]

---

8. Autobiography of Levi Ward Hancock (with additions by his son Mosiah Hancock, "Farmington Davis Co Co [sic], 1896"), 61–64, writing of Mosiah Hancock.
9. Ibid., 48–57, writing of Levi Hancock.
10. Ibid., 63, writing of Mosiah Hancock.
11. An 1833 timing for Fanny Alger move to the Smith home may also draw support from an 1876 statement of Eliza Webb, in whose home Fanny stayed when she left the Smith's. Wrote Webb, "Fanny Alger had lived in Joseph's family several years." (Eliza J. Webb [Eliza Jane Churchill Webb], Lockport, New York, to Mary Bond, April 24, 1876. Biographical Folder Collection, P21,

The account also has weaknesses. The author could have known of the events only indirectly and recorded them sixty-three years after the fact. Although he recorded what he believed his father *should* have put into his autobiography, the father does not appear to have agreed. Rather than report the historically significant first plural marriage in the church, reveling in his role in such an event, as Joseph B. Noble did, Levi Hancock omitted it altogether.

The Mosiah Hancock account is also anachronistic to the Mormonism of 1833. His narrative assumes an established polygamous culture, in which an unrelated girl living in a married man's house might be *expected* to become his wife and in which parents would readily agree to such a marriage.[12] Although these social conventions made sense to Mosiah, who came of age in polygamous 1840s–1850s Nauvoo and Utah, they would have made no sense to Mormons of the 1830s, who were still thoroughly immersed in the larger pre-Victorian monogamous culture.

The account also places Joseph Smith's marriage to Fanny Alger under Emma's nose for at least two and a half years before its discovery, and contradicts earlier information attributed to Mosiah's aunt, Clarissa—Fanny Alger's mother. Clarissa Hancock Alger, according to an 1876 letter from Eliza Jane Churchill Webb to Mary E. Bond, "says Fanny was sealed to Joseph by Oliver Cowdery in Kirtland in 1835—or 6."[13]

---

f11, item 7, 8, Community of Christ Library-Archives, Independence, Missouri, transcription courtesy of Ron Romig.) Clarissa Alger's reported identification of 1835 or 1836 as the year of marriage (also per Webb, cited below) may reflect Fanny having not joined the Smith household until 1835 or may reflect her knowledge that the relationship did not begin until a couple years after her daughter's removal to the Smith home.

12. Note the assumption of polygamous norms that runs through Mosiah Hancock's account. He recounts that his mother, living as she did at the prophet's home, "had thought that perhaps she might be one of the Prophet's wives as herself and Sister Emma were on the best of terms.... Father [Levi Hancock] goes to the Father Samuel Alger—his Father's Brother in Law and [said] 'Samuel[,] the Prophet Joseph loves your Daughter Fanny and wishes her for a wife what say you'—Uncle Sam Says—'Go and talk to the old woman about it twi'll be as She says' Father goes to his Sister and said 'Clarissy, Brother Joseph the Prophet of the most high God loves Fanny and wishes her for a wife what say you' Said She 'go and talk to Fanny it will be all right with me'—Father goes to Fanny and said 'Fanny Brother Joseph the Prophet loves you and wishes you for a wife will you be his wife'? 'I will Levi' Said She." Ibid., 63.

13. Webb to Bond, April 24, 1876 April. Compare the Eliza Webb letter to the following from her daughter Ann Eliza Webb Young, doubtless reflecting information from Eliza: "Fanny's parents considered "it the highest honor to have their daughter adopted into the Prophet's family, and her mother has always claimed that she was sealed to Joseph." Ann Eliza Webb Young, *Wife Number 19; or, The Story of a Life in Bondage, Being a Complete Exposé of Mormonism, and*

The author, Eliza Webb, had been close to Fanny and was an insider regarding Fanny's relationship with Smith: when Emma threw her out, it was Eliza who took her in. To the extent that Eliza Webb's letter is accepted as reflecting the mother's understanding, Mosiah's account must be questioned. If Levi Hancock had secured her permission for and performed the marriage in 1833, she should have known Cowdery had not performed it in 1835 or 1836. Though her reported belief that Cowdery was the officiator is problematic in itself, it is one that, on Mosiah Hancock's account, she should have known better.[14] Given the lateness and difficulties of Hancock's narrative of the origin of the Smith-Alger pairing, it is unfortunate that it is the only one available.

Though the beginning of the relationship eludes us, its ending can be more definitively pegged. Sources on Emma's discovery of Joseph and Fanny and her eviction of the girl are less detailed but more abundant, closer to the event, and more trustworthy.

The few scholars who have attempted to date the discovery of this relationship have generally placed it around summer to fall 1835, on the basis of four evidentiary dots connected by Richard S. Van Wagoner.[15] First, Benjamin F. Johnson, writing at the turn of the twentieth century, recalled being told in 1835, when he was a youth of about Fanny Alger's age that biblical polygamy was to be restored and hearing it "whispered" of Fanny "that Joseph Loved her."[16] Second, it is evident from the "Article on Marriage" drawn up and published in the Doctrine and Covenants in August 1835 that an embarrassing polygamy incident had occurred before that time. The article reads in part: "Inasmuch as this church of Christ has been reproached with the crime of fornication, and polygamy: we declare that we believe, that one man should have one wife; and

---

Revealing the Sorrows, Sacrifices and Sufferings of Women in Polygamy (Hartford, Conn.: Dustin, Gilman, 1876), 67.

14. It is probable that if parental consent were obtained, parents would have been present for the ceremony and would have known who officiated. And even without her attendance at the wedding, it would be surprising if she did know not that her brother, who arranged it, was also the one who performed it.

15. Richard S. Van Wagoner, *Mormon Polygamy: A History*, 2d ed. (Salt Lake City: Signature Books, 1989), 4–16.

16. Dean R. Zimmerman, ed., *I Knew the Prophets: An Analysis of the Letter of Benjamin F. Johnson to George F. Gibbs, Reporting Doctrinal Views of Joseph Smith and Brigham Young* (Bountiful, Utah: Horizon, 1976), 38–39.

one woman, but one husband, except in case of death, when either is at liberty to marry again."[17] Third, Joseph Smith left Kirtland for Pontiac, Michigan shortly before the special conference that voted on the Article and returned not long after, possibly suggesting the Article was passed in his absence to minimize embarrassment.[18] And fourth, Joseph Smith's diary for October 17, 1835, alludes to his dealing with household issues including evicting non-family residents: "called my family together aranged my domestick concerns and dismissed my boarders."[19]

These fragments fit together neatly, but an 1835 dating of the incident is not above critique and serious challenge. Johnson's recollection, written sixty-eight years after the fact, may be imprecise as to the exact timing of the rumors. And Smith's reference to dismissing his boarders, though referring to multiple persons, is completely ambiguous on their identity and why they were required to leave. Mark Ashurst-McGee, an editor with the Joseph Smith Papers Project, suggested the boarders evicted from the Smith home were employees at the nearby printing office, where Smith had reported attempting to settle some "difficulties" the previous day.[20] This coheres perfectly with the autobiographical account given by one of the printers, Ebenezer Robinson:

> In May, 1835, went to Kirtland, Ohio, and obtained a situation in the Latter-day Saints' Church printing office.... The firm consisted of Joseph Smith, Jr., F. G. Williams and Oliver Cowdery. We engaged to work by the month and be boarded by our employers....
>
> We boarded the first two months in the family of Oliver Cowdery, the second two months in the family of F. G. Williams, and the third two months in the family of Joseph Smith, Jr.[21]

---

17. Doctrine and Covenants, 1835 edition, Section CI, 251–252. The Article was removed from the 1876 Utah edition when the revelation on marriage (LDS D&C 132) was added.
18. See the discussion of Smith's trip to Pontiac, Michigan, in Compton, "Fanny Alger Smith Custer: Mormonism's First Plural Wife?" 181, 196–97.
19. Dean C. Jessee, ed., *The Papers of Joseph Smith*, Volume 2, Journal, 1832–1842 (Salt Lake City: Deseret Book, 1992), 52.
20. Personal communication with Mark Ashurst-McGee, July 16, 2010. Smith's diary for Friday, October 16, 1835, reads "was called into the printing office to settle some difficulties in that department, at evening on the same day I baptised Ebenezer Robinson the Lord poured out his spirit on us and we had a good time." The corresponding entry for October 17, reads "called my family together and aranged my domestick concerns and domestic dismissed my boarders."
21. Ebenezer Robinson, "Items of Personal History of the Editor," *The Return* (Davis City, Iowa), 1:4 (April 1889):58.

Robinson's account yields a timetable something like this for the printers' mid-1835 boarding arrangements:

May–June: Oliver Cowdery household
July–August: Frederick G. Williams household
September–October: Joseph Smith household

Robinson's narrative places the printing employees in the Smith home as boarders during October and likely leaving the home that month, making it more than probable they were in fact the boarders evicted after the October 16 "difficulties" at the printing office.

Also problematic for the 1835 timeline of the discovery of the Fanny Alger relationship is the story that Joseph Smith left town to avoid embarrassment over the Alger rumors—this occurring during the Article on Marriage vote. Brian C. Hales, in the most extensive examination of the Article on Marriage to date, demonstrates that there may have been other polygamy-related incidents in early Mormonism aside from Smith's to which the Article responded, that Smith's trip to Pontiac at the time the Article passed appears to have been for family and ecclesiastical reasons, and that the Article had to be hastily drawn up and voted on in his absence because the Doctrine and Covenants was about to go to press.[22]

An alternative dating of the relationship discovery, to 1836, is supported by other evidence. As discussed below, rumors of the relationship appear to have peaked in 1837, when Oliver Cowdery was most actively discussing it, a peak which better fits an 1836 discovery date than an 1835 date. Fanny Alger left Ohio around September 1836, establishing that as the outside date. Also in 1837, likely in response to those rumors, Smith published a list of frequently asked questions about the Mormons in the *Elders' Journal*, including the question "Do the Mormons believe in having more wives than one?"[23]

---

22. Hales, "Fanny Alger and Joseph Smith's Pre-Nauvoo Reputation," 177–187.

23. Joseph Smith, Editorial, *Elders' Journal* 1:2 (November 1837): 28–29. A similar inference on the date of the discovery was made by researcher H. Michael Marquardt in an October 19, 1995, letter to Gary J. Bergera: "It appears that whatever occurred with Fanny Alger probably happened in the year 1836 with Fanny leaving Kirtland, Ohio. This year is closer to the events relating to Oliver Cowdery since Cowdery had discussed the matter with Joseph Smith and others in the summer and fall of 1837." H. Michael Marquardt Collection, J. Willard Marriott Library, University of Utah, Salt Lake City.

Cowdery's 1837–1838 complaints of Smith's "dirty, nasty, filthy" relationship with Alger are also significant by their *absence* in early 1836, when Cowdery had no apparent trouble accepting Smith's purity and worthiness to dedicate the Kirtland temple on March 27, and to see Christ with him on April 3.[24] This too suggests a later dating for the "outing" of the relationship, placing it probably between April 3, 1836, and September of the same year.

Other sources also support an 1836 dating for the relationship's end. Clarissa Hancock Alger's dating of the relationship's *beginning* to 1835 or 1836 also weighs against an 1835 discovery. If Clarissa Alger believed the marriage might not have *begun* until 1836, she could not have understood it to be *discovered and terminated* in 1835. And Benjamin Winchester, a plural brother-in-law to Smith and a church leader in Philadelphia, later an apostate, stated of his Kirtland days that in the *summer of 1836* "there was a good deal of scandal prevalent among a number of the Saints concerning Joseph's licentious conduct," which led to some schism within the church.[25]

Additional testimony, collected by Andrew Jenson, also strongly confirms the 1836 date. As mentioned above, Jenson was the first to publish Fanny Alger's name as one of Joseph Smith's plural wives, and others have followed in his footsteps.[26] What has not been known is *why* Jenson included her on his list—on what authority he made the identification. This source was Eliza R. Snow, president of the LDS Relief Society and herself one of the prophet's plural widows. At Jenson's request, Snow

---

24. Cowdery's journal or "sketchbook" for the period leading up to the temple dedication says little directly about Smith, but gives every indication that he believed in the sanctity of the temple and Smith's worthiness to dedicate it. Oliver Cowdery, Sketchbook, January–March 1836, LDS Church History Library, Salt Lake City, Utah. For the text of the sketchbook and Leonard Arrington's comments on it, see Leonard J. Arrington, "Oliver Cowdery's Kirtland, Ohio 'Sketchbook,'" in John W. Welch and Larry E. Morris, eds., *Oliver Cowdery: Scribe, Elder, Witness* (Provo, Utah: The Neal A. Maxwell Institute for Religious Scholarship, Brigham Young University, 2006), 241–262. Had Smith and Cowdery seen Christ in the temple *after* Cowdery became aware of Smith's relationship with Fanny Alger, then it is likely that Cowdery would have viewed Smith as unworthy of his role in the temple dedication and/or would have regarded Christ's visitation to Smith, in company with Cowdery, as an indication that Smith had nevertheless been divinely forgiven, something Cowdery's subsequent behavior indicates he did not believe.

25. Benjamin Winchester, "Primitive Mormonism," *Salt Lake Tribune*, September 22, 1889.

26. Ann Eliza Webb's discussion of Fanny Alger in her 1875 *Wife No. 19*, cited herein, mentions a girl named "Fanny," apparently as a wife. And the 1881 *Anti-Polygamy Standard*, also cited herein, uses the name "Fanny Alger or Olger," but describes her as a mistress, rather than a wife.

recorded for him a handwritten list of her "sister wives," including Fanny Alger.²⁷ When Jenson subsequently interviewed Eliza Snow about Fanny's life and relationship with Joseph Smith, she told him, per his interview notes, that Fanny Alger was "one of the first wives Joseph married," one whom "Emma made such a fuss about." Most significantly, Eliza R. Snow explained how she knew about Fanny Alger and the relationship: Eliza "was well acquainted with her as she lived with the Prophet at the time".²⁸

Snow's presence in the house at the time of the discovery establishes the range for when it could have occurred. According to her autobiography, Eliza Snow lived in the Smith's Kirtland home twice, once in mid-1836 while teaching a school term that began in the spring and again at the first of 1837.²⁹ By 1837 Fanny Alger was living in Indiana and married to Solomon Custer; so it was during the first of these two stays, in mid-1836, that Snow and Alger shared the house and the great "fuss" occurred.

The testimony of a contemporary member of the household that the relationship was discovered during her 1836 residence effectively confirms a relationship occurred, as well as the time of its discovery and consequent termination.

---

27. This list appears as Document #1 in Jenson's folder on Joseph Smith's polygamy in the newly available Andrew Jenson Papers at the LDS Church History Library. Jenson made a list of Joseph Smith's wives in his own hand and then turned it over to Eliza R. Snow (likely on a visit with her that he records in his journal for February 14, 1887) who added an additional fourteen names to the list, including that of Fanny Alger. I identified Snow's handwriting by comparing this portion of the document to other documents in her hand and then met with Brian C. Hales and Jill Mulvay Derr, Snow's biographer, on July 25, 2008, to examine the documents with them. After making the comparisons, she confirmed that "there is every indication" the fourteen additional names on Jenson's list are in Eliza R. Snow's hand.

28. Jenson Papers, Joseph Smith polygamy folder, Document #10. For further information on the Jenson notes see, Hales, "Fanny Alger and Joseph Smith's Pre-Nauvoo Reputation," 142–145, and the present author's extensive work in progress on Andrew Jenson's Joseph Smith polygamy research materials.

29. "In the Spring of 1836, I taught a select school for young ladies, and boarded with the Prophet's family: at the close of the term [likely that summer or fall] I returned to my parental home.... The 1ˢᵗ of January 1837…I bade a final adieu to the home of my youth, to share the fortunes of the people of God." Eliza R. Snow, "Sketch of My Life," 7. "Utah and Mormons" collection, Bancroft Library, University of California Berkeley, microfilm copy in LDS Church History Library.

This timing for the discovery has important implications for the subject to be addressed next—the *nature* of Smith and Alger's relationship.[30]

The Nature of the Relationship

Scholars are divided over when Smith's earliest non-monogamous relationships occurred and whether they were marital or extramarital. Compton and Hales have argued for a formal marital relationship; Van Wagoner has argued for an informal marital relationship (a mutual understanding of marriage without a wedding ceremony); and George D. Smith, Gary J. Bergera, and Janet Ellingson have argued that the Smith-Alger pairing was an affair that preceded formal polygamy.[31] On the latter argument, the relationship occurred too early to be a marriage, before the theological and authority basis for polygamy was sufficiently developed; and later identifications of the relationship as marital constitute a respectable overlay on an otherwise scandalous connection.

Evidence of Adultery

The earliest rumors about the relationship between Joseph Smith and Fanny Alger appear to have identified it as an extramarital affair. And some contemporaneous or nearly contemporaneous evidence supports this.

The earliest evidence that the relationship was an extramarital affair may be found in Emma's reactions to it. Her rage at discovering Joseph and Fanny Alger together indicates the relationship had been formed in secret and that she saw it as a violation of his wedding vows. A view on her part that the relationship was immoral, and likely adulterous, can be inferred from the closings of letters she sent him while he was in hiding because of Kirtland difficulties the following year: on April 25, "I pray

---

30. A more precise dating of the relationship's end is made in my presentation at the 2010 Salt Lake City Sunstone Symposium, "Dating Fanny Alger: The Nature, Timing, and Consequences of an Early Polygamous Relationship."

31. George D. Smith, *Nauvoo Polygamy: "... but we called it celestial marriage,"* Salt Lake City: Signature Books, 2008, 39–43; Gary James Bergera, "Identifying the Earliest Mormon Polygamists, 1841–44," *Dialogue: A Journal of Mormon Thought* 38 (Fall 2005): [1–74] 30 n75; Janet Ellingson, "Alger Marriage Questioned," Letter, *Journal of Mormon History* 23 (Spring 1997), vi–vii.

that God will keep you in purity and safety till we all meet again"; and on May 2, "I hope that we shall be so humble and pure before God that he will set us at liberty to be our own masters."³²

Another datum suggestive of an extramarital relationship between Smith and Alger is the absence of an obvious officiator to perform a polygamous marriage at that time. No one performing any Mormon polygamous marriages prior to 1841 has been identified, and, aside from Smith's counselor Sidney Rigdon (a strong opponent of polygamy in the 1840s), Latter Day Saint ministers were not known to perform marriages in Kirtland until the fall of 1835. Even Fanny Alger's family appears to have been unable to identify a likely officiator. The first-cousin account identifying her uncle Levi Hancock as the officiator seems problematic and doubtful. And her mother's reported identification of the officiator as Oliver Cowdery—arguably the person most agitated about the incident after Emma—seems more doubtful still.

Janet Ellingson, responding to Todd Compton's arguments that the relationship was a plural marriage, has argued that Alger's behavior in the wake of its discovery provides a neglected contemporaneous demonstration that *she* saw it as an extramarital affair. Had she believed herself married to Smith, she would not have promptly married Solomon Custer in Indiana.³³ Ellingson is surely right to this extent: the fact the relationship was dissolved after being discovered and hastily replaced for Alger by her legal marriage to Solomon Custer would be more typical of an affair than a marriage.

In addition to contemporaneous behavioral indications of a nonmarital relationship between Smith and Alger, there are early reminiscences to that effect. One that unequivocally accuses the prophet of sexual immorality is the 1842 affidavit by Boston LDS convert Fanny Brewer, who describes circumstances in Kirtland upon her visit in 1837, at the peak of the gossip regarding Smith and Alger: "There was much excitement against the Prophet on another account, likewise, — an un-

---

32. Emma Hale Smith to Joseph Smith, April 25 and May 2, 1837, Joseph Smith Letterbooks, LDS Church History Library, photocopy of holograph in Linda King Newell Collection, Marriott Libary, University of Utah, as cited in Linda King Newell, "Emma Hale Smith and the Polygamy Question," *John Whitmer Historical Association Journal* 4 (1984): 4. This connection was suggested by Brian C. Hales.

33. Ellingson, "Alger Marriage Questioned," vi–vii.

lawful intercourse between himself and a young orphan girl residing in this family, and under his protection!!!"[34]

According to the April 12, 1838, trial minutes for Oliver Cowdery, who was reportedly called in by Joseph Smith to help calm Emma after she discovered him with Alger, Cowdery circulated rumors of immoral behavior between Smith and Alger implying the relationship constituted adultery. All of the testimonies describe the 1837 conversations in which the affiant asked Cowdery about the rumors. Cowdery affirmed they were true and that Smith's behavior had been abominable. When asked explicitly if Smith had confessed to adultery, Cowdery reportedly answered, "No," but only after hesitation and "considerable winking" that would tend to undermine the literal meaning of the word.[35]

Smith and Oliver Cowdery argued over the accuracy of the latter's rumors months before Cowdery was brought to trial. In a letter to his brother Warren three months before his trial, Oliver reported on "some conversation" held with Smith "in which in every instance I did not fail to affirm that which I had said was strictly true. A dirty, nasty, filthy affair of his and Fanny Alger's was talked over in which I strictly declared that I had never deserted from the truth in the matter, and as I supposed was admitted by himself."[36] The letter clearly represents the relationship as sexually immoral, and its reference to an impure "*affair*" is almost always read as a direct accusation of adultery.

Another category of evidence that the Fanny Alger relationship was extramarital is that of late reminiscences. Such reminiscences are given by William E. McLellin, a "Mr. Moreton[,] one of the first Apostles" as cited by Disciples of Christ minister and critic of Mormonism, Clark Braden, and "Lewis and Ezra Bond," also as cited by Braden.

McLellin claimed to have heard stories in the 1830s of Joseph Smith's "polygamy and adultery" and to have confirmed these in conversation with Emma Smith in 1847. In an 1872 letter to the prophet's eldest son and presumptive heir, Joseph Smith III, McLellin related the two cases Emma had reportedly verified, the first a relationship between Smith

---

34. Fanny Brewer, Letter, September 13, 1842, Boston, printed in John C. Bennett, *The History of the Saints: Or an Exposé of Joe Smith and Mormonism* (Boston: Leland & Whiting, 1842), 85–86, capitalization standardized.
35. Cannon and Cook, eds., *Far West Record*, 167–168.
36. Oliver Cowdery to Warren Cowdery, January 21, 1838.

and the daughter of a thus far unidentifiable Hill family and the second with Fanny Alger.³⁷ The Hill relationship he understood to be adultery: Smith, he said "committed an act with a Miss Hill — a hired girl" around the time of Joseph Smith III's birth in November 1832. When caught, Smith is said to have called in Oliver Cowdery and other church leaders to mollify Emma, and next to have "confessed humbly and begged forgiveness" of Emma and the church leaders, after which "Emma and all forgave him."³⁸ Regarding Fanny Alger, McLellin was less specific but later described her relationship with Smith as "polygamy."³⁹

The two narratives are closely parallel and often thought to be variant tellings of a single event.⁴⁰ The earliest published association of the name "Fanny Alger" with Joseph Smith supports this identification, narrating the story of a hired girl having a sexual relationship with Joseph Smith, a discovery which so distressed Emma that Oliver Cowdery had to be called in to keep the peace.⁴¹ This source is an 1881 piece in the *Anti-Polygamy Standard* by the pseudonymous "Historicus."⁴² "Historicus"

---

37. Regarding unsuccessful attempts to identify a candidate "Miss Hill" besides Fanny Alger, see Hales, "Fanny Alger and Joseph Smith's Pre-Nauvoo Reputation," 145–146 and 146 n86.

38. "William E. McLellan, M.D., to President Joseph Smith [III]," Independence, Missouri, July 1872, typescript in "Letters and documents copied from originals in the office of the Church Historian, Reorganized Church," LDS Church History Library; from originals in Community of Christ Library-Archives. If indeed Oliver Cowdery was involved in the event described, it cannot have been around the birth of Joseph Smith III, as here narrated. Cowdery left Ohio for Missouri nearly a year before the birth of Joseph Smith III and returned when the namesake Joseph was ten months old. Cowdery was present in Kirtland in the spring and summer of 1836, making it possible for him to have intervened that point. See the Oliver Cowdery biographical sketch on the Saints Without Halos website, http://saintswithouthalos.com/b/cowdery_o.phtml, accessed July 23, 2010.

39. J[ohn]. H[anson]. Beadle, "Jackson County," *Salt Lake Tribune*, October 6, 1875, 4.

40. For a discussion of this question, see Linda King Newell and Valeen Tippetts Avery, *Mormon Enigma: Emma Hale Smith, Prophet's Wife, "Elect Lady," Polygamy's Foe* (New York: Doubleday & Co., 1985) 66; Smith, *Nauvoo Polygamy*, 40–42; and Hales, "Fanny Alger and Joseph Smith's Pre-Nauvoo Reputation," 145–147.

41. McLellin's account to J. H. Beadle identifies *Fanny Alger* as a hired girl, as his own earlier letter to Joseph Smith III had identified "Miss Hill," suggesting the conflation or identity of the two. Beadle, "Jackson County," *Salt Lake Tribune*, October 6, 1875, 4.

42. Another author writing near the same time under this pseudonym was William Gill Mills, a merchant, poet, and Irish LDS convert who abandoned Mormonism and his plural wife while on a mission to England. Mills signed his pamphlet *Blood atonement. Fully established as a doctrine and practice of the Mormon Church* "Historicus. Salt Lake City, Oct. 25, 1884" (Salt Lake City, 1884). An examination of other *Anti-Polygamy Standard* pieces by "Historicus" suggests he was a missionary who worked in the Liverpool mission office, but probably in the 1870s, after Mills had left the church. His identity is as yet undetermined.

relates that when Joseph Smith III was a young infant, "Emma Smith, Joseph's Wife, had a young girl in her employment by the name of Fanny Olger or Alger," and "she [Emma] discovered that Joseph had been celesitalizing with this maiden, Fanny." Emma consequently "became terrible worked up about it. She was like a mad woman, and acted so violently that Oliver Cowdery and some of the elders were called in to minister to her and 'cast the devil out of sister Emma.'"[43] The author narrates Joseph Smith's relationship with "Fanny Olger or Alger" as a case of adultery, but, like McLellin, backdates the affair to the infancy of Joseph Smith III. There are thus variant narratives of the Fanny Alger relationship in which she is clearly McLellin's "Miss Hill."

McLellin himself may have received two versions of the scandal, one in which Fanny Alger was described by name and identified as Smith's plural wife and another in which she was given the name "Hill" (plausibly "Fanny Hill," in conflation with the heroine of John Cleland's famous 18th century erotic novel[44]), identified as Smith's adulterous paramour, and said to have been discovered in a relationship with him around 1833, more plausibly the time she *moved into* the Smith home, rather than the time the relationship was discovered by Emma.[45]

Clark Braden's first source on Joseph Smith's alleged adultery, a "Mr. Moreton," referred to by Braden as one of Smith's "first Apostles," is described in the 1884 transcription of a debate with RLDS apostle E. L. Kelley as having "told his daughter and her husband that Emma Smith detected Joseph in adultery with a girl by the name of Knight, and that

---

43. "Historicus," *Anti-Polygamy Standard*; "Sketches from the History of Polygamy: Joseph Smith's Especial[?] Revelations," *Anti-Polygamy Standard* 2: 1 (April 1881): 1.

44. Newell and Avery, in a widely adopted interpretation, suggest that the elderly McLellin, conflated "Fanny Alger, with Fanny Hill of John Cleland's 1749 novel and came up with the hired girl, Miss Hill." *Mormon Enigma*, 66. See Smith, *Nauvoo Polygamy*, 40 n90; and Hales, "Fanny Alger and Joseph Smith's Pre-Nauvoo Reputation," 145–147. Conflation of Fanny Alger with the salacious Fanny Hill could also explain why McLellin was emphatic that "Miss Hill," unlike Fanny Alger, had been an adulterous paramour of Smith, rather than a wife.

45. As discussed above, an 1833 timing for the Fanny Alger move to the Smith home appears to be supported by the Mosiah Hancock account and dovetails with Eliza Webb's report that Fanny "had lived in Joseph's family several years." But Webb also indicates a close family understanding that Fanny's relationship with Smith began no sooner than 1835.

Joseph confessed the crime to the officers of the church," another likely garbled reference to the Alger incident.[46]

Braden also reports information he received from members of the Bond family, who lived in Kirtland at the time of the Fanny Alger incident:

> Lewis Bond and Ezra Bond have repeatedly stated that their father and mother, who were amongst the first Mormons in Kirtland, repeatedly declared that Smith practiced polygamy in Kirtland, and that he followed a girl into a privy and committed fornication with her. Mrs. Bond made such declarations to Mrs. Hansbury and others.[47]

Ezra Bond was a member of the Ira and Charlotte Bond family, and it was his sister Mary E. Bond whose correspondence with Eliza Webb on Fanny Alger is quoted above.[48] The Bonds were apparently present in Kirtland at the time of the Alger incident, and in a position to hear the gossip. In her letter to Mary Bond, Eliza Webb stated, "I suppose your mother will remember what a talk the whole affair made."[49] So the girl Smith supposedly followed "into a privy" is likely Fanny Alger, with whom he was actually caught in another out building, the barn.

There is thus evidence of an extramarital affair between Joseph Smith and Fanny Alger in roughly contemporaneous events, in the Brewer and Cowdery testimonies within a few years of the event, and in further testimonies in succeeding decades. But before the sum of this evidence can be properly weighed it must be properly critiqued.

---

46. E. L. Kelley and Clark Braden, *Public Discussion of the Issues between The Reorganized Church of Jesus Christ of Latter Day Saints and the Church of Christ (Disciples) Held in Kirtland, Ohio, Beginning February 12, and Closing March 8, 1884, between E. L. Kelley, of the Reorganized Church of Jesus Christ of Latter Day Saints and Clark Braden, of the Church of Christ* (St. Louis: Clark Braden, 1884), 202.

47. Ibid.

48. Among the useful sources on the Bond family is the Bond message board at Ancestry.com: http://boards.ancestry.com/surnames.bond/1204/mb.ashx, accessed July 22, 2010.

49. Eliza J. Webb to Mary E. Bond, April 24, 1876. The content of the letter suggests that the mother, Charlotte Bond, was a believing member of the RLDS Church, and perhaps therefore disinclined to believe Smith had been a polygamist. Yet, according to Braden, she acknowledged a relationship between Joseph Smith and this girl, apparently Fanny Alger.

Review and Critique of the Evidence for Adultery

The evidence for an extramarital affair between Joseph Smith and Fanny Alger is of varying quality. While the evidence of contemporaneous behavior provides some direction, the direct testimony, despite surface appearances, is largely ambiguous, failing to distinguish between an extramarital affair and a secret polygamous marriage.

Even the vehement oral accusations and letter by Cowdery, for instance, fall short of stating that Smith's behavior constituted adultery. In his trial, Cowdery was charged with *"insinuating"* that Smith's relationship with Alger was adulterous, accused of this in the testimony, and convicted of making insinuations rather than assertions that Smith had committed adultery. Though said to have given his verbal answer with incongruous body language, he stated "no" when asked point blank if Smith's confessions to him amounted to an admission of adultery. There is nothing to indicate that "adultery" was *his* term. This reluctance to use the term "adultery" seems out of line with his emphatic condemnation of Smith's "dirty, nasty, filthy" behavior and his insistence that his reports had been "strictly true" and "never deserted from the truth of the matter."

Because Cowdery was alienated from Joseph Smith at the time of his trial and was being expelled from the church, it is not likely that the best construction was being placed on his words and actions. And Cowdery was not in attendance at his trial, rendering him unable to defend himself from exaggeration and misunderstanding. The wrong he saw in Smith might thus have not been adultery, but polygamy.

Evidence coincident with Cowdery's return to the church eight years later indicates his revulsion to polygamy and his incredulity that it would be allowed as a religious practice.[50] For Cowdery, polygamy was a sexual

---

50. Cowdery wrote regarding polygamy in an 1846 letter, "I can hardly think it possible, that you have written us the truth, that though there may be individuals who are guilty of the iniquities spoken of—yet no such practice can be preached or adhered to, as a public doctrine." Oliver Cowdery to Daniel and Phebe Jackson, July 24, 1846, original letter unlocated, photographs of original letter, RLDS Archives, as quoted in Scott H. Faulring, "The Return of Oliver Cowdery," in Welch and Morris, eds., *Oliver Cowdery: Scribe, Elder, Witness*, 332. For more on Oliver Cowdery's attitude toward polygamy, see Brian C. Hales, "Guilty of Such Folly?": Accusations of Adultery and Polygamy Against Oliver Cowdery," *Mormon Historical Studies* 9:1, Spring 2008, 41–57.

sin in itself, and perhaps *arguably constituted* adultery. Such an uncertain definition on Cowdery's part would account for his curious mix of vehemence against Smith's "dirty, nasty, filthy" behavior on the one hand and reticence to directly call it "adultery" on the other.

Though Cowdery's letter, with its talk of Smith's "dirty, nasty, filthy affair," would seem to explicitly identify the relationship as an extramarital affair, it does not. The letter stops short of an accusation of adultery. The key word is "affair." Although it has hitherto escaped comment, that word in Oliver's January 21, 1838, letter *overwrites* a pre-existing word. An examination of the overwriting on the manuscript letter, in the Oliver Cowdery Letterbook at the Huntington Library by Christopher C. Smith, confirms that the copyist first wrote another word after "dirty, nasty, filthy" and then replaced it with "affair."[51] The original, underlying word appears to have been "scrape," a word also used in the trial testimony to narrate Cowdery's description of the trouble Smith and Alger had gotten themselves into. Noah Webster in his 1828 dictionary of American English defined a "scrape" as a "difficulty; perplexity; distress; that which harasses," adding that it was "*a low word.*"[52] The letter's original use of this word is significant for how one should interpret the replacement term "affair."

Oliver Cowdery essentially wrote, in his original letter to Warren, that Smith and Alger had gotten themselves entangled in "a filthy mess." But this was changed during or subsequent to the copying of the original text into Oliver's letterbook. Someone thought the better of this word choice, presumably because "scrape" was, as Webster termed it "a low word," not one indicative of breeding and education. And it is not clear that this someone was Oliver. The letter was recorded in the letterbook by his nephew, Warren F. Cowdery, and it is not clear whether the decision to replace the word "scrape" was made by the author or by

---

51. Personal communication from Christopher C. Smith, October 2, 2009, regarding Oliver Cowdery to Warren Cowdery, January 21, 1838, Oliver Cowdery Letterbook, Henry E. Huntington Library, San Marino, California. At my request, Smith reviewed the letter. Although the overwriting is visible on the microfilm copy of this document available at the LDS Church Historical Library, the underlying text can be discerned only on the manuscript.

52. Noah Webster, *An American Dictionary of the English Language* (New York: S. Converse, 1828). Emphasis in original.

the copyist.[53] Whoever it was, replaced it with the word "affair," the primary definition of which at the time was, per Webster's, "Business of any kind; that which is done, or is to be done; a word of very indefinite and undefinable signification." The word "affair" was also occasionally used to refer to a *love* affair in the modern sense (though not so often for this definition to appear in Webster's), but does not appear to have been in its modern sense connoting an *extramarital* love affair.[54] Thus the word substitution did not turn the Smith-Alger trouble into adultery, but into an ill-defined, if still "dirty, nasty, filthy," equivalent to McLellin's 1872 term "transaction" or the 1838 trial term (from Smith or the clerk) "business." Only the phrase "dirty, nasty, filthy scrape" can be traced directly to Oliver Cowdery. But neither of the phrases—"dirty, nasty, filthy scrape," or "dirty, nasty, filthy affair"—provide any information that would distinguish between the sin of adultery and the sin of polygamy, as he saw it.

The 1842 Fanny Brewer affidavit, likely reflecting Cowdery's reported 1837 "insinuations," identifies Smith's crime as "unlawful intercourse."

The much later testimony of William McLellin, "Mr. Moreton," and the Bond family is more ambiguous. Although McLellin's 1872 letter to Joseph Smith III described his father committing adultery when it spoke of the involved girl as "Miss Hill," it was less specific in characterizing his relationship with "Fanny Alger." But in McLellin's conversation with J. H. Beadle of the *Salt Lake Tribune* three years later, as narrated by Beadle, he described Joseph Smith's relationship with Fanny Alger as "the first well authenticated case of *polygamy*."[55] Thus McLellin appears to describe two relationships, one adulterous and one polygamous, with Fanny Alger's being the latter. However, if, as most interpreters have concluded, the stories *both* refer to Fanny Alger, then McLellin describes her relationship with Joseph Smith inconsistently, as adultery and as polygamy, providing ambivalent witness to an extramarital affair.

---

53. My thanks to H. Michael Marquardt and Brian C. Hales for the information that Warren F. Cowdery served as copyist for this letter.

54. An extensive search by the author of pre-1840 texts in electronic databases fails to shows the occasional use of the term "affair" in the sense of "love affair," but without any evident connotation of adultery.

55. Beadle, "Jackson County," *Salt Lake Tribune*, October 6, 1875, 4. Emphasis added. McLellin reportedly also referred (though perhaps only facetiously) to the intimacy Emma witnessed between Joseph and Fanny as a "sealing."

Braden's "Mr. Moreton," cited third hand, is more explicit that Smith's crime was "adultery." But the source is problematic. There was no "Moreton" among the first of the LDS Twelve Apostles, nor among any of the subsequent apostles. And research by the author and Brian C. Hales has failed to identify a likely "Moreton" (or "Morton") to provide this information. William E. McLellin *was* one of "the first Apostles" in the LDS Church. The father of Braden's "Mrs. Hansbury" was almost certainly not a "Moreton" but a McLellin.[56] McLellin's identity as Braden's "Moreton" would explain Moreton's reported status as one of Smith's "first Apostles" and account for the information Braden claims to have received by way of him. Like William McLellin's "Miss Hill," Moreton's lady of the "Knight" was caught with Joseph by Emma, after which he "confessed" his sin to other church authorities. "Moreton" is thus not an additional source, and this third hand account adds little that is not found in McLellin's firsthand testimonies.

Members of the Bond family, as reported by Braden, described Smith's act with a girl, likely Fanny Alger, as "fornication." Yet they also affirmed that Smith practiced "polygamy" during the Kirtland era, again communicating ambiguity over whether Smith's relationship with Alger was marital or non-marital in nature. As in the larger body of testimony reporting an adulterous relationship between Smith and Alger, the description is equivocal. Likely such ambiguities express the mixed understandings of the period when the event first became known: stories circulated of both polygamy and adultery.

The stronger evidences that Smith had an extramarital relationship with Alger are the contemporaneous events: Emma's expulsion of the girl and expressions of concern that her husband remain "pure"; Smith and Alger's termination of their relationship shortly after its discovery; and Alger's prompt marriage to another man.

It is possible that Emma Smith may have viewed polygamy *as* adultery during the Kirtland period, as she apparently did several years later in Nauvoo.[57] Whatever she knew or thought regarding the nature of

---

56. The daughter's name "Hansbury" is erroneous as well. Braden's informant was likely Helen Rebecca McLellin, who married Lafayette W. Clarke.

57. Emma's Nauvoo view that her husband's polygamy was an "indulgence" comparable to an extramarital affair on her part was described by Joseph Smith to William Clayton, and recorded

Joseph's relationship with Fanny, it raised concerns in her mind that his absence from her could lead to infidelity.

Janet Ellingson's argument about Fanny Alger's behavior also has probative force. A relationship that is, by appearances at least, readily abandoned when discovered and promptly replaced would be quite atypical for a marriage.

But Ellingson makes too much of these data, arguing that Alger's marriage to Custer just a few months after her split from Smith demonstrates unequivocally that she had not regarded herself as married to Smith. Although their separation was not typical for a marriage, *any* marriage they had would, of necessity, been atypical, given its unusual circumstances, much like Smith's heavily documented yet atypical Nauvoo marriages. Though inaugurated with formal wedding ceremonies by elders with legal status as ministers, even these Nauvoo marriages themselves were non-legal and socially scandalous, and therefore carried out in secret. When these relationships were discovered, the consequences could be similar to those for Joseph and Fanny Alger's relationship: Emma's understandable rage, the expulsion of a plural wife from the Smith home, pressure to terminate the relationship, and the rapid spread of rumor. Eliza R. Snow, for instance, who had witnessed Emma's "fuss" over Fanny Alger in the Smiths' Kirtland home, faced her own "fuss," eviction, and demand the relationship cease when her marriage to Joseph was discovered by Emma in the Smiths' Nauvoo home.[58] Snow's relationship with Joseph Smith survived the turmoil. Not all plural marriages did.

Even in the Utah period, when polygamy was an established, public system of marriage, polygamous marriages were contracted and abandoned more readily than monogamous marriages. And early, secret marriages were still more precarious. Seven years after Smith's relationship with Alger ended, his relationship with two other wives was similarly terminated. In August 1843, Emma gave Joseph an ultimatum, requiring that he give up his polygamous marriages with Emily and Eliza Partridge, to which she had explicitly consented at the ceremony, and demanding the girls immediately *remarry* in order to preempt possible resumption

---

in Clayton's journal. George D. Smith, ed., *An Intimate Chronicle: The Journals of William Clayton* (Salt Lake City: Signature Books, 1995), 108, entry for June 23, 1843.

58. Newell and Avery, *Mormon Enigma*, 132–135, 155.

of their relationship with Smith. Under this pressure from his first wife, Smith relented. He and the Partridge sisters parted with an understanding and a handshake.[59]

Smith's relationship with Fanny Alger seven years earlier, contracted without Emma's knowledge or consent and before Smith had taught polygamy's doctrinal rationale, was at least as vulnerable to such pressure. If Smith and Alger did marry, their secret marriage was likely destined for a similar private or even *de facto* "divorce"—physical separation with the understanding the relationship could not persist in the face of domestic and communal uproar.

In either case, whether Fanny Alger regarded herself as having left a marriage to Smith or an affair with him, she had considerable motive to promptly contract a legal marriage. Pregnant and single, a swift marriage was her only chance to avoid the stigma that an illegitimate birth would bring to her and the child.[60]

The evidence that Joseph Smith and Fanny Alger had an extramarital affair may be summarized as follows. In 1837 and 1838, Oliver Cowdery believed Smith and Alger to have committed sexual sin and reportedly insinuated that their relationship constituted adultery but refused to assert it as a fact. Others later ambivalently characterized the relationship as adultery *and* as part of his Kirtland establishment of "polygamy." More significantly, when the relationship was discovered, Joseph Smith, Emma Smith, and Fanny Alger took actions less typical for a marriage than for an affair, though also somewhat typical of later secret polygamy.

Evidence of Marriage

The evidence for a marriage between Joseph Smith and Fanny Alger also temporally divides into contemporaneous evidence, early testimony, and late testimony. But this, more extensive body of evidence also divides into further types. Some of the relevant evidence addresses the larger question of whether Joseph Smith preached and practiced polygamy at Kirtland, providing a backdrop against which claims of polygamy between Smith and Alger can better be assessed. Other evidence directly

---

59. Compton, *In Sacred Loneliness*, 409–411.
60. The child whose fortunes likely guided Fanny in this decision does not appear with the Custers on the census and was probably stillborn or deceased in infancy.

addresses the Smith-Alger relationship. This may be divided into evidence from the following sources: Oliver Cowdery's trial, Fanny Alger's family, contemporaneous Kirtland residents, and contemporaneous members of the Smith household. Also bearing on the question of marriage is the *timing* of the relationship.

Evidence of Kirtland Polygamy

Evidence for Kirtland polygamy predates the 1836 discovery of Joseph Smith's relationship with Fanny Alger. One of the earliest and clearest sources of such evidence is the August 1835 "Article on Marriage" inserted into the Doctrine and Covenants. The Article, quoted above, responds to a case in which some unidentified persons entered a polygamous relationship and thus brought "reproach" upon the Church. The Article makes clear that polygamy, as distinct from adultery, emerged in Mormonism during the Kirtland period, but does not state whether Joseph Smith was one of those involved or provide details of the case.[61] It does, however, offer a significant, if overlooked, clue regarding the incident in the following statement: "According to the custom of all civilized nations, marriage is regulated by laws and ceremonies: therefore we believe, that all marriages in this church of Christ of Latter Day Saints, should be solemnized in a public meeting, or feast prepared for that purpose."[62] The Article's explicit directive that marriages be solemnized at public events suggests that the case in question was not one of bigamy, in which a married person obtains an ostensibly legal marriage to a second spouse, nor one of mere adultery. In forbidding *marriages performed in secret*, the Article suggests the "crime of polygamy" to which it responds was likely such a secret marriage.

Additional evidence of Kirtland polygamy can be found in reminiscent accounts from the 1840s, two of them made during Joseph Smith's lifetime. The first, appearing in Oliver Olney's 1843 *Absurdities of Mormonism*, asserted, "Polygamy was first introduced in Kirtland, Ohio,

---

61. Smith was not the only individual in Kirtland said to have practiced or attempted to practice polygamy. Benjamin F. Johnson claims that Jared Carter pursued this course in 1835. Zimmerman, ed., *I Knew the Prophets*, 38. And Oliver Cowdery's 1834 letters and the 1837 Kirtland Seventies' quorum minutes may hint at individuals entering this practice. See Hales, "Fanny Alger and Joseph Smith's Pre-Nauvoo Reputation," 175–177, 188.
62. Doctrine and Covenants, 1835 edition, Section CI, 251–252.

about eight years ago. ... it was first said to be too strong meat for the Latter Day Saints to bear."⁶³ Olney, who had been a Kirtland resident with in-law connections to prominent Saints, understood polygamy to have originated around 1835.⁶⁴ The second, the pseudonymous letter of "An Exile" published in the *Warsaw Signal* two months before Joseph Smith's death, also identified the mid-1830s as the time polygamy first emerged, similarly stating that it had been prematurely introduced, and adding that it re-emerged in 1838:

> In the year 1834, at Kirtland Ohio, the aforementioned step in the heavenly stairway was located. Much excitement grew out of this measure; many of the Saints demurred.... The doctrine was hushed up, as being sent before its time.... The next glimpse I obtained of this hellish Spiritual Wife doctrine, was in the year 1838, just on the eve of hostilities in Missouri.⁶⁵

The letter appears to have been written by the disaffected Ebenezer Robinson, who shared its author's dissenter or "exile" status, close knowledge of and dissent from Nauvoo polygamy, and critical attitude toward the practice of tithing and the city's vast temple-building project.⁶⁶ His source of information regarding an 1834 marriage is unknown, but his 1834 date for the initial preaching or introduction of polygamy

---

63. Oliver H. Olney, *Absurdities of Mormonism* (Hancock Co., Illinois: [no publisher], 1843), 10.

64. Whether because of his family connections or other sources, Olney had an unusual amount of "inside" information on Joseph Smith, including inklings of the temple endowment two months before it was instituted and 1842 hints that Joseph Smith was making plans to send an expedition to the Rocky Mountains. See his journal writings for the period in the Oliver Olney Papers, originals at Yale; microfilm at LDS Church History Library.

65. An Exile, "The Nauvoo Block and Tackle," *Warsaw Signal*, April 24 ["25"], 1844, 2.

66. "The Nauvoo Block and Tackle" reflects Ebenezer Robinson's experiences and idiosyncratic concerns, including his rejection (from the Nauvoo period forward) of the system of tithing for purportedly providing funds for the church leaders but not for the poor, his objection to the revelation that the Saints would be "rejected with their dead" if they did not complete the temple within the appointed time (LDS D&C 124), his view that the latter idea was a threat to generate fear and provide "incentive" for the payment of tithes, his rejection of polygamy, his recent meeting alongside his wife with Hyrum Smith who had taught them polygamy and likely sealed them in eternal marriage at that time. Compare the content of "The Nauvoo Block and Tackle" to Robinson's personal history and religious reflections in *The Return* (Davis City, Iowa) 1:9 (September 1889): 136–137; 1:10 (October, 1889): 149–151; 1:11 (November, 1889): 174–175; 2:7 (July, 1890): 298–299; 3: 1 (January, 1891): 12–13.

dovetails well with Olney's 1835 date and the Article on Marriage.[67] And his mention of "obtaining a glimpse" of polygamy in Missouri in 1838 can be explained by Robinson's involvement in the Cowdery trial, for which he clerked and at which he would have heard Smith's full, and unrecorded, explanation of what he had confidentially "entrusted" to his "bosom friend" Cowdery regarding his relationship with Alger.

John Whitmer, who was the official historian of the church during and in the aftermath of the Smith-Alger relationship, later (probably in 1847) wrote of that very time, "In the fall of 1836, Joseph Smith Jr., S. Rigdon, & others of the Leaders of the church at Kirtland, Ohio…were lifted up in pride, and lusted after the forbidden things of God such as…[the] Spiritual wife doctrine, that is pleurality [sic] of wives…."[68]

Friendlier sources of later decades similarly report that polygamy was understood, if not practiced, by Joseph Smith in the Ohio period. Several of them place the initial polygamy revelation in or around 1831[69], and William W. Phelps is said to have identified its origin in the 1835 translation process for the Book of Abraham:

> Elder W. W. Phelps said the in Salt lake Tabernacle, in 1862, that while Joseph was translating the Book of Abraham, in Kirtland, Ohio, *in 1835*, from the papyrus found with Egyptian mummies, the Prophet

---

67. Though Robinson did not, by his own account, arrive in Kirtland until March 1835, he was one of the printers of the 1835 Doctrine and Covenants, including the Article on Marriage, and was thus unusually well positioned to know what incident prompted W. W. Phelps, with whom he worked on the publication, to include it.

68. Bruce N. Westergren, *From Historian to Dissident: The Book of John Whitmer* (Salt Lake City: Signature Books, 1995), Chapter XX, 183. Robin Jensen, of the Joseph Smith Papers Project, has dated this portion of Whitmer's book to between February 21, 1847 (a date given at the beginning of Chapter 21), and Whitmer's early spring 1848 rejection of James J. Strang (whom he calls Smith's successor in the manuscript *after* the reference to 1836 "lusting" after plural wives). Personal communication, June 23, 2010.

69. For example, Joseph Bates Noble, at a quarterly stake conference held at Centerville, Davis County, Utah, June 11, 1883, cited in Andrew Jenson, *Historical Record* (May–August 1887): 232–33; Orson Pratt, *Millennial Star*, "Report of Elders Orson Pratt and Joseph F. Smith," 40 (December 16, 1878): 788; Joseph F. Smith, sermon in *Deseret News*, May 20, 1886; quoted in Andrew Jenson, *Historical Record*, 6:219; Helen Mar Kimball Whitney, *Why We Practice Plural Marriage*, (Salt Lake City: Juvenile Instructor Office, 1884), 53; Orson Pratt, sermon, October 7, 1869, G. D. Watt, *Journal of Discourses by Brigham Young, President of the Church of Jesus Christ of Latter-day Saints, His Two Counselors, the Twelve Apostles, and Others*, 26 volumes (Liverpool: F. D. Richards, 1855), 13:193.

became impressed with the idea that polygamy would yet become an institution of the Mormon Church.[70]

Benjamin F. Johnson attributed his own first awareness of polygamy to a conversation with his well-connected brother-in-law during the same time period: "In 1835, at Kirtland, I learned from my sister's husband, Lyman R. Sherman,[71] who was close to the Prophet, and received it from him, 'that the ancient order of Plural Marriage was again to be practiced by the Church.'"[72]

Smith's plural wife Mary Elizabeth Rollins Lightner did not learn of polygamy from him until early 1842, but recalled that he said he had first been commanded by an angel to take her as a wife during the middle of the Kirtland period, in 1834.[73]

A voluminous but late and often confused set of testimonies to the Kirtland teaching and practice of polygamy is also provided by late non-Mormon recollections. G. S. Pelton recalled a Mormon man who acknowledged having two wives, and stated, incorrectly, that "[t]here was no secret about Mormons having plural wives in Kirtland."[74] Clark Braden cited J. M. Atwater's recollection of being told about polygamy

---

70. T. B. H. Stenhouse, *Rocky Mountain Saints* (New York: Appleton and Company, 1873), 182n, emphasis added. Stenhouse states: "Elder W. W. Phelps said in Salt Lake Tabernacle, in 1862, that while Joseph was translating the Book of Abraham, in Kirtland, Ohio, in 1835, from the papyrus found with the Egyptian mummies, the Prophet became impressed with the idea that polygamy would yet become an institution of the Mormon Church. Brigham Young was present, and was much annoyed at the statement made by Phelps, but it is highly probable that it was the real secret which the latter then divulged. The Conscientious Mormon who calmly considers what is here written on the introduction of polygamy into the Mormon Church will readily see that its origin is probably much more correctly traceable to those Egyptian mummies, than to a revelation from heaven. The first paragraph of the Revelation has all the musty odour of the catacombs about it, and that Joseph went into polygamy at a venture there cannot be the slightest doubt."

71. Sherman was called by Joseph Smith as an apostle but died before learning of the calling. See Lyndon W. Cook, "Lyman Sherman—Man of God, Would-Be Apostle," *BYU Studies* 19:1 (1978): 121–124.

72. As Johnson recalled, this disclosure regarding polygamy was made at the same time rumors were circulating that Joseph "loved Fanny."

73. "He said I was the first woman God commanded him to take as a plural wife in 1834. He was very much frightened about until the angel appeared to him three times." Mary Elizabeth Rollins Lightner to Emmeline B. Wells, summer 1905, photocopy of manuscript in Linda King Newell Collection, Ms 447, Box 9, Fd. 2, Marriott Library.

74. G. S. Pelton affidavit, March 21, 1885, in Arthur B. Deming, *Naked Truths About Mormonism* (Oakland, California), 1:12 (April 1888): 203, Col. 3–1.

in Kirtland by disaffected witness to the Book of Mormon, Martin Harris, who said polygamy was first announced by Smith's counselor Sidney Rigdon, that it was then "taught and practiced by Smith and in Kirtland under the name of 'spiritual wifery.'"[75]

Kirtland Justice of the Peace J. C. Dowen recalled in an affidavit solicited by anti-Mormon author Arthur B. Deming that the Mormons were performing extra-legal marriages and also that he had once known "the names of Joe Smith's two spiritual wives in Kirtland."[76]

Charlotte Bond, who (as noted above) was present in Kirtland at the time of the Fanny Alger incident, is reported by Braden to have "repeatedly declared" to her children and other of his sources "that Smith practiced polygamy in Kirtland," citing the example of a girl he followed into "a privy," though incongruously labeling his sexual relationship with her as "fornication."[77]

More than one of the witnesses recalled hearing of Joseph Smith's rumored polygamy in 1837, when gossip about Smith's relationship with Fanny Alger reached its zenith. Nancy Smith Alexander recalled in an affidavit the source, place, and timing of learning the prophet was a polygamist: "I heard Mrs. Betsy Gilett, say in our house in Kirtland before the Prophet Jo Smith left for Mo. [at the end of 1837] [t]hat he practiced a plurality of wives. There was very much talk among the old women about plurality of wives...."[78] Nancy's brother, Warren, told Braden of having heard the same or similar reports: "W[arren]. S. Smith and others testify that the practice of sealing women to men was so much talked of at Kirtland, while Smith was there, that it became a by-word on the streets."[79]

Distinguished educator Alfred Holbrook recounted in his autobiography what he learned of polygamy during his 1837 visit to Kirtland as young man: "The doctrine was first broached in Kirtland by the revelation of Joe Smith, with reference to the daughter of one of the old inhab-

---

75. Kelley and Braden, *Public Discussion of the Issues*, 202.

76. J. C. Dowen affidavit, January 2, 1885, Deming, *Naked Truths about Mormonism*, 2:1 (December, 1888):301, Col. 1–3 through 1–5. Dowan was elected Justice of the Peace in 1833 and 1836.

77. Kelley and Braden, *Public Discussion of the Issues*, 202.

78. "Mrs. Alexander's Statement," ca. 1886, A. B. Deming Papers, Utah State History Division (copy of material in the Chicago Historical Society).

79. Kelley and Braden, *Public Discussion of the Issues*, 202.

itants of Kirtland, who was sealed to Joe as his spiritual wife."[80] Though the Algers were not "old inhabitants of Kirtland," the coincidence of visitor Holbrook hearing this rumor at the time Oliver Cowdery and others were most actively spreading the story of Fanny Alger strongly suggests she is the one referred to.

Tending to confirm these late accounts of prophetic polygamy rumors in Kirtland, Smith, as editor of the *Elders' Journal*, published a list of frequently asked questions, including this: "Do the Mormons believe in having more wives than one?"[81] Though rumor had long held that the Saints practiced group marriage, Smith eluded specific questions about "a community of wives" in favor of a question about "having more wives than one." Consistent with the accounts of Nancy Smith and Alfred Holbrook, the more salient rumor at the time was not one of free love, but of polygamy.[82] These sources collectively identify 1837 as a time when polygamy gossip about the prophet spread widely in Kirtland and reached its peak. And it is not coincidental that rumors of his polygamy and his relationship with a woman later said to be his polygamous wife peaked at the same time.[83]

---

80. Alfred Holbrook, *Reminiscences of the Happy Life of a Teacher* (Cincinnati: Elm Street Printing, 1885), 223–24: "I do not think, however, that Mr. Rigdon ever favored the idea of polygamy. . . . The doctrine was first broached in Kirtland by the revelation of Joe Smith, with reference to the daughter of one of the old inhabitants of Kirtland, who was sealed to Joe as his spiritual wife. It was not the prevalent doctrine, nor generally received as binding upon other persons than those who were called by a distinct revelation."

81. Joseph Smith, Editorial, *Elders' Journal*, 1:2 (November 1837): 28–29. Smith's response to this question, in the succeeding issue of the *Elders' Journal* (printed July 1838) was, "No, not at the same time. But they believe that if their companion dies, they have a right to marry again." Joseph Smith, Editorial, *Elders' Journal* volume 1:3 (July 1838): 43.

82. Although the standard "community of wives" charge is not among those Smith addresses Brian Hales suggests that the polygamy question should nonetheless be read in light of that charge, particularly given that the polygamy question is preceded by one on whether the Saints believe in "having all things in common." Hales, "Fanny Alger and Joseph Smith's Pre-Nauvoo Reputation," 172–175, 188. The issues of "plurality of wives" and "community of wives" are distinct, if often associated, and the question on having more wives than one suggests that rumors of the former were at least as much a concern as the latter.

83. It should not be assumed that polygamy rumors were universally distributed in Kirtland, nor even that everyone heard about Joseph Smith and Fanny Alger. Brian Hales has documented several Kirtland residents of the mid-1830s who later reported no recollection of polygamy talk in Kirtland. And an extensive newspaper search by Hales and the present author shows no media awareness of Mormon polygamy until 1842. See Hales, "Fanny Alger and Joseph Smith's Pre-Nauvoo Reputation," 165–172. Rumors of adultery were likely the most widespread in Kirtland after the Fanny Alger "fuss" began, and some individuals apparently heard no rumors of relation-

Other evidence that the prophet and Fanny Alger were secretly married is given by the 1838 Oliver Cowdery trial, in testimony by her parents, brother, and cousin, and in late testimony by contemporaneous residents of Kirtland and even in the Smith home.

The 1838 trial proceedings in which Oliver Cowdery was found guilty of insinuating that Smith committed adultery offer distinct lines of evidence, ironically, not only that Joseph Smith's relationship with Fanny Alger was extramarital, but also that it was marital. Though Smith plainly denied to the high council that he and Alger had engaged in an adulterous relationship, it is not clear that he denied they had *any* relationship. His comment to the council about having entrusted many things to Cowdery implies the opposite—that he *had* confided the relationship to Cowdery: "Joseph Smith jr testifies that Oliver Cowdery had been his bosom friend, therefore he entrusted him with many things. He then gave a history respecting the girl business." Though the council clearly felt, on the basis of Smith's testimony, that Cowdery had indeed "*falsely* insinuated" he was guilty of adultery, the possibly sensitive details of what Smith had "entrusted" to his "bosom friend" were omitted by high council clerk Ebenezer Robinson from the trial record.[84]

If Smith did broach the idea of polygamy in his explanation to the high council, this would account for Robinson's later affirmation that he "glimpsed" polygamy in 1838—which is when *he* would have learned the relationship was polygamous.[85] Robinson's statement might conceivably also refer to Smith's later reported 1838 relationship with Lucinda Harris. But it seems doubtful that this case, if it did occur at that time, would

---

ship at all. But the early accounts of Whitmer, Olney, and Robinson suggest that some were in the know regarding the relationship's polygamous nature, and the broadly agreeing resident and visitor reminiscences, along with the *Elder's Journal* question, indicate that polygamy rumor also spread among the wider populace.

84. Cannon and Cook, eds., *Far West Record*, 162–169.

85. A similar interpretation is made by Richard Bushman: "[Joseph Smith] contended that he had never confessed to adultery. . . In contemporaneous documents, only one person, Cowdery, believed that Joseph had had an affair with Fanny Alger. Others may have heard the rumors, but none joined Cowdery in making accusations. David Patten, who made inquiries in Kirtland, concluded the rumors were untrue. No one proposed to put Joseph on trial for adultery. . . . On his part, Joseph never denied a relationship with Alger, but insisted it was not adulterous. He wanted it on record that he had never confessed to such a sin. Presumably, he felt innocent because he had married Alger." Richard L. Bushman, *Joseph Smith: Rough Stone Rolling* (New York: Alfred A. Knopf, 2005), 324–25.

have been either well known or identified as *polygamy*. The relationship is not discussed in any available contemporaneous documents. And if it had been known, Lucinda's legal marriage to George W. Harris would have framed it as adultery, rather than polygamy. The only known case at all likely to have provided a "glimpse" of polygamy at that time was, therefore, of Joseph Smith and Fanny Alger. Given Robinson's access to confidential information on that relationship, through the Cowdery trial, it very likely constitutes his "glimpse."

In understanding Fanny Alger's relationship with Joseph Smith as polygamous, Robinson would certainly not have been alone. Alger's family, in later years and likely at the time, understood it as such. When Fanny's mother and father retrieved her from Kirtland and took her to Indiana, Fanny was pregnant and at the center of a scandal. Nevertheless, Fanny's mother is said, on the authority of Eliza J. Webb, to have "always claimed that she was sealed to Joseph."[86]

Fanny's brother was reportedly a more ambivalent witness. Benjamin F. Johnson, sharing his knowledge of Joseph Smith's life in 1903, reported that her brother's inquiries about the relationship after Smith's death were met with the answer, "That is all a matter of my own, and I have nothing to communicate."[87] But John Hawley, reporting on a conversation with the brother, John Alger, wrote, "what I heard [from] John Olger one of the first (or among the first) members of the Church toald me his Sister was Seald to Joseph in Curtlin, this he Said to me in 1868 [sic]."[88]

---

86. Ann Eliza Webb Young, *Wife No. 19, or the Story of a Life in Bondage, being a Complete Expose of Mormonism, and Revealing the Sorrows, Sacrifices and Sufferings of Women in Polygamy*, (Hartford, Connecticut: Dustin, Gilman & Co., 1875), 66–67. See also Eliza Jane Webb's report to Mary E. Bond (Webb to Bond, 24 April 1876) that Fanny's mother "says Fanny was sealed to Joseph" in 1835 or 1836. That Eliza Webb had continued communication with the Algers regarding Fanny seems evident from her knowledge of the fate of Fanny's child by Joseph Smith. The letter communicates Eliza's understanding that none of Joseph's children by polygamous wives survived, indicating either that Fanny's pregnancy ended without a live birth or that the child died. Although Chauncey Webb, as quoted in note 4 above indicates that Alger was pregnant when she left the Smith home (and went to the Webb home), his wife wrote, "…Emma Smith turned Fanny out of her house because of Joseph's intimacy with her. Joseph never had any living children by his polygamous women…."

87. Zimmerman, *I Knew the Prophets*, 33.

88. John Hawley Autobiography, January 1885, Community of Christ Library-Archives, excerpts typed March 1982 by Lyndon W. Cook, in Scott H. Faulring Papers, Marriott Library, Accn 2316. Box 19, Folder 11, 97. Spelling as in original.

The account by Fanny's first cousin Mosiah Hancock also communicates the family understanding that she was secretly married to Joseph Smith. And however problematic Hancock's account is in several of its details, it seems more likely that he related garbled stories from his father, aunt, and other family than he created his entire elaborate family narrative *ex nihilo*.

Another type of evidence that the relationship was marital comes from witnesses who had been aware of the relationship at the time and recalled it years later to have been polygamy. Despite his ambivalence noted above, William McLellin qualifies as one of these, having described the relationship, according to the *Salt Lake Tribune*'s J. H. Beadle, as "the first well authenticated case of polygamy."[89]

Eliza Jane Churchill Webb was another. Webb, with whom Fanny Alger stayed after she left the Smith home, knew from Alger's explanations that Emma had evicted her because of her intimacy with Smith. While not committing herself to believing that Fanny's case was also one of full-blown "sealing," Webb was open to the "sealing" interpretation and expressed herself as "perfectly satisfied that something similar commenced" in Kirtland and particularly in the case of Fanny Alger. Though Eliza Webb's primary reason for holding this position appears to be that she knew Smith and Alger had a sexual relationship, her phrasing indicates that she believed a new relationship *practice* began in Kirtland, and not merely that Smith and Alger had a spontaneous extramarital affair.[90]

Chauncey G. Webb, Eliza's husband, who was similarly situated to know what Fanny Alger said of her relationship with Joseph Smith, stated that Smith "was sealed there [in Kirtland] secretly to Fanny Alger." Further wording by Webb about the couple's "celestial relation" that

---

89. *Salt Lake Tribune*, October 6, 1875.
90. Eliza J. Webb to Mary Bond, 24 April 1876; and Eliza J. Webb, Lockport, New York to Mary Bond, 4 May 1876, Biographical Folder Collection, P21, fi1 [Myron H. Bond], item 9. Eliza appears to have been responding to a question from her correspondent Mary Bond regarding whether the practice of sealing really began in Kirtland, as suggested in Webb's previous letter. To this implied question Webb responded: 'I do not know that the "sealing" commenced in Kirtland but I am perfectly satisfied that something similar commenced and my judgment is principally formed from what Fanny Alger told me herself concerning her reasons for leaving 'sister Emma.'" Members of the Bond family, with whom Eliza Webb corresponded regarding Fanny Alger and who were evidently in Kirtland at the time of the stir over Fanny Alger, also believed the relationship to have been polygamous.

resulted in Fanny's pregnancy is obviously facetious, but his statement about a secret sealing appears to be intended at face value. Webb, unlike McLellin, uses the term "sealed" to refer to something that happened *to* Smith and Alger, rather than to refer to what they did together in a hay loft. Webb also adds the qualifier "secretly" to the sealing of Smith and Alger, which would be otiose if his term "sealing" is meant to refer only to sexual relations between the two. While Webb may not have understood the Smith-Alger relationship to have begun under the rubric of *eternal marriage*, he does appear to have understood it to have begun under the rubric of *marriage*.[91]

Even closer to the relationship between Joseph Smith and Fanny Alger is a witness, mentioned above, from within the Smith household, one of Fanny's co-residents in the home, the then newly baptized Eliza R. Snow. As two single women living with the Smiths, Fanny and Eliza are likely to have roomed together. And Eliza affirmed that she had known Fanny, lived in the home at the time the mistress of the house learned of the latter's relationship with Joseph Smith, and known of the "fuss" the discovery created.

Significantly, it was on Eliza's authority that Fanny Alger's name was presented to the world by Andrew Jenson as that of a plural wife of Joseph Smith. When Snow provided Jenson with the names of such wives, she omitted at least one wife she thought doubtful or problematic and then, before completing the list, deleted others.[92] Had she felt uncertain or troubled over Fanny's status as a wife, or feared that including her as a wife might prove embarrassing, she had the option of omitting or removing her name as well. But she did not. Notably, Snow appears to have believed Fanny Alger was likely to be living at the time she presented Alger's name for publication, increasing the danger that a false identification of Alger as a plural wife might lead to embarrassment. Thus, in a few ways, Snow's inclusion and retention of Fanny Alger on her list of Joseph Smith's plural wives demonstrated considerable confidence that Fanny did indeed belong in this category.

---

91. Wyl, *Mormon Portraits*, 57.
92. This may be demonstrated by an analysis of the changes made to the list in current work in progress by the author.

Eliza R. Snow's confidence that Smith was not an adulterer who had used girls living in his home is also indicated by another, more momentous action she undertook. Six years after the Alger incident, while again living in the Smith home, she married Joseph Smith. She then, following a course eerily like Fanny's, reportedly found herself pregnant with his child and expelled from the home by Emma.[93] Though there is no doubt that Eliza Snow was taken with Joseph Smith's charisma and awed by his prophetic mantle, her action bespeaks a degree of trust in both Smith's revelations and his intentions that reasonably might, and ought, to have been lacking had she observed evidence that he seduced his former boarder, Fanny Alger.

While it is unclear whether Eliza R. Snow understood in 1836 that Joseph Smith was plurally married to Fanny Alger, it does seem evident that whatever she knew or observed of their relationship at the time did not prevent her from presenting Alger's name to the world as that of a plural wife nor from accepting a polygamous proposal from Smith herself.

The final line of evidence supporting a marriage between Joseph Smith and Fanny Alger is provided by the indications by Eliza R. Snow and others that the relationship was discovered in mid-1836. The *timing* of the relationship, or at least the timing of one bookend of the relationship—its termination, has implications for its *nature*.

The relationship of Joseph Smith and Fanny Alger was discovered and terminated later than has generally been believed. As noted, historians have usually identified the August 1835 Article on Marriage's declaration against polygamy as a response to rumor about the Smith family drama over Fanny Alger. But given that Emma did not make her "fuss" over Alger until mid-1836 and that rumors over that situation appear not to have gathered to a full head of steam until 1837, this cannot be correct. Thus polygamy had *demonstrably* entered Mormondom sometime before the Smith-Alger blow-up, from *at least* the time of the 1834–1835 events to which the Article on Marriage responded. It is senseless to argue that their relationship had to be extramarital when discussion, and

---

93. Brian C. Hales identifies five accounts indicating that Eliza was pregnant at the time of the conflict with Emma that preceded her expulsion from the Smith home, but questions their accuracy. See Hales, "Emma Smith, Eliza R. Snow, and the Reported Incident on the Stairs," *Mormon Historical Studies* 10:2 (2009): 63–75.

even incidents, of polygamy (however little known) were underway in the church sometime before their relationship was discovered, and likely before it even began.

Another implication of the late ending date for the Joseph Smith-Fanny Alger relationship is that it increases the plausibility the relationship would have been solemnized by a third-party officiator in a formal, though private, wedding ceremony. Early Latter-day Saint elders believed they were within their rights to perform marriages, as ministers of the Gospel, and did so where this was legally permissible. But they were long denied this privilege in Kirtland, barred from obtaining licenses to perform marriages under ministerial authority (likely because their religious body was not properly incorporated with the county). Among the Saints, only Sidney Rigdon, who still possessed a license from his days as a "Campbellite" minister, used ministerial authority to perform public marriages. But ultimately even Rigdon was blocked from doing so and was indicted in June 1835 for performing a marriage on a license that was presumed revoked, because of his change of denomination. *Any* Latter Day Saint who performed a marriage in Geauga County on ministerial authority was subject to prosecution.[94]

The publication of the Article on Marriage two months later changed this. Ohio marriage statute provided that officiators could act without a license so long as the ceremony was done "agreeable to the rules and regulations of their respective churches." Because the Saints now *had* official rules and regulations regarding marriage, their ministers could assert the right to perform marriages accordingly.[95] Indeed, this was likely an *intended* effect of the Article on Marriage and may account for the urgency of including the Article in the Doctrine and Covenants and even the need for it to disclaim the recent incident or incidents of polygamy. The Saints *needed* an official statement of marriage rules in order to legally perform their own marriages, and a public impression that the Saints would use this legal right to form quasi-legal polygamous marriages may

---

94. M. Scott Bradshaw, "Joseph Smith's Performance of Marriages in Ohio," *Brigham Young University Studies* 39:4 (2000): 23–24.

95. Hartley, William G. "Newel and Lydia Bailey Knight's Kirtland Love Story and Historic Wedding." *BYU Studies* 39 (2000): [6–22], 18; and, Bradshaw, "Joseph Smith's Performance of Marriages in Ohio," 23–69.

have undermined their ability to assert it.⁹⁶ Though the Article on Marriage responds in part to an early incident of polygamy in the church, it is not *about* polygamy. Its purpose, and effect, was to enable the Saints to exercise in the legal domain an authority they believed they already held in the spiritual—the power to marry.

With the Article in place and the Doctrine and Covenants printed, the prophet began asserting his rights of marriage, first in performing the nuptials of Newel Knight and Lydia Goldthwaite Bailey on November 24. In doing so he declared, on Lydia's recollection:

> Our elders have been wronged and prosecuted for marrying without a license. The Lord God of Israel has given me authority to unite the people in the holy bonds of matrimony and from this time forth I shall use that privilege to marry whomsoever I see fit.⁹⁷

Newel similarly recalled that the prophet performed the marriage in "the name of the Lord, & by the authority of the preisthood [sic]."⁹⁸

That Smith claimed his authority to marry from God rather than from the state is significant. If he claimed authority solely *from* the state, then he would be justified only in performing marriages duly authorized *by* the state. But since he claimed authority from God, he could feel justified in performing, or delegating the performance of, any marriage he believed to be *authorized* by God—including a polygamous one.

There were several months between Smith's November 1835 public assertion that he (and "our elders") held divine authority to perform marriages and the discovery of his relationship with Alger, during which he could have had a marriage performed for them.⁹⁹ But there is no reason to suppose that Smith only came to believe he held *divine* authority to perform marriages when he acquired *legal* authority to perform them. Smith's November 1835 announcement celebrated his new ability to *use*

---

96. This purpose for the Article on Marriage appears to have gone previously unremarked. I am indebted to the works of Bradshaw, Hales, and Hartley for providing the basis for this reinterpretation.
97. Hartley, 17.
98. Newel Knight, "Autobiography and journal [ca. 1846];" MS 767, Folder 1, item 4, 59; LDS Church History Library.
99. Chauncey Webb's implication that Fanny Alger was visibly pregnant at the time she stayed in the Webb home suggests the relationship began no later than the end of April 1836, allowing five months in which a marriage could have been performed.

his divine marriage authority legally, not a new bestowal of divine authority. An account from Justice of the Peace J. C. Dowen suggests Smith may have begun marrying the Saints "according to the law of God" before that time, with the understanding that the legality of the marriage depended on its being also solemnized by one licensed to marry. In any case, Smith claimed divine authority to marry under God's law *no later than* November 1835, making a marriage between himself and Fanny Alger after that date perfectly plausible.

Smith's self-understood authority to bind family relationships may have expanded still further before his relationship with Alger began when on April 3, 1836, he and Oliver Cowdery experienced the delivery of divine "keys" or authority from Elijah, the authority under which later Mormons would receive eternal marriage "sealings." A mid-1836 termination date for the Smith-Alger relationship thus makes it possible that it was not only a marriage but also a sealing, as suggested by the Webbs and others.[100] In either case the mid-1836 end date for the relationship is significant. As the plausible time frame for the relationship's inception comes to encompass Joseph Smith's early public performance of marriages in fall 1835, and even the reception of "sealing keys" in early spring 1836, the plausibility that it was initiated with a marriage ceremony rises sharply.

Review and Critique of the Evidence for a Marriage

The evidence for Kirtland polygamy, and for polygamy between Joseph Smith and Fanny Alger in particular, needs to be examined critically so its true value can be assayed. The first evidence to be critiqued is that provided by the Article on Marriage. Because the Article precedes the Alger "fuss" it cannot refer directly to that incident; and it may not even refer to a relationship entered into by Joseph Smith. But polygamy ideas afloat in 1834–1835 Kirtland likely reflect Smith's private teachings and demonstrate that polygamy was even then resonant with Mormon

---

100. A post-April 3, 1836, date for the beginning of the Smith-Alger relationship is certainly possible, but, given her relatively advanced state of pregnancy later that summer, is less probable than an earlier beginning date. For a more precise date of the relationship's ending, consult Bradley, "Dating Fanny Alger: The Nature, Timing, and Consequences of an Early Polygamous Relationship," which narrows the discovery to a two-week window in 1836, sets it in its immediate context, and works out its implications in detail.

restorationism. Smith's reported entry into polygamy by spring 1836 fits the context of the time.

The early testimony of Kirtland polygamy is one of the more impressive lines of evidence in its favor. Oliver Olney and Ebenezer Robinson, both dissenters against non-monogamous practices, had no reason to whitewash as polygamy what their knowledge suggested was only adultery. Yet both, writing during Smith's life and with reasonable claim to inside information, attested to Kirtland polygamy. John Whitmer, similarly unsympathetic to Smith and to polygamy and writing within four years of Smith's death, had as little reason to recast adultery as polygamy, yet referred to polygamy being taught in Kirtland at almost the precise time rumor of the Alger incident began to ripple out from the Smith house.

The circa 1835 testimony of Lyman Sherman on polygamy to Benjamin F. Johnson and Smith's own 1842 testimony that he had been commanded to wed Mary Rollins in 1834 are more problematic because they are reported secondhand and late.[101] Johnson heard Sherman's statement while quite young, reported it nearly seventy years later and after many years' awareness of subsequent polygamy. Yet Johnson's numerous other late reminiscences are treated as valuable historical sources because of his general accuracy, and Lyman Sherman's early death and personal non-involvement in polygamy pinpoint the remembered conversation as occurring before the Nauvoo institution of polygamy and bolsters Johnson's recollection. Mary Rollins Lightner is also a widely used, informed and evidently accurate, source. And it seems likely that she recalled when, on Smith's account, the angel had first commanded him to marry her.

Less reliable and more problematic are the late testimonies of Kirtland residents and visitors. The testimony of G. S. Pelton that Mormons were *open* in their practice of polygamy in Kirtland is clearly false. The testimonies collected by Clark Braden and Arthur Deming are identifiably colored by John C. Bennett's popular 1842 exposé *The History of the Saints* and by subsequent news reports on polygamy. Some of these testimonies anachronistically place the Nauvoo term "spiritual wives" on the

---

101. On Lyman Sherman, see Lyndon W. Cook, "Lyman Sherman—Man of God, Would-Be Apostle," *BYU Studies* 19:1 (1978):121–124.

lips of the Kirtland Saints and backdating Smith's early 1840s proposal to Nancy Rigdon to the mid-1830s.[102]

Yet these recollections presumably reflect, to some extent, the rumors that raged over the Alger incident. And it seems unlikely that so many witnesses hostile toward Smith would have converted rumors of mere adultery into a more formal practice which, though alien to their own sensibilities, had some biblical claim to respectability.

The late resident accounts may also be inaccurate in describing Rigdon as a supporter of polygamy, something the Nauvoo sources do not show. Yet the claim is made in a few of these accounts, and also in John Whitmer's earlier, "inside" history, and this despite the Nauvoo-era narrative of Rigdon's anger when Smith proposed to his daughter. The accounts provide some evidence that Rigdon may have supported polygamy for a time during the Kirtland era, which, if true, might make him a candidate for performing Kirtland-era plural marriages.

Though none of the Kirtland residents' testimonies of Mormon polygamy pre-date the Bennett exposé, this puts them on par with the resident testimonies of Mormon adultery, which are also late and confused. The polygamy reports are more numerous and less ambiguous than those of adultery. Some of them tend to suggest 1837 as a peak time for polygamy rumors in Kirtland, which, as described above, is also the time when the Fanny Alger rumors peaked and when Joseph Smith found it necessary to respond in the *Elders' Journal* to the "common" question of whether the Saints believed in polygamy. Such consistency between late Kirtland resident/visitor accounts, early insider accounts, and denials in near-contemporaneous LDS press indicate the presence of contemporaneous rumors that Smith practiced polygamy.

The evidence of the 1838 Cowdery trial and his letter to his brother is inarguably mixed. The several affiants giving testimony for the trial appear to have understood Cowdery to imply that Smith had committed adultery with Alger. And though he would not explicitly affirm this, he did not deny it either, except in one dubious instance in which his nonverbal actions reportedly contradicted the verbal denial. Oliver's letter to

---

102. For discussion of the backdating of the Nancy Rigdon incident and discussion of sealing from Nauvoo to Kirtland, see Hales, "Fanny Alger and Joseph Smith's Pre-Nauvoo Reputation," 127–129.

his brother Warren, weeks before the trial, indicates that he and Joseph Smith argued vehemently over the *meaning* of Smith's behavior, implying they took different positions on whether it was adulterous. Smith's behavior, it appears, was not an open-and-shut case of adultery, but a matter of interpretation.

Smith's unrecorded disclosures to the high council regarding what he had "confided" in his "bosom friend" Cowdery and what had happened in "the girl business," imply he did not deny having a relationship with Alger, but only that the relationship was not adultery. Later and even contemporaneous rumors of his polygamy indicate the grounds on which he could have made such a denial. And high council clerk Ebenezer Robinson's remembered "glimpse" of polygamy in 1838, having no other readily plausible referent, provides significant evidence that Smith acknowledged to the council that Alger had been his polygamous wife.

The testimony of various members of the Alger family also provides evidence, but is nearly always indirect. The statements of Fanny's mother, brother John, and uncle Levi are all reported secondhand.[103] The only direct family testimony comes from her first cousin, Mosiah, who was not alive at the time of the events he narrates and necessarily relies on his memories of his parents' stories.

These family members are consistent in affirming a marriage. Yet they appear to have been largely in the dark regarding any marriage details. The Mosiah Hancock account seems confused and attributes performance of the marriage to his father, who failed to claim such a thing for himself in his own autobiography. The mother's reported belief that Oliver Cowdery performed her daughter's marriage to Smith is inconsistent with Cowdery's documented rage over the relationship. And Fanny reportedly refused to offer her brother any clarification on the matter.

Possible explanations for this reported ignorance among close family are that 1) Fanny never disclosed anything to them about a marriage and they inferred from the later practice of polygamy that it must have been one, 2) the reports are erroneous (e.g., on Clarissa Alger believing her daughter's marriage to Joseph Smith had been performed by

---

103. Research identifying first-hand family testimony on Fanny Alger's relationship with Joseph Smith would be one of the most valuable further contributions that could be made on the question.

Cowdery, Fanny refusing to discuss the matter with John, etc.), and 3) Fanny's mother and possibly others were told she had married Smith, but further details were kept secret. Although any of these are plausible, it seems unlikely that Fanny refused to say *anything* to her mother and other family during her pregnancy about how she came to carry Smith's child. So she likely said something at least consistent with the marriage interpretation.

The testimony of those who were aware of the Fanny Alger blow-up in the Smith household at the time it occurred is also valuable in assessing the nature of the relationship. McLellin's testimony is, as discussed above, ambiguous. He appears to believe that Smith's relationship with Fanny Alger was polygamous while at the same time holding that his relationship with "Miss Hill" (identified in other sources with Alger) was adulterous, seemingly testifying himself to a standstill.

Whatever Chauncey and Eliza J. Webb knew from Fanny Alger and from whomever had arranged her stay with them was at least consistent with polygamy, and perhaps suggestive of it. Both Webbs offered their testimony as *opponents* of Mormonism, and, like the non-Mormon and other ex-Mormon residents of Kirtland, had no reason to whitewash as polygamy what their information suggested to be only adultery.

Eliza R. Snow's identification of Fanny Alger as a wife was important but in two ways potentially problematic. First, Eliza may have only inferred after the fact that Alger had been Smith's wife, rather than paramour. And, second, in her autobiography she expresses the shock and dismay she experienced on learning, in Nauvoo, that polygamy "was to be introduced into the church" and reveals that she first thought this restoration was far off, probably even beyond the term of her natural life.[104] Whatever experience Eliza may have had of polygamy in Kirtland, she did not understand from it that polygamy was to become a church

---

104. Eliza R. Snow, "Sketch of My Life," in *The Personal Writings of Eliza Roxcy Snow*, ed. Maureen Ursenbach Beecher (Logan, UT: Utah State University Press, 2000), 13: "In Nauvoo I first understood that the practice of plurality of wives was to be introduced into the church. The subject was very repugnant to my feelings—so directly was it in opposition to my educated prepossessions, that it seemed as though all the prejudices of my ancestors for generations past congregated around me: But when I reflected that I was living in the Dispensation of the fulness of times, embracing all other Dispensations, surely Plural Marriage must necessarily be included, and I consoled myself with the idea that it was far in the distance, and beyond the period of my mortal existence."

practice, and may not have even recognized it as polygamy at the time (if indeed it was there). Yet such expressions of shock are a stock theme in the autobiographies of Nauvoo Saints, even when those Saints had prior inklings of polygamy. Benjamin F. Johnson and Brigham Young, who both report prior understanding that polygamy would be practiced, felt thunderstruck when they confronted it up close. The point of such narratives, which undoubtedly express genuine turmoil from the time, is that polygamy was not *sought after* or *chosen*, but dropped on the unwilling narrator, who accepts it only because God requires it. Given this function of the stock "polygamy shock" motif, Snow's autobiographical use of it tells little about previous encounters she may have had with polygamy, including whether she knew or heard in 1836 that Fanny Alger had been Joseph Smith's plural wife.

Despite her averred surprise, Snow demonstrated confidence in following Fanny's relationship course in Nauvoo and later in publishing her name as that of Smith's wife, even while she might well yet be living, suggesting that if she did not actually know from her Kirtland experience in the Smith household that her erstwhile housemate had been Joseph Smith's wife, what she knew from that experience was, at minimum, *consistent* with that conclusion.[105]

The final evidence favoring a marriage between Joseph Smith and Fanny Alger is that the relationship ended much later than previously believed. This allows, and may suggest, that the relationship *began* relatively late as well. Given that the relationship did not end until approximately summer 1836, it plausibly began after the summer 1835 Article on Marriage reacting to polygamy within the church, and quite likely after the 1834–1835 case or cases of polygamy to which the Article responds. It also plausibly began after Smith publicly proclaimed his divine rights of marriage in November 1835, and probably after Smith began to *believe* he held such rights, increasing the odds that he saw *it* as a divinely authorized polygamous marriage.

---

105. Significantly, in 1899 Eliza's brother, Lorenzo Snow, had Fanny Alger posthumously sealed to Smith in the Salt Lake Temple as an earthly wife for whom there had been no sealing record, likely reflecting Eliza's view that Alger had been a plural wife to Smith in this life. Also, the delay in her temple sealing to Smith until after her death suggests some awareness by the Snows and others that Fanny was still living during the 1880s.

Evidence that Joseph Smith and Fanny Alger contracted a marital relationship in mid-1830s Kirtland is of several types. Diverse lines of evidence, most of them strong in themselves, join in indicating this same conclusion. Contemporaneous evidence and late evidence, testimony and inference, family and stranger, friend and foe, all primarily affirm a marital relationship. The consilience or convergence of such lines of evidence is itself the best evidence that Smith and Alger married. This evidence is not without ambiguity or contradiction. There is evidence pointing in other directions. Yet given the mass and strength of this evidence and its solid preponderance in favor of a marriage, a marriage provides the best model for integrating the variegated data into a single picture. It seems unlikely that the voluminous and complex evidence for a polygamous marriage can all be integrated into a framework of simple adultery. The prognosis for integrating the evidence for adultery into the framework of an unfolding system of secret polygamy is much more promising. The evidence consistent with the hypothesis of adultery may not, and seems quite unlikely ever to, indicate that the relationship between Smith and Alger was a spontaneous extramarital affair, but it should inform and enrich understanding of how secret polygamy worked "on the ground."

The difficulty of identifying an officiator for the marriage, a difficulty apparently shared even by Fanny's family, may be read as indicating that there was no marriage to be officiated, but is almost certainly better understood to indicate the secrecy of the relationship and perhaps the nonstandard nature of its ceremony.[106] The behavior by Smith and Alger that seems atypical of marriage and could reflect adulterous intent better reflects the infeasibility of carrying on an individual marriage *relationship* outside of an established marriage *system* and demonstrates the contradictions of attempting to establish one marriage system in the shadows

---

106. One possibility that has been suggested regarding the origin of the relationship is that Smith and Alger entered a mutual covenant of marriage, without the need for an officiator, a less formalized version of polygamy that later Latter Day Saints equated with the biblical "concubinage." Another possibility is that Smith felt authorized, in an exceptional case, to officiate for his own marriage, much as Smith and Cowdery initially made exceptions to baptismal and ordination rules, Smith baptizing Cowdery before he had himself been baptized, etc. But given that Smith claimed divine authority to marry in the fall of 1835 (and probably much earlier) and could delegate any authority he held, it seems as likely, if not more so, that he employed a third-party officiator who has not yet been clearly identified. Possible candidates for the officiator role include Levi Hancock and Sidney Rigdon.

of another. Marriage, by its nature, is not only a personal contract but also an institution of society, helping to build societies, one familial block at a time, but also drawing strength from society, its recognition, norms, and traditions.

Conclusion

A polygamous marital relationship between Joseph Smith and Fanny Alger is better evidenced by the data than an extramarital affair, better fits the contemporaneous context, and holds greater explanatory power. It is more voluminous, of more distinct types, from a greater range of persons, and less ambiguous. The evidence demonstrates that the relationship between Joseph Smith and Fanny Alger, when we know of it existing in spring-summer 1836, was carried out in a church into which polygamy had entered and in which non-legal marriages could be justified as divinely sanctioned.

In such a case, where the evidence is thoroughly mixed, a key interpretive question is, "Which of these hypotheses best explains the evidence for the *other?*" The polygamy interpretation of Joseph Smith's and Fanny Alger's relationship accounts for the rise of its opposite, and for a great deal of data the other cannot.

Rumors and assertions that Smith and Alger committed adultery are readily explained under the polygamy interpretation *if not everyone was in the know regarding the marital relationship or regarded it as legitimate.* In this case, the relationship would be assumed adulterous by default. But the adultery interpretation does not similarly explain contemporaneous rumors, early accounts, family accounts, and numerous reminiscences of *polygamy*, which is decidedly not the default interpretation for an intimate relationship between a married person and someone besides his or her legal spouse.

Though secret, atypical, and of uncertain officiator and date, Joseph Smith's relationship with Fanny Alger merits identification as his earliest known polygamous marriage. Polygamy appears to have commenced in Kirtland, which requires that scholars interpret the practice in the light of Kirtland theology, as well as that of Nauvoo, and that they interpret Kirtland theology in light of this unorthodox marital practice.

What occurred at the veil of Kirtland temple, behind which Joseph Smith and Oliver Cowdery, still brothers, met Christ and the biblical worthies and what occurred behind the veil of secrecy that covered polygamy, and parted the brothers, are two sides of that same uniquely Mormon work, "the restoration of all things."

Section 132 of the LDS Doctrine and Covenants: Its Complex Contents and Controversial Legacy

BY NEWELL G. BRINGHURST

AMONG THE MOST "doctrinally complex" and controversial documents attributed to Mormon leader Joseph Smith is his 1843 revelation "relating to the new and everlasting covenant," ultimately included as Section 132 in the LDS Doctrine and Covenants.[1] In the words of historian Danel W. Bachman "no document has created more controversy than has the revelation on eternal and plural marriage...."[2] More important, this revelation was of primary significance in that it not only provided the basic theological framework for Mormon polygamy, but outlined a number of other fundamental beliefs and doctrines—many

---

1. The Doctrine and Covenants is a book of scripture first published in 1835 with 102 sections, which has been added to and changed by Latter Day Saint tradition churches in divergent ways. As a result, the Doctrine and Covenants published by the LDS Church is significantly different from the Doctrine and Covenants published by the Community of Christ.

2. Danel W. Bachman, "New Light on an Old Hypothesis: The Ohio Origins of the Revelation on Eternal Marriage," *Journal of Mormon History*, 5 (1978), 19.

considered essential to Mormonism as practiced today. It has been characterized as Smith's "most epoch-making revelation" in the words of controversial biographer Fawn M. Brodie.[3]

This being said, the revelation when initially issued as a handwritten manuscript on July 12, 1843, received limited exposure, and was presented to just a small, select group of Smith's most trusted associates. It remained unknown to the vast majority of Latter Day Saints, not made public until the early 1850s—some eight years following Smith's death. In 1852 Brigham Young, as leader of the largest group of Latter Day Saints, authorized publication of the revelation through the pages of the church's semi-official *Deseret News*—doing so to announce plural marriage as official Mormon doctrine and acknowledging its extensive practice among his followers.[4] The entire text of the revelation itself was reprinted in two other Mormon Church periodicals, specifically, the Washington, D.C.-based *The Seer*, under the editorial direction of Apostle Orson Pratt, Mormonism's leading advocate of plural marriage; and in the *Millennial Star*—the church's premier international organ, based in Liverpool, England.[5] The revelation received additional publicity over the following three decades through numerous sermons delivered by Young and other church leaders, many of which were published in the *Journal of Discourses* and other church publications.[6]

In 1876 the revelation was recognized as canonized scripture with its incorporation into the LDS Doctrine and Covenants as Section 132—such status continuing down to the present.[7] Two years later the same

---

3. Fawn M. Brodie, No *Man Knows My History: The Life of Joseph Smith* (New York: Alfred A. Knopf, 1945), 340.

4. *Deseret News*, Extra, September 14, 1852, 25–47.

5. "CELESTIAL MARRIAGE; A Revelation on the Patriarchal Order of Matrimony, or Plurality of Wives," *The Seer*, January 1853; *Millennial Star*, January 1, 5, 12, November 1859, April 28, 1866, February 13, 1869, November 22, 1875; *Deseret News*, January 21, 1857. For an overview of the publication history of the revelation see: Robert J. Woodford, "The Historical Development of the Doctrine and Covenants, (Ph.D. Dissertation: Brigham Young University, 1974), "Table 132," 1738–1741.

6. G. D. Watt, *Journal of Discourses by Brigham Young, President of the Church of Jesus Christ of Latter-day Saints, His Two Counselors, the Twelve Apostles, and Others*, 26 volumes (Liverpool: F. D. Richards, 1855). See, for example: Brigham Young, 1:188; 6:281; 6:281; 17:198; Orson Pratt, 13:192–94; George Q. Cannon, 13: 198; and Joseph F. Smith, 20: 29.

7. "Revelation on the Eternity of the Marriage Covenant, including Plurality of Wives, Given through Joseph the Seer, in Nauvoo, Hancock County, Illinois, July 12th, 1843," 463–74, Doctrine and Covenants, Section 132, 1876 edition.

revelation was placed in a second Mormon scriptural work—The Pearl of Great Price.[8] As such, the importance of the revelation as essential Mormon canon was further enhanced.

While the 1843 Revelation provided "scriptural justification for polygamy" in the words of Richard L. Bushman,[9] the precise date that Smith, himself, commenced promoting polygamy is unclear. The process certainly began during the early 1830s, shortly after the Mormon Church was organized.[10] Also in dispute is the exact date that that Smith took his first plural wife.[11] What is clear is that beginning in 1841, the Mormon leader directed a small cadre of his most trusted followers to take plural wives of their own.[12] And by July 1843 Smith had married some 29 to 31 women, according to the most credible estimates—this representing the vast majority of the total 33 to 37 plural wives he would ultimately marry.[13]

---

8. It was placed under the heading: "REVELATION ON THE ETERNITY OF THE MARRIAGE COVENANT INCLLUDING THE PLURALITY OF WIVES..." Pearl of Great Price, 1878, 64–70. The revelation continued to be placed in four subsequent editions of the Pearl of Great Price over the following twelve years, 1879 to 1891.

9. Richard L. Bushman, *Joseph Smith: Rough Stone Rolling* (New York: Alfred A. Knopf, 2005), 443.

10. Danel W. Bachman in two works asserts that Smith began to advocate the practice of polygamy in 1831, prompted by the Mormon leader's transcription of the Old Testament. See Bachman's, "New Light on an Old Hypothesis," and his "A Study of the Mormon Practice of Plural Marriage before the Death of Joseph Smith," (MA Thesis, Purdue University, 1975).

11. Both Todd Compton and Richard Bushman assert that Smith "married" or took Fanny Alger as his first plural wife in the mid-1830s—this occurring while the Mormon leader was living in Kirtland, Ohio. See Todd Compton, *In Sacred Loneliness: The Plural Wives of Joseph Smith* (Signature Books, 1997), 4; and Bushman, *Joseph Smith*, 323. Whereas George D. Smith argues that Smith did not take his first plural wife until 1841 with his marriage to Louisa Beeman. George D. Smith, *Nauvoo Polygamy: "...but we called it celestial marriage"* (Salt Lake City: Signature Books, 2009).

12. According to George D. Smith, the Mormon leader by 1843 "had spoken to at least twelve of the brethren about practicing polygamy," *Nauvoo Polygamy*, 47. Included in this group were several members of the Quorum of the Twelve, including Brigham Young and Heber C. Kimball, who were commanded to take plural wives immediately after their return to Nauvoo in 1841 subsequent to their missionary service in Great Britain.

13. Estimates of the total number of women that Smith married vary widely, from as few as 27 to as many as 84—this noted by Jessie L. Embry in *Mormons and Polygamy* (Orem, UT: Millennial Press, 2007), 33. For example, in his seminal work, *In Sacred Loneliness*, Todd Compton asserts the lower number of 33, but George D. Smith estimates a slightly higher total of 37 in his own study, *Nauvoo Polygamy*. For a detailed discussion of the number of Joseph Smith's plural wives, see the appendix of this volume, 290–98.

Not in dispute is the immediate situation prompting Joseph to bring forth the revelation in July 1843, specifically severe marital difficulties with his wife, Emma as a result of her husband's involvement in polygamy. He was urged by older brother, Hyrum, who suggested that Emma would be convinced of the truthfulness of the practice, if presented with the fact of the revelation in print, and thereafter, Joseph would have peace.[14] Some fifteen of the sixty-six verses of the revelation were, in fact, directed to Emma. "The burden of the revelation" in the words of Emma Smith's biographers, Linda King Newell and Valeen Tippetts Avery, was to inform Smith's wife that "only by receiving a fullness of the priesthood" that is, accepting the fact of her husband's plural marriages, could she "have claim on her husband in the eternities."[15]

The revelation was, in the opinion of Newell and Avery, "threatening and strident" in addressing and instructing Emma.[16] It stated: "Let mine handmaid, Emma Smith, receive all those [wives] that have been given unto my servant Joseph, and who are virtuous and pure before me;…" going on to warn that if she failed to comply, Joseph would receive from the Lord "an hundred-fold" in this world of wives.[17] In essence, Emma "could either accept more wives willingly or she could have them forced on her."[18] The revelation further commanded "mine handmaid, Emma Smith, to abide and cleave unto my servant Joseph, and to none else," warning that "if she will not abide this commandment she shall be destroyed, saith the Lord."[19] This command has been interpreted as a reaction to an apparent threat Emma made to Joseph during an argument over polygamy—its precise nature unclear. According to Newell and Avery, quoting a statement made by William Clayton many years later, Emma told Joseph that if he continued to "indulge himself, she would too," that is, involve herself with other men.[20] Whereas according to Danel Bachman's reference to William Clayton's 1843 journal, Emma in

---

14. Donna Hill, *Joseph Smith: The First Mormon* (New York: Doubleday, 1977), 336.
15. Linda King Newell and Valeen Tippetts Avery, *Mormon Enigma: Emma Hale Smith, Prophet's Wife, "Elect Lady," Polygamy's Foe* (New York: Doubleday, 1984), 152.
16. Ibid.
17. Doctrine and Covenants 132: 52, 55.
18. Newell and Avery, *Mormon Enigma*, 153.
19. Doctrine and Covenants 132: 54.
20. This is according to William Clayton's statement in Andrew Jenson, *Historical Record*, 1886 as quoted in Newell and Avery, *Mormon Enigma*, 153.

rejecting "the principle of plural marriage totally…threatened to divorce" her husband "if he did not give it up."[21]

Also pertaining to Emma's situation were verses 64–65, while not addressing her directly, alluded to her in discussing "the position of the first wife." Specifically the verses stated: "If any man have a wife…and he teaches unto her the law of my priesthood, as pertaining to these things, then shall she believe and administer unto him, or she shall be destroyed, saith the Lord your God." It then addressed the condition of the husband whose wife refused to accept additional wives. "It shall be lawful in me, if she receive not this law, for him to receive all things whatsoever I, the Lord his God, will give unto him." Specifically this exempted a man from the so-called "law of Sarah" which "required a husband to ask his wife for permission to take another wife. If the first withheld her consent, the revelation authorized the husband to proceed without it."[22] Earlier in the revelation Emma was told to "forgive my servant Joseph his trespasses" and then pointing to her willful behavior, most especially her resistance to polygamy, it stated, "then shall she be forgiven her trespasses, wherein she has trespassed against me…."[23]

The revelation also referenced Emma, albeit in a more oblique manner, in a verse immediately following its admonishment of her. Specifically, it stated: "And, again, I say, let not my servant Joseph put his property out of his hands, lest an enemy come and destroy him."[24] This portion of the revelation suggests that Emma "pressured Joseph to transfer deeds to some of his property." According to Newell and Avery, "Joseph knew that open disclosure of plural marriage would endanger his life. Emma may have tried to punctuate that eventuality in Joseph's mind by insisting on financial security for her and the children."[25]

In addition to the problem of Emma Smith, the revelation provided Joseph Smith with "answers to at least three separate questions" he had "asked the Lord"—according to Danel Bachman.[26] The first question, contained at the beginning of revelation in verse one, clearly states that

---

21. Bachman, "New Light on an Old Hypothesis," 26, referencing Clayton, Journal, August 16, 1843.
22. Doctrine and Covenants 132: 64–65; Newell and Avery, *Mormon Enigma*, 153.
23. Doctrine and Covenants 132:56
24. Ibid, 132:57
25. Newell and Avery, *Mormon Enigma*, 154.
26. This according to the analysis of Bachman in, "New Light on an Old Hypothesis," 23.

Smith wanted "to know and understand wherein I, the Lord, justified my servants Abraham, Issac, and Jacob, as also Moses, David and Solomon, my servants, as touching the principle and doctrine of their having many wives and concubines."[27] The genesis of this question goes back to 1831, resulting from Smith's revision of the Bible, specifically his encounter with Genesis and other Old Testament passages "relating to plural marriages of the ancients."[28] Such revision "may have aroused his curiosity regarding the patriarchs and the problem of marriage in the resurrection" and given his "native inquisitiveness" acted as a "sufficient stimulus for him to ask questions…about marriage."[29] According to the revelation, the ancients—beginning with Abraham and his immediate descendants, Isaac and Jacob—and continuing on down through David, Solomon, and Moses—were each justified in taking additional wives because the marriages of each were sanctioned by divine revelation and performed by proper authority—"the law of my Holy Priesthood."[30]

The revelation further addressed the situation of Abraham and how it related to Joseph Smith, stating:

> Abraham received promises concerning his seed, and of the fruit of his loins…This promise is yours also, because ye are of Abraham, and the promise was made unto Abraham; and by this law is the continuation of the works of my Father, wherein he glorifieth himself. Go ye, therefore, and do the works of Abraham; enter ye into my law and ye shall be saved.[31]

A second question of major concern was adultery. The "probable stimulant for the question may well been his [Joseph Smith's] own domestic difficulties" notes Danel Bachman, adding that "accusations of adultery" against the Mormon leader came from his increasingly alienated wife, Emma.[32] The revelation addressed this issue in a number of

---

27. Doctrine and Covenants 132:1.
28. Bachman, "New Light on an Old Hypothesis," 24.
29. Ibid.
30. Doctrine and Covenants 132:29–39
31. Ibid., 132:30–32.
32. Bachman, "New Light on an Old Hypothesis," 26. Bachman further suggests that other factors may have stimulated Smith in this regard, specifically "his work with the difficult teaching of Jesus on that subject in the New Testament" going back to the 1830s. But then Bachman points to the "close proximity to" and connection with "the 1843 Nauvoo situation" specifically "the [John C.] Bennett scandal of 1842 which brought to the fore the issues of plural marriage and adultery"

specific verses outlining the instances in which men and women would or would not be guilty of committing adultery, all within the context of "the new and everlasting covenant." These rules were outlined in specific legalistic terms. "If a man receiveth [sic] a wife in the new and everlasting covenant, and if she be with another man, and I have not appointed unto her by the holy anointing, she hath committed adultery and shall be destroyed." It further stipulated that if the woman in question "be not in the new and everlasting covenant, and she be with another man, she has committed adultery." Turning to the male, it stated that "if her husband be with another woman, and he was under a vow, he hath broken his vow and hath committed adultery." In that case, his wife, or wives would be taken away from him and given to another.[33]

Conversely, the revelation addressed those situations in which a polygamist male would not be guilty of adultery according "to the law of the priesthood." Specifically, "if any man espouse a virgin, and desire to espouse another, and the first [wife] give her consent, and if he espouse the second, and they are virgins, and have vowed to no other man, then is he justified; he cannot commit adultery…." It further states:

> And if he have ten virgins given unto him by this law, he cannot commit adultery, for they belong to him…But if one or either of the ten virgins, after she is espoused, shall be with another man, she has committed adultery, and shall be destroyed; for they are given unto him to multiply and replenish the earth, according to my commandment.[34]

This section, according to historian Jessie Embry, "implied that a plural wife should not have been married before. If a man wanted more children…a wife's age would be important."[35] Or in the words of legal scholar Sarah Barringer Gordon, such "additional virgins…sanctified

---

along with the "problem of undivorced people with bad marriages, who wanted permission to remarry without a divorce." Additional factors included "considerable criticism from Gentiles" concerning "rumors of plural marriage in Nauvoo, and doubts [that] existed in the minds of some of Joseph's most trusted followers." Bachman, 25–26.

33. Doctrine and Covenents 132: 41–44.

34. Ibid., 132: 61–63.

35. Jessie L. Embry, *Mormons and Polygamy: Setting the Record Straight* (Orem Utah: Millennial Press, 2007), 75.

their union...in the interest of procreation," conforming with the behavior of the "righteous patriarchs...of old."[36]

In assessing the various penalties for adultery, writer Melodie Moench Charles sees an "imbalance" between those mandated for men in contrast to those imposed on women. Specifically, a woman married in "the new and everlasting covenant," notes Charles, "who commits adultery should be destroyed, while a man married in 'the new and everlasting covenant' who commits adultery suffers only the much softer penalty of having his betrayed wife bestowed on another man." This "imbalance continues" in other ways, specifically:

> The punishment for the adulterous man seems to require that the wife has remained faithful; thus, his incurring a penalty is as dependent upon his wife's actions as upon his own....Yet the adulteress's penalty apparently comes automatically on the heels of her sin. Moreover, the innocent wife whose husband has been unfaithful is not consulted about her fate. She is simply transferred from an unworthy man to a worthy one.[37]

In addition to adultery or "sexual relations outside the bounds of Church supervised law" viewed as a "heinous sin," the revelation discussed two other types of grievous behavior.[38] Specifically, these were: (1) murder, or shedding innocent blood and; (2) "blasphemy against the Holy Ghost. While even murder is forgivable in the next world, blasphemy against the Holy Ghost "shall not be forgiven in this world nor out of the world." The perpetrator "can in nowise enter into my glory, but shall be damned" and "delivered unto the buffetings of Satan unto the day of redemption, saith the Lord God."[39]

Also addressed in the revelation was a third question, the status in the hereafter of those individuals who never married in this mortal existence. Joseph Smith's concern over this issue was apparently stimulated

---

36. Sarah Barringer Gordon, *The Mormon Question: Polygamy and Constitutional Conflict in Nineteenth Century America* (Chapel Hill, North Carolina: University of Illinois Press, 2002), 22.

37. Melodie Moench Charles, "Precedents for Mormon Women from Scriptures," in Maureen Ursenbach Beecher and Lavina Fielding Anderson, eds., *Sisters in Spirit: Mormon Women in Cultural and Historical Perspective* (Urbana and Chicago: University of Illinois Press, 1992), 46.

38. These the words of Lawrence Foster, *Religion and Sexuality: Three American Communal Experiments of the Nineteenth Century* (New York and Oxford: Oxford University. Press), 146.

39. Doctrine and Covenants 132: 27, 26.

by his reading of a passage in the twenty-second chapter of Matthew, detailing a confrontation between Jesus and Sadducees over the doctrine of the resurrection. Jesus's reply was "in the resurrection they neither marry, nor are given in marriage, but are as the angels of God in Heaven."[40] The situation of such individuals in the hereafter as stated in the revelation was: "when they are out of the world they neither marry nor are given in marriage; but are appointed angels in heaven, which angels are ministering servants, to minister for those who are worthy of a far more, and an exceeding, and an eternal weight of glory."[41]

Of central importance, indeed "at the heart" of the revelation was a fourth interrelated concept—the eternal nature of "marriage relationships."[42] According to Lawrence Foster, marriage was raised to a position of "supreme importance as the only means by which the highest status and glory could be achieved in heaven."[43] Two types of marriage were defined. The first, ordinary secular marriages, or marriages without proper priesthood authority, would not endure beyond mortality or "are not of force when they are dead, and when they are out of the world."[44] The status of such individuals in the hereafter would be akin to that of those who had never married as "'ministering angels' a sort of perpetual servant class...."[45] In essence: "The worldly-wed became single again, and a permanent cap limited their progress."[46] In the words of the revelation: "these angels" that "did not abide my law...cannot be enlarged, but remain separately and singly, without exaltation, in their saved condition, to all eternity; and from henceforth are not gods, but are angels of God forever and ever."[47]

The second type, "'celestial' form of marriage" sealed by proper Priesthood authority, was for "time and eternity" and would endure "in heaven as well as on earth." The men of such marriages would in heaven "be great patriarchs having 'all power' surrounded by their own families as

---

40. Bachman, "New Light on an Old Hypotheis," 23; Matthew 22:30.
41. Doctrine and Covenants 132:16.
42. Foster, *Religion and Sexuality*, 145.
43. Ibid., 145.
44. Doctrine and Covenants 132:15.
45. Foster, *Religion and Sexuality*, 145.
46. In the words of Richard L. Bushman in *Rough Stone Rolling*, 443.
47. Doctrine and Covenants 132:17.

well as by…ministering angles who lack wives or progeny."[48] Such men would "inherit thrones, kingdoms, principalities, and powers, dominions, all heights, and depths" ultimately becoming "gods, because they have no end" and are "above all" with "all power."[49]

In espousing the possibility of godhood, the revelation interrelated with, and underscored the all-important concept of exaltation. Through "eternal increase…godlike patriarchs by means of their children, grandchildren, and so forth would move on to rule over whole new worlds, achieving full godhood in conjunction with their wives in what could be easily seen as a kind of cosmic 'manifest destiny.'"[50] Indeed, the revelation "was integral with [Mormonism's evolving] cosmology." A Latter Day Saint "portrait of the universe as a field for dominion by the patriarchal family had begun to take form."[51]

The revelation, in fact, "culminated the emergence of [a] family theology"—this the characterization of Richard L. Bushman. "More than any previous revelation, this one put the family first." Indeed, the family was "the one institution sure to survive death" and destined to be "the fundamental governing unit in the hereafter."[52] Within this eternal family structure, such married men and women would retain the capacity to bear offspring. Through their capacity to "enlarge" their dominion, they would be assured "a continuation of the seeds forever and ever."[53] In other words: "They kept bearing children. This capacity to 'enlarge' made them, in effect gods" with "procreation…lifted to the highest level of human and divine endeavor."[54]

As for the intended status of women within this eternal family structure, there is disagreement among historians. Interpreting their status in positive terms is Richard L. Bushman, who asserts: "Before the marriage revelation, women were in the shadows in Joseph's theology, implied but

---

48. Foster, *Religion and Sexuality*, 145.
49. Doctrine and Covenants 132:19–20.
50. These the words of Lawrence Foster in *Religion and Sexuality*, 145.
51. As stated by B. Carmon Hardy in *Solemn Covenant: The Mormon Polygamous Passage* (Urbana and Chicago: University of Illinois Press, 1992), 10–11.
52. Bushman, *Rough Stone Rolling*, 445. For a more in-depth discussion of this theological concept, see the following essay by Craig L. Foster, titled, "Doctrine and Covenants Section 132 and Joseph Smith's Expanding Concept of Family."
53. Doctrine and Covenants 132:17, 19.
54. As stated by Bushman, *Rough Stone Rolling*, 448.

rarely recognized…Now they moved to the center." Bushman further states that the revelation "did not overturn the family order. If anything, women were more entrenched in the roles of mother and wife" but conceding that the revelation "gave husbands the upper hand…."[55] Further enhancing their status, women were assured exaltation, specifically: "Men would not become gods alone." Through the eternal perpetuation of the family structure, including procreation, "husbands and wives passed by the angels and became 'gods' together—and only together."[56]

Viewing the revelation *vis-à-vis* women in a less positive light is writer Melodie Moench Charles. While acknowledging that the revelation through verses 19 and 20 promises "the same exaltation to godhood for both men and women" other parts of it consider "women as if they were merely the instruments which aid men to fulfill their mortal religious obligations and enable them to produce kingdoms to rule over in heaven."[57] Specific examples include Abraham's concubines "given unto him" so that he could fulfill God's law; women given to Joseph Smith so that he could be ruler "over many things," and the women given to worthy Mormon men, in general, "for their exaltation in the eternal worlds" so that "they may bear the souls of men."[58] Such teachings, according to Charles, "view women as property rather than individuals with inherent importance."[59]

The revelation's effect on women has been considered from yet another perspective by Margaret and Paul Toscano. According to the Toscanos the revelation granted "priesthood" and/or the powers thereof "to men and women jointly."[60] In making this assertion, the authors refer specifically to that portion of the revelation describing the marriage of men and women through sealing by "the Holy Spirit" under "the new and everlasting covenant" through the "power and the keys of this priesthood."[61] Joseph Smith, in the words of the Toscanos, "connected polygamy" with "the concept of the fullness of the priesthood" whereby "the

---

55. Ibid., 444, 446.
56. Ibid., 445.
57. Charles, "Precedents for Mormon Women from Scriptures," 46–47.
58. Doctrine and Covenants, 132 37, 53, 63.
59. Charles, "Precedents for Mormon Women from Scriptures," 47.
60. Margaret and Paul Toscano, *Strangers in Paradox: Explorations in Mormon Theology* (Salt Lake City: Signature Books, 1990), 183.
61. Doctrine and Covenants 132: 19.

full range of divine gifts and powers can be realized only when men and women are united with each other and with God on an equal footing."[62] Such views have proven controversial. The extent and limits of priesthood power granted women through the revelation and other actions by Smith during the crucial Nauvoo period continue to generate heated debate.[63]

Not in debate is that the revelation further affirmed the importance of Mormon priesthood authority while enhancing the power of Joseph Smith, himself. "At [its] base was priesthood sealing, the practice of binding people together by priesthood authority"—these the words of Richard L. Bushman.[64] Smith, moreover, "insisted that [such] sealing authority be tightly controlled"; notes Brian C. Hales.[65] Accordingly, the revelation declared: "There is never but one on the earth at a time on whom this power and the keys of this priesthood are conferred.... Behold, mine house is a house of order, saith the Lord God, and not a house of confusion."[66] It further stated that the Mormon leader was conferred "the keys and power of the priesthood" adding that, "whatsoever you [Smith] seal on earth shall be sealed in heaven; and whatsoever you bind on earth, in my name and by my word, saith the Lord, it shall be eternally bound in the heavens."[67] In general, Smith was divinely commissioned through "appointment" to "restore all things."[68] Turning to the specific problem of adultery, Smith was empowered by the "Holy Priesthood" to punish male members found guilty of this sin, by taking away the offending male member's wife and giving "her unto him that hath not committed adultery but hath been faithful" provided the woman in question had not herself committed adultery "but is innocent and hath not broken her vow."[69]

---

62. Margaret and Paul Toscano, *Strangers in Paradox*, 259.
63. For a brief discussion of this controversy see: Newell G. Bringhurst, "Joseph Smith's Ambiguous Legacy: Gender, Race, and Ethnicity as Dynamics for Schism within Mormonism after 1844," *John Whitmer Historical Society Journal*, 27 (2007), 5–8.
64. Bushman, *Rough Stone Rolling*, 443.
65. Brian Hales, *Modern Polygamy and Mormon Fundamentalism* (Salt Lake City, UT: Greg Kofford Books, 2006),
66. Doctrine and Covenants 132:7–8
67. Ibid., 132:45–46.
68. Ibid., 132:40.
69. Ibid., 132:43–44.

The revelation through two other verses further affirmed both the power and exalted status of Joseph Smith. The first declared that "whomsoever you [Smith] bless I will bless, and whomsoever you [Smith] curse I will curse, saith the Lord...."[70] Through a second, the Mormon leader was divinely guaranteed exaltation. Specifically it stated that "the Lord thy God...will be with thee even unto the end of the world, and through all eternity; for verily I seal upon you your exaltation, and prepare a throne for you in the kingdom of my Father, with Abraham your father."[71]

Portions of the revelation reflected concern about the coming of the millennium or end times, which appeared imminent given the unsettled political and social climate of Jacksonian America during the mid-1840s.[72] Specifically the revelation stated:

> Everything that is in the world, whether it be ordained of men, by thrones, or principalities, or powers, or things of name, whatsoever they may be...shall be thrown down, and shall not remain after men are dead, neither in nor after the resurrection.[73]

It earlier stated that:

> All covenants, contracts, bonds, obligations, oaths, vows, performances, connections, associations, or expectations, that are not made and entered into and sealed by the Holy Spirit of promise...are of no efficacy, virtue, or force in and after the resurrection from the dead; for all contracts that are not made unto this end have an end when men are dead.[74]

Such verses reflect a "combination of legal exceptionalism...and state-building," in the words of Sarah Barringer Gordon, all of which anticipated the building of a new political order, or Mormon Kingdom of God on earth "based on an alternative structure of private governance."[75] Joseph Smith's decision to run for U. S. President in 1844, coupled with

---

70. Ibid., 132:47
71. Ibid., 132:49
72. For a good overview of developments in the larger American society see: Daniel Walker Howe, *What Hath God Wrought: The Transformation of America, 1814–1848* (New York: Oxford University Press, 2007).
73. Ibid., 132:13
74. Ibid., 132:7
75. Gordon, *The Mormon Question*, 22–23.

the formation of the secret Council of Fifty, reflect the Mormon leader's preoccupation with political matters, albeit within the context of millenarian expectations.[76]

In overall terms, the revelation, as perceived in "Joseph's mind...functioned like law" and, indeed, was a "divine commandment."[77] The revelation was couched in highly legalistic terms. At its beginning it declares: "I [the Lord] reveal unto you [Joseph Smith] a new and an everlasting covenant; and if ye abide not that covenant, then are ye damned."[78] Another verse further affirms: "I [the Lord thy God] give unto you this commandment—that no man shall come unto the Father but by me or by my word, which is my law, saith the Lord."[79] The "bulk of this" revelation according to Lawrence Foster "was devoted to reminding the Mormons that strict obedience to God's commands was required...."[80] Underscoring its status as divine law was its concluding verse stating:

> As pertaining to this law, verily, verily, I say unto you, I will reveal more unto you, hereafter; therefore, let this suffice for the present. Behold, I am Alpha and Omega. Amen.[81]

The overall contents of the revelation have been described as all that Joseph Smith "had been thinking and dreaming over the past years, everything that he had conceived about heaven and hell and sex, which he had never before dared commit to paper...."—these the words of Smith biographer, Fawn Brodie.[82] Whereas, George D. Smith has suggested that "Smith's words perhaps implied separate revelations received at different times, of which the culminating 1843 statement gave *ex post*

---

76. For an overview of Joseph Smith's 1844 Presidential Campaign, see: Newell G. Bringhurst and Craig L. Foster, *Mormon Quest for the Presidency* (Independence, MO: John Whitmer Books, 2008), 7–49. The definitive study of the Council of Fifty is Klaus J. Hansen, *Quest for Empire: The Political Kingdom of God and the Council of Fifty in Mormon History* (East Lansing Michigan: Michigan State University Press, 1967). For two perspectives of Mormon Millenarianism see: Grant Underwood, *The Millenarian World of Early Mormonism* (Urbana, Ill: University of Illinois Press, 1993); and Dan Erickson, *"As a Thief in the Night": The Mormon Quest for Millennial Deliverance* (Salt Lake City, UT: Signature Books, 1998).
77. This according to Bushman in *Rough Stone Rolling*, 441.
78. Doctrine and Covenants 132:4.
79. Ibid., 132:12
80. Foster, *Religion and Sexuality*, 146
81. Doctrine and Covenants 132: 66.
82. Brodie, *No Man Knows My History*, 340.

facto validation to previous instances."[83] Similarly, Carmon Hardy asserts: "It is clear that the 1843 revelation was a selective accumulation of the prophet's thought on the subject."[84] Assessing the revelation from a somewhat different perspective is Lawrence Foster who asserts that many of Smith's "statements reveal a basically positive attitude toward sexual expression as well as the difficulty he [the Mormon leader] had in keeping his impulses in check."[85]

Whatever interpretation is given its contents, the revelation itself was kept secret from the vast majority of church members. The revelation, moreover, proved controversial, upon its disclosure to a limited number of individuals closest to Smith. Particularly upset was the Mormon leader's first wife, Emma, to whom a significant portion of the revelation had been directed. When shown the revelation, immediately following its transcription in July 1843, she became so upset that she reportedly destroyed the copy she had been shown.[86] Emma, "said that she did not believe a word of it, and appeared very rebellious" according to the contemporary journal account of Joseph Smith's scribe, William Clayton.[87] The following month, Hyrum Smith read the revelation to the thirteen-member Nauvoo High Council. Three of that number rejected it outright, specifically Council President William Marks, Austin A. Cowles, one of his counselors, and fellow member, Leonard Soby.[88]

Such opposition was the forerunner of a rift among the Latter Day Saints, leading to outright schism and the formation in April 1844 of the True Church of Jesus Christ of Latter Day Saints under the leadership of William Law, a wealthy Canadian convert who had been a special counselor in the First Presidency of the LDS Church. Law was joined by a number of other dissidents, including his brother, Wilson, and Austin Cowles. These dissidents proclaimed their opposition to plural mar-

---

83. Quoted in George Smith's *Nauvoo Polygamy*, 46.
84. Hardy, *Solemn Covenant*, 10.
85. Foster, *Religion and Sexuality*, 126.
86. Newell and Avery, *Mormon Enigma*,
87. George D. Smith, ed., *An Intimate Chronicle: The Journals of William Clayton* (Salt Lake City, UT: Signature Books, 1995), entry for "July 12, 1843, Wednesday," 110.
88. Foster, *Religion and Sexuality*, 177. Among the ten members who approved of it were: Samuel Bent, George W. Harris, Dunbar Wilson, William Huntington, Levi Jackman, Aaron Johnson, Thomas Grover, David Fullmer, Phineas Richards, and James Allred. This according to an affidavit given by David Fullmer on June 15, 1869, as reprinted in Charles Shook, *The True Origins of Mormon Polygamy* (Cincinnati, Ohio: Standard Publishing Co., 1914), 97.

riage, as well as Smith's involvement in politics, declaring the Mormon leader a "fallen prophet."[89]

Through the pages of their newspaper, the *Nauvoo Expositor*, these dissenters provided information concerning the still-secret revelation. Specific details were contained in three separate affidavits given by William Law, his wife, Jane Law, and Austin Cowles. In his statement William Law asserted that Hyrum Smith had read to him "a certain written document which he said was a revelation from God." Law further stated: "The revelation (so called) authorized certain men to have more wives than one at a time, in this world and in the world to come. It said this was the law and commanded Joseph to enter into the law.—And also that he should administer to others." Jane Law, in her own affidavit, affirmed that she had also read the revelation, noting that "it is sustained in strong terms the doctrine of more wives than one at a time, in this world, and in the next" further noting that the document "authorized some to have up to the number of ten, and set forth that those women who would not allow their husbands to have more wives than one should be under condemnation before God."[90]

Austin Cowles in his statement recalled the August 1843 occasion during which the revelation was read by Hyrum Smith to members of the Nauvoo High Council, of which Cowles was a member. Cowles noted that the revelation contained two basic "doctrines." One was "the sealing up of persons to eternal life, against all sins, save that of shedding innocent blood or of consenting thereto…" The second was "the doctrine of a plurality of wives, or marrying virgins; that 'David and Solomon had many wives, yet in this they sinned not, save in the matter of Uriah.'" Cowles dismissed such teachings as "heresies…taught and practiced in the Church" causing him "to leave the office of first councilor to the president of the Church at Nauvoo." He "dared not teach or administer such laws."[91]

Portions of the revelation were also disclosed in a second publication, specifically, the *Warsaw Message*, a non-Mormon newspaper in the

---

89. For a brief overview of this schism, see Newell G. Bringhurst and John C. Hamer, "Introduction," 4, in *Scattering of the Saints: Schism within Mormonism*, eds. Newell G. Bringhurst and John C. Hamer (Independence, MO: John Whitmer Books, 2007).
90. *Nauvoo Expositor*, June 7, 1844, 2.
91. Ibid.

neighboring town of Warsaw, Illinois. They were presented through satire—a thirteen stanza poem entitled "Buckeye's Lamentation for Want of More Wives." The following two stanzas referred directly to essential portions of the revelation:

> I once thought I had knowledge great,
> But now I find 'tis small,
> I once thought I'd religion too,
> But now I find I've none at all—
> For I have but ONE LONE WIFE,
> And can obtain no more;
> And the doctrine is I can't be saved,
> Unless I've HALF A SCORE.
>
> * * *
>
> A TENFOLD glory—that's the prize!
> Without it you're undone!
> But with it you will shine as bright
> As the bright shining sun,
> There you may shine like mighty Gods,
> Creating worlds so fair
> At least a WORLD for every WIFE
> That you take with you there.[92]

"Buckeye's Lamentation" was published anonymously. But the author appears to have been Francis Higbee, a one-time Latter-day Saint, who in 1844 joined with William Law and other dissidents in opposition to Joseph Smith's introduction of plural marriage.[93]

While Joseph Smith was unable to prevent publication of "Buckeye's Lament," and its disclosure of the still-secret revelation, he wasted little time in moving against the *Nauvoo Expositor*. Before a second issue could be published, Smith, acting in his capacity as Nauvoo City Mayor, at a June 10, meeting of the city council declared the *Nauvoo Expositor* "a nuisance" and issued an order for the city marshal "to destroy the *Expositor*"

---

92. *Warsaw Message*, February 7, 1844, as quoted in Brodie's *No Man Knows My History*, 344.
93. For an thorough, incisive discussion of both the contents of and circumstances surrounding the publication of "Buckeye's Lamentation" see: Gary James Bergera, "Buckeye's Lament: Two Early Insider Exposes of Mormon Polygamy and their Authorship," *Journal of the Illinois State Historical Society* 96 (Winter 2003): 350–90.

which was done by removing "the press, type, and printed papers, and fixtures" into the nearby street.[94]

In that same June 10 city council meeting, Joseph Smith along with his brother, Hyrum responded to the matter of the revelation itself as described in the *Expositor's* affidavits of William Law and Austin Cowles. The minutes of that meeting acknowledged the Mormon leader as the "author of a revelation on marriage." It was not concerned with "plural marriage as such" but rather "with marriage in eternity and in biblical times."[95] Smith, himself, stated that "he had never preached the revelation in private, as he had in public—had not taught it to the anointed in the church in private, which statement many present confirmed."[96] As for William Law's statement in the *Expositor*, the Mormon leader dismissed it as blasphemy whereby "the truth of God was transformed into a lie concerning this thing." Smith also assailed the credibility of Austin Cowles, asserting that "he had never had any private conversation with…Cowles on these subjects," stating that he, Smith, "preached on the stand from the bible, showing the order in ancient days having nothing to do with the present times…" And Hyrum Smith echoing his brother "proceeded to show the falsehood of Austin Cowles…in relation to the revelation referred to, that it was in reference to *former* days, and not the present times, as related by Cowles…"[97]

Joseph Smith's summary action in ordering the destruction of the *Nauvoo Expositor* led directly to his arrest and incarceration in the jail in nearby Carthage, thereby setting the stage for his assassination at the hands of a well-organized anti-Mormon mob on June 27, 1844. Underlying this fatal sequence of events, was controversy surrounding Smith's efforts to promote plural marriage, and in particular his attempt to elevate it to the status of essential Mormon doctrine through his July 1843 Revelation. Affirming this fact was Sidney Rigdon, a former member of the church's First Presidency and close confident to Smith, who after becoming estranged from the Mormon leader over the whole issue of plural marriage, characterized the system as "the thing which put [Jo-

---

94. Bushman, *Rough Stone Rolling*, 541–2.
95. As described by Richard P. Howard, "The Changing RLDS Response to Mormon Polygamy: A Preliminary Analysis," *The John Whitmer Historical Association Journal*, 3 (1983), 22.
96. *Nauvoo Neighbor*, June 19, 1844.
97. Ibid.

seph and Hyrum Smith] into the power of their enemies, and was the immediate cause of their death."[98]

The July 1843 revelation on the "New and Everlasting Covenant" itself, particularly the way in which its various complex verses were interpreted, became a continuing source of controversy among Latter Day Saints, particularly as the movement fragmented following Joseph Smith's death. The largest group, the Utah-based Church of Jesus Christ of Latter-day Saints, under the leadership of Brigham Young, made public its specific provisions beginning in 1852. Young and his followers were motivated by several factors in publicizing the revelation in conjunction with acknowledging polygamy as essential Mormon doctrine. The first involved the "end of Mormon isolation" with the establishment of Utah as a federal territory in 1850, and related influx of "outside" federal officials. A second related factor was that a number of these officials, so-called "runaway federal appointees" disclosed to their superiors in Washington D.C. the existence of polygamy among the Utah Saints. Also prompting the Mormons to publicize the practice was an increased sense of millenarian expectations, with polygamy viewed as an essential component of the earthly Kingdom of God to be established in anticipation of the End Times and Second Coming.[99]

Brigham Young led the way in publicizing plural marriage as an essential practice based on Joseph Smith's 1843 Revelation. At the August 29, 1852, Church Conference in which the revelation was first made public, Young gave a brief history of the revelation, itself, concluding with the declaration that "no man could be exalted in heaven without the application of the principles involved."[100] The revelation, itself, was printed in its entirety under the title: "The Principle and Doctrine of Having Many Wives and Concubines, A Revelation to Joseph Smith, Jr., July 12, 1843."[101]

To further publicize the newly disclosed doctrine of plural marriage and the revelation on which it was based, Brigham Young dispatched a number of his most trusted lieutenants to major urban centers through-

---

98. *Latter Day Saints' Messenger and Advocate*, June 1846.
99. As discussed in David J. Whittaker, "The Bone in the Throat: Orson Pratt and the Public Announcement of Plural Marriage," *The Western Historical Quarterly*, 18:3 (July 1987), 293–301.
100. As described by Whittaker, "The Bone in the Throat," 302.
101. *Deseret News Extra*, September 14, 1852.

out the United States, assigning them to establish church-sponsored periodicals. Most noteworthy was Mormon Apostle Orson Pratt, considered Mormonism's most articulate theological spokesman, who traveled to Washington, D.C., where he established *The Seer*. "CELESTIAL MARRIAGE: A Revelation on the Patriarchal Order of Matrimony, or Plurality of Wives," appeared in *The Seer's* January 1853 issue, followed by a series of articles elaborating on the doctrinal principles affirming plural marriage.[102] Similarly, Apostle John Taylor was dispatched to New York City, where he published *The Mormon* from February 1855 to September 1857. Concurrently, Apostle George Q. Cannon traveled west to San Francisco where he oversaw the *Western Standard*. And, a fourth Mormon Apostle, Erastus Snow, was dispatched to the Midwest where he brought forth the *St. Louis Luminary*.[103]

Underscoring the essential importance of the revelation, itself, Brigham Young asserted on more than one occasion that it was the "Prophet Joseph Smith who revealed this holy law and order to the Latter-day Saints" as he "received it from Israel's God."[104] Young preached that polygamy was essential for exaltation, declaring that "the only men who become Gods, even the Sons of God, are those who enter into polygamy." In direct reference to Smith's "revelation on *celestial marriage*," Young both chastised and threatened those were "determined not to enter into a plural marriage" stating that such individuals could look forward to an eternal life "single and alone, for ever, and ever, and be made servants, while others receive the highest order of intelligence and are bringing worlds into existence."[105]

On another occasion, Apostle Wilford Woodruff, referred to a discussion with Brigham Young and other church leaders relative to that portion of "the revelation on patriarchal marriage" indicating that "all shall be damned that do not keep this law unto who it is revealed." Woodruff rhetorically asked the Mormon leader: "Does it mean that they shall take more wives than one or be damned?" The inquiring apostle recorded that group's decision that the "law" in question consisted of "the whole law

---

102. *The Seer*, January 1853.
103. Whittaker, "A Bone in the Throat," 304.
104. Brigham Young, *Journal of Discourses*, 3:266.
105. Brigham Young, *Journal of Discourses*, 11:272.

with all its covenants."[106] By 1879 Woodruff harbored no doubts whatsoever on this question, asserting: "God our heavenly father, knowing that this was the only law ordained by the Gods of eternity that would exalt immortal beings, commanded Joseph Smith the Prophet and the Latter-day Saints to obey this law or you shall be damned."[107] Referring to the revelation itself, William Clayton, who had served as Joseph Smith's scribe when it was initially recorded, recalled:

> From him [Joseph Smith] I learned that the doctrine of plural and celestial marriage is the most holy and important doctrine ever revealed to man on the earth and that without obedience to that principle, no man can ever attain to the fullness of exaltation in celestial glory.[108]

By the late 1870s, the revelation was clearly Mormonism's *premier* scriptural proof text affirming the practice of plural marriage. In 1876 the revelation's status as canonized scripture was affirmed with its inclusion as Section 132 in the Utah Doctrine and Covenants. And in 1878 it was included in a second scriptural work, The Pearl of Great Price, under the title "Revelation on the Eternity of the Marriage Covenant including the Plurality of Wives"—thus achieving the unique status as the only revelation published concurrently in two Mormon scriptural works.[109]

At the same time Utah Mormon leaders mandated the removal of an earlier LDS Church declaration entitled "On Marriage" from the Doctrine and Covenants. Previously known as Section 101, it had been included in every edition of the Doctrine and Covenants since its initial publication in 1835. The removed section clearly at variance with current church practice stated:

> Inasmuch as this Church of Christ has been reproached with the crime of fornication, and polygamy; we declare that we believe that one man should have one wife; and one woman but one husband, except in case of death, when either is at liberty to marry again.

---

106. Journals of Wilford Woodruff 4:411 as quoted in Stephen C. Taysom, "A Uniform and Common Recollection: Joseph Smith's Legacy, Polygamy, and the Creation of Mormon Public Memory, 1852–2002," *Dialogue: A Journal of Mormon Thought*, 35:3 (Fall 2002), 125–26.

107. Journals of Wilford Woodruff, February 22, 1879, 7:456 as quoted in Taysom, "A Uniform and Common Recollection, 129.

108. Statement by William Clayton made on February 16, 1874, reprinted as "William Clayton's Testimony," *Historical Record* 6 (May 6, 1887): 225–26.

109. Pearl of Great Prince, 1878 Edition, 64–70.

It had further declared that all marriages in the church "should be solemnized in a public meeting or feast, prepared for that purpose" and that it was "not right to prohibit members of this church from marrying out of the church if it be their determination so to do" although such "persons [would] be considered weak in the faith...."[110]

As for the revelation affirming plural marriage, the primary motive for including it in the Doctrine and Covenants as well as in the Pearl of Great Price was a desire on the part of LDS leaders to "reinforce [the church's] claim that patriarchal marriage [i.e., polygamy] was an entirely religious tenet" in conformity with religious liberty as guaranteed by the First Amendment to the United States Constitution—all of this prompted by pending litigation culminating in the landmark U.S. Supreme Court case, *Reynolds vs United States* (1879). Unfortunately for the Latter-day Saints, the high court ruled against them, condemning polygamy as a "non-Western" practice "contrary to the nation's traditions, and if permitted could lead to suttee and other forms of barbarous behavior."[111] This decision opened the way for a vigorous anti-polygamy crusade by federal officials, which ended only when Utah Mormon leaders publicly agreed to suspend the practice of plural marriage beginning with the issuance of the 1890 Manifesto.[112]

In the wake of the Manifesto, Mormon perceptions relative to the meaning and significance of Joseph Smith's 1843 revelation underwent a radical transformation.[113] In 1891 the text of the revelation was completely removed from Pearl of Great Price. Although the revelation retained its place as Section 132 in the Doctrine and Covenants, there was a conscious effort on the part of Utah Mormon leaders to place less emphasis on those parts dealing with plural marriage. In this regard, there were

---

110. Doctrine and Covenants 101:1–4, 1835 Edition. This section was not a revelation, but was prepared while the original edition of the Doctrine and Covenants was being prepared and presented to a general assembly of the church on August 17, 1835, which approved of it unanimously. It has been included in every edition of the RLDS (now Community of Christ) Doctrine and Covenants as Section 111.

111. B. Carmon Hardy, ed., *Doing the Works of Abraham: Mormon Polygamy, Its origin, practice, and demise* (Norman Oklahoma: The Arthur H. Clark, 2007), 263.

112. An excellent discussion of this process is Gordon, *The Mormon Question*.

113. The most important work tracing this development is Stephen Taysom's "A Uniform and Common Recollection: Joseph Smith's Legacy, Polygamy, and the Creation of Mormon Public Memory, 1852–2002."

changes in the superscript preceding the revelation. Initially this involved a slight change in the wording from the original "Revelation on the Eternity of the Marriage Covenant, including Plurality of Wives" to "Revelation on the Eternity of the Marriage Covenant, as also Plurality of Wives." This seemingly slight change from "including" to "as also" clearly reflected a reduced emphasis on plural marriage in favor of eternal marriage minus polygamy.[114]

And in time, additional text was added to the superscript preceding Section 132, dealing with various other issues collectively described as "relating to the new and everlasting covenant." These included such doctrinal issues as "power of the Holy Priesthood, as being operative beyond the grave," the importance of marriage being performed by proper authority to be valid beyond death, and "essentials for the attainment of the status of godhood," and "the sin of adultery." Also added was the statement: "Plurality of wives acceptable only when commanded by the Lord"—this was clearly designed to emphasize the fact that polygamy was no longer an authorized practice within the LDS Church.[115]

Despite efforts by LDS Church leaders to deemphasize those parts of the revelation dealing with polygamy, the church found itself under attack by outsiders for the mere fact that the revelation continued to be included in the Doctrine and Covenants—such criticism particularly evident in the early twentieth century during the controversy over the seating of Mormon Apostle Reed Smoot as a United States Senator.[116] Critics pointed out that Section 132 had been retained in the Doctrine and Covenants whereas the 1890 Manifesto, calling for the suspension of plural marriage was nowhere present.[117] All such controversy led to the issuing of a Second Manifesto, by then-LDS Church President Joseph F. Smith. In this 1904 document Smith decried plural marriage affirming that "all such marriages [were] prohibited and threatening excommunication to any church official performing such marriages."[118] And some

---

114. As noted by Carmon Hardy, *Solemn Covenant*, 16.
115. See Superscript to Section 132 as contained in editions of the Doctrine and Covenants that appeared beginning in the early twentieth century.
116. The most important work discussing this controversy is Kathleen Flake, *The Politics of American Religious Identity: The Seating of Senator Reed Smoot, Mormon Apostle* (Chapel Hill: University of North Carolina Press, 2004)
117. Hardy, *Solemn Covenant*, 297.
118. Taysom, "A Uniform and Common Recollection," 131.

four years later, the 1890 Manifesto was placed in the 1908 edition of the Doctrine and Covenants. It was however, not included as a "revelation" or "section" in the main part of that scriptural work, but, instead, placed as an "Official Declaration" in the back.[119]

Also during the late nineteenth and early twentieth centuries, efforts were made by various church spokesmen to de-emphasize the importance of polygamy, in particular the connection between plural marriage and celestial marriage, previously emphasized as a central tenet of Joseph Smith's 1843 revelation.[120] Leading the way was premier church intellectual and future Mormon Apostle, James E. Talmage. In his classic doctrinal work, *The Articles of Faith*, published in 1899, Talmage defined celestial marriage as "the system of holy matrimony, involving covenants as to time and eternity," representing "the order of marriage that exists in the celestial worlds."[121] In referencing Section 132, Talmage "skillfully avoided mentioning plural marriage, emphasizing instead the eternity of the marriage covenant."[122] Actually, Talmage had intended to include in *The Articles of Faith* a section entitled "Items on Polygamy" which, however, was omitted from the final version of the book as published. It is not clear if the decision to omit it was his, a Church committee on publications, or that of the First Presidency, notes Talmage biographer, James P. Harris.[123] Two years later Talmage, in a church magazine article, further down-played the importance of polygamy, dismissing it variously as not "a vital tenet of the Church" and "an incident—never an essential." Talmage concluded that "plural marriage" was "practiced by a limited proportion" of Latter-day Saints "under [the] sanction of Church ordinance."[124]

Other church writers also de-emphasized polygamy as an aspect of the revelation. John Henry Evans "argued that eternity of the mar-

---

119. "Official Declaration," Doctrine and Covenants (1908), 543–44
120. Taysom, "A Uniform and Common Recollection," 132.
121. James E. Talmage, The Articles of Faith (Salt Lake City, UT: Deseret News Press, 1899), 458.
122. These the words of Stephen Taysom in "A Uniform and Common Recollection," 133.
123. James P. Harris, "Foreward," printed in James E. Talmage, *The Articles of Faith* (Salt Lake City, UT: Signature Books, 2003), xxvi.
124. James E. Talmage, "The Story of Mormonism," *Improvement Era* 4 (October 1901);12. Talmage's views were expanded and reprinted some six years later in a pamphlet entitled *The Story of Mormonism* (Liverpool, England: Millennial Star Office, 1907), 86.

riage covenant and not polygamy, was the chief theme of Joseph Smith's 1843 revelation."[125] Mormon Apostle and prolific writer Joseph Fielding Smith in his widely used textbook, *Essentials in Church History*, first published in 1921, stated that the "the primary point of the revelation...was to teach that marriage between a man and a woman can be eternal and that people may become like God in every way," although he did acknowledge that "this revelation also contains the doctrine of plural wives."[126] Brigham H. Roberts, another church leader and historian, in his massive *Comprehensive History of the Church of Jesus Christ of Latter Day Saints* brought forth in 1930 asserted that the revelation had as its "primary purpose...the eternity of the marriage covenant," which he claimed had been "obscured by the discussion of and the popular clamor concerning the plurality feature of the new marriage system." He further argued that "plural marriage was a conditional, temporary, and relatively minor aspect of 'celestial marriage.'"[127] Some three years earlier a less well-known Mormon writer, J. M. Sjodahl, had gone even further in his extreme claim that the "'revelation of celestial marriage' dealt solely with the 'eternal duration of the marriage relation.'"[128]

Generating even more controversy in discussing the revelation was an officially sanctioned scriptural work entitled, *Latter-day Revelations: Selections from the Book of Doctrine and Covenants of the Church of Jesus Christ of Latter-day Saints*. Published in 1930 under the imprint of the LDS Church, the volume was actually compiled by James E. Talmage, who by this time was a senior apostle in the Quorum of the Twelve. This work was characterized as containing "Sections and parts of Sections from the Doctrine and Covenants, the sections comprising scriptures

---

125. As stated by B. Carmon Hardy, *Solemn Covenant*, 298. See John Henry Evans, *One Hundred Years of Mormonism: A History of the Church of Jesus Christ of Latter-day Saints from 1805 to 1905* (Salt Lake City, UT: Deseret Sunday School Union, 1905), 476–77.
126. Joseph Fielding Smith, *Essentials in Church History* (Salt Lake City, UT: Church of Jesus Christ of Latter-day Saints, 1921), 341, as quoted in Taysom, "A Uniform and Common Recollection," 135.
127. Brigham H. Roberts, *A Comprehensive History of the Church of Jesus Christ of Latter-day Saints*, 6 volumes (Salt Lake City, UT: Church of Jesus Christ of Latter-day Saints, 1930), 2:93–95, as quoted in Taysom, "A Uniform and Common Recollection," 135.
128. J. M. Sjodahl, "Temple Marriage an Antidote Against Divorce," *Improvement Era* 30 (October 1927): 12.

of general and enduring value...."[129] Its purpose, in the words of Talmage, was "to make the strictly doctrinal parts of the Doctrine and Covenants of easy access and reduce its bulk."[130] Accordingly some ninety-five sections of the Doctrine and Covenants were completely omitted, along with parts of twenty-one others. The most noteworthy of these omissions was the entire text of Section 132! Fundamentalist Mormons were outraged, "accusing the [LDS] church of changing the scriptures." In response, then Church President Heber J. Grant, ordered the work immediately "withdrawn" from sale and the remaining copies "shredded to avoid further conflict with the fundamentalists," according to Talmage biographer, James P. Harris.[131]

Such conciliatory gestures toward Fundamentalist Mormons were short-lived, for within three years, LDS Church leaders were asserting an increasingly hard line toward those dissidents advocating plural marriage. This was most evident in an "Official Statement" issued by the LDS First Presidency in 1933. Known as "The Final Manifesto," the text of the document was crafted by J. Reuben Clark, a lawyer by training and a nationally prominent Mormon political figure, recently sustained as second counselor in the LDS First Presidency.[132] Clark was motivated by his own strong antipathy toward the fledgling, increasingly active fundamentalist movement, in which two of his close relatives had played leading roles, specifically, his uncle, John Woolley, and cousin, Lorin C. Woolley. As for Clark, over the course of some twenty years, before entering the church First Presidency, he had urged stringent measures against Fundamentalist Mormons whom he considered a serious threat to the LDS Church.[133]

As authored by Clark, the "Official Statement" conceded that "the revelation of July 1843...provided that under certain conditions, which are clearly defined, a man may receive more than one woman to be his wife" and as such "plural marriage became a recognized doctrine of the

---

129. Latter-day Revelations: Selections from the Book of Doctrine and Covenants of the Church of Jesus Christ of Latter-day Saints (Salt Lake City, UT: Church of Jesus Christ of Latter-day Saints, 1930), iv.
130. As quoted in James P. Harris, "Forward" to James E. Talmage, The Articles of Faith, xxx.
131. Ibid., xxix–xxx.
132. The definitive biography of Clark is D. Michael Quinn, *Elder Statesman: A Biography of J. Reuben Clark* (Salt Lake City, UT: Signature Books, 2001).
133. Quinn, *Elder Statesman*, 237–44.

church." But as a result of legislation enacted by the federal government to suppress "the practice...President Woodruff promulgated... The Manifesto" of 1890. In addition, Latter-day Saint leaders agreed to a provision in the constitution for the newly created state of Utah, forever prohibiting the practice of polygamy. All of this reflected "the church's pledge to discontinue polygamy" and "obey the civil law." Clark then denounced those whom he classified as a "few misguided members of the church...who had secretly associated themselves together for the avowed purpose of perpetuating the practice of polygamy or plural marriage in defiance of the pledge made to the government." The document further declared that such individuals were acting without proper authority, noting that their actions in authorizing polygamy were both "illegal and void because the Lord has laid down without qualification the principle that 'there is never but one on the earth at a time on whom this power and the keys of this priesthood are conferred.' The Lord has never changed this rule."[134] In referring to the "one man" possessing "the power and keys of the priesthood, the 1933 statement, with no little irony, was quoting directly from the 1843 revelation![135]

Clark further alluded to the same revelation in asserting that "Celestial marriage"—that is, marriage for time and eternity—and polygamous or plural marriage are not synonymous terms. "Monogamous marriages for time and eternity, solemnized in our temples in accordance with the word of the Lord and the laws of the Church are celestial marriages."[136] In affirming a distinction between "Celestial" and polygamous or plural marriages, the statement was in agreement with the similar distinction made by James E. Talmage some three decades earlier.

In essence, the current position of the LDS Church concerning Section 132 of the Doctrine and Covenants follows the parameters laid down by various LDS Church spokesmen in the wake of the 1890 Manifesto. John Henry Evans, James E. Talmage, and J. Reuben Clark asserted that the concept of "celestial marriage" is distinct and separate from "plural or polygamous marriage" while putting new emphasis on various theological concepts contained in the revelation other than polygamy. In par-

---

134. "An Official Statement from the First Presidency of the Church of Jesus Christ of Latter-day Saints," *Deseret News*, June 17, 1933, Church Section, 1–4.
135. Doctrine and Covenants, 132: 7
136. "An Official Statement from the First Presidency..." 3–4.

ticular, they stressed the power of priesthood authority in performing ordinances effective beyond death and the prime importance of marriage for time and eternity as essential for "exaltation" — the attainment of the highest degree of glory in the Celestial Kingdom. All of these concepts continue to be essential tenets of modern Mormon belief.

Reflective of the current LDS position is the way in which Section 132 is discussed in *Teachings of the Presidents of the Church: Joseph Smith*—an official guide published for the benefit of church members in 2007. Specifically this work states that:

> In 1843 the Prophet [Joseph Smith] dictated a revelation that describes the eternal nature of the marriage covenant (see D&C 132). The doctrines in this revelation had been known by the Prophet since 1831. As commanded by God, he also taught the doctrine of plural marriage.[137]

Indeed, Latter-day Saint emphasis on the non-polygamous aspects of Doctrine and Covenants 132 stands in contrast to the interpretation given the same document by present-day Fundamentalist Mormons who emphasize the prime importance of those features concerned with plural marriage. In this regard Fundamentalist Mormons are more akin to nineteenth century Latter Day Saints who affirmed plural marriage as an essential Mormon tenet than with their twenty-first century counterparts in the Church of Jesus Christ of Latter-day Saints.[138]

---

137. *Teachings of the Presidents of the Church: Joseph Smith* (Salt Lake City, UT: The Church of Jesus Christ of Latter-day Saints, 2007), 22. In the introduction of this same work, under the heading "Teachings for Our Day" the LDS Church issued the following disclaimer: "This book...does not discuss plural marriage." It then goes on to state: "The doctrines and principles relating to plural marriage were revealed to Joseph Smith as early as 1831. The Prophet taught the doctrine of plural marriage, and a number of such marriages were performed during his lifetime. Over the next several decades, under the direction of the Church Presidents who succeeded Joseph Smith, a significant number of Church members entered into plural marriages. In 1890, President Wilford Woodruff issued the Manifesto, which discontinued plural marriage in the Church (see Official Declaration 1). The Church of Jesus Christ of Latter-day Saints no longer practices plural marriage." xii.

138. For a Fundamentalist Mormon perspective on Section 132 of the Doctrine and Covenants see: Anne Wilde, *An Essential For Exaltation: Celestial Plural Marriage Essential for the Highest Degree of the Celestial Kingdom* (Salt Lake City, UT: Pioneer Press, 1998).

Doctrine and Covenants Section 132 and Joseph Smith's Expanding Concept of Family

by Craig L. Foster

THE POWERFUL, almost haunting, words of the old folk gospel song, "Will the Circle be Unbroken," express the intense longing to be reunited in the presence of God with deceased loved ones in the hereafter. "Will the circle be unbroken; by and by, Lord, by and by; there's a better home awaiting; in the sky, Lord, in the sky."[1] The early Saints of the Restoration had the same yearning to return to God and continue marital and familial bonds beyond death.

The majority of early church members had personally experienced death of loved ones and the ensuing emotional and spiritual pain. Members of the Smith family were certainly not strangers to death, and their perception of death, like so many other Americans from that era, re-

---

1. The author would like to thank Richard E. Bennett, David Choules, Brigham Young University's Religious Studies Center, and Brian C. Hales for their generous assistance. Nitty Gritty Dirt Band, "Will the Circle be Unbroken," Lyrics Freak, http://www.lyricsfreak.com/n/nitty+gritty+dirt+band/will+the+circle+be+unbroken_20101271.html, accessed March 6, 2010.

flected what was known as the "beautiful death." The "beautiful death emphatically focused on the family ties and friendships about to be dissolved."[2]

The doctrines and ordinances introduced by Joseph Smith demonstrated his expanding theology regarding the importance of the eternal family in the gospel of Jesus Christ. Layer upon layer, Smith revealed further knowledge and understanding of what has been described as a celestial "kinship-based covenant system" which fit in well with the early Saints' concept of family and kinship.[3] As one historian explained, "Mormonism, in its earliest decades, was for the most part, a collection of families."[4]

According to David Hackett Fischer, in his ground-breaking work, *Albion's Seed: Four British Folkways in America,* "the nuclear family was the normal unit of residence" in Anglo-American culture. Although similar in many ways, American family patterns, differed by region in the United States due to differing British influences. For example, in the Delaware Valley, Quaker influence on the nuclear family was stronger than in Anglican Virginia, where families tended to be smaller and weaker than in Puritan New England where families were larger. Extended families, however, were more important in Virginia and the Tidal basin region than in New England, while Quakers in the Delaware Valley "submerged the nuclear and extended family into a larger sphere which was their 'family of God.'"[5]

In New England, which was the heritage of the majority of early Latter Day Saints, the Puritan idea of a covenanted family created an "obsession with family and genealogy" which dominated the culture. This "special intensity" was the result of what historian Edmund Morgan

---

2. Samuel Brown, "The 'Beautiful Death' in the Smith Family," *BYU Studies* 45:4 (2006): 123, 124.

3. Rex Eugene Cooper, *Promises Made to the Fathers: Mormon Covenant Organization* (Salt Lake City: University of Utah Press, 1980), 108, as quoted in Gary James Bergera, "The Earliest Eternal Sealings for Civilly Married Couples Living and Dead," *Dialogue: A Journal of Mormon Thought* 35:3 (Fall 2002): 41.

4. Ronald O. Barney statement found on the back cover of Stephen L. Prince, *Gathering in Harmony: A Saga of Southern Utah Families, Their Roots and Pioneering Heritage, and the Tale of Antoine Prince, Sheriff of Washington County* (Spokane, Washington: Arthur H. Clark, 2004).

5. David Hackett Fischer, *Albion's Seed: Four British Folkways in America* (New York: Oxford University Press, 1989), 482, 274–275, and 68–69.

called "Puritan tribalism" as the early founders of New England believed they were "God's chosen people." Because of the Puritan belief in being a chosen people, a blessing which would descend to their children and future generations, there was an "obsession with family and genealogy" which became an "enduring part of New England's culture."[6]

As the nation evolved, so did the dynamics and interpretation of the family. Although some regions of the country still reflect the cultural influence of their pioneering ancestors regarding family, the majority of modern America appears to have adopted the Puritan New England family model where the emphasis is on the inner ring or nuclear family. Within this framework, "normally, the kinship circle is confined [at the most] to a small group of kin consisting of grandparents, aunts, uncles, and cousins. The members of this group are considered kindred." In "American cultural conception, kinship is defined as biogenetic." Thus, the idea of kindred being someone directly related by blood is "quite explicit in American culture."[7]

---

6. Ibid., 69. Fischer's discussion on the Puritan concept of family, kinship and genealogy demonstrates how Puritans put special emphasis on "the innermost nuclear ring" within the concentric set of nuclear and extended rings which made up the traditional Puritan family (70). In regard to the obsession of genealogy, as early as the seventeenth-century a Puritan writer proclaimed, "The Books that shall be opened at the last day will contain Genealogies among them. There shall be brought forth a Register of the Genealogies of New Englands sons and daughters." In the nineteenth-century, Harriet Beecher Stowe observed, "Among the peculiarly English ideas which the Colonists brought to Massachusetts . . . was that of family. Family feeling, family pride, family hope and fear and desire, were . . . strongly marked traits. Genealogy was a thing at the tip of every person's tongue, and in every person's mind . . ." William Stoughton, *New England's True Interest, Not to Lie* (Cambridge, 1670), 33 and Harriet Beecher Stowe, *Uncle Tom's Cabin or, Life among the Lowly; The Minister's Wooing; Oldtown Folks* (New York: Library of America, 1982), 1102, both as quoted in Richard E. Turley Jr. and Craig L. Foster, "The History of Genealogy in America," in Tien-Wai Lin, ed., *Collected Articles on Collected Materials* (Haikou City, China: Nanfang Publishing Co., 2002), 829–830. The book is published in Chinese and English.

7. Jackie Smith Arnold, *Kinship: It's All Relative*, 2nd ed., (Baltimore, MD: Genealogical Publishing, 1990, 1996), 27; and David M. Schneider, *American Kinship: A Cultural Account*, 2nd ed., (Chicago: University of Chicago Press, 1980), 23, 25. Arnold states that "Kinship is figured bilaterally in the United States, which means an individual is affiliated with and descent traced through relatives on both the maternal and paternal sides (27)." It should also be noted that Schneider includes marriage and marriage partners as the definition for a relative in American culture (25). Defining kinship has proven to be a little more complicated among various scholars. Even so, most people recognize kinship as a consanguine or blood relative, having come from a common ancestor. In other words, "kinship is based on the biological blood we share with others," according to George H. Amber, *Blood Kin and In-Laws: All relationships revealed, named, and explained* (West Bloomfield, Michigan: Succinic Press, 1993), 96; Burton Pasternak et al.,

While in American kinship, the nuclear family and the small group of kin most often represents the family unit, such is not always the case. Moreover, with the concept of blood kin (grandparents, aunts, uncles, and cousins) as the unifying symbol of kinship and family, that means that "every member of the family is at the same time a relative and every relative is, in this sense, a member of the family." Thus kinship can and, in some parts of the country, does, both symbolically and in practice, represent a large extended family.[8]

Although extended family was important to the settlers of Virginia's Tidal Basin region, it did not match the importance placed on it by those of America's back country culture.

From the perspective of an individual within this culture, the structure of the family tended to be a set of concentric rings, in which the outermost circles were thicker and stronger than among other English-speaking people. Beyond the nuclear core, beyond even the extended circle, there were two rings which were unique to this culture. One was called the derbfine. It encompassed all kin within the span of four generations. For many centuries, the laws of North Britain and Ireland had recognized the derbfine as a unit which defined the descent of property and power. It not only connected one nuclear family to another, but also joined one generation to the next.[9]

The term derbfine means "true kin" and that is exactly how those of America's back country viewed their extended family. As with the settlers of Puritan New England and Quaker-influenced eastern Pennsylvania and the Delaware Valley, those who settled on colonial America's western frontier (western Pennsylvania, Virginia, the Carolinas, Tennessee, etc.) transplanted their British culture from what is commonly known as

---

Sex, Gender, and Kinship: A Cross-Cultural Perspective (Upper Saddle River, New Jersey: Prentice Hall, 1997), 255; and Arnold, *Kinship*, 29. According to Melvin P. Thatcher in his dissertation, "Kinship and Government in Chu during the Spring and Autumn Era, 722–453 B.C.," (University of Washington: PhD dissertation, 2004), 412, some cultural anthropologists (David M. Schneider being a leading example) have criticized the kinship theory as having no theoretical or comparative value because the concept of kinship itself is rooted in the "European and American cultures of the anthropologists." However, most social anthropologists (C. C. Harris being a leading example) "have not been persuaded by these arguments and continue to use the term." For his part, Thatcher agrees with Harris and other cultural anthropologists.

8. Ibid., 12.
9. Fischer, 663.

the "Celtic Fringe." The concept of derbfine was significant to this group of people who, both in the British Isles and in America recognized it as one of the two types of family structure. The other, which was the familial ring beyond the derbfine, was the clan.[10]

A modified clan system reminiscent of the old world spread rapidly and flourished in the eighteenth-century and nineteenth-century mountainous regions and southern frontiers of America. In fact, in some parts of this region, such as the Ozarks and the Appalachians, "clans became stronger rather than weaker" through the nineteenth century and well into the twentieth century. These clans or family networks usually had large nuclear households which often included "more than one nuclear family living under the same roof." Moreover, "these clans fostered an exceptionally strong sense of loyalty."[11]

While this kinship system was prevalent in America's Southern backcountry, the Puritan family model was, nevertheless, what most influenced Joseph Smith and other early Mormons as they brought these concepts of the family and kinship into their new religious movement. The family, as a sacred unit, played an important role in the restoration of the gospel. While the family played a significant role in the present, reflecting that yearning for bonds to continue beyond death, Joseph Smith also taught how the family unit could be eternal.

In April 1836 the sealing keys to "turn the hearts of the fathers to the children, and the children to the fathers" were restored to Joseph Smith during a series of visions in the Kirtland Temple.[12] Elijah the prophet

---

10. "Celt law 3," http://www.flash.net/~bellbook/faolcu/celtlaw03.html, (accessed June 24, 2002). According to "Tuath na Ciarraide-Mactíre: Tuath Structure," http://tuathamactire.org/tuatha.html (accessed January 31, 2003), the derbfine was made up of two or more fine. A fin in Celtic culture is a family unit. Plural for fin is fine, thus a derbfine being two or more fin and "traditionally encompassed all people descended from a common ancestor, out to four generations." Two or more derbfine, and often as many as five or six, was a tuath. "The tuath is, basicly [sic], the unified extended families that are the derbfine, connected through fosterage, marriage, or blood." In other words, a tuath is a tribe or clan. As described in Treubh Gealach Coille, "Writings: The Family Way," http://users.indigo.net.au/darke/treubh/art_familyway.html (accessed June 24, 2002), "kinship and lineage are of great value to the Celts." Indeed, for the Celts, "it was essentially about the Clann or Fine." It should also be noted that Great Britain's "Celtic Fringe" was made up of the lower part of England's southwest tip in what is traditionally Cornwall, Wales, Ireland, Isle of Man, and Scotland.

11. Fischer, 663, 665–667.

12. Doctrine and Covenants 110:13–16. Julie B. Beck, in a talk titled, "Teaching the Doctrine of the Family," Seminaries and Institutes of Religion Satellite Broadcast (August 4, 2009), 3, sug-

had returned, thus fulfilling the prophecy of Malachi that Elijah would return before the great and dreadful day of the Lord.[13] The power of the sealing keys was to bind families, both intragenerational and intergenerational, together forever. Thus marriage and familial bonds would extend beyond the grave.

The restoration of the sealing keys set in motion the restoration and introduction of other doctrines and ordinances aimed at ensuring the eternal family. In order to be together eternally, former generations that had lived and died without hope of salvation had to have a way back into the presence of God. As early as 1835, Oliver Cowdery wrote, "Do our fathers, who have waded through affliction and adversity…[have] an inheritance in those mansions? If so, can they without us be made perfect?" In 1838, Joseph Smith taught that all who had lived and not had a chance to hear the gospel and "be administered to by an inspired man in the flesh" must do so before being judged.[14]

In August 1840, Smith introduced a way to save those who had passed on when preaching at the funeral of Seymour Brunson. In January 1841, he dictated a revelation he received wherein he discussed baptism for the dead.[15] He then taught the principles behind the salvation for the dead. In an address to the Saints, Smith announced:

> This is the spirit of Elijah that we redeem our dead & connect ourselves with our fathers which are in heaven & seal up our dead to come forth in the first resurrection & here we want the power of Elijah to

---

gests that Joseph Smith understood the "theology about the family" when he was 17 and began to be taught by heavenly messengers, such as "the fathers" who "were Adam, Abraham, Isaac, Jacob, Noah—those ancient prophets who understood the doctrine of eternal families." This is probably not too accurate. Evidence shows Joseph Smith's understanding of the eternal family developed over time as he gained more spiritual knowledge. Nevertheless, Beck positively demonstrates how the "doctrine of the family" is an integral part of Latter-day Saint theology.

13. James B. Allen, Jessie L. Embry, Kahlile B. Mehr, *Hearts Turned to the Fathers: A History of the Genealogical Society of Utah, 1894–1994* (Provo, Utah: BYU Studies, Brigham Young University, 1995), 17.

14. "LETTER VII to W. W. Phelps, Esq." *Latter Day Saints' Messenger and Advocate* (July 1, 1835): 156 and *Elders' Journal* 1 (July 1838): 43, as both are quoted in D. Michael Quinn, *The Mormon Hierarchy: Origins of Power* (Salt Lake City: Signature Books, 1994). 163.

15. According to Jeffrey A. Trumbower, *Rescue for the Dead: The Posthumous Salvation of Non-Christians in Early Christianity* (New York: Oxford University Press, 2001), 35–39, proxy baptisms were indeed practiced by ancient Corinthians and said practice appears to have been generally approved during the first couple of centuries. It was later that proxy baptism was considered heretical.

seal those who dwell on earth to those which dwell in heaven. This is the power of Elijah & the keys of the kingdom of Jehovah.[16]

Words cannot adequately describe the joy early members of the church felt when they learned about baptism for the dead and the other saving ordinances. For example, Brigham Young later recalled:

> It made me glad when it was revealed through his servant Joseph, that I could go forth and officiate…for my ancestors, of the earliest generation, who have not had the privilege of helping themselves.[17]

Members who heard Joseph Smith's teachings about redeeming the dead literally rushed from the meeting down to the Mississippi River to be baptized for departed loved ones. "From that time forward, Saints in Nauvoo waded knee-deep into the Mississippi River to be baptized as proxy for their deceased kindred and friends." There was a fervor and enthusiasm among the Nauvoo Latter-day Saints that was almost palpable. After a short time, the Saints were told they could no longer perform baptisms in the river but had to wait until a font was built in the Nauvoo Temple. Work quickly moved ahead for the completion of the font which, after being dedicated, was used extensively.[18]

In Nauvoo, Wilford Woodruff commenced a prodigious work of performing (and overseeing the work of) the saving ordinances for his numerous kith and kin. He later wrote about the first days after baptisms for the dead had been taught:

> Joseph Smith himself…went into the Missisippi river one Sunday night after meeting, and baptized a hundred. I baptized another hundred. The next man, a few rods from me, baptized another hundred. We were strung up and down the Mississippi baptizing for our dead…

---

16. Susan Easton Black, "'A Voice of Gladness for the Living and the Dead,' D&C 128:19," Brigham Young University, Center for Family History & Genealogy, http://familyhistory.byu.edu/feb21.asp (accessed April 17, 2005). This address was the King Follett discourse by Joseph Smith and is considered by many historians to be Smith's greatest sermon. D&C 124:29–42 also discussed the building of the Nauvoo Temple. D&C 127:5–12 discussed witnessing and recording baptisms for the dead, while D&C 128, an epistle from Joseph Smith, along with giving more details about baptisms for the dead, revealed how Elijah restored the power to baptize for the dead and that all the rights, keys, and power of the priesthood had been restored on earth.

17. Speech delivered by Brigham Young in Nauvoo, 6 April 1845, and reported in *Millennial Star* 6 (October 1, 1845):119–22, as quoted in *Hearts Turned to the Fathers*, 18.

18. Black, 2.

Why did we do it? Because of the feeling of joy that we had, to think that we in the flesh could stand and redeem our dead.[19]

In the process of performing the saving ordinances, the Saints believed they were not only going through the necessary steps and ritual of temple work, they were, in reality, also saving themselves by reaching out to those on the other side. As Joel Hills Johnson later wrote in the hymn, "High on the Mountain Top," "And save ourselves with all our dead." As a result of turning hearts one to another, the Saints believed they would not only physically be connected by blood, but also spiritually connected. They would be an eternal family, with one generation sealed to another in a continuous chain from God the Father to Adam and from Adam down to the present.[20]

As early as 1840, Joseph Smith was teaching that "families were... to be transformed into eternal units." He explained that "a man could be sealed to his wife and after death God would recognize the validity of their union." God had joined Adam and Eve together for eternity and had placed them at the head of the human family. Couples sealed through the authority of the priesthood and their offspring were "recognized by God as legitimate members of his family and legal heirs to his kingdom." They became:

> another link in the chain of families stretching back to Adam, who was linked to God. Thus the 'family of God' became more than metaphor. Exaltation depended on being part of that chain. While one could reach the celestial kingdom by being baptized and enduring to the end, one had to be sealed to enter the highest level of heaven.[21]

One Nauvoo member wrote enthusiastically about marriages being "everlasting." He explained:

---

19. Wilford Woodruff, Journal, 6 April 1891, Archives of the Church of Jesus Christ of Latter-day Saints, Salt Lake City, Utah, as quoted in Black, 3. Woodruff's work in behalf of the dead was not surprising in light of his reaction to the doctrine of redemption of the dead. "I remember well the first time I read the revelation given through the Prophet Joseph Smith concerning the redemption of the dead—one of the most glorious principles I had ever become acquainted with on earth ... Never did I read a revelation with greater joy than I did that revelation." (Wilford Woodruff, Journal, 6 April 1891).

20. "High on the Mountain Top," *Hymns of The Church of Jesus Christ of Latter-day Saints* (Salt Lake City, Utah: The Church of Jesus Christ of Latter-day Saints, 1985), 5.

21. Gordon Irving, "The Law of Adoption: One Phase of the Development of the Mormon Concept of Salvation, 1830–1900," *BYU Studies* 14:3 (Spring 1974): 293.

> The parties (if the[y] belong to the Church) and will obey the will of God in this relationship to each other; are to be married for both Time and Eternity; they have the privilege to be married to their deceased husbands, or wives (as the case may be) for eternity, and if it is a man who desires to be married to his deceased wife; a Sister in the Church stands as Proxy, or as a representative of the deceased in attending to the marriage ceremony....[22]

The sealing powers had been restored to earth, giving the possibility of the circle being unbroken. Proxy baptisms had been introduced allowing those who had died without the gospel to enter into the Kingdom of God. These principles were a significant part of what Richard L. Bushman has described as "the most striking of the Nauvoo doctrinal developments"—the "emphasis on the family."[23] But, in order to achieve exaltation and enter into the highest degree of Celestial glory, "man" must enter into the new and everlasting covenant of marriage.[24]

Section 132 introduced a complex theology that "appears to be an amalgamation of several separate communications to Joseph Smith, each given at separate times and under different circumstances."[25] As scholar Robert L. Millet explained:

> The profound truths contained in section 132 of the Doctrine and Covenants (when read in conjunction with other revelations, particularly section 131) constitute the scriptural authority for the unique and exalted concept of marriage and family among the Latter-day Saints.

He further elaborated regarding the sealing powers:

> Eternal Marriage is the ordinance and covenant which leads to the consummate blessings of the gospel of Jesus Christ; it is that order of the priesthood which, when put into effect, will bind ancestry to

---

22. Jacob Scott letter to Mary Warnock, January 5, 1844, Paul M. Hanson Papers, P12–1, f5, Community of Christ Archives, Independence, Missouri, as quoted in Brian C. Hales, *Joseph Smith's Polygamy* (forthcoming from Greg Kofford Books).
23. Richard Lyman Bushman, *Joseph Smith: Rough Stone Rolling* (New York: Alfred A. Knopf, 2005), 421.
24. Doctrine and Covenants 131:1. Eternal increase can be had only by entering into the covenant.
25. Danel W. Bachman, "New Light on an Old Hypothesis: The Ohio Origins of the Revelation on Eternal Marriage," *Journal of Mormon History* 5 (1978): 23–24.

posterity and thus prevent the earth from being utterly wasted at the time of the Savior's Second Coming.[26]

So, according to the Doctrine and Covenants, only when a couple enters into the new and everlasting covenant of marriage by one who has the power and keys of the priesthood do they have hope to achieve God's promises. These promises include coming forth in the first resurrection, inheriting:

> thrones, kingdoms, principalities, ands dominions …[and they shall receive] their glory in all things, as hath been sealed upon their heads, which glory shall be a fullness and a continuation of the seeds forever and ever. Then shall they be gods, because they have no end; therefore shall they be from everlasting to everlasting, because they continue.[27]

In other words, celestial marriage, according to Mormon doctrine, was and is a prerequisite to exaltation. But what exactly was defined as celestial marriage? Was it only plural marriage or, the plurality of wives? Or was it more? Doctrine and Covenants 132, itself, gives a good clue. The new and everlasting covenant of marriage is discussed beginning in verse nineteen. Discussion regarding the plurality of wives was not broached until the thirtieth verse nor explicitly given as a commandment until the sixty-first verse, thus appearing to differentiate between the concept of celestial marriage and then one of the forms of celestial marriage (ie. plural marriage).[28]

While early Saints used the phrases "celestial marriage" and "plural marriage" interchangeably, it is apparent they recognized these as two different things that went hand in hand. For example, Orson Pratt, in an 1859 discourse defending plural marriage, acknowledged, "There is such a principle as marriage for eternity, which may imply one wife or many. The marriage covenant is indissoluble; it is everlasting; it is not limited

---

26. Robert L. Millet, "A New and Everlasting Covenant (D&C 132)," [1], in Robert L. Millet and Kent P. Jackson, *Studies in Scripture, vol. 1: The Doctrine and Covenants* as accessed at http://ldsbooks.narod.ru/books/Studies-in-Scripture-Vol-1-The-Doctrine-and-Covenants-by-Robert-L-Millet-Kent-P-Jackson.html#30453 (accessed March 18, 2010).

27. Doctrine and Covenants 132:19–20.

28. The sole exception is the first verse, which notes that Joseph Smith had sought understanding regarding the Old Testament practices relating to "many wives and concubines."

to time; but it is a covenant to exist while eternity exists: it pertains to immortality as well as mortality."[29]

In 1843, Joseph Smith taught:

> Except a man and his wife enter into an everlasting covenant and be married for eternity, while in this probation, by the power and authority of the Holy Priesthood, they will cease to increase when they die...but those who are married by the power and authority of the priesthood...will continue to increase.[30]

This teaching was repeated by Smith and other church leaders on a number of occasions. Hyrum Smith exalted, "I rejoice that what is done by the Lord has an endless duration," and John Taylor reflected on expected associations beyond death, "We believe in an everlasting covenant, and in an everlasting gospel."[31]

Joseph Smith, as quoted by John Taylor, explained:

> We could be sealed to one another through time and eternity; we could prepare ourselves for an exaltation in the Celestial Kingdom of God. It is one of the greatest blessings that ever was conferred upon the human family.[32]

Wilford Woodruff insisted the sealing ordinances had indeed been revealed to Joseph Smith and "will have effect after death" and "will reunite men and women eternally in the family organization."[33] Brigham

---

29. Orson Pratt, "Polygamy," in G. D. Watt, *Journal of Discourses by Brigham Young, President of the Church of Jesus Christ of Latter-day Saints, His Two Counselors, the Twelve Apostles, and Others*, 26 volumes (Liverpool: F. D. Richards, 1855), 6:357.

30. Joseph Fielding Smith, comp., *Teachings of the Prophet Joseph Smith* (Salt Lake City, Utah: Deseret Book Company, 1976), 300–301.

31. Hyrum Smith, discourse of April 8, 1844, as quoted in Richard E. Turley Jr., *Selected Collections from the Archives of the Church of Jesus Christ of Latter-day Saints* (Provo, Utah: BYU Press, 2002), DVD no. 1, vol. 6, 1984–91, and John Taylor, *Journal of Discourses* 21:10, November 30, 1884, as quoted in Hales (forthcoming).

32. John Taylor, "The Work of God," *Journal of Discourses* 24:229. The introduction of these new doctrines and ordinances was not always easy for the Saints. Jedediah M. Grant explained regarding temple sealings and plural marriage in "The Power of God and the Power of Satan," *Journal of Discourses* 2:13, that "when the family organization was revealed from heaven—the patriarchal order of God, and Joseph began, on the right and on the left, to add to his family, what a quaking there was in Israel."

33. Wilford Woodruff, "The Holy Ghost—Laboring in Faith—The Kingdom of God—Patriarchal Marriage," *Journal of Discourses* 13:167. It should be noted that on the same page, Woodruff commented that only through the "sealing ordinance" and "the patriarchal order of marriage" would people obtain "a fullness of celestial glory."

Young also spoke of "the greatest blessing" being "to live for ever and enjoy the society of wives, children, and children's children, to a thousand generations, and for ever..."[34]

Eternal marriage binds "ancestry to posterity." As Millet explained, Doctrine and Covenants 132 made it clear that "Salvation consists in the blessing of eternal lives, the continuation of the family unit in eternity."[35] This could only be accomplished by performing the saving ordinances and sealing one to another.

"Nothing in his later life excited Joseph [Smith] more than the idea of joining together the generations of humanity from start to finish."[36] The human yearning for the circle to truly be unbroken pushed the early Saints to seek out how they could be together with loved ones forever. Joseph Smith's expanding theology regarding salvation and the eternal family allowed Latter Day Saints to believe family relationships did not stop with mortality nor with the traditional nuclear family. The concept of family extended to more distant relations; as well as went beyond the grave and became multigenerational. This was eventually accentuated even further by the numerous and intricate family relationships created through plural marriage which, in many ways, supplanted for the Saints the earlier Puritan family model with a religious or spiritual variation of the larger family model of derbfine emphasizing intra- and intergenerational connections.

The doctrines and ordinances of sealings, baptisms for the dead and other temple ordinances focused on eternal relationships and redefined the parameters of the family. All of this culminated with Doctrine and Covenants 132 and the path to exaltation through the new and everlasting covenant of marriage.

---

34. Brigham Young, "Privileges of the Sabbath...," *Journal of Discourses* 8:63.
35. Millet, [2] and [4].
36. Bushman, 422.

Joseph Smith and the Puzzlement of "Polyandry"

by Brian C. Hales

HISTORICAL EVIDENCE indicates that Joseph Smith was sealed to several women who had legal husbands. Generally called "polyandry," this paper will explore these relationships, attempting to discern the nature of the marriages. Polyandry will be discussed in light of early Mormon teachings concerning morality and marriage. The possibility of polyandrous sexual relations existing in these unions will be investigated. In 1854, First Presidency Counselor Jedediah M. Grant instructed:

> Did the Prophet Joseph want every man's wife he asked for? He did not, but in that thing was the grand thread of the Priesthood developed. The grand object in view was to try the people of God, to see what was in them... A man who has got the Spirit of God, and the light of eternity in him, has no trouble about such matters."[1]

---

1. G. D. Watt, *Journal of Discourses by Brigham Young, President of the Church of Jesus Christ of Latter-day Saints, His Two Counselors, the Twelve Apostles, and Others*, 26 volumes (Liverpool: F. D. Richards, 1855) 2: 14.

Todd Compton identified twelve women who were civilly married to another man at the same time they were sealed to Joseph Smith. Included are Sylvia Sessions, Ruth Vose, Mary Elizabeth Rollins, Sarah Kingsley, Presendia Lathrop Huntington, Sarah Ann Whitney, Zina Diantha Huntington, Patty Bartlett, Marinda Nancy Johnson, Elivira Annie Cowles, Elizabeth Davis, and Lucinda Pendleton.[2]

Lawrence Foster wrote:

> Perhaps the most puzzling and difficult-to-interpret behavior of Joseph Smith during this period [of Nauvoo polygamy] is the evidence that he asked some of his closest associates to give their wives to him...[3] How are such actions to be explained? Of course, one easily could make the assumption that most non-Mormons and anti-Mormons have that Smith simply was letting his sexual impulses get away with him in these or other cases. Or, as most Mormon writers have done, one could ignore the evidence entirely and hope that it would be forgotten.[4]

Kathryn Daynes echoed: "Perhaps nothing is less understood than Joseph Smith's sealings to women already married, because the evidence supports conflicting interpretations."[5]

"Ceremonial Polyandry" versus "Sexual Polyandry"

Before looking specifically at Joseph Smith's "polyandrous" marriages, we must determine the meaning of "polyandry." Todd Compton defines "marriage as any relationship solemnized by a marriage ceremony of some sort."[6] Therefore a woman married in a civil *ceremony*, who is subsequently married in a religious *ceremony*, would be considered to be practicing *ceremonial* polyandry. A legal divorce would be necessary to

---

2. Todd Compton, *In Sacred Loneliness: The Plural Wives of Joseph Smith* (Salt Lake City: Signature Books, 1997), 4–7.

3. Lawrence Foster, "Sex and Prophetic Power: A Comparison of John Humphrey Noyes, Founder of the Oneida Community, with Joseph Smith, Jr., the Mormon Prophet," *Dialogue: A Journal of Mormon Thought*, 31:4 (Winter 1998): 76–77 [65–83].

4. W. Lawrence Foster, "Between Two Worlds: The Origins of Shaker Celibacy, Oneida Community Complex Marriage, and Mormon Polygamy" (Ph.D., University of Chicago, 1976), 256.

5. Kathryn M. Daynes, *More Wives Than One: Transformation of the Mormon Marriage System, 1840–1910* (Urbana: University of Illinois Press, 2001), 29.

6. Compton, *In Sacred Loneliness*, 632.

prevent ceremonial polyandry because it would nullify the actions of the civil ceremony (the legal marriage).

While defining "polyandry" as ceremonial polyandry might have a few advantages, overall it seems to generate confusion, because it does not address the issue of sexuality. Theologically, there is a huge difference between ceremonial polyandry and sexual polyandry. If in the case above, the woman ceases to sleep with her legal spouse because of the religious marriage, even without a legal divorce, she would not be practicing *sexual* polyandry. Proving the presence of *ceremonial* polyandry does not prove the presence of sexual polyandry. Specific evidence of sexual polyandry is required.[7]

Too often readers assume sexual relations are included when they hear the term "polyandry." However, they may or may not be present depending upon the meanings of the words employed. One could argue that practically speaking, a marriage without sexuality is not a marriage and the woman would not be truthfully married to two men at the same time. With respect to Joseph Smith's "polyandry," antagonists sometimes show that he practiced ceremonial polyandry and then imply he was also practicing sexual polyandry. For several reasons, such assumptions may not be warranted.

If sexual relations were absent in "polyandrous" marriages as defined by Compton, they might be more accurately characterized as "pseudo-polyandrous."[8] LDS scholar Andrew Ehat agreed that Joseph's sealings to married women were, in fact, "pseudo-polyandrous," because of the absence of physical relations.[9]

Perhaps a more useful definition of marriage is "a union between a man and a woman such that children born to the woman are the recog-

---

7. Documenting the presence of sexual relations between two people is often difficult. Even more challenging is proving that such relations occurred over one-hundred-and-sixty years ago. Accordingly, verifying the presence of polyandrous sexuality (of one woman's sexual relations with two husbands during the same period of time) in the 1840s will be even more formidable. The lack of evidence does not prove that the absence of sexual polyandry as it is impossible to prove a negative. However, without such evidence, caution must be exercised when making assumptions and conjectures.

8. See Andrew F. Ehat, "Pseudo-Polyandry: Explaining Mormon Polygyny's Paradoxical Companion," presented at the 1986 Sunstone Salt Lake Symposium; copy of typescript in possession of the author, 1–29. SL86300. Available for download at http://www.sunstoneonline.com/symposium/symp-mp3s.asp (SL86300).

9. Ehat, "Pseudo-Polyandry," 4-12.

nized legitimate offspring of both partners."[10] Using this classification, polyandry would require the presence of sexual relations with both husbands during the same time period. While Joseph Smith undoubtedly practiced "ceremonial polyandry," the question remains did he also practice "sexual polyandry?" Was he sleeping with other men's wives during the same season those women were also experiencing connubial relations with their legal husbands?

Did Joseph Smith Practice Sexual Polyandry? Differing Opinions

Anti-Mormon literature composed toward the end of the nineteenth century often leveled the accusation of sexual polyandry at Joseph Smith. Usually the claim appeared as one item on their laundry lists of the Prophet's alleged indiscretions. However, the allegation was not always taken seriously by historians.

Notwithstanding, in her 1945 biography of Joseph Smith, *No Man Knows My History*, Fawn M. Brodie treated the behavior as a documented actuality, giving it new credibility as an acknowledged reality, in the minds of many of her readers. She penned: "Joseph could with a certain honesty inveigh against adultery in the same week that he slept with another man's wife, or indeed several men's wives, because he had interposed a very special marriage ceremony."[11]

Since 1945, many other authors have repeated Brodie's seemingly secure position. George D. Smith gave this regal explanation in 1994: "Beginning in 1841, Joseph Smith took as plural wives several married women, as if exercising a variant of the feudal *droit du seigneur*: a king's right to [have sexual relations with] the brides [betrothed to other men] in his domain. This option was presented to the married woman as a favor to her."[12] Similarly, D. Michael Quinn reflected certainty that Mary

---

10. Royal Anthropological Institute, *Notes and Queries on Anthropology* (1951), 110. Quoted in Stephanie Coontz, *Marriage, a History: from Obedience to Intimacy or How Love Conquered Marriage* (New York: Viking, 2005), 27.

11. Fawn M. Brodie, *No Man Knows My History: The Life of Joseph Smith, the Mormon Prophet*, 2nd rev. ed. (New York: Knopf, 1971), 308.

12. George D. Smith, "Nauvoo Roots of Mormon Polygamy, 1841–46: A Preliminary Demographic Report." *Dialogue* 27:1 (Spring 1994): 10.

Elizabeth was "cohabiting with both" Adam Lightner and Joseph Smith, but unfortunately does not provide any corroborating evidence.[13]

George D. Smith's most recent publication, *Nauvoo Polygamy "... but we called it celestial marriage,"* advances the concept beyond Brodie's conjectures. Smith chronicles the initial introductions between Joseph and several of his future "polyandrous" wives. For example, he notes the ages of the women when they first met the Prophet. Sarah Ann Whitney was only five, Mary Elizabeth Rollins twelve, Nancy Marinda Johnson fifteen, Sylvia Sessions nineteen, Ruth Vose twenty-four, etc.[14] The implication seems clear. George D. Smith indicates that for many years, Joseph Smith had his eye on these girls/women and developed sexual polyandry in order to establish conjugal relations with them, even though they were already married.

Todd Compton was less than positive: "It seems probable that Joseph Smith had sexual relations with his polyandrous wives."[15] Regarding one polyandrous sealing, he speculates:

> Nothing specific is known about sexuality in their [Zina Diantha Huntington and Joseph Smith] marriage, though judging from Smith's other marriages, sexuality was probably included.[16]

Other researchers have been more hesitant, but they leave the door open. Martha Sonntag Bradley and Mary Brown Firmage Woodward provided this view concerning one relationship: "Sexual relations with Joseph Smith [and Zina Diantha Huntington Jacobs, legal wife of Hen-

---

13. D. Michael Quinn, *The Mormon Hierarchy: Extensions of Power* (Salt Lake City: Signature Books, 1997), 184–85. Specifically Quinn writes: "Mary Elizabeth Rollins Lightner also claimed that she 'was sealed to Joseph for Eternity.' However, this statement for the public was an effort to conceal the polyandrous circumstances of her marriage to Smith at a time when the twenty-five-year-old woman was also married to Adam Lightner and cohabiting with both men" (ibid.). Quinn provides no documentation to explain his certainty that Mary Elizabeth was concealing anything. Nor is evidence offered to demonstrate that in fact she was sleeping with both men. Neither have I encountered any documentation for either allegation.
14. George D. Smith, *Nauvoo Polygamy: "...but we called it celestial marriage"* (Salt Lake City: Signature Books, 2008), 36.
15. Todd Compton, "Fawn Brodie on Joseph Smith's Plural Wives and Polygamy: A Critical View," in Newell G. Bringhurst, ed., *Reconsidering No Man Knows My History: Fawn M. Brodie and Joseph Smith in Retrospect* (Logan, Utah: USU Press, 1996), 165.
16. Compton, *In Sacred Loneliness*, 82.

ry B. Jacobs], if any, had been infrequent and irregular."[17] In 1975, Danel Bachman wrote concerning the marriage of Joseph Smith to Mary Rollins Lightner, who was legally married to Adam Lightner: "She [Mary Elizabeth] may well have had conjugal relations with Smith."[18]

In 2004, anti-Mormon writer Richard Abanes provided this extreme interpretation:

> Although the wives continued to live with their husbands, they would receive conjugal visits from Smith whenever the need arose... Wife-swapping was eventually looked upon as wholly acceptable if an influential church authority was involved.[19]

No credible evidence of wife-swapping has been located in manuscript sources.

Evidence of Sexual Polyandry

A review of the literature identifies several allegations of sexual polyandry leveled at Joseph Smith. Notably, all are from anti-Mormon or unsympathetic writers and none are first-hand. Three of the allegations are simple assertions. Ann Eliza Webb Young wrote in her expose, *Wife No. 19*: "One woman said to me not very long since, while giving me some of her experience in polygamy: 'The greatest trial I ever endured in my life was living with my husband and deceiving him, by receiving Joseph's attentions whenever he chose to come to me.'"[20] Wilhelm Wyl quoted Sarah Pratt claiming that Lucinda Pendleton Morgan Harris stated in 1842, "Why I AM HIS [Joseph Smith's] MISTRESS SINCE FOUR YEARS"

---

17. Martha Sonntag Bradley and Mary Brown Firmage Woodward, *Four Zinas: A Story of Mothers and Daughters on the Mormon Frontier* (Salt Lake City: Signature Books, 2000), 132–33.

18. Danel Bachman, "A Study of the Mormon Practice of Plural Marriage Before the Death of Joseph Smith" (M.A. thesis, Purdue University, 1975), 135. He also suggests that Presendia's seventh child, may have been "sired" by the Prophet. (Ibid., 139).

19. Richard Abanes, *Becoming Gods: A Closer Look at 21st-Century Mormonism* (Eugene, Oregon: Harvest House Publishers, 2004), 237.

20. Ann Eliza Webb Young, *Wife No. 19* (Hartford, Conn: Dustin, Gilman & Co., 1875), 71. In 1887, Zina referred to Ann Eliza's claims stating flatly: "She was not truthful... she has convicted herself out of her own mouth... Ann Eliza knew she was misrepresenting the facts..." ("J.J.J.", "Two Prophet's Widows," August 8, 1887, *Globe Democrat*). See also Eliza Jane Churchill Webb Letter of August 27, 1876, Myron H. Bond Papers, Community of Christ Archives.

(emphasis in original).²¹ And a third author asserted she heard Presendia Huntington "say afterwards in Utah, that she did not know whether Mr. Buell [her legal husband] or the Prophet was the father of her son."²²

Reviewing these alleged quotations raises important questions including problems with credibility and plausibility. In the nineteenth century, for a woman to mention her personal sexual involvement was rare. To admit to a polyandrous relationship would be rarer, but to openly refer to a polyandrous sexual involvement would be very extraordinary. The listeners to such admissions would have had no context to evaluate the declarations except to consider the behaviors plainly immoral. Even in the secret teachings of plurality in Nauvoo, there is no evidence that a doctrinal foundation for sexual polyandry was ever discussed. Hence, the women would be essentially declaring themselves to be unchaste. Zina, Lucinda, and Presendia all partook of the conservative Victorian standards of the time and were devout Latter-day Saints. It seems highly un-

---

21. Wilhelm Wyl quoting Sarah Pratt in *Mormon Portraits* (Salt Lake City: Tribune Printing and Publishing Co., 1886), 60. Several problems exist with Pratt's recollection. In 1842, she reported that Joseph's proposal (later called a "dastardly attempt") occurred prior to her husband's return from his mission to England. (John C. Bennett, *The History of the Saints: Or an Exposé of Joe Smith and Mormonism* [Boston: Leland & Whiting, 1842], 230–31.) Orson Pratt arrived in Nauvoo on July 19, 1841, B. H. Roberts, ed., *History of the Church of Jesus Christ of Latter-day Saints*, 7 volumes (Salt Lake City: Deseret News, 1902), 4:389. Hence, Sarah's alleged conversation with "Mrs. Harris" must have occurred prior to that date. Counting back four years establishes the described mistress-hood as beginning in the first half of the year 1837. However, Joseph Smith did not meet Lucinda until March 14, 1838, when the Smith family moved permanently from Ohio to Missouri (*History of the Church*, 3:8–9). Accordingly, the beginning of a four year adulterous relationship in 1837 between Joseph Smith and Lucinda Harris was a geographic impossibility.

22. Nelson Winch Green quoting Mrs. Mary Ettie V. Smith in, *Fifteen Years Among the Mormons: Being the Narrative of Mrs. Mary Ettie V. Smith* (New York: D.W. Evans, 1860), 35. Anti-Mormon writer Fanny Stenhouse described Ettie Smith in 1875 as "a lady who wrote very many years ago and in her writings, so mixed up fiction with what was true, that I was difficult to determine where the one ended and the other began." (Fanny Stenhouse, *"Tell It All": The Story of a Life's Experiences in Mormonism* [Hartford: A. D. Worthington & Co., 1875], 618.) Fawn Brodie theorized that the child was Oliver Buell (Brodie, *No Man Knows My History*, 301–02). However, genetics researcher Ugo A. Perego, has shown through DNA testing that Oliver was not Joseph Smith's son. (Ugo A. Perego, Jayne E. Ekins, and Scott R. Woodward, "Resolving the Paternities of Oliver N. Buell and Mosiah L. Hancock through DNA," *The John Whitmer Historical Association Journal* 28 [2008]: 128–36.) Further research shows Mary Ettie Smith could only have been referring to John Hiram, who was born July 13, 1843, at Adams, Illinois, over sixty miles south of Nauvoo. Other than speculation, nothing has been found to support a connection between Joseph and Presendia during that period.

likely that these women would make such comments. A review of other allegations suggests that none rises above the level of tabloid reporting.

Other acknowledged anti-Mormon authors made similar claims. John Bowes quoted William Arrowsmith in a confusing narrative that alleged sexual polyandry between Joseph Smith and Marinda Nancy Johnson Hyde that apparently bothered only Arrowsmith, since all other described participants remained true to Joseph Smith.[23] William Hall accused the Prophet of impregnating Zina Huntington Jacobs in an account that contains factual errors and has been recently shown to be false through DNA testing.[24] John Hyde paired Joseph Smith with Hannah Ann Dubois Smith Dibble in a story based upon hearsay evidence.[25]

No Complaints from Legal Husbands

Despite several allegations, research fails to identify complaints of sexual polyandry from any of the described participants, including the women or their legal husbands. Todd Compton acknowledges that true polyandrous relationships would be difficult for the men involved: "One wonders why these 'first husbands' apparently acquiesced to their wives' marriages to Smith."[26] He recognized that "If polygyny offended against the American cult of true womanhood, polyandry offended even more."[27] In addressing the legal husbands' reactions, we are confronted with the question, "Did they know of their wives' sealings to Joseph?" Richard Van Wagoner wrote in 1985: "The legal husband did not usually know about the extralegal husband."[28] Richard L. Bushman penned in 2005:

---

23. John Bowes, *Mormonism Exposed* (London: R. Bulman, 1850), 63.
24. William Hall, *The Abominations of Mormonism Exposed* (Cincinnati: I. Hart, 1851), 43; Ugo A. Perego, Natalie M. Myres, and Scott R. Woodward. "Reconstructing the Y-Chromosome of Joseph Smith: Genealogical Applications," *Journal of Mormon History* 31:3 (Fall 2005): 59–60 [42–60].
25. John Hyde, *Mormonism: Its Leaders and Designs* (New York: W.P. Petridge, 1857), 84–85. I have found no evidence to corroborate Hyde's assertion. Hyde was capable of extreme claims, asserting that proxy marriages for the dead had "to be consummated in the same manner as that of the living... And as a marriage ceremony is not valid till completed, there is practice in consequence more abomination" (Ibid., 88–89). This claim is unfounded and contradicted by more reliable evidence.
26. Compton, *In Sacred Loneliness*, 21.
27. Ibid., 80.
28. Van Wagoner, Richard S. "Mormon Polyandry in Nauvoo," *Dialogue: A Journal of Mormon Thought* 18:3 (Fall 1985): 81 [67–83].

Legal Husband	In Sacred Loneliness Commentary	Page
George Harris	"George Harris may have given permission for the marriage, since he was a close friend of Smith and a church leader"	49
Henry B. Jacobs	"Apparently, Henry knew of the marriage and accepted it"	81
Norman Buell	"Norman, a man bitterly opposed to Mormonism, was probably not told of Presendia's marriage."	123
David Sessions	It is not known "whether he [David] knew it or not."	185
Adam Lightner	"He [Adam] was out of town, 'far away' at the time, so probably did not know about it."	213
Orson Hyde	"Four writers offer no consensus on the issue of whether Orson was aware of the marriage"	239
Jabez Durfee	"He may have known about the marriage"	260
John Cleveland	"Because he [John] was a non-Mormon... it is unlikely that Sarah or Joseph told him about their marriage."	278
Edward Sayers	"Whether Edward knew about the marriage is entirely unknown"	383
Jonathan Holmes	"The fact that Holmes was so close to Joseph Smith suggests that he knew of Smith's marriage to his wife and permitted it..."	548
Windsor Lyon	"Nothing is known of Windsor's reaction to the marriage, if he knew of it."	179

CHART 4.1: *Todd Compton's assessments of whether the legal husband knew of their wives' relationships with Joseph Smith. From the chart, it appears that we have no reliable evidence describing the husbands' knowledge of or immediate response to their wives' sealings to the Prophet in eleven cases.*

*Martha Sonntag Bradley and Mary Brown Firmage Woodward wrote: "Henry gave tacit approval, believing that whatever the prophet did was right. We do not know if Zina told Henry about Smith's earlier proposals before their marriage or if he fully understood what the sealing meant." (Four Zinas: A Story of Mothers and Daughters on the Mormon Frontier, Salt Lake City: Signature Books, 2000, 113.) Benjamin F. Johnson provided this interesting recollection: "Of the Prophet's partiality or love for Sister Zina, I will only say she was always in his favor. And that after a two and half years mission to Canada and the middle states, I returned to learn she had but recently married, which perhaps did not quite please the Prophet. For in answer to his great love for her, she soon became his own wife. [She] was among the first to accept the plural order of marriage." ("'Aunt Zina' as I Have Known Her from Youth—By 'Uncle Ben'" [Benjamin F. Johnson], in Zina Card Brown Family Collection, MS 4780, Box 3, Folder 6 , LDS Church Archives.)

Husband	Husband's church membership	Civil marriage	Wife	Wife's sealing to Smith	Husband's history	Husband's Death	Complaints about polyandry
Henry B. Jacobs	Yes baptized in 1832	Mar. 7, 1841	Zina Diantha Huntington	Oct. 1841	Henry stood as a witness as Zina was married to Joseph Smith for eternity and Brigham Young for "time," on Feb 2, 1846.	1886 Utah	None
Norman Buell	Yes; baptized in 1836; disaffected in 1838	Jan. 6, 1827	Presendia Lathrop Huntington	Dec. 11, 1841	Norman "felt the difficulties were too much, and would have persuaded her, if possible, to leave the Church, but she remained firm and steadfast."**	1872	None
Adam Lightner	No	Aug. 11, 1835	Mary Elizabeth Rollins	Feb. 1842	Adam apparently remained a non-member his entire life.	1885 Utah	None
Windsor Lyon	Yes; Excommun. Nov 1842; Rebaptized Jan. 1846	April 21, 1838	Sylvia Sessions	Feb. 8, 1842	Windsor fathered three children with Sylvia prior to his excommunication and two after his 1846 rebaptism. The only child conceived while he was out of the Church was Josephine—allegedly the daughter of Joseph Smith.	1850 Utah	None
David Sessions	Yes; baptized in 1834	Jun. 28, 1812	Patty Bartlett	Mar. 9, 1842	David married two wives polygamously and largely abandoned Patty.	1850 Utah	None
Orson Hyde	Yes; reinstated in 1839	Sept. 4, 1834	Marinda Nancy Johnson	Apr. 1842	Served as apostle and member of the Quorum of the Twelve. Marinda divorced Orson in 1870.	1878 Utah	None†

CHART 4.2: *Additional information concerning the husbands of Joseph Smith's "polyandrous" wives. (Continued on following page.)*

**"Death of Presendia Kimball," *Deseret News Weekly*, Feb. 6, 1892, vol. XLIV, no. 7, page 14. † A letter from John L. Smith to First Presidency, Mar. 8, 1895, supports that Sarah was sealed to Joseph for only "eternity": "In the days of Joseph, Mother [Sarah M. Kingsley (Howe)] Cleveland by advice, was sealed to the prophet in Nauvoo but lived with her husband John Cleveland..." (D. Michael Quinn Papers—Addition—Uncat WA MS 244 [Accession:19990209-c] bx 1.) The author of this letter is likely John Lyman Smith (1823–98), who was both a son-in-law to Sarah Kingsley Cleveland and a first cousin to Joseph Smith Jr. John L. married Sarah's daughter Augusta Bowen Cleveland; and he was a son of John Smith, and brother to George A.

THE PUZZLEMENT OF POLYANDRY

Husband	Husband's church membership	Civil marriage	Wife	Wife's sealing to Smith	Husband's history	Husband's Death	Complaints about polyandry
Jabez Durfee	Yes	Mar. 3, 1834	Elizabeth Davis	<June 1842?	Jabez and Elizabeth divorced prior to Jan. 1846.	1867 Kansas	None
John Cleveland	No; friendly at first but turned bitter	June 10, 1826	Sarah Kingsley	<June 29, 1842?	On August 2, 1850, Sarah wrote: "Your Father would by no means go to live with the Mormons, therefore I beg of you not to ask us any more, it offends him."	1860 Illinois	None
George Harris	Yes; baptized in 1834	Dec. 3, 1830	Lucinda Pendleton	?	Served on Nauvoo High Council. George stood proxy as his wife was sealed to Joseph Smith for eternity on Jan 22, 1846. Divorced by 1853.‡	1857 Iowa	None
Edward Sayers	No**	Jan. 23, 1841	Ruth Vose	Feb. 1843	Edward lived among the Saints until his death.	1861 Utah	None
Jonathan Holmes	Yes; baptized in 1832	Dec. 1, 1842	Elvira Annie Cowles	June 1, 1843	Jonathan was always a faithful Mormon, serving as a bodyguard and pallbearer to the Prophet. He stood as proxy when Elvira was sealed to Joseph Smith in the Nauvoo temple.	1880 Utah	None
Joseph C. Kingsbury	Yes	April 29, 1843	Sarah Ann Whitney	July 7, 1842	This marriage was simply a front, apparently to dispel suspicions then focused on the Prophet. Sarah Ann and Joseph C. Kingsbury never consummated the union.	1898 Utah	None

‡A letter from John L. Smith to First Presidency, Mar. 8, 1895, supports that Sarah was sealed to Joseph for only "eternity": "In the days of Joseph. Mother [Sarah M. Kingsley (Howe)] Cleveland by advice, was sealed to the prophet in Nauvoo but lived with her husband _ohn Cleveland..." (D. Michael Quinn Papers—Addition—Uncat WA MS 244 [Accession:19990209-c] bx 1.) The author of this letter is likely John Lyman Smith (1823–98), who was both a son-in-law to Sarah Kingsley Cleveland and a first cousin to Joseph Smith Jr. John L. married Sarah's daughter Augusta Bowen Cleveland; and he was a son of John Smith, and brother to George A. **Andrew Jenson's personal notes state Edward was not a member. (Andrew Jenson Papers [ca. 1871–1942], LDS Archives).

"In most cases, the husband knew of the plural marriage and approved."[29] Todd Compton provided his own assessments (see chart 4.1).

From chart 4.1, it appears that we have no reliable evidence describing the husbands' knowledge of or immediate response to their wives' sealings to the Prophet in eleven cases. Chart 4.2 provides additional historical information. The twelfth "polyandrous" sealing occurred before the legal marriage (see below).

Reviewing these twelve "polyandrous" husbands, we find great diversity respecting their relationships to the Church and its leaders. There are friendly non-members (Cleveland, Lightner, and Sayers), antagonistic (Buell), unpredictable (Jacobs),[30] active (Durfee, Harris, and Sessions), cyclic (Hyde), and stalwart (Kingsbury and Holmes).

Despite their differences, research suggests that these men shared two things in common. First, their legal wives were sealed to Joseph Smith during the Prophet's lifetime. The second is that they all seem to have reacted to the relationship with the exact same response: *nothing*.

It might be argued that the historical record is so incomplete that such complaints could have been made but were not recorded or have not yet been located. However, grievances are usually designed to publicize a perceived injustice. Protests against a man's sexual involvement with another man's legal wife would have constituted juicy gossip that could have easily resulted in backwoods justice endangering the life of the non-husband. Undoubtedly, rumors of either the behavior or the repercussions would have been exploited by newspapermen scrounging for titillating details about the Mormons, if any such tales had reached their ears. To date, no gripes from any of these legal husbands have been identified in the historical documents.

After evaluating the available evidence regarding conjugal relations in Joseph Smith's polyandrous sealings, Todd Compton wrote that "theo-

---

29. Richard L. Bushman, *Joseph Smith: Rough Stone Rolling* (New York: Alfred A. Knopf, 2005), 439.

30. Jacobs experienced several failed marriages besides his union to Zina. Caroline Barnes Crosby wrote of one in her diary, January 11, 1852: "There were two couples married in our chamber. Mr. John M Horner officiated. Henry B. Jacobs to Mary Clawson..."; March 20, 1852: "Mary Clawson called. She looked very sad, said she had been weeping, gave us an account of her late husband Henry B. Jacobs leaving her in consequence of his old wife [Asenath Babcock married n 1848] coming and claiming her previous right." (Diary of Caroline Barnes Crosby, USHS, 17–30, December 1852 to March 1853.)

retically" it might be argued that in eleven cases of polyandry "there is no evidence for sexuality. In only one case do we have evidence."[31] That "one case" has been touted as an undeniable example of polyandrous sexual relations with the implication that conjugality was probably present in some or all of the rest.

Josephine Rosetta Lyon—Biological Daughter of Joseph Smith?

The marriage in question involves Sylvia Sessions Lyon and her daughter Josephine Rosetta Lyon. In 1915, Josephine signed the following statement:

> Just prior to my mother's death in 1882 she called me to her bedside and told me that her days on earth were about numbered and before she passed away from mortality she desired to tell me something which she had kept as an entire secret from me and from all others but which she now desired to communicate to me. She then told me that I was the daughter of the Prophet Joseph Smith...[32]

All researchers do not agree that this statement clearly declares Josephine to be the biological daughter of the Prophet.[33] It is true that words reflect some ambiguity and could possibly be interpreted to mean that Josephine was to be Joseph Smith's daughter only in eternity, without implying an actual paternal physical connection.[34] However, other de-

---

31. Todd Compton, "Truth, Honesty and Moderation in Mormon History: A Response to Anderson, Faulring and Bachman's Reviews of *In Sacred Loneliness*, section 'Sexuality in the Polyandrous Marriages'" http://www.geocities.com/athens/oracle/7207/rev.html (accessed February 11, 2007). Compton deals with eleven cases of "polyandry," having eliminated one, the marriage to Sarah Ann Whitney. See discussion below.

32. Affidavit of Josephine F. Fisher, February 24, 1915, Archives of The Church of Jesus Christ of Latter-day Saints (LDS Archives), Ms 3423, folder 1, images 48–49; see also Bachman, "A Study of the Mormon Practice of Plural Marriage Before the Death of Joseph Smith," 141. See discussion in Van Wagoner observed: "Mormon Polyandry in Nauvoo," 78 n12.

33. For an alternate view see, "Sylva Porter Sessions Lyon Kimball," in *Our Pioneer Heritage* (Salt Lake City: Daughters of Utah Pioneers, 1967), 10:415.

34. Historian Rex E. Cooper writes: "I find the evidence to be less convincing on three different grounds. First, although the possibility that Josephine was a daughter of Joseph Smith was being discussed as early as 1905, the statement reports a conversation that took place twenty-three years before in 1882. Second, since the statement is transmitted through Andrew Jenson, it is a third-hand account of Sylvia P. Sessions's statement. And third, the statement is unclear about what it meant to be 'a daughter of Joseph Smith.' For example, because of his mother's matrimo-

Sylvia Sessions Lyon (Photo courtesy Clark Layton.)

Josephine Lyon (Courtesy of Clark Layton.)

tails support that Josephine was the literal offspring of the Prophet. For example, if no genetic connection existed between Josephine and Joseph Smith, it is strange that Sylvia would wait until her deathbed to dramatically divulge that the Prophet was to be Josephine's father only in the next life. If Josephine "was the daughter of the Prophet Joseph Smith" only because of a sealing ordinance, rather than through physical siring, all of Sylvia's children would be equally his offspring. However, none of them reported any similar divulgences from their dying mother, nor would there be any compelling reason to keep such knowledge secret.[35] Josephine's name also supports the relationship.

In addition, other sources, beyond the 1915 affidavit, corroborate the story. In 1886, future BYU president George H. Brimhall recorded: "Went to Spanish Fork... Evening had a talk with Father Hales, who told me that it was said that Joseph Smith had a daughter named Josephine living in Bountiful, Utah... Soon the contemporaries of the

---

nial sealing to Joseph Smith, Heber J. Grant was regarded as a 'son of Joseph Smith' even though he was born twelve years after the prophet's death." (Rex E. Cooper, *Promises Made to the Fathers: Mormon Covenant Organization* [Salt Lake City: University of Utah Press, 1990], 144 n1.)

35. Windsor and Sylvia reunited after his January 1846 rebaptism. Byron Windsor Lyon was born September 4, 1847, and David Carlos Lyon on August 8, 1848. However, these children would be part of Joseph Smith's family in eternity.

Prophet Joseph will be all gone."³⁶ The Hales and Fisher families both emigrated from Kent, England, and may have known each other prior to their arrival in the United States. In 1905, Stake President Angus M. Cannon had an interview with Joseph Smith III, wherein he stated:

> I will now refer you to one case where it was said by the girl's grandmother that your father has a daughter born of a plural wife. The girl's grandmother was Mother Sessions, who lived in Nauvoo and died here in the valley. She was the grand-daughter of Mother Sessions. That girl, I believe, is living today in Bountiful, north of this city. I heard Prest. Young, a short time before his death, refer to the report and remark that he had never seen the girl, but he would like to see her for himself, that he might determine if she bore any likeness to your father."³⁷

Since Sylvia said she had never told anyone prior to revealing Josephine's paternity to her, these accounts suggest that rumors of Josephine's true biological father arose from other sources that received limited private circulation prior to Sylvia Sessions' death. In other words, several historical documents support a genetic relationship between the Prophet and Josephine, besides Sylvia's affidavit.

Joseph Smith and Sylvia Sessions—Polyandry or Polygyny?

Sylvia Sessions wedded Windsor Lyon in a civil ceremony on 21 April 1838. Together they moved to Nauvoo and were comfortably established there by July 1840. At some point thereafter, Sylvia was sealed to the Prophet. The question is when did that sealing occur and what was the status of her marriage to Windsor at that moment. If they had experienced a religious divorce prior to her sealing to Joseph Smith, a religious divorce that would have curtailed sexual relations between the two, then Sylvia would be guilty of ceremonial polyandry, but not sexual polyandry.

---

36. Jennie H. Groberg, ed., *Diary of George H. Brimhall*, vol. 1, Bound typescript, undated, no publisher, copy in Harold B. Lee Library, Special Collections, 2 volumes; George H. Brimhall Journal, Jan. 1, 1888, CA, MS d 1902, Harold B. Lee Library, Special Collections. The most likely identity of "Father Hales" is Charles Henry Hales (1817–1889), Brian C. Hales' great-great grandfather.

37. Angus Munn Cannon, "Statement of an interview with Joseph Smith, III, 1905," regarding conversation on October 12, 1905, MS 3166, LDS Church Archives.

Todd Compton wrote: "On February 8, 1842, when Sylvia was twenty-three, she was sealed to Joseph Smith."[38] Other authors have agreed with this date.[39] The source of this information is an unsigned document written in 1869 in an affidavit book.[40] Importantly, within that same collection of affidavit books is a second unsigned document that specifies an February 8, 1843 date, a full year later.[41] Research shows that neither of the documents is more reliable than the other and therefore, should not be treated preferentially. In addition, Josephine was born on February 8, 1844 raising additional questions about the reliability of the month and day written on the two manuscripts. Taken together, it appears that the documents present conflicting years and suspicious dates that are unconfirmed. Consequently, they provide contradictory information regarding the timing of Joseph Smith's and Sylvia Sessions sealing ceremony.

Without the assistance of the affidavit books, other sources must be consulted. In a document undoubtedly used to write his 1887 *Historical Record* article on plural marriage, independent historian Andrew Jenson referred to Sylvia as "formerly the wife of Windsor Lyons."[42] He also penned: "Sessions, Sylvia Porter, wife of Winsor [sic] Palmer Lyon, was born July 31, 1818... [She] Became a convert to 'Mormonism' and was married to Mr. Lyons — When he left the Church she was sealed to the

---

38. Compton, *In Sacred Loneliness*, 681–82; Todd Compton, "Remember Me in My Affliction": Louisa Beaman and Eliza R. Snow Letters, 1849," *Journal of Mormon History* 25:2 (Fall 1999): 60 [46–69].

39. Gary J. Bergera, "Identifying the Earliest Mormon Polygamists, 1841–1844," *Dialogue: A Journal of Mormon Thought* 38:2 (Fall 2005): 66; Michael Marquardt, *The Rise of Mormonism: 1816–1844* (Longwood, Florida: Xulon Press, 2005), 561; George D. Smith, "The Summer of 1842: Joseph Smith's relationships with the 12 Wives He Married After His First Wife, Emma," Sunstone Symposium presentation, Salt Lake Community College, July 31, 1998, 5; Danel W. Bachman, "A Study of the Mormon Practice of Plural Marriage Before the Death of Joseph Smith;" D. Michael Quinn lists on the year, 1842 in *The Mormon Hierarchy: Origins of Power*, 587.

40. Joseph F. Smith Affidavit Books 1:60, Church History Library of The Church of Jesus Christ of Latter-day Saints. See also Todd Compton, "A Trajectory of Plurality: An Overview of Joseph Smith's Thirty-three Plural Wives," *Dialogue: A Journal of Mormon Thought* 29:2 (Summer 1996): 34.

41. Joseph F. Smith Affidavit Books, 4:62. See discussion in Brian C. Hales, "The Joseph Smith—Sylvia Sessions Plural Sealing: Polyandry or Polygyny?" *Mormon Historical Studies* 9:1 (Spring 2008): 41–57; www.JosephSmithsPolygamy.com.

42. Andrew Jenson Papers, LDS Archives.

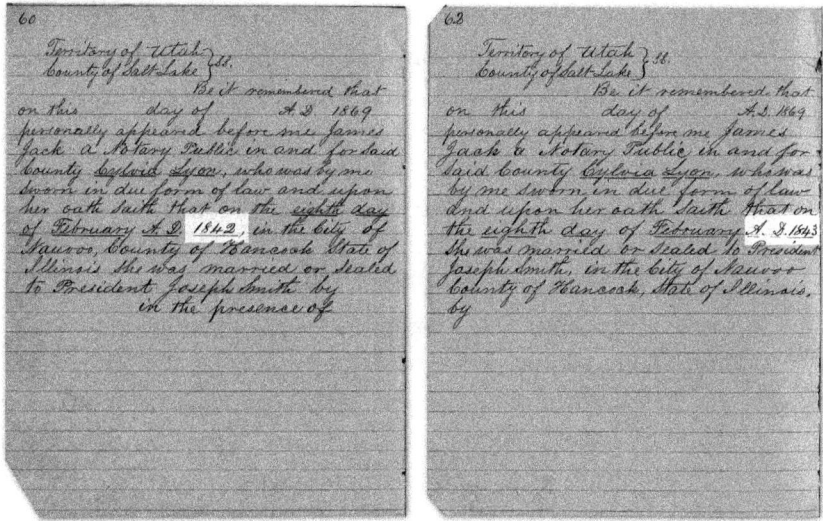

Pages from Joseph F. Smith Affidavit Books, 1:60, 4:62 showing conflicting dates. (Courtesy LDS Church History Library.)

Prophet Joseph Smith."[43] A second corroboration is found in the 1915 statement from Josephine. She remembered her mother also "told me that I was the daughter of the Prophet Joseph Smith, she having been sealed to the Prophet at the time that her husband Mr. Lyon was out of fellowship with the Church."[44] Accordingly, these documents place the sealing after Windsor's excommunication.

Windsor had a falling out with Stake President William Marks over a financial negotiation in the fall of 1842. In the end Windsor sued Marks in the civil courts—a violation of Church standards since such matters were to be resolved between members within the Church. In response, Marks brought Windsor up for a Church court. On November 19, 1842, Windsor was excommunicated.[45] One question arises: "Did Windsor and Sylvia obtain a civil divorce after his excommunication?"

---

43. Biographical Information on Windsor and Sylvia Lyon, undated sheet in Andrew Jenson Collection, LDS Archives.
44. Josephine R. Fisher, certificate, February 24, 1915. Original in Vault Folder LDS Archives, Ms 3423, folder 1, images 48–49; see also Bachman, "A Study of the Mormon Practice of Plural Marriage Before the Death of Joseph Smith," 141, 350.
45. Fred C. Collier, *The Nauvoo High Council Minute Books of the Church of Jesus Christ of Latter Day Saints* (Hanna, Utah: Collier's Publishing Co., 2005), 74.

Currently, no documentation of a legal divorce between Windsor and Sylvia after his excommunication has been found. Such divorces required a hearing before the circuit court in Carthage. In fact, it is doubtful that Joseph Smith or Sylvia Sessions seriously considered the need prior to her sealing to the Prophet. After introducing celestial marriage in Nauvoo, the validity of civil ceremonies in comparison to eternal sealings was often questioned. Stanley B. Kimball penned: "Some church leaders at that time considered civil marriage by non-Mormon clergymen to be as unbinding as their baptisms. Some previous marriages… were annulled simply by ignoring them."[46]

There is no question that in special circumstances, Joseph Smith, as President of the Church, believed himself capable of granting permission to ignore legal unions (constituting a religious divorce). In October 1835, the Prophet was consulted regarding the status of Lydia Goldthwaite Bailey's marriage to her abusive husband, Calvin Bailey, who had deserted her three years earlier. At that time, Lydia had received a marriage proposal from Newel Knight and didn't know what to do, since a formal divorce had not occurred. Hyrum Smith was acting as an intermediary. Newel Knight recorded:

> Bro Hiram came to me said he had laid the affair before Bro Joseph, who at the time was with his council. Broth Joseph after p[ray]or & reflecting a little or in other words enquiring [of the] Lord Said it is all right, She is his & the sooner they [are] married the better. Tell them no law shall hurt [them]. They need not fear either the law of God or man for [it] shall not touch them; & the Lord bless them. This [is the] will of the Lord concerning that matter… I told her all that had transpired, & we lifted our hearts with gratitude to our heavenly Father for his goodness towards us, & that we live in this mometuous age, & as did the ancients, so we have the privilege of enquireing through the prophet, & receiveing the word of the Lord concern\ing/ us.[47]

After prayer and reflection, Joseph declared that Lydia was capable of remarrying. Interwoven within his directive was the acknowledgement that Lydia was, from a religious standpoint, divorced from Calvin Bai-

---

46. Stanley B. Kimball, *Heber C. Kimball: Mormon Patriarch and Pioneer* (Urbana: University of Illinois Press, 1981), 95.

47. Newel Knight, "Autobiography and journal [ca. 1846];" MS 767, Folder 1, item 4, 57–58; LDS Archives.

THE PUZZLEMENT OF POLYANDRY   117

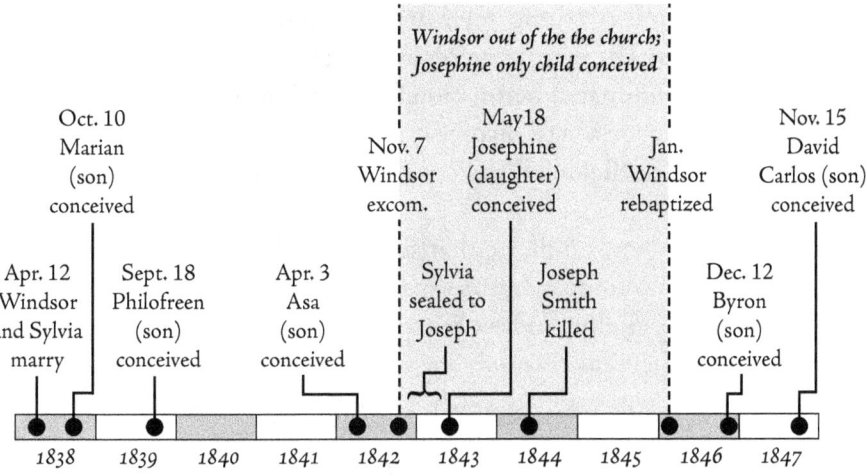

CHART 4.3: *Timeline showing the approximate conception dates of Sylvia's children and important activities of Joseph Smith and Windsor Lyon.*

ley.⁴⁸ Given that the Prophet's jurisdiction concerned only religious laws, the separation or divorce granted could only be considered ecclesiastical. However, Joseph instructed that thereafter they needed to no longer "fear either the law of God or man." Joseph Smith evidently considered his judgment in that matter to satisfy all pertinent concerns including state and federal laws, so far as the participants were concerned. Throughout the proceedings, there is no hint of approved polyandry, sexual or otherwise. On occasion, the Nauvoo High Council also assumed authority to allow a new matrimony to a man still legally married.⁴⁹

In addition, it appears that for most Latter-day Saints, the sealing ceremony constituted a matrimonial upgrade sufficient to dissolve previously contracted earthly matrimonies. For them, priesthood authority

---

48. Evidence shows that the Latter Day Saints never considered full marital polyandry to be acceptable to God. Nor is there any manuscript documentation to suggest that any Church members ever viewed themselves as being polyandrously marriage. Accordingly, there is no doubt that a divorce from her first husband was acknowledged by Latter Day Saints.

49. See the case of Henry H. Wilson tried on January 21, 1843. Even without a legal divorce, "it was decided by President Hyrum Smith and William Marks, that if he feels himself justified and can sustain himself against the laws of the land, that he is clear as far as they were concerned (i.e. the jurisdiction of the High Council) and was at liberty to marry again on the aforesaid conditions." Collier, *The Nauvoo High Council Minute Books of the Church of Jesus Christ of Latter Day Saints*, 80.

was so superior as to trump any marriage ceremony sanctioned only by worldly powers. The eternal union authorized conjugality in the sealed marriage and eliminated permission for sexual relations in the previous union. The need for a legal divorce was ignored in the wake of an eternal nuptial, but the religious divorce was binding, prohibiting sexual relations.

Several evidences indicate that some sort of divorce or termination was inherent in Windsor Lyon's excommunication or at least accompanied it chronologically. Andrew Jenson's notes reflect this perspective as he referred to Sylvia as "formerly the wife of Windsor Lyons,"[50] also writing that Sylvia "was married to Mr. Lyon. When he left the Church she was sealed to the Prophet Joseph Smith."[51]

Josephine Lyon's 1915 statement also implies that the excommunication invalidated her marriage to Windsor, allowing her to be legitimately sealed to Joseph Smith and bare a child with him. Sylvia told Josephine that she was "sealed to the Prophet at the time that her husband Mr. Lyon was out of fellowship with the Church."[52]

Researchers who accept Josephine's 1915 statement as evidence that she was Joseph's offspring cannot easily reject the timeline presented or the implication that Windsor's church estrangement was interpreted by Josephine as an official separation or divorce, thus legitimizing her mother's ability to be sealed to the Prophet. Neither is there any indication that Josephine thought her mother was simultaneously married to two men polyandrously or that Sylvia continued to cohabit with Windsor after his excommunication. Importantly, there is no evidence of sexual polyandry in this relationship.[53]

---

50. Andrew Jenson Papers, LDS Church History Library.
51. Biographical Information on Windsor and Sylvia Lyon, undated sheet in Andrew Jenson Collection, LDS Archives.
52. Josephine R. Fisher, certificate.
53. Some researchers may dismiss the two Jenson accounts and Josephine Fisher's recollection indicating that an official separation or religious divorce occurred between Windsor and Sylvia as simply attempts to cover-up sexual polyandry. They might also assume that since they had children together, both before his November 1842 excommunication and after his January 1846 rebaptism, that they continued to cohabit while Windsor was out of the Church. However, no evidence exists to support continued conjugality between Sylvia and Windsor after his excommunication and prior to Joseph Smith's death.

LDS Theology: Sexual Polyandry is *Non-Doctrinal* and *Anti-Doctrinal*

Besides the lack of credible evidence of sexual polyandry, other observations make such a practice less likely among the Latter-day Saints. Foremost is that from the standpoint of LDS theology, sexual polyandry is easily classified as *non-doctrinal* and *anti-doctrinal*. An evaluation of scriptures and Joseph Smith's teachings fails to identify any statements that would authorize its practice. No ceremonies are described that would solemnize a true polyandrous relationship wherein a woman was authorized to be sexually involved with both husbands.

The revelation on eternal marriage, Utah Doctrine and Covenants section 132: 63 defines sexual polyandry as adultery saying that if a woman: "after she is espoused, shall be with another man, she has committed adultery, and shall be destroyed" (see also v. 42).

Early Utah Church leaders condemned polyandry. Brigham Young stated in 1852: "What do you think of a woman having more husbands than one? This is not known to the law."[54] On October 8, 1869, Apostle George A. Smith taught that "a plurality of husbands is wrong."[55] Six years later Orson Pratt instructed: "God has strictly forbidden, in this Bible, plurality of husbands, and proclaimed against it in his law."[56] Pratt further explained:

> Can a woman have more than one husband at the same time? No: Such a principle was never sanctioned by scripture. The object of marriage is to multiply the species, according to the command of God. A woman with one husband can fulfill this command, with greater facilities, than if she had a plurality; indeed, this would, in all probability, frustrate the great design of marriage, and prevent her from raising up a family. As a plurality of husbands would not facilitate the increase of posterity, such a principle never was tolerated in scripture.[57]

Bathsheba Smith, wife of Apostle George A. Smith, was asked in 1892 if it would "be a violation of the laws of the church for one woman

---

54. *Journal of Discourses*, 1:361.
55. Ibid., 13:41.
56. Ibid., 18:55–56.
57. Orson Pratt, "Celestial Marriage," *The Seer*, 1:4 (April 1853): 60.

to have two husbands living at the same time…" She replied: "I think it would."[58]

Importantly, all of these individuals were involved with Nauvoo polygamy and several were undoubtedly aware of Joseph Smith's sealings to legally married women. There is also evidence that he may have discussed eternal plural marriage with Orson Pratt's legal wife, Sarah.

Hyrum Smith's son, Joseph F. Smith, wrote in 1889: "Polyandry is wrong, physiologically, morally, and from a scriptural point of order. It is nowhere sanctioned in the Bible, nor by the law of God or nature and has not affinity with 'Mormon' plural marriage."[59]

One of the ways sexual polyandry is anti-doctrinal comes as it creates confusion regarding the paternity of the wife's offspring. Charles W. Penrose wrote in the Utah Church's publication, the *Millennial Star*, in 1867: "Polyandry is contrary to nature, that it strikes at the foundation of the object of marriage—the propagation of the race, that, if it be productive of any increase whatever, the paternal identity is destroyed, or made so doubtful, as to annihilate those natural sympathies which properly should exist between the father and his offspring."[60]

Mormon theology assigns specific responsibilities to parents regarding their own children. "And again, inasmuch as parents have children in Zion, or in any of her stakes which are organized, that teach them not to understand the doctrine of repentance, faith in Christ the Son of the living God, and of baptism and the gift of the Holy Ghost by the laying on of the hands, when eight years old, the sin be upon the heads of the parents" (Utah D&C 68:25). Correspondingly, a father is not held accountable for teaching and disciplining his neighbor's children. Instead, "great things" are expected from fathers concerning their own offspring (Utah D&C 29:48). Polyandry would unavoidably introduce confusion into this strict injunction. How could either husband be held stringently responsible for the mandated fatherly duties in a polyandrous family?

---

58. Bathsheba Smith, Testimony given in the Temple Lot Case, part 3, 347, question 1142.

59. Joseph F. Smith to Zenos H. Gurley, June 19, 1889, digitally published in Richard E. Turley Jr., *Selected Collections from the Archives of The Church of Jesus Christ of Latter-day Saints* (Provo, Utah: BYU Press), vol. 1, DVD #29.

60. Charles W. Penrose, "Why We Practice Plural Marriage," *The Latter-day Saints' Millennial Star*, N. 37 (September 14, 1867) XXIX, 578 [577–80].

In light of these doctrinal difficulties, it appears that foisting a new moral standard of sexual polyandry upon LDS women in Nauvoo might have been difficult, even for Joseph Smith. As observed, no religious precedent could be recruited to use as an example. There were no Biblical prophetesses and priestesses who practiced it who could be used as examples. No scriptures were available to justify it. Joseph Smith would have been starting from scratch to defend such a principle to women who possessed an understanding of the Old Testament and a devout dedication to Biblical standards.

Joseph's eternal sealings involved witnesses and officiators, often family members of the women involved. They too would have needed to be convinced of the propriety of sexual polyandry. Dimick Huntington performed the ceremony as two of his already married sisters, Zina and Presendia, were sealed to Joseph, while his wife, Fanny, willingly served as a witness.[61] How readily would these individuals have accepted and participated in a process that they could have viewed only as adultery, except their natural inclinations had been turned 180 degrees? Importantly, there is no credible documentation that any of these women saw themselves as practicing practical polyandry or that sexual polyandry was acceptable to them.

Some Researchers Readily Ignore Theology

One common thread running through the reports of researchers who depict Joseph Smith as practicing sexual polyandry is a willingness to ignore his theology. Many authors may feel justified because they believe Joseph Smith was a deceiver.

Dan Vogel in his *Joseph Smith: The Making of a Prophet*, reflects this view: "One cannot ignore Smith's capacity to deceive. One of the clearest evidences of this is his repeated public denial during the early 1840s of his own and other's plural marriages."[62] Vogel is correct in observing that the Prophet carefully denied the practice of plural marriage several times publicly during his lifetime, even though privately, evidence shows he was involved. When asked in July 1838, "Do the Mormons believe in

---

61. Joseph F. Smith Affidavit Books, LDS Archives, 1:5, 1:7.
62. Dan Vogel, *Joseph Smith: The Making of a Prophet* (Salt Lake City: Signature Books, 2004), ix.

having more wives than one?" He replied: "No, not at the same time."[63] Five months later, the Prophet wrote to the Saints saying: "Was it for committing adultery that we were assailed? We are aware that that false slander has gone abroad, for it has been reiterated in our ears. These are falsehoods also."[64] In 1844, one month before the martyrdom, the Prophet stated: "What a thing it is for a man to be accused of committing adultery, and having seven wives, when I can only find one."[65]

Regarding these statements, Danel Bachman observed: 'Most of these denials stressed semantical and theological technicalities. That is, the language of the defense was carefully chosen to disavow practices that did not accurately represent Church doctrines."[66] Todd Compton concurred: "Faced with the necessity of keeping polygamy secret, the Mormon authorities generally chose to disavow the practice, sometimes using language with coded double meanings."[67] Lawrence Foster wrote: "Smith himself most characteristically made indirect denials of polygamy in which he said simply that such statements were too ridiculous to be believed. But he always carefully refrained from saying that such statements weren't true."[68]

Regardless, Dan Vogel and other writers seem willing to assume that since Joseph Smith was not strictly abiding his public declarations on polygamy, his public declarations and private teachings need not be taken too seriously. In other words, the Prophet's theology can be essentially ignored under the assumption that he was not living it. Their approach often reflects the idea that writers can compose their historical

---

63. *Elders' Journal*, 1:3 (Kirtland, Ohio, July 1838): 43.

64. Joseph Smith's letter to the Church, December 16, 1838, as quoted in *History of the Church*, 3:230.

65. Andrew F. Ehat and Lyndon W. Cook, eds., *The Words of Joseph Smith: Contemporary Accounts of the Nauvoo Discourse of the Prophet Joseph Smith* (Provo, Utah: BYU Religious Studies Center, 1980); and *History of the Church* 6:408–12. For other general denials of the practice of polygamy see *Millennial Star*, August 1, 1842, 74; January 15, 1850, 29–30; July 1, 1845, 22–23; *Times and Seasons*, September 1, 1842, 909; October 1, 1842, 939–40; March 15, 1843, 143; February 1, 1844, 423; March 15, 1844, 474; November 15, 1844, 715; May 1, 1845, 893–94.

66. Bachman, "A Study of the Mormon Practice of Plural Marriage Before the Death of Joseph Smith," 197. Fawn Brodie agreed: "The denials of polygamy uttered by the Mormon leaders between 1835 and 1852, when it was finally admitted, are a remarkable series of evasions and circumlocutions involving all sorts of verbal gymnastics." (Brodie, *No Man Knows My History*, 312.)

67. Compton, *In Sacred Loneliness*, 643.

68. Foster, "Between Two Worlds," 208 n1.

reconstructions of Joseph Smith's actions and behaviors, largely independent of the doctrines he taught.

Two problems emerge with this methodology. First, while it appears that Joseph Smith did in fact use careful language to secretly defy public laws that contradicted divine laws, to conclude that similar tactics spread to other aspects of his life requires specific evidence. Stated another way, in order to obey God, Joseph Smith may have publicly feigned obedience to the laws of the land while privately disobeying them. However, assuming that he also publicly feigned obedience to God's laws while privately disobeying them is not justified. The two processes are very dissimilar.[69]

An August 1, 1831, revelation states: "Let no man break the laws of the land, for he that keepeth the laws of God hath no need to break the laws of the land" (Utah D&C 58:21). Critics sometimes allege that this directive would prohibit the secret practice of polygamy because it violated state laws in Ohio and Illinois. However, a revelation received two years later specifies which laws are to be embraced and which "cometh of evil": "Therefore, I, the Lord, justify you, and your brethren of my church, in befriending that law which is the constitutional law of the land; And as pertaining to law of man, whatsoever is more or less than this, cometh of evil" (Utah D&C 98:7).

Plural marriage is not prohibited by the United States Constitution; in addition, the Bill of Rights guarantees religious freedom. It appears that Church members viewed state laws against it, laws that were passed in the 1830s, as "extra-constitutional" or as "more or less than" the constitution and therefore "evil." The Saints felt little compulsion to obey unconstitutional laws if it interfered with the practice of their religion. Using subterfuge to hide compliance with divine mandates undoubtedly generated inner conflict, but there was never any real question which of the laws (the laws from God or the laws of the land) the Latter-day Saints were going to follow.

The second problem with assuming Joseph was not living his theology is that the religious men and women surrounding him apparently observed no such inconsistency. Many antagonistic writers reconstructing the Nauvoo period assert that Church members were very gullible

---

69. See Hales, *Joseph Smith's Polygamy: Theology*, appendix.

dupes. George T. M. Davis wrote in 1844: "From personal observation, I am convinced that there are many poor, unfortunate, deluded beings there, who are naturally honest, and who, under the influence of good example and upright leaders, would 'act well their part' in society. That class, however, are, generally speaking, of weak intellect, to a great extent uneducated, and easily made the dupes of the vicious."[70] Similarly, Mrs. B. G. Ferris asserted twelve years later: "Anyone with half an eye can see the object of the prophet Smith, in promulgating such a doctrine [of plural marriage]; and the wonder is, that its transparency is not obvious to all… The effect of the Mormon creed is, evidently, to gather together a low class of villains, and a still lower class of dupes."[71]

However, individuals who have closely studied the lives of Nauvoo polygamists can usually see that such descriptions are not accurate.[72] The men and women who lived close to Joseph Smith and were involved with the first plural marriages generally reacted to the principle with the same revulsion most of us do today. In addition, they were men and women of piety and strong convictions. Non-Mormon Bernard Devoto observed in 1930: "[Joseph Smith] attracted to his support not only the ordinary fanatics who gave the American Pentecost its hundreds of sects and supported them all, but also such superior and more significant men as [Sidney] Rigdon, Orson and Parley Pratt, Orson Hyde, W.W. Phelps, and Brigham Young."[73] Fawn Brodie agreed: "The best evidence of the magnetism of the Mormon religion was that it could attract men with the quality of Brigham Young, whose tremendous energy and shrewd intelligence were not easily directed by any influence outside himself."[74]

---

70. George T. M. Davis, *An Authentic Account of the Massacre of Joseph Smith* (St. Louis: Chambers and Knapp, 1844), 38.

71. Mrs. B. G. Ferris, *The Mormons at Home; With some Incidents of Travel from Missouri to California* (New York: Dix and Edwards, 1856), 130–31. William Harris referred to the Mormons as "dupes and fanatics" (*Mormonism Portrayed* [Warsaw: Sharp Gambel, 1841], 35). See also Rev. F. B. Ashley, *Mormonism: An Exposure of the Impositions Adopted by the Sect Called "The Latter-day Saints"* (London: John Hatchard, 1851), 8.

72. See Steven C. Harper, "By No Means Men of Weak Minds: The Gullible Bumpkin Thesis and the First Mormons," *Nauvoo Journal* 7:2 (Fall 1995): 39–48.

73. Bernard DeVoto, "The Centennial of Mormonism," *American Mercury* 19 (January 1930): 5.

74. Brodie, *No Man Knows My History*, 126–27. Joseph Johnson writing in 1885 disagreed: "[Brigham Young] must have been an idiot, or thought he was addressing idiots." (*The Great Mormon Fraud* [Manchester, Butterworth and Nodal, 1885], 17.)

Accordingly, to assume that Joseph Smith could have blithely transgressed his own theological teachings without disillusioning followers like Brigham Young, Eliza R. Snow, and many others is problematic. Most of Joseph's closest followers were too perceptive to be bamboozled and too religious to become accomplices in a deliberate deception. When asked in 1859: "Is the system of your church [a plurality of wives] acceptable to the majority of its women?" Brigham Young replied: "They could not be more averse to it than I was when it was first revealed to us as the Divine will. I think they generally accept it, as I do, as the will of God."[75] On August 18, 1887, Eliza R. Snow declared: "It [plural marriage] is so great and grand an institution that only the good and god-like can understand and appreciate it."[76] Excusing these comments as the babblings of dupes or the cover-ups of confederates seems insufficient. The documented behavior of men and women like Brigham and Eliza suggests that from their viewpoint, Joseph Smith lived his religion.

The historical record shows there were a few Church members who dissented along the way, but they constituted a small minority when compared to the numbers who embraced Joseph Smith's teachings as bona fide revelations from the heavens. It could be argued that even the Prophet could not have convincingly dressed up immorality in divine garb without more than a few people becoming rattled and breaking ranks.

In view of these observations, it seems unwise to ignore Joseph Smith's theological teachings concerning polygamy and sexuality under the assumption that he didn't live them and no one really cared. Joseph Smith taught in D&C 132:63 that sexual polyandry is adultery. For authors to assert that he disobeyed this teaching without concomitantly explaining the lack of disgust from the Nauvoo polygamy insiders to the Prophet's alleged hypocrisy is problematic.

---

75. Horace Greeley, "Overland Journey. XXI. Two Hours with Brigham Young," *New-York Daily Tribune*, August 20, 1859, 19:5,718, 5/6–6/1–2; cited in Horace Greeley, *An Overland Journey from New York to San Francisco in the Summer of 1859* [New York: H. H. Bancroft & Co., 1860], reprinted with Charles T. Duncan, ed. (New York: Ballantine Books, 1963), 138. This interview was reprinted in the *Millennial Star* 21:38, September 17, 1859, 608–11, with the following qualification: "Although the wording of the conversation might not be exactly as spoken, on the whole, we have no hesitation in endorsing it by republication" (Ibid., 605).

76. "Two Prophets' Widows A Visit to the Relicts of Joseph Smith and Brigham Young," J. J. J., in *St. Louis Globe-Democrat* (Thursday, August 18, 1887) 85:6.

Eternal Sealings in the New and Everlasting Covenant

If Joseph Smith lived his theology, then why did he engage in ceremonial polyandry? Historical evidence shows that Joseph Smith taught of eternal marriages called the "new and everlasting covenant."[77] It allows two forms of eternal marriage. One is for "time and eternity," which comprises earth life and beyond. The second is for "eternity" only, meaning a marriage that exists only after death.

For reasons that are unclear, a few authors have taken the position that none of the sealings in Nauvoo including any of the Prophet's could have been exclusively for "eternity."[78] Todd Compton explained: "There are no known instances of marriages for 'eternity only' in the nineteenth century."[79] D. Michael Quinn agreed: "If the phrase 'eternity only' ever appeared in an *original* record of LDS sealing in the nineteenth century, I have not discovered it while examining thousands of such manuscript entries."[80]

While these observations may be technically true, they probably have little application to sealings solemnized in Joseph Smith's time. Prior to his death, several dozen plural sealing ceremonies were performed for approximately thirty men and their polygamous wives.[81] Unfortunately, only one contemporary document is available specifying the terminology that was used.[82] The ceremonial prayer uniting Joseph to previously

---

77. See D&C 131:2, 132:6 and George D. Smith, ed. *An Intimate Chronicle: The Journals of William Clayton* (Salt Lake City: Signature Books, 1995), 102, 110, 111, 115, 119, 123, 151, etc.

78. See Compton, *In Sacred Loneliness*, 298 (see also 295) for Delcena's "time only" marriage to Joseph Smith, although no evidence exists to verify it. Contrast pages 14 and 500 for an argument citing the lack of evidence as showing "eternity" only sealings may never have occurred. See also Gary James Bergera, "The Earliest Eternal Sealings of Civilly Married Couples Living and Dead," *Dialogue: A Journal of Mormon Thought* 35:3 (Fall 2002): 51, 59.

79. Compton, *In Sacred Loneliness*, 14; see also 500.

80. Quinn, *The Mormon Hierarchy: Extensions of Power*, 184; italics in original. See also D. Michael Quinn, "Organizational Development and Social Origins of the Mormon Hierarchy, 1832–1932. A Prosopographical Study," University of Utah, 1973, 154–55; D. Michael Quinn, "The Mormon Hierarchy, 1832–1932: An American Elite" (Ph.D. diss., Yale University, 1976), 64.

81. Thirty-four were for Joseph Smith (Compton, *In Sacred Loneliness*, 4–7) and fifty-one for an additional twenty-nine men (See Brian C. Hales, *Joseph Smith's Polygamy: History*, chapter one, Salt Lake City: Greg Kofford Books, forthcoming.)

82. The words are found in a revelation given through Joseph Smith to Newel K. Whitney specifying the language of the sealing ceremony he was to use in solemnizing the plural marriage of his daughter, Sarah Ann to Joseph Smith. Quoted in Michael Marquardt, *The Joseph Smith Revelations: Text and Commentary* (Salt Lake City: Signature Books, 1999), 315–16; see also Reve-

unmarried Sarah Ann Whitney was dictated by written revelation stating: "You both mutually agree calling them by name to be each others companion so long as you both shall live... and also through out all eternity."[83] Otherwise, it does not appear that the terminology employed in the dozens of plural sealing ceremonies during Joseph Smith's lifetime was written down, either at the time they were performed or shortly thereafter. If any such original records were kept, they apparently have not been preserved. In short, we do not have a record of the specific language used in the rest of these sealings.

It is true that some later reminiscences state that their sealings in Nauvoo were for "time and eternity." However, to assume that the women were remembering the exact language may not be warranted. When asked in 1892 if she could remember the words used to seal her to Joseph Smith, Malissa Lott replied: "I don't know that I can go and tell it right over as it was... I don't remember the words that were used."[84] Similarly, Emily Partridge testified: "I can't remember the exact words, that he said."[85] Most late recollections were recorded at a time when sealing ceremonial language had been standardized utilizing the phrase "time and eternity." Whether individuals would have recalled early variations in the wording of the prayers is unclear. Furthermore, to presuppose that sexual relations were present based solely on a late memoir that declared a Nauvoo marriage ("polyandrous" or not) was for "time and eternity" would be unjustified by the documents alone. More specific evidence would be required.

Evidence for "Eternity" Only Sealings in Joseph Smith's "Polyandrous" Marriages

Manuscript documentation has been identified supporting that "eternity" only sealings occurred during Joseph Smith's lifetime and even within his own "polyandrous" marriages. Nauvooan Justus Morse recounted in an affidavit dated March 23, 1887:

---

lations in Addition to Those Found in the LDS Edition of the D&C on *New Mormon Studies: A Comprehensive Resource Library*, CD-ROM (Salt Lake City: Smith Research Associates, 1998).

83. Quoted in Marquardt, *The Joseph Smith Revelations*, 315–16; see also Revelations in Addition to Those Found in the LDS Edition of the D&C.

84. Malissa Lott, Testimony in the Temple Lot Case, part 3, pages 95–96, questions 54, 70.

85. Emily Partridge, Testimony in the Temple Lot Case, part 3, page 359, question 198.

In the year 1842, at Nauvoo, Illinois, Elder Amasa Lyman, taught me the doctrine of *sealing*, or marrying for eternity, called *spiritual wifery*,[86] and that within one year from that date my own wife and another woman were sealed to me for eternity in Macedonia, by father John Smith, uncle to the Prophet. This woman was the wife of another man, but was to be mine in eternity and the said father John Smith, also taught me that if an unmarried woman was sealed to me that she was mine for *time* as well as eternity and that I was not limited as to number."[87]

In an 1895 letter to his Aunt, Joseph Riley Morse wrote of his father, Justus Morse: "He was a good man. His word was as good as his note any place we ever lived."[88] Nevertheless, Gary Bergera discounts the accuracy of Justus' memory by observing: "John Smith did not take his first plural wife until August 1843, and Lyman not until September 1844."[89] While Bergera's observations appear to be correct, the historical record demonstrates that Joseph Smith did not require men to be polygamists in order to teach the principle to others or to perform plural sealings. Joseph B. Noble, Dimick B. Huntington, Brigham Young, Willard Richards, Newel K. Whitney, and William Clayton all performed plural marriages for others prior to becoming polygamists themselves.[90] Brigham Young, and members of the Quorum of the Twelve, learned of the restoration of plural marriage in 1841 and shared that information with others before individually entering into plurality.

---

86. Lawrence Foster observed: "This author has never encountered the term 'plural marriage,' and almost never encountered the term 'celestial marriage,' in Mormon or non-Mormon accounts from the Nauvoo period." (W. Lawrence Foster, "Between Two Worlds," 277, n3 continued).

87. Affidavit, March 23, 1887, in Charles A. Shook, *The True Origin of Mormon Polygamy* (Cincinnati: Standard Publishing Company, 1914), 169–70; italics in original. Morse served as an Elder, a Seventy, and a High Priest under Joseph Smith and joined the RLDS Church in 1870.

88. Quoted in Michael S. Riggs "'His Word Was as Good as His Note' The Impact of Justus Morse's Mormonism(s) on His Families," *John Whitmer Historical Association Journal* 17 (1997): 80 [49–80].

89. Gary James Bergera, "'Illicit Intercourse,' Plural Marriage, and the Nauvoo Stake High Council, 1840–1844," *The John Whitmer Historical Association Journal* 23 (2003): 74 n73 [59–91].

90. All of the men listed performed plural marriages for Joseph Smith and perhaps others. See Compton, *In Sacred Loneliness*, 59, 81, 122, 179, 213, 298, 348 for marriage performance dates and sealer identities. Cross reference this with Smith, "Nauvoo Roots of Mormon Polygamy," 52–74 and Bergera, "Identifying the Earliest Mormon Polygamists, 1841–1844," 1–74, for the dates the sealers themselves became polygamists.

Specific evidence exists supporting that Joseph Smith personally experienced sealings for "eternity," not "time and eternity" and therefore without sexual relations.[91] Within the research papers of Andrew Jenson, author of the 1887 *Historical Record* article on Joseph Smith's plural wives, is the following statement:

> \Sister Ruth/ ~~Mrs. Sayers~~ was married in her youth to Mr. Edward Sayers, a thoroughly practical horticulturist and florist, and though he was not a member of the Church, ~~yet~~ he willingly joined his fortune with her and they reached Nauvoo together some time in the year 1841;
> While there the strongest affection sprang up between the Prophet Joseph and Mr. Sayers. The latter not attaching much importance to \the/ theory of a future life insisted that his wife \Ruth/ should be sealed to the Prophet for eternity, as he himself should only claim [page2—the first 3 lines of which are written over illegible erasures] her in this life. She \was/ accordingly ~~the~~ sealed to the Prophet in Emma Smith's presence and thus ~~were~~ became numbered among the Prophets plural wives. ~~She however~~ \though she/ \continued to live with Mr. Sayers / ~~remained with her husband~~ \until his death.[92]

Another document from Jenson's hand corroborated that concerning Joseph's plural sealing to Ruth Sayers: "Joseph did not pick that woman. She went to see whether she should marry her husband for eternity."[93] Other documents from Zina Huntington, Patty Bartlett, and Mary

---

91. Recognizing that Joseph Smith's marriages could have been for either "time and eternity" or just "eternity," P. P. Kelley questioned Malissa Lott in 1892 regarding the type of sealing ceremony that she experienced with the him: "Did you live with Joseph Smith as his wife, or were you just simply sealed to him for eternity?" (Temple Lot Case, complete transcript, part 3, pages 97, questions 94.) Malissa, who was single at the time of her sealing to the Prophet, had earlier stated: "I was married to him for time and all eternity." (*Ibid.*, page 95, question 56.)

92. Andrew Jenson Papers [ca. 1871–1942], LDS Archives. It appears that the documents in these folders were used to compile Jenson's 1887 *Historical Record* article on plural marriage. See Joseph F. Smith affidavit books, LDS Archives, 1:9, for date of this sealing "February A.D. 1843." However the affidavit states that the sealing was performed by Hyrum Smith, which is unlikely because Hyrum did not accept plural marriage until May of that year.

93. Recorded by D. Michael Quinn. See D. Michael Quinn Papers, Yale University, Addition—Uncat WA MS 244 (Accession:19990209-c) bx 1. I have been unable to identify the primary document to verify this quotation.

Elizabeth Rollins indicate their marriages may also have been "eternity" only sealings as well.[94]

Another example, apparently unknown to Todd Compton in 1997 and not included on his list of "polyandrous" wives, occurred between Esther Dutcher and Joseph Smith.[95] Esther was the legal wife of Albert Smith. She died in 1856; years later her widowed husband described her circumstances to Daniel H. Wells who thereafter wrote to Joseph F. Smith concerning the matter:

> He [Albert] is… much afflicted with the loss of his first wife. *It seems that she was sealed to Joseph the Prophet in the days of Nauvoo, though she still remained his wife*, and afterwards nearly broke his heart by telling him of it, and expressing her intention of adhering to that relationship. He however got to feeling better over it and acting for Joseph had her sealed to him, and to himself for time.[96]

Wells' description indicates that Esther was "sealed" to Joseph, but was the "wife" of Albert, implying an eternity sealing. Unfortunately, we have no other information regarding the circumstances surrounding the sealing including when it might have occurred or who performed the ceremony.

The "Pretend" Marriage of Joseph C. Kingsbury and Sarah Ann Whitney

Returning to Todd Compton's list of twelve "polyandrous" wives, evidence indicates that Sylvia Sessions' relationship was not polyandrous and Joseph Smith's sealing to Ruth Vose Sayers was an "eternity" only marriage. That leaves ten more to investigate.

---

94. See Zina Huntington in Wight interview, "Evidence from Zina D. Huntington Young," *Saints Herald* (January 11, 1905), 29; Patty Bartlett in Donna Toland Smart, ed., *Mormon Midwife: The 1846–1888 Diaries of Patty Bartlett Sessions* (Logan, Utah: Utah State University, 1997), 276; and Mary Elizabeth Rollins in "Remarks at B.Y.U., April 14, 1905," copy of original signed typescript, Vault Mss 363, fd 6, Harold B. Lee Library, Brigham Young University, 7.

95. I am indebted to Michael Marquardt for bringing this to my attention. It constitutes a new plural wife on my list of Joseph Smith's polygamous marriages, previously unreported by any researcher. See forthcoming *Joseph Smith's Polygamy: History*, Greg Kofford Books, 2010.

96. Daniel H. Wells to Joseph F. Smith, June 25, 1888, LDS Church History Department; italics added.

THE PUZZLEMENT OF POLYANDRY   131

The relationship between Sarah Ann Whitney, Joseph Smith, and Joseph C. Kingsbury is unique. It is the only eternal "polyandrous" marriage where the eternal sealing preceded the legal marriage. That is, Joseph Smith was sealed to Sarah and then months afterwards, she was legally married to Kingsbury. Researcher Michael Marquardt summarized:

> Sarah Ann Whitney was married to Joseph Smith on July 27, 1842. Nine months later on April 29, 1843, she was [legally] married to Joseph C. Kingsbury with the Prophet Joseph Smith officiating. She was then eighteen years old. It seems that Joseph Smith married Sarah Ann Whitney for time and for all eternity and then relinquished her for time, in a pretended marriage ceremony to Joseph C. Kingsbury.[97]

Evidence supports that this civil marriage was never consummated. Todd Compton wrote:

> One wonders what the dynamics of a pretend marriage would have been—there would have been no sexual dimension, but Joseph Kingsbury and Sarah must have lived as close friends.... We do know that Sarah Ann continued to live with her parents after the marriage to Smith; and Kingsbury, the day after the "pretend" marriage, apparently moved in the Whitney house also. Sarah became generally known as Mrs. Kingsbury, and she and Joseph C. attended public functions together. Outsiders would have suspected nothing unusual in the relationship.[98]

Years later in 1880, Kingsbury submitted a bill to the Church for his financial support of Sarah Ann. The bill read: "Nov 23, 1880, Joseph C. Kingsbury asked John Taylor that an $8000 debt to the church be remitted in consideration of services he had rendered in Nauvoo, and after leaving there, to the Prophet Joseph, in keeping one of his wives, Sarah Whitney, daughter of Bishop N. K. Whitney."[99] It is not known if Church President John Taylor honored the claim.

---

97. H. Michael Marquardt, *The Strange Marriages of Sarah Ann Whitney to Joseph Smith the Mormon Prophet, Joseph C. Kingsbury, and Heber C. Kimball* (Salt Lake City: Modern Microfilm, 1973; rev. ed., Salt Lake City: Utah Lighthouse Ministry, 1982), 18.

98. Compton, *In Sacred Loneliness*, 352.

99. L. John Nuttall Notes for J. Taylor Office Jrnl, HDC, d1346; quoted in D. Michael Quinn Papers—Addition—Uncat WA MS 244 (Accession:19990209-c) Box 1, Yale University Special Collections.

This episode demonstrates that Joseph Smith facilitated the creation of at least one "front husband" and perhaps others. It is possible that after Windsor Lyon's excommunication and religious separation from Sylvia Sessions Lyon, Joseph Smith asked him to serve as a front husband to Sylvia.

Kingsbury's relationship with Sarah Ann shows that Joseph Smith's plural wives could feign legal matrimony to someone else in order to shield the Prophet from suspicion from law enforcement officers. Importantly, it demonstrates that observing that a woman lived under the same roof with a man does not verify a sexual connection between her and her legal husband. In other words, assuming conjugality from outward appearances may not be warranted. Accordingly, documenting sexual polyandry requires specific evidence of sexuality in both relationships. That is, conjugality between the woman and both husbands during the same time period must be confirmed. Such evidence will not be easy to obtain, but should be the standard for any writer affirming that Joseph Smith engaged in sexual polyandry. Authors who are willing to *assume* sexual polyandry should inform their readers that their conclusions are speculative, without specific supportive evidence.

The Four Women Married to Non-Members or Anti-Mormons

Besides Ruth Vose Sayers' "eternity" sealing to Joseph Smith, several other "polyandrous" wives appear to have experienced "eternity" only marriage to the Prophet. Historical documents show that he began teaching about eternal marriage (independent of plural marriage) as early as January 1840.[100] As the Prophet carefully explained those teachings to

---

100. Parley P. Pratt Jr., ed., *Autobiography of Parley Parker Pratt, One of the Twelve Apostles of the Church of Jesus Christ of Latter-day Saints* (Salt Lake City: Deseret Book Co., 1985), 259–60. In their book *Four Zinas: A Story of Mothers and Daughters on the Mormon Frontier*, 108. Martha Sonntag Bradley and Mary Brown Firmage Woodward wrote that Joseph Smith proposed plural marriage to Zina Huntington three times in 1840. However, supporting historical documents are not available to corroborate this story and Zina contradicted it in her own testimony (Zina D. H. Young, Interviewed by John W. Wight, October 1, 1898, "Evidence from Zina D. Huntington-Young," *Saints' Herald* 52:2 [January 11, 1905]: 28–30. Also in J. D. Stead, *Doctrines and Dogmas of Brighamism Exposed*, [Lamoni, Iowa: RLDS Church, 1911], 212–14). Accordingly, this family tradition should be quoted with caution.

selected listeners, there were three other women (in addition to Ruth Vose) who could not be eternally sealed to their earthly spouses. Both Mary Elizabeth Rollins and Sarah Kingsley were married to non-Mormons and Presendia Huntington's husband, Norman Buell, was an avid anti-Mormon, who would never have participated in a church-sponsored marriage of any kind. Norman's brother-in-law left this report:

> [While] Norman Buell was in Clay Co. saying good Lord and kind devil, for a time; but the time finally came that he must choose a side, so he chose the Master that would give him the most money then, and in whos hands he thought he would be the safest. He even got to the pitch that he would not let his wife say a word in favor of her brethren, and would say all manner of evil of them himself. He was once an Elder in the church of Jesus Christ.[101]

All four of these women had ample reason to seek an "eternity" sealing to Joseph Smith.

Antagonistic writers have alleged that sexual relations might have existed in these relationships. If so, such intimacies could not have occurred with the consent of the respective legal husbands—they simply would not have allowed it. Some authors have suggested Joseph Smith might have contracted clandestine sexual encounters, which seems unlikely for several reasons.

First, there is no persuasive evidence to support it. Second, Joseph Smith's previous experience with mobbings and the complications of the Fanny Alger relationship in Kirtland, Ohio, years before undoubtedly generated powerful memories informing him of the inherent risks and possible consequences. Third, the Prophet knew how readily a man would grab a gun or otherwise threaten the life of another male who takes sexual advantage of his wife. Even Church member Benjamin F. Johnson, who greatly admired the Prophet, threatened deadly retaliation should anything improper happen between his sister and Joseph. In 1869 he recalled:

> I sincerely believed him [Joseph Smith] to [be] a prophet of God, and I loved him as such, and also for the many evidences of his kindness

---

101. Oliver B. Huntington, "Oliver B. Huntington Diaries," Ms 162, Harold B. Lee Library, Manuscripts and Special Collections, volume 2—"History of Oliver Boardman Huntington"—"commenced December 10th 1845," 45.

to me, yet such was the force of my education, and the scorn that I felt towards anything un-virtuous that under the first impulse of my feelings, I looked him calmly, but firmly in the face and told him that, "I had always believed him to be a good man, and wished to believe it still, and would try to;"—and that, "I would take for him a message to my sister, and if the doctrine was true, all would be well, but if I should afterwards learn that it was offered to insult or prostitute my sister I would take his life." With a smile he replied "Benjamin, you will never see that day, but you shall live to <u>know</u> that it is true, and rejoice in it."[102]

Historian Craig L. Foster described an 1851 incident of a man who was caught sleeping with another man's wife:

> Howard Egan… in 1851, killed James Monroe. Monroe had an affair with Egan's first wife, Tamson. Monroe wisely chose to get out of town before Egan's return from a prolonged journey to California. However, Egan followed Monroe and finally caught up with him close to the Utah border, where he shot and killed him. Egan was later brought to a trial… During the closing arguments, Smith [George Albert Smith, his defense attorney] stated, "In this territory it is a principle of mountain common law, that no man can seduce the wife of another without endangering his own life… The man who seduces his neighbor's wife must die, and her nearest relative must kill him!" Egan was acquitted.[103]

In 1855, Apostle Parley P. Pratt was sealed to Eleanor Mccomb McLean as a plural spouse. She had been civilly married to an abusive and angry anti-Mormon, Hector McLean.[104] Upon learning of the plural marriage, Hector tracked down Parley, stabbing and shooting him to death. T. B. H. Stenhouse wrote that shortly after the cold blooded

---

102. Joseph F. Smith Affidavit Books, 2:3–4, 1869, CA MS 3423 fd 5. On another occasion Johnson remembered telling Joseph Smith: "If I even Should know that you do this [plural marriage] to Dishonor & debauch my Sister I will kill you as Shure as the Lord Lives." (Dean R. Zimmerman, ed., *I Knew the Prophets: An Analysis of the Letter of Benjamin F. Johnson to George F. Gibbs, Reporting Doctrinal Views of Joseph Smith and Brigham Young* [Bountiful, UT: Horizon, 1976], 41.)

103. Craig L. Foster, "The Butler Murder of April 1869: A Look at Extralegal Punishment in Utah," *Mormon Historical Studies* 2:2 (Fall 2001): 109. [105–114] See also Kenneth L. Cannon II, "'Mountain Common Law': The Extralegal Punishment of Seducers in Early Utah," *Utah Historical Quarterly* 51:3 (Fall 1983): 308–27.

104. Steven Pratt, "Eleanor McLean and the Murder of Parley P. Pratt," *Brigham Young University Studies* 15:4 (Winter 1975): 225–234 [225–256.]

murder, Hector "walked through the town with his friends, and in the evening took the passing steamer for the South. No one seemed to think that he should be arrested... There is always a feeling of sympathy for the injured when domestic intrusions are before the public."[105] "Domestic intrusions" in Joseph's day were not tolerated by legal husbands or the public in general.

As can be seen, it seems to have been a common reaction and expectation in nineteenth-century America for husbands and brothers to avenge women who were coerced into extra-marital intimacies or ravished.[106] It is unlikely that any of the husbands of these four women would have accepted an explanation of plural marriage had they learned that Joseph Smith was sexually involved with their wives. Retribution to the Prophet and perhaps even the man's wife might have been swift and destructive.

It appears the fear of frontier justice would be a natural deterrent to Joseph Smith were he to contemplate a sexual polyandrous arrangement in these four instances. It is impossible to prove a negative but it seems Joseph would be hesitant to accept the associated risks. Certainly such recklessness does not characterize the Prophet's life.

Fourth, correspondence in 1892 between Mary Elizabeth Rollins Lightner and John Henry Smith, implies an "eternity" only sealing between her and the Prophet:

> I hope you will not think me intrusive, I am sure I do not wish to be– If I could have an oportunity of conversing with you, and Brother Joseph [F. Smith] I could explain some things in regard to my living with Mr L, after becoming the *Wife* of *another*, which would throw light, on what *now* seems mysterious—and you would be perfectly

---

105. T. B. H. Stenhouse, *The Rocky Mountain Saints* (New York: D. Appleton and Company, 1873), 430.

106. In another example, the record of the Morgan County, Utah, Probate Court, Book "A", March 1869 term, pages 17–22, reports that Charles A. Walker was convicted of rape on a married woman and the jury recommended a prison term of 15 years, which sentence was pronounced by Probate Judge Haven. Sentence was pronounced on March 16 and the prisoner ordered committed to the penitentiary. But when court convened on March 20, "Josiah Eardly Sheriff stated before the court that the prisoner, Charles A. Walker, had been killed while in his custody by one Neils Swenson (husband of Palia Swensen, raped by said Charles Walker)." On March 22, the grand jury indicted Swensen for murder. He was tried the same day and the jury reported that they "do hereby return a verdict of 'not guilty' it being justifiable homicide." Cited in Stanley S. Ivins Collection, notebook #8, 166.

satisfied with me. I write this; because I have heard that it had been commented on to my injury. I have done the best I could, and Joseph will sanction my action—I cannot explain things in this Letter—some day you will know *all*. That is, if I ever have an oportunity of conversing with either of you.[107]

Mary Elizabeth doesn't explain what information would make John Henry Smith "perfectly satisfied" regarding the apparent polyandrous arrangements, but it seems the only possible explanation would be that her sealing was for the next life and did not include intimate relations during mortality. She could not have expected Smith to be "perfectly satisfied" if the answer was that she was sleeping with two husbands during the same time period. In 1892, Church members would have considered sexual polyandry to be a sin next to murder (see D&C 132:61–63).

The Remaining Six "Polyandrous" Wives

Of the thirteen "polyandrous" marriages compiled, evidence supports that one was a pretend marriage (Sarah Whitney), another was simply non-polyandrous (Sylvia Sessions), and five were for "eternity" only (Ruth Vose, Esther Dutcher, Presendia Huntington, Mary Elizabeth Rollins, Sarah Kingsley). The remaining six present a more complex picture, creating questions that are not easily answered without additional information. One thing they all had in common was that the women's legal husbands were all very active Latter-day Saints. It is not known how any of those men might have initially reacted to a situation wherein their wives sought to be sealed to Joseph Smith for "eternity" (like Ruth Vose

---

107. Mary Elizabeth Rollins Lightner to John Henry Smith, January 25, 1892, in George A. Smith Family Papers, MS 36, Box 7, Folder 12 (John Henry Smith, incoming correspondence); Marriott Library; emphasis in original. This quotation is referenced in Bachman, "A Study of the Mormon Practice of Plural Marriage Before the Death of Joseph Smith," 135. Bachman lists the recipient as John A. Young in the text and John A. Smith in the footnote (ibid.) Also cited by Richard S. Van Wagoner as a letter to "John R. Young," in "Mormon Polyandry in Nauvoo," *Dialogue: A Journal of Mormon Thought* 18:3 (Fall 1985): 77, 82 [67–83]. Van Wagoner's second reference in the article lists the date as "January 25, 1892," as does his citation in *Mormon Polygamy: A History*, 43, 232. Apparently Van Wagoner did not locate the original, but repeated Bachman and assumed the recipient was John R. Young. Dan Bachman was unable to recall the precise primary reference (e-mail to author June 14, 2008). I am indebted to Don Bradley for solving this mystery.

THE PUZZLEMENT OF POLYANDRY

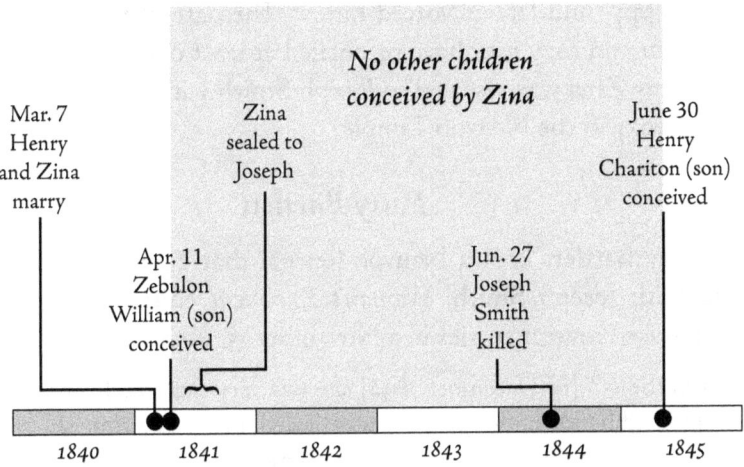

CHART 4.4: *Timeline of Zina Huntingdon showing the approximate conception dates for her children.*

Sayers) or even for "time and eternity," with its accompanying ramifications. A review of their marital relationships provides few clues.

Zina Huntington

Zina married Henry Bailey Jacobs March 7, 1841 and became pregnant the following month.[108] However, according to available evidence, she did not conceive any additional children with Henry until well past Joseph Smith's death.

Interestingly, Zina testified that her sealing to Joseph Smith was performed twice. The first time was on October 27, 1841, by Dimick Huntington, her brother. She also affirmed: "When Brigham Young returned from England, he repeated the ceremony for time and eternity."[109] The timeline is problematic because Brigham arrived from England in July 1841. Zina Huntington described her marriage to Henry B. Jacobs

---

108. See Allen L. Wyatt, author of "Zina and Her Men: An examination of the Changing Marital State of Zina Diantha Huntington Jacobs Smith Young," Mesa, Arizona: FAIR, 2006 FAIR Conference, available at http://www.fairlds.org/FAIR_Conferences/2006_Zina_and_Her_Men.html, (accessed August 16, 2007).

109. Zina D. Huntington, John Wight interviewer, "Evidence from Zina D. Huntington Young," Interview with Zina, October 1, 1898, *Saints' Herald* 52 (January 11, 1905): 29.

as "unhappy" and later divorced him.[110] The date of their separation is unknown and they may have reconciled at least once. Henry stood as a witness as Zina was resealed to Joseph Smith with Brigham Young acting as proxy in the Nauvoo Temple.

Patty Bartlett

Patty Bartlett kept a Nauvoo journal that mentioned her interactions with Joseph Smith. *Woman's Exponent* editor Emmeline Wells paraphrased several entries in a November 15, 1884, article:

> On the 13th [of December, 1842] she was very sick, the Prophet came and laid hands on her and she was healed. From that time she speaks of Joseph having visited at her house almost daily… On the 30th [June 1843] she says Bro. Joseph is at home again; she went to see him, and then heard him address the people… Oct. 3rd [1843] she took dinner at the Prophet Joseph's…[111]

The whereabouts of the original Nauvoo journal is unknown; neither have Emmeline's prepublishing notes for the *Woman's Exponent* articles been located. Many documents housed in the *Woman's Exponent* office were destroyed due to a fire and a flood, but whether the Sessions diaries or other important manuscripts were among them is not clear.[112]

It is interesting that David and Patty Sessions attended the Nauvoo Temple together, receiving their endowments on December 15, 1845, but they were not sealed in marriage, nor did Patty participate in a resealing to Joseph Smith at that time. Had Patty lost interest or was her sealing to Joseph Smith a point of contention with David? We do not know. Patty's diary recounts many struggles in their relationship after Nauvoo.[113]

---

110. Wight interview, "Evidence from Zina D. Huntington Young," *Saints' Herald*, January 11, 1905, 29; Zina also reported: "It was a most unhappy and ill-assorted marriage, and she subsequently separated from the husband who was so little suited to be a companion for her through life. Joseph Smith taught her the principle of marriage for eternity, and she accept it as a divine revelation , and was sealed to the Prophet…" [Emmeline B. Wells] "A Distinguished Woman, Zina D. H. Young," *Woman's Exponent* (Dec. 1, 1881): 99.

111. [Emmeline Wells], "Patty Session," *Woman's Exponent* (November 15, 1884): 95.

112. Personal communication with Carol Cornwall Madsen, October 5, 2008.

113. Donna Toland Smart, ed., *Mormon Midwife: The 1846–1888 Diaries of Patty Bartlett Sessions*, (Logan, Utah: Utah State University, 1997).

Marinda Nancy Johnson

Little is known concerning Marinda Nancy Johnson Hyde's relationship with the Prophet. Records provide two different sealing dates during his lifetime. The first is "Apr 42," which is written by Thomas Bullock on one of the blank pages at the back of the second of four small books Willard Richards used to record Joseph Smith's journal between December 1842 and June 1844.[114] It follows the July 14, 1843, entry and could also be transcribed: "Spri 42." The accuracy of the record is unknown, but Marinda's involvement with the Prophet's proposal to Nancy Rigdon in April 1842 is supportive that Marinda had been initiated into Nauvoo polygamy's inner circle by that time.

The second sealing date is a year later and is documented in an affidavit signed by Marinda in 1869 that records the date of May 1843.[115] A late second-hand report of questionable accuracy supports the earlier sealing date. It states that upon learning of the sealing, Orson Hyde was irate. Exposé author Ann Eliza Webb Young wrote:

> When Joseph Smith first taught polygamy, and gave the wives as well as the husbands opportunity to make new choice of life-partners, Mrs. Hyde, at that time a young and quite prepossessing woman, became one of the Prophet's numerous fancies.... Hyde was away on a mission at the time, and when he returned, he, in turn, imbibed the teachings of polygamy also, and prepared to extend his kingdom indefinitely. In the mean time it was hinted to him that Smith had had his first wife sealed to himself in his absence, as a wife for eternity. Inconsistent as it may seem, Hyde was in a furious passion."[116]

Whether this account contains any elements of truth is unknown. It may describe a situation where Joseph's "polyandrous" sealing was not immediately approved by the legal husband. John D. Lee remembered that

---

114. See Richard E. Turley Jr., *Selected Collections from the Archives of The Church of Jesus Christ of Latter-day Saints*, Provo, Utah: BYU Press, vol. 1, DVD # 20, MS155_1_6_320.jpg.; it is written in the hand of a different scribe from previous entries. Scott H. Faulring, ed. *An American Prophet's Record: The Diaries and Journals of Joseph Smith* (Salt Lake City: Signature Books, 1989), 396;

115. Joseph F. Smith Affidavit Books, 1:15, LDS Church History Department, MS 3423.

116. Ann Eliza Webb Young, *Wife Number 19, or, The Story of a Life in Bondage, Being a Complete Exposé of Mormonism, and Revealing Sorrows, Sacrifices and Sufferings of Women in Polygamy* (Hartford: Dustin, Gilman, and Co., 1876), 325–26.

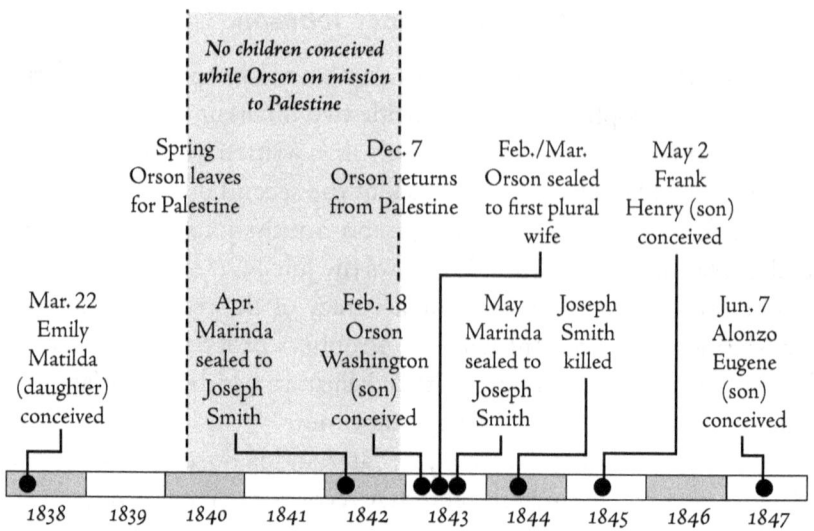

CHART 4.5: *Timeline showing important events for Orson Hyde, Marinda Johnson, and Joseph Smith*

Orson gave his permission: "Hyde's wife, with his consent, was sealed to Joseph for an eternal state."[117] Whatever misgivings Orson Hyde might have possessed, if any, must have been assuaged soon. Within months, Orson appealed to Joseph to perform his own plural marriage, stating in 1869: "In the month of February or March, 1843, I was married to Miss Martha R. Browitt, by Joseph Smith, the martyred prophet, and by him she was sealed to me for time and all eternity in Nauvoo, Illinois."[118] Interestingly, a Hyde family tradition states that "before Orson Hyde married Marinda, Joseph Smith cautioned him against marrying her, as she was his celestial wife, but Orson married her anyway."[119]

The reproductive history of Marinda shows that Orson Washington Hyde was born November 9, 1843; conception would have occurred approximately February 16, 1843. No evidence has been found to connect

---

117. John D. Lee, ed., *Mormonism Unveiled, or, The Life and Confessions of the Late Mormon Bishop* (St. Louis: Byron, Brand, 1877), 147. Lee added "but I do not assert the fact."

118. Affidavit of Orson Hyde, September 15, 1869, MS 3423_2_7s.jpg, LDS Church History Department; Joseph F. Smith Affidavit Books, 2:45; published in Joseph Fielding Smith, *Blood Atonement and the Origin of Plural Marriage* (Salt Lake City: Deseret News, 1905), 74.

119. Myrtle Stevens Hyde, *Orson Hyde: The Olive Branch of Israel* (Salt Lake City: Agreka Books, 2000), 160.

Joseph Smith with this child. Todd Compton observes: "It is striking that Marinda had no children while Orson was on his mission to Jerusalem, then became pregnant soon after Orson returned home. (He arrived in Nauvoo on December 7, 1842, and Marinda conceived Orson Washington Hyde two to three months later.)"[120]

A second son, Frank Henry Hyde, has been proposed as a child of Joseph Smith.[121] However, *The Ogden Standard*, June 29, 1908, contains an article entitled: "Frank H. Hyde Dies Suddenly." While obituaries can contain inaccurate information, it states: "Mr. Hyde was the eldest son of the late Apostle Orson Hyde and Marinda Johnson Hyde, and was born sixty-two years ago, at Nauvoo, Illinois."[122] Working back sixty-two years from June 1908 corresponds to a birth year of 1846 for his January 23, birth date. That would correlate with a roughly May 2, 1845, conception date, which is almost a year after Joseph Smith's death.

Elvira Annie Cowles

Elvira Annie Cowles married her legal husband, Jonathan Holmes, on December 1, 1842. Jonathan was a close friend of the Prophet and served as a pall bearer at Joseph Smith's funeral. Elvira signed an 1869 affidavit saying she was sealed to Joseph Smith on June 1, 1843. A letter written on June 2, 1931, from a Church member, William Wright records:

> I was well acquainted with two of Joseph's wives, LaVina [Elvira] and Eliza. I came to Utah in '69, and rented LaVina Holmes farm. Before Joseph was shot, he asked Jonathan Holmes if he would marry and take care of LaVina, but if LaVina wanted him to take care of her he would take her. He would fill that mission to please his Father in Heaven.[123]

---

120. Compton, "Fawn Brodie on Joseph Smith's Plural Wives and Polygamy," 165.
121. See below and, Brodie, *No Man Knows My History*, 345; Ugo A. Perego, Natalie M. Myres, and Scott R. Woodward. "Reconstructing the Y-Chromosome of Joseph Smith: Genealogical Applications," *Journal of Mormon History* 31:3 (Fall 2005): 43[42–60].
122. "Frank H. Hyde Dies Suddenly," *The Ogden Standard* (June 29, 1908): 5.
123. Undated holograph letter of William Wright, stampted as received in the First Presidency Office on June 2, 1931, in Box 65, CR 1/44, Misc. Corresp. Of 1st Pres., at the LDS Church History Library; copy in D. Michael Quinn Papers, Yale University, Special Collections, Uncat WA MS Uncat. WA MS. 98, 881028, bx3, fd 2.

Despite her 1842 wedding date to Jonathan, Elvira did not conceive her first child until seven months after the Prophet's death. The couple went on to have a total of five children together. Jonathan respected his wife's sealing to the Prophet, standing proxy for Joseph Smith in the Nauvoo temple as she was resealed to the Prophet vicariously for eternity.[124]

Elizabeth Davis

The date of Joseph Smith's sealing to Elizabeth Davis Durfee has not been verified. There is no doubt that she was a member of the polygamy inner circle in Nauvoo, however, that she was actually sealed to Joseph has been questioned.[125] After Emily Partridge was sealed to the Prophet, she related a conversation demonstrating Durfee's ignorance of restored plural marriage:

> Mrs. Durfee invited my sister Eliza and I to her house to spend the afternoon. She introduced the subject of spiritual wives as they called them in that day. She wondered if there was any truth in this report she heard. I thought I could tell her something that would make her open her eyes if I chose, but I did not choose to. I kept my own counsel and said nothing.[126]

Even though Elizabeth's legal husband, Jabez Dufee, was an active Latter-day Saint, he was endowed on a different day than Elizabeth when the Nauvoo Temple opened in the winter of 1845.[127] The two formally divorced the next year, but it appears a separation had occurred previous to that time. Elizabeth was resealed by proxy to Joseph Smith in the Nauvoo Temple on January 22, 1846, but Jabez did not participate

---

124. Lisle Brown, *Nauvoo Sealings, Adoptions, and Anointings: a Comprehensive Register of Persons Receiving LDS Temple Ordinances, 1841–1846* (Salt Lake City: Signature Books, 2006), 282 n268, 284 n306.

125. Richard Lloyd Anderson and Scott H. Faulring, "Review of In Sacred Loneliness: The Plural Wives of Joseph Smith, by Todd M. Compton," *FARMS Review of Books*, 10:2 (1998): 74–76. [67–104]

126. Emily D. P. Young, autobiographical sketch, "Written Especially for My Children, January 7, 1877," Marriott Library, University of Utah, manuscript owned by Emily Young Knopp, copy of typescript in possession of the author.

127. Brown, *Nauvoo Sealings, Adoptions, and Anointings: a Comprehensive Register of Persons Receiving LDS Temple Ordinances, 1841–1846*, 88.

either as a proxy husband or witness. Cornelius Lott represented the Prophet in the vicarious ordinance.[128]

Lucinda Pendleton

The sealing date for Lucinda Pendleton is also unknown. Evidence supporting her inclusion as a plural wife of Joseph Smith is the weakest of all thirty-four women. Regardless, her legal husband, George Harris, stood proxy for Joseph Smith in the Nauvoo temple as Lucinda was sealed to the Prophet for eternity.[129] The couple divorced sometime in the early 1850s.

Hopefully additional evidence concerning these six women will be discovered in the future helping to clarify the nature of their relationships with Joseph Smith and their respective legal husbands after their sealings to the Prophet.

"Polyandry" and Joseph Smith's Behaviors

Concerning the confusion surrounding some of Joseph Smith's "polyandrous" wives, Todd Compton insightfully observes: "It would help [the] case [that their sealings were only for 'eternity'] if they found polyandrous wives who explicitly, unambiguously stated that their marriages were for eternity only, not for time."[130] Comments by Mary Elizabeth Rollins Lightner suggest that the Prophet instructed her not to talk about it. In a letter to Emmeline B. Wells, Mary Elizabeth explained: "I could tell you why I stayed with Mr. Lightner. Things the leaders of the Church does not know anything about. I did just as Joseph told me to do, as he knew what troubles I would have to contend with."[131]

Amidst the silence are certain clues from Joseph Smith's behavior that might shed some light on what was happening in Nauvoo. For ex-

---

128. Ibid., 282.
129. Ibid., 282 n268, 284 n306.
130. Todd Compton, "Truth, Honesty and Moderation in Mormon History: A Response to Anderson, Faulring and Bachman's Reviews of *In Sacred Loneliness*," section "Sexuality in the Polyandrous Marriages," http://www.geocities.com/athens/oracle/7207/rev.html (accessed February 11, 2007).
131. Excerpts from a letter from Mary Elizabeth Rollins Lightner dated November 21, either 1870 or 1880, Mary Elizabeth Rollins Lightner Collection; MS 752, Folder 4; LDS Church History Department. Location of original letter is unknown.

ample, evidence indicates that Joseph Smith was just as motivated to be sealed to a woman for "eternity," as he was to be sealed to her for "time and eternity." Brigham Young recalled the non-polyandrous sealing of his sister Fanny to the Prophet:

> I recollect a sister conversing with Joseph Smith on this subject [plural marriage]. She told him: "Now, don't talk to me; when I get into the celestial kingdom, if I ever do get there, I shall request the privilege of being a ministering angel; that is the labor that I wish to perform. I don't want any companion in that world; and if the Lord will make me a ministering angel, it is all I want." Joseph said, "Sister, you talk very foolishly, you do not know what you will want." He then said to me: "Here, brother Brigham, you seal this lady to me." I sealed her to him. This was my own sister according to the flesh.[132]

Fanny Young was then fifty-six years of age. There is no indication that sexual relations were in any way contemplated or experienced by the participants, yet Joseph instantly requested the participation of both Fanny and Brigham in effectuating the ordinance. Todd Compton observed that this sealing "shows how casual and unromantic polygamy could be."[133]

Another observation is that the Prophet respected women's desires and choices. When turned down in his plural marriage proposals, as in the case of Sarah Kimball, he departed saying simply he would pray for her.[134] While he gave Lucy Walker a twenty-four hour time limit to make a reply, this ultimatum came only after she had vacillated for over a year.[135]

Todd Compton wrote: "Sometimes these sacred marriages were felt to fulfill pre-mortal linkings and so justified a sacred marriage superim-

---

132. *Journal of Discourses*, 16:166–67.
133. Compton, *In Sacred Loneliness*, 616.
134. See "Sarah M. Kimball's Testimony," in Andrew Jenson, "Plural Marriage," *Historical Record* 6 (July 1887): 232. When accused of improper behavior by women such as Sarah Pratt and Nancy Rigdon, Joseph Smith defended himself. However, women who quietly spurned his proposals were in no way disciplined for their choices.
135. See Lyman Omer Littlefield, *Reminiscences of Latter-day Saints: Giving an Account of Much Individual Suffering Endured for Religious Conscience* (Logan, Utah: Utah Journal Co, 1888), 46–48; see also testimony in Jenson, "Plural Marriage," 229–30.

posed over a secular one."¹³⁶ "Heavenly marriages in the pre-existence required earthly polyandry here. Certain spirits were 'kindred,' matched in heaven, were born into this life, and, because of unauthorized marriages performed without priesthood sealing power, became linked 'illegally' to the wrong partners."¹³⁷ There is documentation for this in one of the marriages. Mary Elizabeth Lightner remembered Joseph saying to her that, "I was created for him before the foundation of the Earth was laid."¹³⁸ On another occasion she recalled: "Joseph said I was his, before I came here and he said all the Devils in Hell should never get me from him."¹³⁹ And she noted her own feelings: "I had been dreaming for a number of years I was his wife."¹⁴⁰

Evidence also indicates that he gave his consent for one of his other plural wives to separate from him and marry another man. Malissa Lott, one of Joseph Smith's plural wives, wrote to Andrew Jenson on June 27, 1887: "Flora Ann Woodworth... married Carlos Gove at Navoo with the consent of the Prophet."¹⁴¹ Don Bradley explains:

> This statement tells us... that he [Joseph Smith] was at least in some cases willing to release an unhappy plural wife and allow her to remarry. Flora Woodworth is known to have married again after her marriage with Joseph Smith, but this marriage has sometimes been understood to have occurred after his death. However, if Malissa Lott is regarded as a credible witness on the subject, Flora not only remarried during Joseph's lifetime, but also with his consent. In this case, the Prophet would presumably have granted Flora divorce, at least "for

---

136. Compton, *In Sacred Loneliness*, 22. Anti-Mormon J. H. Beadle wrote in 1870: "In the pre-existent state souls are mated, male and female, as it is divinely intended they shall fill the marriage relation in this life; or, in more poetic phrase, 'marriages are made in heaven.'" (John Hanson Beadle, *Life in Utah: Or, the Mysteries and Crimes of Mormonism* [Philadelphia: National Publishing Co., 1870], 340.)

137. Compton, *In Sacred Loneliness*, 19.

138. Mary Elizabeth Lightner, Summer 1905 letter to Emmeline Wells, Harold B. Lee Library, Mary Elizabeth Lightner collection, LDS Church History Department.

139. Mary Elizabeth Rollins Lightner, "Statement" signed February 8, 1902, Vesta Crawford Papers, copy, MS 125, bx 1 fd 11, Marriott Library. Original owned by Mrs. Nell Osborne. See also Compton, *In Sacred Loneliness*, 212.

140. Mary Rollins Lightner, Remarks at Brigham Young University, 2, April 14, 1905.

141. Andrew Jenson Papers [ca. 1871–1942], MS 17956; LDS Church Archives, Box 49, Folder 16, document #14. Helen Mar Kimball wrote a conflicting account, that Carlos did not approach Flora until after the death of Joseph Smith. See "Travels Beyond the Mississippi," *Woman's Exponent* (November 1, 1884): 407.

time," and left her free to make her own choices regarding future marriage. Having married Joseph in plural marriage, she was not simply "trapped" if she found this difficult practice intolerable.[142]

In addition, legally married women were given a choice to whom they would be sealed for "eternity" and perhaps even "time and eternity." John D. Lee provided this recollection:

> About the same time the doctrine of "sealing" for an eternal state was introduced [1842–43], and the Saints were given to understand that their marriage relations with each other were not valid. That those who had solemnized the rites of matrimony had no authority of God to do so. That the true priesthood was taken from the earth with the death of the Apostles and inspired men of God. That they were married to each other only by their own covenants, and that if their marriage relations had not been productive of blessings and peace, and they felt it oppressive to remain together, they were at liberty to make their own choice, as much as if they had not been married.[143]

While Lee's declarations cannot always be taken at face value, his description may have been accurate, especially regarding the possibility that a woman could have been sealed for eternity to someone other than her legal husband.[144] With Ruth Vose Sayers serving as an example, other women who were married to non-members or unworthy husbands may have followed her lead, or perhaps preceded her in this practice.[145] Apparently some women with active LDS husbands chose to be sealed to the Prophet, as with Esther Dutcher.

Women's preferences continued to be respected concerning sealings to Joseph Smith after his death. For example, Joseph married two widows, Delcena Johnson Sherman and Martha McBride Knight, presumably only for "time." However, after the Prophet's death, when the women appeared at the Nauvoo Temple to be re-sealed to him for eternity by proxy, Delcena was sealed vicariously to her deceased legal husband,

---

142. Don Bradley, unpublished forthcoming manuscript analyzing the Andrew Jenson Papers MS 17956; LDS Church Archives, Box 49, Folder 16, documents 1–18. Copy in possession of the author.

143. Lee, *Mormonism Unveiled*, 146.

144. Historical evidence shows that John D. Lee's *Mormonism Unveiled* was edited by his attorney, who was paid from the royalties of his book. On many points it may not be reliable.

145. See Justus Morse, Affidavit, March 23, 1887, in Shook, *The True Origin of Mormon Polygamy*, 169–70; italics in original quoted earlier in this article.

Royal Lyman Sherman, while Martha McBride was sealed to Joseph Smith, not her civil spouse, Vinson Knight.[146] It is probable that the individual choices of these women determined who they were to be united to eternally.[147]

Also, when eternal sealings were performed, the Prophet was apparently comfortable either ignoring legal marriages or granting religious divorces as in the cases of Lydia Bailey (Kirtland, Ohio, 1835) and Sylvia Sessions. The legal system would not acknowledge the matrimonial separation or the new marriage, but Church member participants would be bound religiously to follow them. Importantly, they would prohibit sexual polyandry. Once a woman or man was sealed to a new eternal companion, subsequent conjugality with former spouses would be considered adultery. Brigham Young explained: "If after she has left her husband, and is sealed to another, [and] she shall again cohabit with him it is illicit intercourse, and extremely sinfull."[148]

Lastly, documents support that the Prophet was comfortable having a legal husband serve as a caretaker to one of his "time and eternity" spouses, as in the case of Joseph C. Kingsbury. The legal husband would not experience connubial relations with the wife, but could have plural wives of his own besides the one he was sheltering. This process could create a number of "front husbands." Todd Compton discounts the idea:

> The 'pretended' marriage opens up the possibility of other 'front husbands' in Smith's polyandrous marriages. But the evidence generally does not support front husband marriages in the other unions of the Mormon leader. In a pretend marriage we would expect a sealing to Smith, then a subsequent civil ceremony with the front husband, but most of Joseph's polyandrous wives married 'first husbands' before him;

---

146. Brown, *Nauvoo Sealings, Adoptions, and Anointings*, 272, 283. See also Biographical Sketch of Martha McBride Knight, internally titled "Part history of Martha McBride," by Mary Louisa Belnap Lowe, MS 14269, LDS Archives.

147. Todd Compton penned: "Some widows whom Smith married were sealed to their first husbands in the temple, but Martha [McBride] evidently chose the Mormon prophet as her eternal companion, not Vinson." (Compton, *In Sacred Loneliness*, 372).

148. Brigham Young, "A Few Words of Doctrine," October 8, 1861, uncorrected notes of George D. Watt, From "Reports of Speeches ca. 1845–1885," by the Historian's Office, CR 100 317; LDS Church History Department. President Young was speaking of a different but analogous situation.

and there is no evidence that any of them agreed to become front husbands *after* Smith married their wives. In fact, such a marriage—living with a wife and not having sexual relations with her after a period of full marriage—would probably have been impracticable.[149]

In evaluating Compton's observations, it is useful to note that opposite is also true, that "there is no evidence that any of them *declined* to become front husbands *after* Smith married their wives."

Three Interpretations of the Complexities and Incomplete Information

Examining the available evidence concerning these last six "polyandrous" wives and their relationship with Joseph Smith provides incomplete information. It is possible that additional documents will be discovered, like Patty Sessions Nauvoo diaries or other manuscripts, which will bring clarity to these associations. The limited historical data currently identified can be interpreted at least three ways. First, it is probable that some or all of the six women were sealed to Joseph Smith in "eternity" only marriages, like Ruth Vose.

A second reconstruction, popular with detractors, asserts that Joseph Smith practiced sexual polyandry with some (or most or all) of the "polyandrous" wives. This interpretation also affirms Compton's view stated above, that a husband would not suddenly stop conjugal relations with his legal wife, even if confronted with a religious dissolution of the marriage and a request from the wife and the Prophet to do so. Researchers who embrace this view must accept four assumptions:

1. That credible evidence exists beyond the tabloid level accusations supporting it. Most serious researchers would not draw strict conclusions based upon the sensationalized claims that are currently available.

2. That Joseph Smith would blithely disobey a commandment he had dictated, a commandment that labels such behavior as "adultery," stating that women so involved would be "destroyed" (D&C 132:63).

3. That the plural wives and other participants, those who performed and witnessed the sealings, would have condoned the relationships, by

---

149. Compton, *In Sacred Loneliness*, 352.

ignoring Biblical teachings and Joseph Smith's instructions condemning such relations.

4. That all participants would have easily overlooked Joseph Smith's hypocrisy on this point, continuing to follow him as a prophet without apparent complaint.

For decades, anti-Mormon writers have apparently been comfortable with these assumptions, accusing Joseph Smith of sexual polyandry. Doubtless this phenomenon will continue.

The third interpretation acknowledges Joseph's willingness to dissolve legal nuptials through eternal sealings and in one instance, to personally ask one man to serve as a "front husband." It suggests that these processes could have been repeated. Importantly, it asserts that identifying sexuality between the Prophet and a "polyandrous" wife would not demonstrate sexual polyandry unless the persistence of sexual relations was also verified in the legal marriage.

This last explanation proposes the following scenario: A woman is given a choice to be eternally sealed to Joseph Smith or her legal husband. She chooses the Prophet and is sealed, not just for "eternity" only (as seen with Ruth Vose), but for "time and eternity." The sealing nullifies her civil marriage in the eyes of all participants (as seen with Sylvia Sessions). Then, appealing to the legal husband's devotion to him and the Church, Joseph Smith asks the legal husband to support the woman and to carry on a façade to shield the Prophet from suspicion (as seen with Joseph C. Kingsbury). Concerning this possibility, Todd Compton wrote: "One might conjecture that a 'first husband' very devoted to Smith would, at his command, refrain from sexual relations with his wife."[150]

Of the six legal husbands, several may have been willing to serve as "front husbands" for their spouses under these strange but not impossible circumstances. Zina Huntington's spouse, Henry B. Jacobs, believed: "whatever the Prophet did was right, without making the wisdom of God's authorities bend to the reasoning of any man."[151] As already dis-

---

150. Compton, "Fawn Brodie on Joseph Smith's Plural Wives and Polygamy," 165.
151. Zina Diantha Huntington Young, Autobiography, Zina D. H. Young Collection, LDS Church History Department.

cussed, one historical source referred to Jonathan Holmes' willingness to care for Elvira in a way similar to that of a "front husband."[152]

Marinda Nancy Johnson Hyde's childbearing supports a continued marriage to Orson at least until the second sealing date, but thereafter it is less clear. She conceived a child shortly after Orson returned home from his mission to Palestine. He also married polygamously about that same time. However, after the second sealing date, Marinda bore no other children until well after Joseph Smith's death. Patty Sessions' age (47) at the time of her sealing might argue against a sexual relationship with Joseph. The cases of Elizabeth Davis and Lucinda Pendleton are inconclusive due to the lack of evidence.

For three of the wives, Zina Huntington, Marinda Nancy Johnson, and Sylvia Sessions, two sealing dates have been discovered. If two ceremonies were performed, perhaps a first was for "eternity" and then a later second sealing was for for "time and eternity." The depth of these conjectures further illustrates the problems arising from a lack of evidence in these cases.

Summary

A review of Joseph Smith's alleged "polyandrous" marriages demonstrates the importance of clarifying the meaning of "polyandry." The Prophet unquestionably participated in "ceremonial polyandry," whereby a woman was married to him in a second marriage ceremony, without securing a legal divorce from her first husband. However, to assume Joseph also was involved with "sexual polyandry" requires specific evidence because the second nuptial may have been for "eternity" only (without a sexual union) or may have accompanied a religious divorce from the woman's civil husband (prohibiting further sexual relations with the legal husband).

---

152. William Wright letter, ca. May 1931, copy in D. Michael Quinn Papers—Addition—Uncat WA MS 244 (Accession:19990209–c) Box 1—Card file—Topic: Polygamy, Joseph Smith's.

Joseph Smith's "Polyandrous" Wives	Legal Husband	Eternity Only	Religious Divorce/ Sealing	"Front" Husband	Sexual Polyandry
1. Sylvia Sessions	Windsor Lyon		probable	?	no
2. Sarah Ann Whitney	Joseph C. Kingsbury			yes	no
3. Ruth Vose	Edward Sayers	probable			no
4. Mary Elizabeth Rollins	Adam Lightner	probable			no
5. Sarah Kingsley	John Cleveland	probable			no
6. Presendia Lathrop Huntington	Norman Buell	probable			no
7. Esther Dutcher	Albert Smith	probable			no
8. Zina Diantha Huntington	Henry B. Jacobs	?		?	?
9. Patty Bartlett	David Sessions	?		?	?
10. Marinda Nancy Johnson	Orson Hyde	?		?	?
11. Elvira Annie Cowles	Jonathan Holmes	?		?	?
12. Elizabeth Davis	Jabez Durfee	?		?	?
13. Lucinda Pendleton	George Harris	?		?	?

CHART 4.6 outlines the probable and unknown characteristics of Joseph Smith's thirteen "polyandrous" marriages. It appears that one was not polyandrous, a second was based upon a "pretend" marriage, and several were "eternity" sealings. Greater clarification on the remaining relationships will come only as new historical data are discovered. Importantly, to assert that Joseph Smith practiced sexual polyandry is a conclusion that goes beyond available evidence.

The Age of Joseph Smith's Plural Wives in Social and Demographic Context

BY CRAIG L. FOSTER, DAVID KELLER, AND
GREGORY L. SMITH

"I have seen old men with white hair and wrinkled faces, go hunting after young girls...."[1]

—John Hyde

Introduction

FOR THE MODERN reader, perhaps one of the most controversial and shocking aspects of nineteenth-century Mormon polygyny is the relatively young age of some plural wives. Latter Day Saints, especially leaders such as Joseph Smith, have been frequently charged with pedophilia or "statutory rape" by modern readers and critics.

---

1. John Hyde, *Mormonism: Its Leaders and Designs*, (New York: W. P. Fetridge, 1857), 55.

Jon Krakauer's *Under the Banner of Heaven* (2003), for example, discussed the "still pubescent girls" whom Joseph married.[2] Krakauer even went as far as to explain that Smith lied about receiving revelation to convince teenage girls to marry him and commented, "His way of getting laid doesn't reflect well on him."[3] Lawrence O'Donnell, television commentator and actor on the HBO series *Big Love*, went even further when he practically screamed about "the Church's seventy year delight in polygamy and sex with young girls."[4]

Were Joseph Smith's wives' marital ages collectively normal relative to their contemporaries? Did the Latter Day Saints' marriage patterns conform to marriage age patterns in other parts of the United States? We strongly suggest that Latter Day Saint marriage patterns and the age of Joseph's wives was well within the norm for their time and place on the nineteenth-century American frontier.

Joseph Smith's Wives

Various writers have not agreed on the number of Joseph's plural wives. Andrew Jenson's 1887 tally numbered twenty-seven, while Fawn Brodie added twenty-one to Jenson's list.[5] A significantly higher number was given by Mormon writer, Stanley S. Ivins, asserting that Smith was married to some eighty four women![6] Much more conservative was

---

2. Jon Krakauer, *Under the Banner of Heaven: The Story of Violent Faith* (New York: Doubleday, 2003), 120.

3. Chris Nashawaty, "Jon Krakauer Gets Religion," *Entertainment Weekly* (July 18, 2003), 47, as quoted in Craig L. Foster, "Doing Violence to Journalistic Integrity," *FARMS Review* 16:1 (2004), http://maxwellinstitute.byu.edu/publications/review/?vol=16&num=1&id=530 (accessed July 15, 2010).

4. Lawrence O'Donnell, Transcript of *The McLaughlin Group* (December 7, 2007) <http://www.mclaughlin.com/library/transcript.asp?id=629>; O'Donnell, Transcript of Hugh Hewitt Radio Show (December 11, 2007) <http://hughhewitt.townhall.com/talkradio/transcripts/Transcript.aspx?ContentGuid=cb634a31-a45d-47fd-b285-d181b269d10c>; O'Donnell, "Romney and Me," *The Huffington Post* (December 13, 2007) <http://www.huffingtonpost.com/lawrence-odonnell/romney-me_b_76764.html?load=1&page=3> (accessed July 15, 2010).

5. Fawn McKay Brodie, *No Man Knows My History: The Life of Joseph Smith, the Mormon Prophet* (New York: Vintage Books, 1995), 457. On Brodie's handling of the plural marriage evidence, see Todd Compton, "Fawn Brodie on Joseph Smith's Plural Wives and Polygamy: A Critical View," in *Reconsidering No Man Knows My History: Fawn M. Brodie and Joseph Smith in Retrospect*, ed. Newell G. Bringhurst (Logan, Utah: Utah State University Press, 1996), 154–94.

6. Stanley S. Ivins collection, Utah State Historical Society, Box 12, Fd. Ivins' list was reproduced in Jerald and Sandra Tanner, *Joseph Smith and Polygamy* (Salt Lake City: Modern Micro-

Wife	Birth	Marriage	Age	Gap
Helen Kimball	22 Aug. 1828	*1 May 1843*	14.7	22.7
Nancy Winchester	10 Aug. 1828	**30 Jun. 1843**	14.9	22.6
Flora Woodworth	14 Nov. 1826	**1 Mar. 1843**	16.3	20.9
Fanny Alger	20 Sep. 1816	**1 Apr. 1833**	16.5	10.8
Sarah Lawrence	13 May 1826	*1 May 1843*	17.0	20.4
Lucy Walker	30 Apr. 1826	1 May. 1843	17.0	20.4
Sarah Whitney	22 Mar. 1825	27 Jul. 1842	17.4	19.3
Emily Partridge	28 Feb. 1824	4 Mar. 1843	19.0	18.2
Maria Lawrence	18 Dec. 1823	*1 May 1843*	19.4	18.0
Malissa Lott	9 Jan. 1824	20 Sep. 1843	19.7	18.1
Zina Huntington*	31 Jan. 1821	27 Oct. 1841	20.8	15.1
Eliza Partridge	20 Apr. 1820	8 Mar. 1843	22.9	14.3
Sylvia Sessions*	31 Jul. 1818	8 Feb. 1842	23.5	12.6
Mary Rollins*	8 Apr. 1818	25 Feb. 1842	23.9	12.3
Louisa Beaman	7 Feb. 1815	5 Apr. 1841	26.2	9.1
Marinda Johnson*	28 Jun. 1815	*1 Apr. 1842*	26.8	9.5
Olive Frost	24 Jul. 1816	**1 Jul. 1843**	27.0	10.6
Elvira Cowles*	23 Nov. 1813	1 Jun. 1843	29.5	7.9
Hannah Ells	**1 Jan. 1813**	**30 May 1843**	30.4	7.0
Almera Johnson	12 Oct. 1812	*2 Apr. 1843*	30.5	6.8
Presendia Huntington*	7 Sep. 1810	11 Dec. 1841	31.3	4.7
Agnes Coolbrith*	9 Jul. 1808	6 Jan. 1842	33.5	2.5
Desdemona Fullmer	6 Oct. 1809	*1 Jul. 1843*	33.8	3.8
Ruth Vose*	26 Feb. 1808	*1 Feb. 1843*	35.0	2.2
Delcena Johnson*	19 Nov. 1806	**1 Jul. 1842**	35.6	0.9
Lucinda Pendleton*	27 Sep. 1801	**1 Jan. 1838**	36.3	−4.2
Martha McBride*	17 Mar. 1805	*1 Aug. 1842*	37.4	−0.8
Eliza Roxcy Snow	21 Jan. 1804	29 Jun. 1842	38.5	−1.9
Patty Bartlett*	4 Feb. 1795	9 Mar. 1842	47.1	−10.9
Elizabeth Davis*	11 Mar. 1791	**30 May 1842**	51.3	−14.8
Sarah Kingsley*	20 Oct. 1788	**29 Jun. 1842**	53.7	−17.2
Fanny Young*	8 Nov. 1787	2 Nov. 1843	56.0	−18.1
Rhoda Richards	8 Aug. 1784	12 Jun. 1843	58.9	−21.4

FIGURE 5.1: *Joseph Smith's Plural Wives*
Notes: * (previously married), **bold** (broadly estimated date)
italics (estimates are within a month)

scholar Danel Bachman who identified just thirty-one spouses for the Mormon leader.[7] Todd Compton's thorough history of Joseph's plural wives continued Bachman's tradition of a more responsible analysis of the evidence, settling on thirty-three wives.[8]

Despite these caveats, Compton's list is recent, rigorous, and yields a higher percentage of teen brides and a greater age disparity than the more recent estimate offered by George D. Smith, which removes one teenage bride from Compton's list, and adds ten post-teenagers.[9] While increasing the number of plural wives, these alterations lower the average age difference between Joseph and his wives by over two years (from 6.7 years to 4.6), and likewise decrease the percentage of teenage brides (30% to 21%). Since any attempt to ascertain the "normality" of Joseph's wives' ages is best served by a "worst case scenario" approach, we have elected to use Compton's tabulation. The wives and their known or estimated dates of birth and marriage are found in Figure 5.1. The gap signifies the age difference between Joseph Smith and the woman.

Joseph Smith's Critics

For the modern critic, Joseph's young wives are juicy fodder. Jon Krakauer's discussion of "still pubescent girls" marrying Joseph Smith was intended to be shocking, though it is not clear what kind of wives he would prefer early Mormon men to have married—pubescent means

---

film, n.d.), 41–41.

7. Danel W. Bachman, "A Study of the Mormon Practice of Polygamy before the Death of Joseph Smith," (Master's thesis, Purdue University, 1975), 112–116.

8. Todd M. Compton, *In Sacred Loneliness* (Salt Lake City: Signature Books, 1997). We have estimated some dates. Richard Anderson and Scott Faulring have contested four of these wives (fourteen- or fifteen-year-old Nancy Winchester and three non-teens) on the grounds of insufficient evidence. They likewise favor accounts which situate Fanny Alger's marriage in 1835 rather than early 1833. Also of note is an account by Fanny's uncle, which would place her likely birth date at least a year earlier than erroneous family group sheets report. Also see Levi Hancock, "The Life of Levi Hancock," Autobiography (1803–1836) Typescript, Harold B. Lee Library <http://www.boap.org/LDS/Early-Saints/LHancock.html>. While ambiguous about the date, census records side with Levi's account regarding Fanny's birthplace.

9. George D. Smith, "Nauvoo Roots of Mormon Polygamy, 1841–46: A Preliminary Demographic Report," *Dialogue: A Journal of Mormon Thought* 27:1 (1994): 60–61.

"arriving at or having reached puberty." All females of sexual maturity remain "pubescent."[10]

Never one to be overburdened by historical details or interpretive nuance when discussing religion, vocal atheist Christopher Hitchens used candidate Mitt Romney's speech during the 2008 presidential primaries as an opportunity to describe Joseph Smith as a "serial practitioner of statutory rape."[11] Lawrence O'Donnell vehemently attacked Joseph in multiple venues as "a criminal who was...a rapist," and decried "the criminal, adulterous, rapist founder of" Mormonism.[12]

George D. Smith's *Nauvoo Polygamy* likewise emphasized what was called Joseph Smith's "interest in marrying teenagers." For example, the introduction to *Nauvoo Polygamy* mentioned that Joseph "was betrothed to teenage women as young as fourteen."[13]

Compton, whose book, *In Sacred Loneliness*, is a more careful study of the lives of Joseph's plural wives, may have, nevertheless, let his own views color his work[14] when he noted rhetorically that when "looking at

---

10. *Merriam-Webster's Medical Dictionary*, (2002), s.v., "pubescent." See also *American Heritage Stedman's Medical Dictionary* (New York: Houghton Mifflin, 2002), s.v., "pubescent." We note too that to the modern clinician, pedophilia "'involves sexual activity with a prepubescent child (generally age 13 years or younger)," *Diagnostic and Statistical Manual of Mental Disorders*, 4th ed. (Washington, DC: American Psychiatric Association; 1994), 527 <http://www.psychiatryonline.com/DSMPDF/dsm-iv.pdf>.

11. Christopher Hitchens, "Holy Nonsense: Mitt Romney's Windy, Worthless Speech," slate.com (December 6, 2007) < http://www.slate.com/id/2179404/> (accessed July 15, 2010).

12. Lawrence O'Donnell, Transcript of *The McLaughlin Group* (December 7, 2007), Transcript of Hugh Hewitt Radio Show (December 11, 2007) <http://hughhewitt.townhall.com/talkradio/transcripts/Transcript.aspx?ContentGuid=cb634a31-a45d-47fd-b285-d181b269d10c>; O'Donnell, "Romney and Me," *The Huffington Post* (December 13, 2007) <http://www.huffingtonpost.com/lawrence-odonnell/romney-me_b_76764.html?load=1&page=3> (accessed July 15, 2010).

13. George D. Smith, *Nauvoo Polygamy*: "...but we called it celestial marriage" (Salt Lake City: Signature Books, 2009), 226 and xii. In the book, Smith made references to Joseph Smith's marriages as "secret liaisons with women and girls" (55) and also a "tryst" (xi). He went so far as to call the plural marriages of Joseph Smith to Emily and Eliza Partridge a "celestial *ménage-à-quatre*" (180).

14. Reviewers who have seen Compton's treatment of Joseph's plural marriage as overly negative include Richard Lloyd Anderson and Scott H. Faulring, "The Prophet Joseph Smith and His Plural Wives," *FARMS Review of Books* 10/2 (1998); Alma G. Allred, "Variations on a Theme," (paper presented at Mormon History Association, 2 May 1999 [updated December 6, 1999]) <http://www.shields-research.org/Reviews/Rvw-Sacred_Loneliness_Allred.htm>; Danel W. Bachman, "Prologue to the Study of Joseph Smith's Marital Theology (Review of *In Sacred Loneliness: The Plural Wives of Joseph Smith*)," *FARMS Review of Books* 10/2 (1998) <http://farms.byu.edu/display.php?table=review&id=291>; and Danel W. Bachman, "'Let No One...Set on

polygamy from our late-twentieth-century monogamous and feminist perspectives, one wonders why Latter Day Saint leaders did not see more clearly the problematic nature of such relationships and retreat from them."[15] Compton made his own views of such relationships clear elsewhere, writing in response to Jerald and Sandra Tanner that "I strongly disapprove of polygamous marriages involving teenage women...."[16]

Unfortunately, Jon Krakauer, George D. Smith, and other commentators have fallen into the same trap. They impose their values upon another place and time and, when the marriage patterns do not conform to their modern worldview, they look upon and write about marriages with teenaged brides with an open-mouthed, shocked, or offended voice.

For example, Krakauer suggested in an interview that Mormons would be uncomfortable with how he portrayed their history, "They will not like the fact that I point out that Joseph Smith told fourteen-year-old girls 'God says you should marry me, if you don't . . .' His way of getting laid doesn't reflect well on him."[17] In this case, as in many others, Krakauer's verbally evocative analysis is not impeded by factual detail. Informed readers are more apt to dislike his rather flippant analysis because (as Compton,[18] and others have observed[19]) there is no evidence that the marriage with 14-year-old girls was consummated.[20]

My Servant Joseph': Religious Historians Missing the Lessons of Religious History," (paper presented at the Mormon History Association, 2 May 1999) <http://www.shields-research.org/Reviews/Rvw-Sacred_Loneliness_Bachman.htm>. For Compton's reply to Anderson, Faulring, and Bachman's FARMS articles, see Todd M. Compton, "Truth, Honesty and Moderation in Mormon History: A Response to Anderson, Faulring and Bachman's Reviews of *In Sacred Loneliness*," (July 2001) <http://www.geocities.com/Athens/Oracle/7207/rev.html>.

15. Compton, *In Sacred Loneliness*, 455–456.
16. Todd M. Compton, "Response to Tanners," LDS Bookshelf mailing list, n.d., www.ldsmormon.com/compton.shtml (accessed July 28, 2009).
17. Chris Nashawaty, "Jon Krakauer Gets Religion," *Entertainment Weekly* (July 18, 2003): 47.
18. Ibid., also see *In Sacred Loneliness*, 6.
19. Stanley B. Kimball, "Heber C. Kimball and Family, the Nauvoo Years," *Brigham Young University Studies* 15/4 (Summer 1975): 465.
20. For reviews of Krakauer's other historical gaffes, see Foster, "Doing Violence to Journalistic Integrity," and Paul McNabb (editor), and Richard E. Turley Jr., "Faulty History: A Review of *Under the Banner of Heaven: A Story of Violent Faith*," Foundation for Apologetics Information and Research, 2003 < http://www.fairlds.org/pubs/Krakauer.pdf> (accessed July 28, 2009).

Long Term Marriage Trends

It is not surprising that moderns, even respected historians, would look askance at the early age of some of Joseph Smith's wives, given present-day marriage trends. The United States has historically had the highest marriage rate of any other country, and that trend continued into the late twentieth century.[21] Despite this statistic, the United States—like the rest of the west—"has seen a dramatic retreat from marriage." And, among those who do marry, there "have been substantial increases in the mean age at first marriage."[22]

Figure 5.2 shows various long-term marital statistics for white females in the United States[23] based on synthetic birth cohorts in census years.[24] The mean age at first marriage typically occurs at the age at which 60% of the marriage population has already married. The 50% (median), 25%, and 10% marks are also depicted. The mode is an estimate of the most popular marital age. The minimum age of eligibility is a benchmark defined by the Coale-McNeil model for nuptiality as "the earliest age of a significant number of first marriages."[25] Lacking a more direct method, marriage statistics for 1800 to 1840 are projected from

---

21. Carl N. Degler, *At Odds: Women and the Family in America from the Revolution to the Present* (Oxford: Oxford University Press, 1980), 457.

22. Robert Schoen and Vladimir Canudes-Romo, "Timing effects on first marriage: Twentieth-century experience in England and Wales and the USA," *Population Studies* 59:2 (2005): 135.

23. For similar studies see Catherine A. Fitch and Steven Ruggles, "Historical Trends in Marriage Formation: The United States 1850–1990," in *The Ties that Bind: Perspectives on Marriage and Cohabitation*, edited Linda J. Waite (New York: Aldine de Gruyter, 2000), 59–90; Warren C. Sanderson, "Quantitative Aspects of Marriage, Fertility and Family Limitation in Nineteenth Century America: Another Application of the Coale Specification," *Demography* 16 (1979): 339–358; Michael R. Haines, "Long Term Marriage Patterns in the United States from Colonial Times to the Present," *National Bureau of Economic Research* (Cambridge, MA), NBER Working Paper Series, (Historical Paper No. 80. 1996):15–39; Catherine A. Fitch, *Transitions to Marriage in the United States, 1850–2000*, (unpublished Ph.D. Dissertation: University of Minnesota, 2005); J. David Hacker, "Rethinking the 'Early' Decline of Marital Fertility in the United States" *Demography* 40:4 (2003): 605–620.

24. See Technical Note 1. Raw data obtained from Steven Ruggles, J. Trent Alexander, Katie Genadek, Ronald Goeken, Matthew B. Schroeder, and Matthew Sobek. *Integrated Public Use Microdata Series: Version 5.0* [Machine-readable database]. Minneapolis: University of Minnesota, 2010 <http://usa.ipums.org/usa/> (accessed March 18, 2010).

25. Ansley J. Coale, "Age Patterns of Marriage," *Population Studies* 25:2 (1971): 206. See also A.J. Coale and D. R. McNeil, "The Distribution by Age of the Frequency of First Marriage in Female Cohort." *Journal of American Statistical Association* 67 (1972): 743–749.

Daniel Smith's proposal for a mean age of 21.0 years in 1800[26] and holding the minimum age constant at its 1850–1900 average of 13.6 years.

Figure 5.2 shows long term trends for white teenage brides as a percentage of census year marriage cohorts.[27] Marriage cohorts are age dependent, that is, sensitive to a society's age structure created from birth and death rates. Teenage marriage was over four times more common in Joseph Smith's America than it is today. The 1960 baby boom offers a close comparison, but nuptiality has been in rapid decline since.

This shift in marriage patterns, which has gone mostly unnoticed during the past half-century, is reflected in the higher age of first marriage among American men and women. The median age at first marriage has risen by over five years since 1970. It is now twenty-six for women and twenty-eight for men.[28] This later age of marriage for both males and females has become not only accepted but expected in twenty-first century America. While studies show that Latter Day Saints and conservative Protestants currently marry at a younger age than other religious and non-religious groups, they too appear to have been affected by the changing demographics.[29] Demographers call this the "second demographic transition." In societies that "exhibit lengthy economic prosperity, men and women alike begin to lose motivation to marry and have children, and thus avoid one or both."[30]

---

26. Daniel S. Smith, "American family and demographic patterns and the north-west European model," *Continuity and Change* 8:3(1993): 389–415.

27. See Technical Note 2 for details on how figs. 1 and 2 were made. A more advanced paper covering the methods used in this paper is David Keller, "Timely Statistics Vindicate the Prophet," working paper (2010).

28. Ibid. Tellingly, Regnerus wrote in the same article, "Most young Americans no longer think of marriage as a formative institution, but rather as the institution they enter once they think they are fully formed."

29. Xiaohe Xu, Clark D. Hudspeth, and John P. Bartkowski, "The Timing of First Marriage: Are There Religious Variations?" *Journal of Family Issues* 26 (2005): 585 and 588. Latter Day Saints and conservative Protestant women married at earlier ages than their Catholic and mainline Protestant counterparts. All married at a younger age than Jewish women. Of these, there was a more pronounced difference between those born before 1960 and women born after 1960, with those born before 1960 marrying at an even younger age than those born after 1960.

30. Mark Regnerus, "The Case for Early Marriage," *Christianity Today* (August 3, 2009), http://www.ctlibrary.com/ct/2009/august/16.22.html (accessed December 30, 2009). Also see, Regnerus, "Say Yes. What Are You Waiting For?" *The Washington Post* (April 26, 2009), http://www.washingtonpost.com/wp-dyn/content/article/2009/04/24/AR2009042402122.html (accessed December 30, 2009).

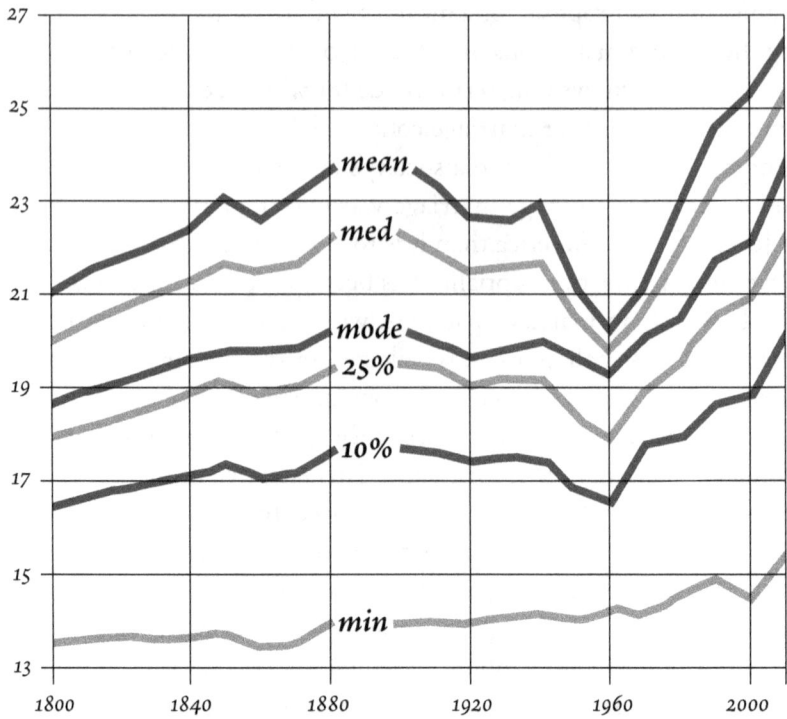

FIGURE 5.2: *Age Independent Marriage Statistics from US Census*

Unlike today, in the mid 19th century teenage brides seldom married someone near their own age. The average age difference between a husband and a wife in her mid-teens was typically 2–3 years higher than the overall average. Rolf and Ferrie[31] charted the decline of the overall age gap from 4.55 years in 1850 to 2.30 years in 2000 after peaking at 4.96 in 1870. They also found the western frontier had an average gap that was two years higher than elsewhere between 1850 and 1880. Higher male to female sex ratios—due to higher male birth rates and life expectancy, as well as immigration[32]—led to the larger age gaps observed in the 19th century.

---

31. Karen Rolf and Joseph Ferrie, "The May–December relationship since 1850: Age homogamy in the U.S.," Working Paper (September, 2008).
32. Albert Esteve and Anna Cabré, "Marriage Squeeze and Changes in Family Formation: Historical Comparative Evidence in Spain, France, and United States in the XXth Century," Paper presented at Population Association of America 2004 Annual Meeting. James Matthew

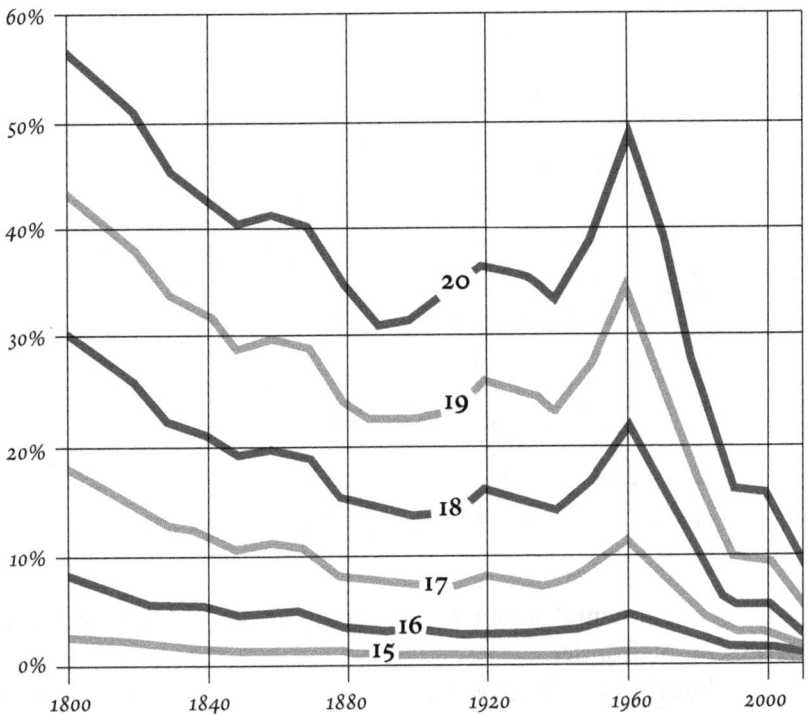

FIGURE 5.3: *Age Dependent Cumulative Marriage Rates from US Census*

Typically men would court across the entire eligible age spectrum younger than themselves. The economic stability of some older men was a factor that helped them be seen as attractive marriage partners. Figure 5.4 compares Joseph Smith's plural marriages to the marriages of his peers (aged 34–38) in various regions of the country according to the 1880 census sample. While on average Joseph Smith married older women than his 1880 peers, his wives' ages were more spread out. Though his percentage of teenage brides (30%) was slightly higher than a reasonable estimate for his peers in 1840s Illinois (20%), it was far from being historically high. One wonders if America could have met its "manifest

---

Gallman, "Relative Ages of Colonial Marriages," *Journal of Interdisciplinary History* 14:3 (Winter, 1984): 616–617, found in a study of communities in New Hampshire and North Carolina that "roughly two thirds of the men" married women within a five year range.

Place	States	N	mean	std	Teen %
Joseph Smith	OH IL MO	33	6.7	12.5	30%
USA		512	10.0	6.5	19%
New England	NH ME VT CT MA RI	39	7.1	7.7	9%
Mid Atlantic	NY PA NJ	72	8.1	5.9	7%
NE Central	OH MI IN WI IL	118	9.4	5.3	10%
NW Central	MN IA MO ND SD NE KS	70	10.9	5.9	20%
S. Atlantic	DE MD VA NC SC GA FL WV DC	75	10.2	5.6	18%
SE Central	AL MS TN KY	60	11.2	6.4	22%
SW Central	OK AR LA TX	62	12.0	6.8	46%
West	AZ CO ID UT NM MT WY NV OR WA CA HI AK	20	14.3	5.8	55%

FIGURE 5.4: *Age gap for husbands aged 34–38 using 1880 IPUMS.*

destiny" of continental settlement so rapidly without adapting marital practices to the frontier.

The thought of early marriage age coupled with a large age gap between spouses is not only foreign but repulsive to most modern Americans.[33] Recent decades' increased awareness of the scourges of child abuse and pedophilia is proper, and can only heighten the modern reader's discomfort with this aspect of LDS history. Nevertheless, in spite of contemporary marriage patterns—as well as exclamations of shock and accusations of Mormon pedophilia from critics of the Church—the indisputable reality is that in a large portion of the world and throughout most of history, marriage at a young age has been the norm.

Biology-based Legal Tradition

Indeed, overall, the age of consent for marriage and sexual activity throughout history has coincided with the onset of puberty. Colonial America inherited customs regarding marital eligibility and statutory

---

33. According to Malini Karkal and S. Irudaya Rajan, "Age at Marriage: How Much Change?" *Economic and Political Weekly* 24:10 (March 11, 1989): 505, internationally and particularly in third-world countries, attempts are being made to raise the legal age of marriage in order to lower the fertility of the population. Nevertheless, most marriages "still take place around the age at menarche."

rape from Christian Europe, which can be traced back to the Greco-Roman period when the age of consent became a legal matter.

In Christian Europe, like other parts of the world, the age of consent was generally based on biological development. Thus European countries traditionally set the right of consent between the age of twelve and fourteen, and followed the Roman tradition of an "absolute minimum at seven."[34] In Islam, the minimum age of consent is age nine. Furthermore, an Islamic apologist stated that the commencement of puberty "genetically ranges from ages 7 to 13 in women." This assessment, however, appears to be quite early compared to most other localities and time-periods.[35] Nevertheless, the age of menarche, or the onset of menstruation, has certainly fluctuated over time.

In ancient Rome the accepted age of menarche was around fourteen years, but was also recognized to occur as early as twelve. This was based on contemporary medical opinion and was ultimately incorporated into Roman law. While Roman girls tended to marry in their early to mid-teens, this appears to not have been the pattern among males. In spite of being legally able to marry as young as fourteen years old, it seems that most males waited at least until their twenties. One reason was probably economic, since the men had to be able to provide for themselves and a family. Anecdotal evidence from the late Roman period of the fourth and fifth centuries A.D. "points to men in their late twenties marrying women who were in their teens." In fact, "it was not unheard of for a man in his fifties or even sixties to marry a woman in her early teens."[36]

Following the Roman precedent, early medieval manuscripts placed menarche around the range of twelve to fourteen years, and colloquial evidence affirms that was indeed the common age range.[37] In fact, canon law—said to be created by the monk Gratian (an ecclesiastical lawyer

---

34. Vern L. Bullough, "Age of Consent: A Historical Overview," *Journal of Psychology & Human Sexuality* 16:2/3 (May 2005): XXX. Between age seven and puberty, there could be consent to marriage but the marriage could not be consummated.

35. Bismillaah al Rahmaan Al Raheem, "Islam Answers: Morality of Marrying Aisha at an Early Age," http://www.muhaddith.org/earlymarriage/Index.html (accessed July 15, 2010).

36. Mathew Kuefler, "The Marriage Revolution in Late Antiquity: The Theodosian Code and Later Roman Marriage Law," *Journal of Family History* 32:4 (October 2007): 348. According to Kuefler, early Christians greatly influenced fourth and fifth century Roman marriage laws.

37. J. B. Post, "Ages at Menarche and Menopause: Some Medieval Authorities," *Population Studies* 25:1 (March 1971): 84, 86.

and teacher who in 1140 published the first definitive collection of Roman Catholic canon law)—also followed Roman law in this matter.[38] British common law, which was in turn influenced by canon law, recognized the onset of puberty and the right to marry at age twelve for girls and fourteen for boys. As late as 1983, the Code of Canon Law (which is binding upon all baptized Catholics) decreed the minimum age of marriage to be sixteen for men and fourteen for women.[39]

Beginning around 1500, "a retardation of menarche began throughout Europe." This was particularly the case in northern and western Europe. The delay in menarche's onset continued in Europe and other parts of the world until about 1830 when "there began a progressive decline in the age of menarche."[40]

These changes in the age of menarche were reflected in the age at marriage over the centuries. "In most human societies…women have entered first marriages around puberty, at about fifteen or so."[41] In some places and times brides were younger. As discussed above, in Europe the legal age of marriage from the Roman period onward was twelve for girls and fourteen for boys; the average age of marriage for girls ranged between thirteen and seventeen. In fact, because marriage tended to occur within a short time after the onset of menarche, and because this commonly occurred by age fourteen, a fourteen year-old girl was regarded as an adult.[42]

---

38. Vern L. Bullough, "Age of Consent," *Encyclopedia of Children and Childhood in History and Society*, http://www.faqs.org/childhood/A-Ar/Age-of-Consent.html (accessed December 30, 2009). Gratian's collection, called the Decretum Gratiani, drew on older local collections, councils, Roman law, and the Church Fathers.

39. Fr. Jason Gray, "Canon Law vs. Illinois State law on Marriage," (December 21, 2005), http://www.jgray.org/docs/IL_marriage.html (accessed on December 30, 2009).

40. Ibid., 83. For example, according to Elise De la Rochebrochard in "Les âges à la puberté des filles et des garçons à partir d'une enquête sur la sexualité des adolescents," *Population* 54:6 (Nov-Dec 1999): 938, age at menarche in 1750 was almost 16 years old. By 1900, it was down to 14 years old and in 2000 had decreased to about 12.5 years.

41. Alan Macfarlane, *Marriage and Love in England: Modes of Reproduction, 1300–1840* (Oxford: Blackwell, 1986), 214.

42. M. K. Hopkins, "The Age of Roman Girls at Marriage," *Population Studies* 18:3 (March 1965): 309, 313. See also Paul Veyne, "The Roman Empire," in P. Veyne, *Histoire de la Vie Privée* (Cambridge: Harvard University Press, 1987), 20.

Throughout the Middle Ages, teenage marriage was common-place, "particularly among more elevated social groups."[43] The sixteenth century's shift to a higher age of menarche was accompanied by a corresponding increase in the age of marriage. This was particularly so in northwest Europe where there was a pattern of late marriage among both men and women, typically in the mid to late twenties on average.[44]

Southern and eastern European marriage patterns did not follow those of northwest Europe. From an early time, and even into the twentieth century, marriages in these parts of Europe took place at a younger age. In Belgrade, Serbia, for example, where girls were regarded as marriageable between thirteen and fifteen, "A third of all girls of the age of fifteen, and over half of the girls age sixteen, already had husbands." Between 1650 and 1750, seventy percent of all women between the ages of fifteen and nineteen were married or widowed.[45]

Although data are sparse for the US in the 19th century regarding the average age at menarche, it likely followed the lowest European trends.[46] Using post-1910 US data, Grace Wyshak[47] determined that the average age at menarche had dropped linearly at 3.2 month/decade, with a value of 13.1 years in 1920. If projected backward, this trend yields 15.2 years in 1840, a figure that closely matches an 1845 clinical survey in Birmingham,

---

43. Diana O'Hara, *Courtship and Constraint: Rethinking the Making of Marriage in Tudor England* (Manchester: Manchester University Press, 2000), 165.

44. Ibid., 164. H. E. Hallam in "Age at First Marriage and Age at Death in the Lincolnshire Fenland, 1252–1478," *Population Studies* 39:1 (March 1985): 55, 59, also discussed an increase in age of marriage near the end of his study. He showed, however, that marriage ages in Lincolnshire tended to be higher than in other parts of England from a very early date.

45. Peter Laslett, "Age at Menarche in Europe since the Eighteenth Century," *Journal of Interdisciplinary History* 2:2 (Autumn 1971): 232, 229, and 227. According to Laslett in Belgrade, "husbands were, on the average, nearly ten years older than their wives... and [sought] out the youngest nubile girls to marry," 230. Interestingly enough, the difference between northern and southern Europe, in terms of marriage patterns, existed even within the Russian Empire. According to Helena Chojnacka in "Nuptiality Patterns in an Agrarian Society," *Population Studies* 30:2 (July 1976). In the late 1800s Russia, girls aged fifteen to nineteen made up 15–25% of the married women in the southern part of Russia while only five percent of the married women in the northern part of Russia were ages fifteen to nineteen.

46. Other useful publications on 19th century menarche statistics include J. M. Tanner, "Menarchial Age," *Science* 214 (1981):604 and Peter Laslett, *Family life and illicit love in earlier generations* (New York: Cambridge University Press, 1977).

47. Grace Wyshak "Secular changes in age at menarche in a sample of US women," *Annals of Human Biology* 10:1 (1983):75–77.

England.[48] As plotted above, the statistical minimum age at marriage was on the rise during the same period, somewhat countering the idea that two trends should always be correlated.

Though the distribution of the onset of menarche consistently follows the familiar bell shaped curve, the higher averages of the 19th century were partially offset by wider spreads—the bell became broader. If Mormon girls in 1840 Illinois roughly followed the Birmingham rates, 10% would have reached puberty before turning 13, 24% before age 14, and 45% before turning 15. Joseph's youngest wife, Helen Mar Kimball, married at an age by which 40% of the female population had already matured, though it is unlikely than even then the marriage was consummated. Nevertheless, Helen's parents would likely never have considered proposing the marriage if she was still prepubescent. Helen's own remarks are strong evidence of her maturity. "I had grown up very fast and my father often took me out with him and for this reason was taken to be older than I was."[49]

Economic and Cultural Factors

Even today, marriage continues to be based not only upon biological factors, but also cultural and economic ones. For example, early marriage is particularly common in Sub-Saharan Africa and parts of South Asia. In Afghanistan, Mali and Niger, half of all girls aged fifteen to nineteen are married, while more than half of the girls in Guinea and Yemen marry by age sixteen. In Nigeria, the national median age of marriage is seventeen but in Kebbe state the median age of marriage is as low as eleven years old.[50]

While social and biological factors help determine the age at time of marriage, one of the major factors continues to be economic. The stability and financial certitude of the present and future generations are a prime consideration. Thus "early age at marriage in pre-industrial societies was

---

48. P. E. Brown, "The Age at Menarche," *British Journal of Preventive and Social Medicine* 20 (1966):9–14

49. Helen Mar Kimball Whitney, "Scenes and Incidents in Nauvoo," *Woman's Exponent* 11 (1882–83). <http://www.boap.org/LDS/Early-Saints/HWhitney.html> (accessed July 15, 2010).

50. Annie Bunting, "Stages of Development: Marriage of Girls and Teens as an International Human Rights Issue," *Social and Legal Studies* 14 (2005): 23.

a social measure to ward off the threat of failure in population replacement." Obviously, "women who marry young are exposed to conceptions throughout the most fecund years of their lives" which encouraged the early marriage patterns.[51]

Along with the basic criteria for survival, another economic factor which encouraged early marriages historically has been the potential availability of land. This is one of the reasons agrarian societies with ample land have traditionally seen younger marriages. Such was the case in the early North American colonies where both the British and French colonists temporarily bucked the western European pattern of late marriage. The marriage age of women in the American colonies was considerably lower than in their native Western Europe.[52]

Marriage Age Patterns in the New World: From Frontier to Settled Regions

Québec

In Québec, Canada, for example, there was a serious dearth of marriageable women during the early years of settlement. To meet this lack, the French government transported in the *"Filles du Roi"* ("King's Daughters"). These mainly poor and orphaned young women had very little opportunity in their native France. Of the 774 women identified as "King's Daughters," seventy-six—almost ten percent—were between the years of twelve and fifteen. Almost forty-two percent of these women were age twenty and younger and eighty-two percent of the women were thirty years and younger.[53] But, by the eighteenth century, the average age of first marriage for women had risen to twenty years in Québec.[54]

New England

This same pattern was also seen in the American colonies. Of a necessity, marriages were entered into at an earlier age than in their land

---

51. Karkal and Rajan, 505.
52. Degler, 6.
53. Silvio Dumas, *Les Filles du Roi en Nouvelle-France: Études Historique avec Répertoire Biographic* (Québec, Québec: Société Historique de Québec, 1972), 67. The ages of 11.5% of the women could not be identified.
54. Gillian Hamilton and Aloysius Siow, " Marriage and Fertility in a Catholic Society: Eighteenth-Century Québec," 1. http://repec.economics.utoronto.ca/files/UT-ECIPA-SIOW-99-01.pdf (accessed March 21, 2009).

of origin, resulting in larger families to work the land and build communities. For example, Lancaster County, Pennsylvania, was the "frontier" prior to 1741—during that period, over thirty-nine percent of the women were under age twenty at the time of their first marriage. By 1771–1800, however, the number of women marrying under age twenty had decreased to only twenty-seven percent.[55]

Over time, as life became more comfortable and land less available, women began "marrying at increasingly later ages, shortening their childbearing years and thus limiting the number of children they were likely to have." This was particularly the case in New England. By the 1830s, the *Universal Traveler* observed, New Englanders had come to "'seldom marry at as early an age as is common' elsewhere."[56]

Nevertheless, New England, like other parts of the United States, continued to base its marriage laws on the "traditional English common-law nuptial-age demarcations" which allowed marriage at twelve for women and fourteen for men. These same statutes became a part of American common law, and "every American state adopted these age boundaries after the Revolution."[57] Over time, individual states altered these ages, moving the ages higher for both females and males. Even so, some states retained the old common law ages into the twentieth century.[58]

As late as 1906, six states still retained a minimum age of twelve for girls. These states included Kansas, Missouri, and Rhode Island. In 1887, New Hampshire changed the permissible marriage age for girls from twelve to thirteen. Eight other states, including Iowa, Texas, and Utah,

---

55. Rodger C. Henderson, "Demographic Patterns and Family Structure in Eighteenth-Century Lancaster County, Pennsylvania," *The Pennsylvania Magazine of History and Biography* 114:3 (July 1990): 357.

56. Jack Larkin, *The Reshaping of Everyday Life, 1790–1840* (New York: Harper & Row, 1988), 69. By the second generation in Andover the average age of marriage was twenty-two years. Of the sixty-six women in his study, twenty-two were married before the age of twenty-one, according to Philip J. Greven Jr., in "Family Structure in Seventeenth-Century Andover, Massachusetts," in Michael Gordon, ed., *The American Family in Social-Historical Perspective*, 3rd ed., (New York: St. Martin's Press, 1983), 140.

57. Michael Grossberg, *Governing the Hearth: Law and the Family in Nineteenth-Century America* (Chapel Hill: University of North Carolina Press, 1988), 106.

58. Ibid., and "Marriage and Divorce in the United States," *The Albany Law Review* 43 (January–July, 1891): 869.

had fourteen as the minimum age for girls.[59] As late as 1905, fourteen was the legal marriage age for girls in Illinois. Interestingly, thirteen states, including Colorado, Massachusetts, New Jersey, Pennsylvania, and Vermont had no fixed minimum marriage age.[60]

THE SOUTHERN STATES

In spite of low or absent minimum marriage age laws in states such as Massachusetts, socio-economic factors encouraged a later age for first marriages. Industrialization and commercialization in New England and the Mid-Atlantic states increased "and by 1800 much of coastal North American society had fallen in line with the European pattern" of late marriages. This was a pattern repeated in many parts of the country as America moved westward—a frontier period of rapid expansion, dropping marriage ages, and large families would be followed by a return to the higher marriage ages of Europe and the long-settled New England states. Nevertheless, there were parts of the United States that continued to have a large number of early marriages.[61]

This was particularly true in the Southern states, especially in the back country, "an area that included a large portion of the population, [where] the pattern of early marriage and large families continued."[62] From the time of the first settlements in the Chesapeake region and even up to the twentieth century, marriage happened at a much younger age than in Europe or even New England. Girls often married at age sixteen and younger.[63] For example, in Virginia "Betty Washington, a good-humored young woman who strikingly resembled her brother George, was just sixteen when she married young widower Fielding Lewis in May, 1750."[64]

---

59. S.N.D. North, comp., and Desmond Walls Allen, ed., *Marriage Laws in the United States, 1887–1906* (Conway, Arkansas: Arkansas Research, 1993).
60. Ibid.
61. John Mack Faragher, *Sugar Creek: Life on the Illinois Prairie* (New Haven: Yale University Press, 1986), 88. Faragher discusses on p. 87 how the pattern of early marriage and large families continued in western Europe until the sixteenth century, at which point the pattern changed significantly. According to him, "Historians do not agree on the exact causes of this trend toward later marriage, but it seemed to characterize societies with increasing commercial life."
62. Ibid., 88.
63. Michael Gordon, *The American Family in Social-Historical Perspective*, 3rd ed. (New York: St. Martin's Press, 1983), 16.
64. James S. Wamsley with Anne M. Cooper, *Idols, Victims, Pioneers: Virginia's Women from 1607* (Richmond, Virginia: Dietz Press, 1976), 63.

There were three significant differences between the upper class women of the North and South in the early 1800s. In the South, where property and wealth was a primary factor in match-making, cousin marriage was prevalent, and the median age of marriage was dramatically lower for women. "Daughters of fifteen and sixteen were frequently married off by anxious parents, or at an impatient bridegroom's insistence. There was no stigma attached to having a child bride, although planters were aware of the [social] disadvantages young wives suffered."[65]

Marriage patterns in the South, like the North, varied depending upon class and locality. Marriage patterns in the Appalachian Mountains and the southern frontier, for example, tended to have an even younger average age than the Chesapeake southern coastal regions: "Girls were thirteen to fifteen, on the average, when they married and the grooms were fifteen to eighteen."[66] Cousin marriage was also common on the southern frontier where people settled and then later moved on as intact "neighborhoods," a large group of people who lived within a certain proximity to each other and were connected by kinship, or at least kithship. Among some of these groups, interfamilial as well as intergenerational marriage took place, partly because the females married at a much younger age than their brothers.[67]

Southerners carried their marriage traditions with them as they moved west into Arkansas, Missouri, Texas and points beyond. There is a plethora of anecdotal evidence of early marriages among emigrants moving west. One example among many was early Oregon settler Mrs.

---

65. Catherine Clinton, *The Plantation Mistress: Woman's World in the Old South* (New York: Pantheon Books, 1982), 59 and 61. On p. 240 are the results of a survey of a sample group of Southern women born before 1759 and born after 1759. Of women born before 1759, 41.7% of all women were married between the ages of thirteen and nineteen. Thirteen percent of all women were married by age sixteen. The number of marriages involving young brides decreased among those born after 1759. Of all marriages, 28.9% were below the age of twenty. Almost seven percent of the women were sixteen or under at the time of marriage.

66. Dallas Bogan, "Early Appalachian Marriage Customs: Most Relationships Prearranged by Family Members," *History of Campbell County, Tennessee*, http://www.tngenweb.org/campbell/hist-bogan/marriage.html (accessed July 21, 2009).

67. Russell M. Reid, "Church Membership, Consanguineous Marriage, and Migration in a Scotch-Irish Frontier Population," *Journal of Family History* 13:4 (1988): 401. According to Reid, the intergenerational marriage was made possible in part because sisters were able to marry and bear children at such a younger age than their brothers. Catherine Clinton in *The Plantation Mistress*, 60, stated, "The onset of adulthood—at least as signaled by marriage—was much earlier for women than for men in southern culture."

John Kirkwood, who described how she married Kirkwood after having only met him several times. Her brother was to be married the next day and John Kirkwood, visiting for the wedding, asked her to marry him at the same time. She later recalled, "I was nearly fifteen years old and I thought it was high time that I got married so I consented."[68]

Mrs. Kirkwood was not alone. Memoirs suggest that fifteen was a typical age for women to marry during the earliest years on the Willamette Valley frontier. One woman recalled that "in those days the young men began wondering why a girl wasn't married if she was still single when she was 16."[69] There appears to have been social pressure to marry young. Furthermore, "[a]necdotal evidence also reveals that young women who migrated to Oregon with their families during their teenage years were sometimes pressured to marry significantly older men, and at least a few young women married men they hardy knew."[70]

This pattern of marriage was the same in other parts of the west, particularly during early settlement. In Colorado, for example, most women were married between the ages of sixteen and twenty-two.[71] While many young women married after their arrival at their destination, some would marry on the trail or even before departing for the west. Juliett Adeline Boston, for example, married at age fourteen to John Sutton Petty in 1838. Their marriage took place in Anderson County, Kentucky, right before they moved west to homestead in Cass County, Texas.[72]

Although Southerners brought a tradition of early marriage, at least for the women, there were other factors involved in marriage timing and mate selection. These centered on economic survival. "Across rural America in the mid-nineteenth century, men and women married at relatively young ages to secure land and a partner in labor. They could not afford to postpone marriage in search of the perfect mate. Uneven

---

68. Lillian Schlissel, *Women's Diaries of the Westward Journey* (New York: Schocken Books, 1982, 1992), 45.

69. Cynthia Culver Prescott, "'Why She Didn't Marry Him': Love, Power, and Marital Choice on the Far Western Frontier," *Western Historical Quarterly* 38 (Spring 2007): 29.

70. Ibid. According to Prescott, 28, historians Paul Burke and Donald DeBats have estimated the median age at first marriage of women living in Washington County, Oregon, in 1860 to be 17.4 years.

71. Julie Jones-Eddy, *Homesteading Women: An Oral History of Colorado, 1890–1950* (New York: Twayne Publishers, 1992).

72. Herbert C. Banks, *Daughters of the Republic of Texas: Patriot Ancestor Album* (Paducah, Kentucky: Turner Publishers, 2001), 219.

sex ratios and acute labor needs placed additional pressure on frontier women to marry early."[73]

Two marriage models

Economics, perhaps even more than tradition, most influenced the age of the bride at the time of marriage. This factor is particularly obvious when studying the pattern of migration westward and settlement in America. There appear to have been two different models regarding age at marriage and family size in American history. The first model involved families that were on the vanguard of westward migration. These were the ones who lived on the frontier and were constantly pushing west looking for new land and economic opportunity. In essence, western migration and the American frontier produced conditions that encouraged "early and continuous marriage of pioneer women." Because "girls married young and were in a constant state of matrimony," these frontier families produced large families.[74] These people were upwardly mobile, but also restless, and their pattern of life was to move from free land to free land, or at least to where land was cheap. This type of economy promoted "early marriage, and higher marital fertility than in areas where land [was] relatively less abundant."[75] Early marriage was common among these pioneers, and it was the pattern that persisted. They usually married "in mid-adolescent years" and produced large families of six or more children because of the need for physical labor in clearing land and making a living.[76]

The second marriage model reflected the lifestyle of families who lived in more settled areas of the country, such as New England and the Atlantic seaboard, as well as other parts of the country that were into the second or third generation of settlement. These families, believing themselves geographically and economically stable[77] and impacted by

---

73. Ibid., 28.
74. James E. Davis, *Frontier America, 1800–1840: A Comparative Demographic Analysis of the Settlement Process* (Glendale, California: Arthur H. Clark, 1977), 52.
75. Guillaume Vandenbroucke, "The American Frontier: Technology versus Immigration," *Review of Economic Dynamics* 11:2 (April 2008): 286.
76. *Women's Diaries of the Westward Journey*, 151–52.
77. Ibid.

"scarce land and low mortality,"[78] of a necessity married later and had fewer children.[79]

Emigrants altered their marriage plan

Although women married at a later age along the Eastern seaboard, those who emigrated from these areas seem to have adopted the same pattern of earlier marriage on the frontier as their Southern counterparts. As the frontier continued to push westward, those in the vanguard married at a younger age and had larger families, despite the marriage patterns of the areas from which they came. "A trip westward was almost a demographic journey back in time; family sizes in communities further west mirrored those in much-longer settled places a generation or two previously. The women of Sugar Creek, Illinois, for example, were marrying four to five years younger on the average than those in Sturbridge or Deerfield, Massachusetts."[80]

In Ohio of the 1820s "girls were generally married before they were seventeen."[81] The same was later true for Illinois and the Midwest and "Oregon's women's ages at first marriage were comparable to those who settled in Sugar Creek, Illinois, earlier in the nineteenth century."[82] For example, Hannah Elizabeth Totten, an early Kansas settler, married George Washington Thorne at the age of fifteen, the same age her own mother had married her father, Joseph Totten. Both of her parents were married in Iowa but were originally from further east.[83] In each locale, the age of brides at marriage slowly increased, due to economic and social progress, as well as changing views on the role of romantic love in

---

78. *The American Family in Social-Historical Perspective*, 16.
79. *Women's Diaries of the Westward Journey*, 151–52.
80. *The Reshaping of Everyday Life*, 69. Most of the Sugar Creek settlers originally hailed from New England. But even emigrants from other countries who settled on the American frontier followed frontier marriage patterns rather than those of their old country. For example, "The fact that [Norwegian emigrants] were able to marry so quickly once they reached the American frontier is itself evidence of the new opportunities for demographic relaxation," according to Jon Gjerde and Anne McCants, "Fertility, Marriage, and Culture: Demographic Processes Among Norwegian Immigrants to the Rural Middle West," *The Journal of Economic History* 55:4 (Dec 1995): 867.
81. *Frontier America*, 51–52.
82. Prescott, 29.
83. "Elizabeth (Totten) Thorne's Life on the Plains," Kansas Collection Articles, http://www.kancoll.org/articles/thorne.htm (accessed August 1, 2009).

mate selection. "In Oregon and throughout the Far West, the children of early settlers increasingly matched their lives to eastern middle-class standards as frontier conditions faded. ... Second-generation Oregonians' rapid adoption of eastern expectations for marriage reveals the rapidity with which the West became incorporated into the American nation during the late-nineteenth century."[84]

For example, by the time of the 1880 census, the common age at first marriage in the American Midwest, like the regions further east, had increased. At the time of the 1880 census, fewer than thirty-six percent of those married had done so by age nineteen. While this number was almost ten percent higher than New England's teen marriage rate, it was ten percent *lower* than it had been in the west when frontier conditions still prevailed.

Loss of the frontier and the rise of marriage ages

Figure 5.5 compares the 1880 marriage cohort cumulative distributions for white females by region. IPUMS classifies three quarters of the 1880 Midwest's marriage aged population as "rural." Marriage for female residents (min = 14.2, mean = 22.5) of rural areas where more land was available occurred substantially earlier than their urban counterparts (15.0, 24.3). (Recall that approximately 60% of age independent first marriages occur between the minimum and mean ages.)

The marriage patterns of the Northeast migrants settling in the Midwest (14.0, 23.1) highly resembled that of Midwest natives (14.3, 22.9), but sharply deviated from Northeast patterns (14.5, 24.5). In contrast, migrants from the South (13.8, 22.1) continued to marry significantly younger than the natives, and preserved all but earliest part of the Southern schedule (13.3, 22.2). From this limited information, it would appear that statistics from the Northeast where Joseph Smith was born and raised are the least suited to assessing the age of his plural spouses in 1840s Illinois. The Northeast had been settled for the longest period, and would be expected to have correspondingly higher ages at marriage. Yet, even emigrants raised under these conditions were quick to adapt to

---

84. Ibid., 45.

the new circumstances in which they found themselves on the frontier, and marriage ages dropped accordingly.

Recent scholarly developments have enabled extraction of accurate marital statistics from the 1850–1870 censuses.[85] It is now clear that marital ages were rising sharply in the U.S., and even more so in the Midwest during this period. Figure 5.6 collects regional statistics for 1850–1870 including the mean, minimum age, and cumulative marriage rates for 14-year-olds. Some entries are calculated over an extended period as sample size dictates. For the entries based on the smallest sample sizes, we have reported the standard deviation of the margin of error. Moving backwards in time, one begins to see the Midwest's statistical picture morph toward the younger marriage rates found on the frontier.

Mormon Conformance to the Pattern

The Midwest is split into an eastern and western division by the census bureau, with Illinois assigned to the more populous eastern division. In settling Nauvoo and its surroundings, Latter Day Saints straddled the divisional boundary at Illinois and Iowa. The two areas the Saints had recently lived in, Ohio and Missouri, were also the most populated states in their respective divisions. By 1880, Illinois had gained a substantial population with a marriage pattern (14.5, 23.3) typical of the eastern Midwest (14.4, 23.3). In 1850, Illinois had marital statistics (13.8, 21.6) that took on intermediate values between the western (13.7, 21.1) and eastern division (13.8, 21.9). As sample sizes are relatively small for Illinois, we combined it with its neighboring states (IA, MO, KY, IN, WI, MI) and obtained even lower results (13.6, 21.5).

Our national assumptions stated earlier amount to the mean age rising almost 0.4 years per decade between 1800 and 1850. The data from 1850 to 1880 show that Illinois mean age was rising more rapidly than that of the US. Thus it is conservative to use the national trend to estimate the 1840 Illinois mean at 21.2 years. The regional trend for Illinois

---

85. Added records in the IPUMS database allow for more precise adjustments for under-imputed marital status. Though done on a national level earlier, J. David Hacker showed that regional analysis for 1850–1870 can be successfully done in "Economic, Demographic, and Anthropometric Correlates of First Marriage in the Mid-Nineteenth-Century United States" *Social Science History* 32:3 (Fall 2008): 307–345.

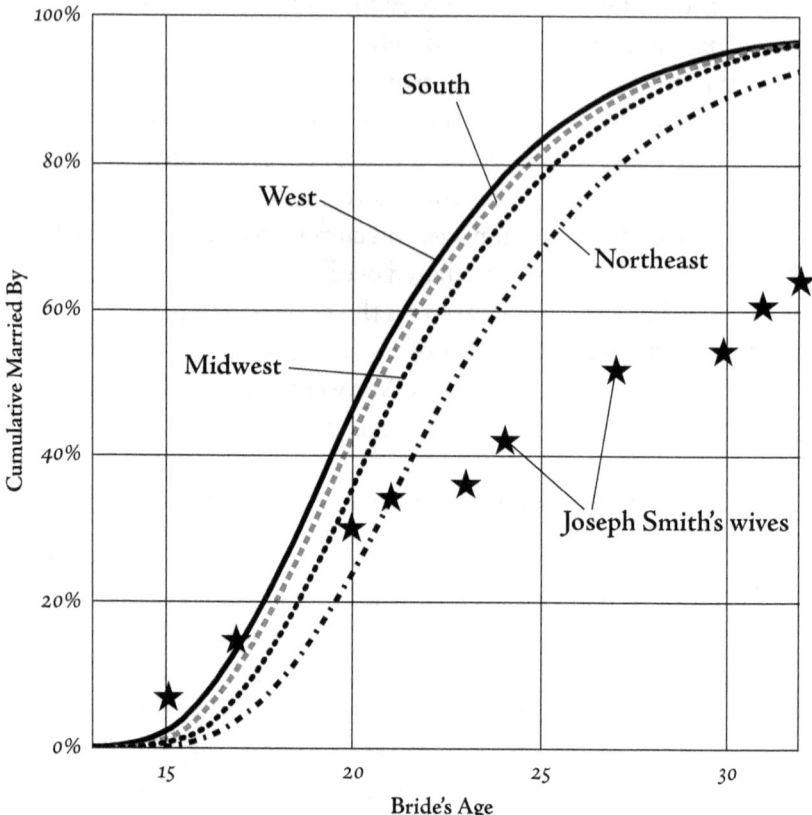

FIGURE 5.5: *1880 Marriage Cohort by Region*

to become increasingly similar to the eastern Midwest division the further one goes back suggests that dropping the minimum age to 13.7 is reasonable. Under these projections the 1840 Illinois marriage cohort consisted of the following cumulative percentage of teens: 14 (1.9%), 15 (6.7%), 16 (15.6%), 17 (27.4%), 18 (40.3%), and 19 (52.6%).

While age-structure dependent, county records have their own sources of bias due to the difficulty of identifying remarriages. Figure 5.7 contains marriage rates of five randomly selected counties (four from Illinois or Iowa and one from late frontier Nebraska). We attempted to cross check marriage pairs in genealogical databases to eliminate higher order marriages, but much less than the expected 12% were removed be-

Place	Mean			Minimum Age			Rate 14 and Under		
	1850	1860	1870	1850	1860	1870	1850	1860	1870
New England	24.4	23.8	24.4	13.5	13.8	14.0	1.0%	0.8%	0.7%
Mid Atlantic	23.6	23.5	23.5	13.7	13.7	13.9	1.0%	1.0%	0.8%
Northeast	23.8	23.6	23.8	13.7	13.7	13.8	1.0%	0.9%	0.8%
NE Central	21.9	22.0	22.5	13.8	13.6	14.1	1.3%	1.6%	0.8%
NW Central	21.1	21.2	21.7	13.7	14.0	13.8	1.9%	1.2%	1.4%
Midwest	21.8	21.9	22.3	13.8	13.7	14.0	1.5%	1.6%	1.0%
South Atlantic	22.3	22.4	22.6	13.5	13.3	13.5	1.7%	2.2%	1.6%
SE Central	22.0	21.9	22.6	13.1	13.4	13.5	3.2%	2.1%	1.8%
SW Central	20.8±0.3			13.1±0.2			3.9±0.9%		
South	22.0	21.9	22.4	13.3	13.3	13.3	2.5%	2.3%	2.1%
West	19.0±0.5			13.4±0.3			4.6±1.8%		
USA	22.7	22.5	22.7	13.5	13.5	13.7	1.5%	1.6%	1.3%

FIGURE 5.6: *Regional Marriage Activity.*

fore charting.[86] This inadequacy, coupled with smaller sample sizes and local variations, is largely why county marriage rates sometimes trail the Illinois estimates for the 1850 and 1880 marriage cohort.

The data: sources and potential Mormon bias

The two Mormon data sets likely overlap somewhat, but the selection criteria go to different extremes. For the Nauvoo (1839–1845) set, all marriages with adequate dating information from a compilation by Susan Easton Black[87] were used, while "Skolnick78" (1835–1845) includes only once-married couples.[88] Mormon monogamous marriages from a

---

86. See Technical Note 3.
87. Susan Easton Black, "Marriages in the Nauvoo Region 1839–1845," on-line database, using sources: Lyndon W. Cook, *Civil Marriages in Nauvoo and some outlying areas (1839–1845)* (Liberty Publishing Co., 1980); with additional data from *Times and Seasons, The Wasp, Nauvoo Neighbor*, and "A Record of Marriages in the City of Nauvoo," located at the Historical Department of The Church of Jesus Christ of Latter-day Saints. <http://www.worldvitalrecords.com/indexinfo.aspx?ix=usa_il_nauvoo_marriages> (accessed July 15, 2010).
88. M. Skolnick, L. Bean, D. May, V. Arbon, K. De Nevers and P. Cartwright, "Mormon Demographic History I. Nuptiality and Fertility of Once-Married Couples," *Populations Studies* 32

Kirtland data set[89] are not shown, but have a teenage marriage rate of almost 50% compared to 33% and 43% for the two that are shown.

While likely not statistically significant, Nauvoo actually had fewer teen brides than in some of the surrounding counties. In Lee County, Iowa, directly across the Mississippi River from Nauvoo, between 1837 and 1850, of the 313 recorded marriages, forty-five percent were women aged thirteen to nineteen. Twelve brides were under sixteen at the time of their marriage, including two thirteen-year-olds who married a twenty-year-old and thirty-three-year-old, respectively.[90]

Of course, there were a number of Latter Day saints residing in Lee County until late 1846 and some moderns might suspect that the high number of young brides was reflective of Mormon culture, rather than frontier demographics. No such Mormon influence existed in Louisa County, Iowa, however, which was also situated on the Mississippi River two counties above Lee County. Mormon settlement here was almost non-existent, even though the country was opened for settlement at almost the same time as Lee County.

In non-Mormon Louisa County, between 1842 and 1852, fifty-one percent of marriages were to brides aged nineteen and younger. In fact, seventeen percent of the females married when they were sixteen and younger.[91] Clearly, young marriage ages seen in Lee County are not a case of Mormons *skewing* the samples, but rather *conforming* to the dominant marriage trends in their frontier society.

(1978): 14. Marriage rates estimated from the published mean (21.35), standard deviation (4.26), and knowledge gained from 1910 about how the GLG shaping parameter changes when only once-marrieds are considered.

89. Milton V. Backman Jr. with Keith Perkins and Susan Easton, "A profile of Latter-day Saints of Kirtland, Ohio and members of Zion's Camp 1830–1839: vital statistics and sources," complied in cooperation with the Department of Church History and Doctrine, Brigham Young University, in Family History Library, Salt Lake City, Utah.

90. Joyce S. Cowles and Karen Kester, *Lee County, Iowa Marriages* v. 1 (Des Moines: Iowa Genealogical Society, 1987). There were a total of 328 women listed between 1837 and 1850. Of those women, fifteen were second marriages and were not included in the final figures. While there were a number of women who did not originally have an age recorded, most were identified using other sources. The ages of five brides were ultimately unidentifiable. 141 women were aged nineteen or younger while 167 women were aged twenty and older.

91. "Louisa County (Iowa) Marriages," 1842–1852, http://iagenweb.org/louisa/LCmarriageage.htm (accessed April 14, 2009). While there were a total of 100 marriages recorded during this time-period, two were second marriages and were not included in the final statistics.

The marriage records from Sangamon County[92] and Cass County[93] come from the same general area, albeit later in the 19th century. These confirm the census suggestion of a rapid decline in teenage marriage rates. Though having a smaller total sample size (32) than encompassed by Joseph Smith's wives (33), the Hitchcock County[94] sample shows that even at such a late date it is possible to find frontier regions of the country with a higher percentage of 14 year old brides. As will now be seen, neither Joseph Smith or Hitchcock county were abnormal for their time.

Comparing Joseph Smith's plural marriages to the marriage patterns of the Illinois area

Figure 5.7 shows the frequency of Joseph's teenage wives by age compared to some contemporary marriage cohorts. In comparison with our estimate for 1840 Illinois, only Joseph's rate for fourteen-year-olds (6.1% vs. 1.94%) is higher, but not so much so that it is abnormal. Although tests for normality are somewhat arbitrary, we will adopt a tough standard of a 95% critical region. Suppose we were to randomly select a group of 33 brides based on 1840 Illinois statistics. We could repeat that processes until a large ensemble of such groups was generated. We wish to determine the expected percentage of those groups containing at least a couple of 14 year old brides. If Joseph Smith's cohort puts him in the top or bottom 2.5% (approximately 2 standard deviations from the mean in a normal distribution), then we would conclude his behavior was abnormal for his time and place.

Since Joseph's profile only ranks in the upper 87 percentile[95] for 14-year-olds, it is not statistically significant. The high cumulative rate can be adequately explained by the small sample size of 33. At the 95%

---

92. Eileen Gochanour, "Sangamon County, Illinois Marriage Applications — March 16, 1879 thru December 31, 1881," < http://sangamon.ilgenweb.net/marr1879.htm > (accessed July 15, 2010).
93. "Cass County [Iowa] Marriages," 1853–1881, <http://iagenweb.org/cass/bmd/mar-1853-1881.htm> (accessed July 15, 2010).
94. "Hitchcock County [Nebraska] Marriages, Courthouse records starting 26 Jan 1888," 1888–1898 <http://www.usgennet.org/usa/ne/county/hitchcock/olres/marr1888.html> (accessed July 15, 2010).
95. See Technical Note 4.

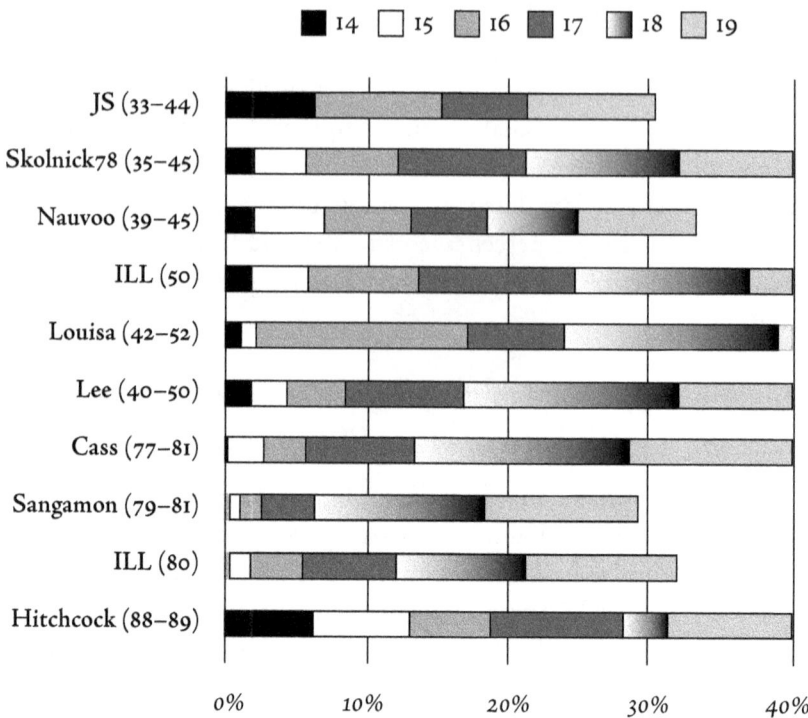

FIGURE 5.7: *Teenage marriage rates for 5 randomly selected counties, Joseph Smith's plural wives, 2 Mormon data sets, and the Illinois census.*

benchmark, Joseph Smith's cohort would be normal for any region with a cumulative rate of at least 0.75% for fourteen-year-olds. Plural marriage aside, Joseph Smith would have been normal in any of the four major areas of the US (Northeast, Midwest, South, West) until as late as 1880. Nationally, marriage at 14 years of age did not become that rare until 1980.

Contemporary anecdotal confirmation

Joseph's polygyny even provides us with an interesting test case of our statistical conclusions. Nine months after marrying seventeen-year-old Sarah Ann Whitney, Joseph arranged for Joseph C. Kingsbury to enter into "a pretended marriage," to disguise their polygamous arrangement.[96] As Compton notes, "[o]utsiders would have suspected nothing unusual in the relationship" between Sarah Ann and her pretended husband. Yet, Kingsbury was born in 1812, and was thus only seven years younger than Joseph Smith. It is implausible that the LDS leader would have chosen a "front husband" for Sarah Ann who would have attracted unwanted attention. Thus, if the age differential between Sarah Ann and Joseph Smith was atypical, strange, or socially risky, it makes little sense to think that a relationship with Joseph Kingsbury would have been much more acceptable. The Prophet's choice of Kingsbury as his marital decoy demonstrates that such differences in age were not likely to attract comment.

Conclusion

We have demonstrated through an analysis of the relevant scholarly literature covering traditional, legal, sociological, and economic trends, that the relatively young marital ages among nineteenth-century Saints did, indeed, fit within the larger historical context of American society. This included Joseph Smith's wives, whose age at marriage was well within the norm for his time and place on the nineteenth-century American frontier.

Given the secrecy which attended Nauvoo polygamy, it would be unusual to find complaints about the bride's marriage age or the age differential during Joseph Smith's lifetime. But if Joseph had married only one of his polygamous wives in a typical monogamous marriage, both the statistical data and historical clues make it unlikely that their ages would have been much remarked upon. Modern historians, critics, or readers must consider marriage ages in the proper historical time *and place*—the American frontier—if they are to properly understand and characterize these relationships.

Technical Notes

1. Cohorts are arranged by segmenting the population into groups (usually by birth year) and then observing events in each individual's

---

96. Compton, *In Sacred Loneliness*, 351–352; citing Joseph C. Kingsbury, "The History of Joseph C. Kingsbury," Marriot Library, MS 522, 13.

life history. A synthetic cohort can be used to approximate these life histories if the conditions found in a calendar year are assumed to remain constant over time. For example, the 1865 birth cohort in the 1880 census would synthetically have the same marriage statistics in 1881 as the 1864 birth cohort did in 1880, and so on. See Fitch (2005) 28–39 for more information about using synthetic birth cohorts.

2. From 1880 onwards, the IPUMS website provides complete information about marital status for each individual in its census samples. Further breakdowns by sex, age, race, and region are possible. From this raw data, synthetic birth cohorts can be formed and cumulative marriage rates (the percentage ever married divided by the total) calculated. Demographers often approximate two statistical measures, the singulate mean age at marriage (SMAM) and the percentage ever married by age 50 (C_o), using Hajnal's method. The spread (or standard deviation) of the distribution about the mean marital age can be determined from optimally fitting the widely used Coale-McNeil model to the raw census data.

From 1850–1870 IPUMS imputes marital status from analyzing households. As this method underestimates actual cumulative marriage rates, Hacker (2003, 2008) has calculated correction factors for the different age groups. For 1800–1840 we assume that SMAM was 21.0 following the discussion in Smith (1993) and Haines (1996) and allow SMAM to drop linearly from its 1850 value. We also assume that the minimum age of eligibility of 13.6 held steady in the 19th century following Sanderson (1979), but using a slightly lower value based on our calculations. These two assumptions are sufficient to estimate the Coale-McNeil nuptiality schedule for 1800–1840.

An additional step was performed to make the cumulative marriage rates dependent on age structure in figs. 1–2. Reconstruction of a census year marriage cohort must take into account that the 19th century was characterized by high birthrates and deathrates. More technical details about our data analysis methods are available in Keller (2010).

3. The 1910 U.S. census was the first to include information about remarriage. About 12% of white brides under age 50 in the previous marriage year cohort were starting a second (or higher) marriage. Removing these brides lowers the mean age by over a year and matches the

cumulative rates found from adjusting synthetic birth year cohorts. Very few teenagers had adequate time to first be married, then be divorced or widowed, then go through a mourning period, and also court and marry a second husband.

4. The percentile (P) of randomly selected marriage cohorts of size N=33 follows a binomial distribution.

For two fourteen-year-olds in 1840 Illinois, p = 1.94% and:

$$P = \sum_{n=0}^{1} \binom{33}{n} p^n (1-p)^n$$

Early Marriage in the New England and Northeastern States, and in Mormon Polygamy: What Was the Norm?

by Todd M. Compton

THE RAID ON the FLDS compound in Texas that took place in April 2008 has brought polygamy to national attention again. Since the FLDS church is a break-off from the Mormon church, this has inevitably led the media to look at polygamy in nineteenth-century Mormonism to give context for the modern practice. And because the raid was spurred by reports of marriages involving underage teenage girls, the question of whether this aspect of FLDS polygamy has roots in nineteenth-century Mormon polygamy has arisen.[1]

In April 2008, historian and journalist Timothy Egan wrote a short opinion piece in the on-line *New York Times* that explicitly found the

---

1. Incidentally, historians of family life call the practice of teenagers marrying "early marriage," a term I will use in this article. I will refer to marriage of girls at ages 14 and 15 as "very early marriage." Some historians refer to girls marrying at the age of 14 and 15 or lower "child marriage." Thomas Patrick Monahan, "One Hundred Years of Marriages in Massachusetts," *The American Journal of Sociology* 56 (May, 1951): 534–545, 540.

roots of questionable FLDS practices in "orthodox" Mormon polygamy in the 1800s.[2] Many conservative Mormons have strongly denied this, though they do not deny that nineteenth-century Latter-day Saints, including church founder Joseph Smith, often married teenagers as plural wives. However, conservatives have stated that young women marrying very early was an accepted part of the culture at the time. Among them is historian Craig Foster, who published a review-article that dealt with the subject in *FARMS Review of Books*.[3] LDS church historian Marlin K. Jensen wrote a reply to Egan that appeared on the LDS church's official website,[4] and general authority Todd Christofferson has also defended Mormon polygamists of the previous century in an interview.[5]

---

2. Timothy Egan, "Faith of Our Fathers," New York Times, April 23, 2008, http://egan.blogs.nytimes.com/2008/04/23/faith-of-our-fathers/?scp=13&sq=Timothy%20Egan&st=cse (accessed March 4, 2009). Egan wrote: "It would have been just another Christian faith had not Smith let his libido lead him into trouble. Before he died at the hands of a mob, he married at least 33 women and girls; the youngest was 14, and was told she had to become Smith's bedmate or risk eternal damnation." He quotes Brodie later on, and is in her camp. See also his "The Persistence of Polygamy," *New York Times*, February 28, 1999, http://query.nytimes.com/gst/fullpage.html?res=9507E1DD133DF93BA15751C0A96F958260&sec=&spon=&pagewanted=1 (accessed March 4, 2009).

3. Craig Foster, "Doing Violence to Journalistic Integrity," *FARMS Review of Books* 16:1 (2004), 149 74, http://farms.byu.edu/publications/review/?vol=16&num=1&id=530 (accessed March 4, 2009.) This is a review of Jon Krakauer, *Under the Banner of Heaven: A Story of Violent Faith* (NY: Doubleday, 2003). Other conservative LDS views of the marriage age question can be found at the FAIR site: [David] Keller, "Lawrence O'Donnell's Charges of Rape," January 13, 2008, at http://www.fairblog.org/2008/01/13/lawrence-odonnells-charges-of-rape/; [David] Keller, "19th century nuptiality and anti-Mormon propaganda," November 5, 2009, at http://www.fairblog.org/2009/11/05/nuptiality-and-propagand/; Gregory L. Smith, "Polygamy book/Age of wives," http://en.fairmormon.org/Polygamy_book_chapter:Age_of_wives. These three authors have written an article in this book which I have not seen. Their work as published on the internet is impressive, though I disagree with arguments and focuses at times. Not having a statistical background, I was not able to follow Keller's statistical analysis, in "19th century nuptiality." This may be the blind spot of a document-oriented historian. For a worthwhile discussion of the issue at the middle-of-the-road Mormon blog, Times and Seasons, see Kaimi Wenger, "Brides Among the Beehives," June 13, 2007, at http://timesandseasons.org/index.php/2007/06/brides-among-the-beehives/ (accessed March 4, 2009).

4. Marlin K. Jensen, "Polygamy Then and Now," May 5, 2008, in the Newsroom of the official LDS website, http://newsroom.lds.org/ldsnewsroom/eng/commentary/polygamy-then-and-now (accessed on January 11, 2010).

5. "Q&A with Mormon Elder," an interview with Reuters, June 11, 2007, http://www.reuters.com/article/idUKFLE15338920070611?pageNumber=1&virtualBrandChannel=0 (accessed March 4, 2009).

Conservative Mormons have had the tendency to make statements like the following: "marriages of younger girls were not uncommon in the past," as Foster writes. It seems to me that there were two problems with this kind of statement. First, it is so general that it doesn't help much. In Foster's statement, "Not uncommon" and "the past" are very broad, vague terms. If we say that marriages at an early age were "common," what does common mean? Ten percent of marriages? Five? Two percent? So it would be better to progress from broad generalizations to some kind of specificity, in time and place. (And in different places and times, percentages will vary a great deal.)

Second, often the evidence for such statements comes from cultures very different from nineteenth-century New England and northeastern America (the cultural background for Mormonism).[6] The fact that colonists in *seventeenth-century Quebec* or gypsies in Serbia arranged marriages for their children in their early teens is not the evidence needed to examine nineteenth-century American marriage practice.[7] If one argues that early marriage was common in Joseph Smith's environment, one would need to produce statistical evidence that it was common in the nineteenth-century New England and northeastern states. The data from exotic cultures may be interesting and worth discussing, but they are not directly relevant to nineteenth-century American culture.

Third, conservative Mormons have sometimes argued from a legal basis—for instance, stating that the age of consent for young women was twelve in such and such countries and states at such and such times. If early marriage was legal, yet was extremely rare, the legal data, while interesting, are not directly relevant.

Therefore, I would like to frame the question in this way: Mormon polygamy, from its earliest beginnings,[8] often included "early marriage" or "very early marriage." Were such early marriage ages typical of nine-

---

6. For the specific states I am considering, see the IPUMS section below.

7. For examples of early marriage outside the European marriage pattern, see Craig Foster, "Doing Violence to Journalistic Integrity."

8. Of Joseph Smith's thirty-three plural marriages that can be reliably documented (in my view), ten were marriages to teen-age girls (including a marriage to fourteen-year-old Helen Mar Kimball, daughter of apostle Heber C. Kimball, and a marriage to Nancy Winchester, who was probably fifteen when she married Joseph). Todd Compton, *In Sacred Loneliness: the Plural Wives of Joseph Smith* (SLC: Signature Books, 1997). See also Richard Bushman, *Joseph Smith: Rough Stone Rolling* (New York: Knopf, 2005), 644n1, who counts 32 plural marriages, and George

teenth-century New England and northeastern states culture? Was marriage age in plural marriage lower, equal to, or higher than non-Mormon marriage in northeast America?

I should state at the outset that I am not a social historian specializing in the family, but I will refer to the work of respected social historians of America who do answer this question. In addition, social historians' conclusions often are based on statistics derived from vital records, and I am not trained as a statistician. I will try to reflect their conclusions accurately. Readers interested in further analysis of the numbers I give below should refer to demographic historians I cite to examine their methodology and the records they are reflecting.

I will also directly report some census data, from U.S. census database IPUMS, in a limited way.

Statistical evidence can have great value and yet have limitations; it obviously can be difficult to understand, and can be misleading. According to a joke that statisticians tell, a statistician, a historian and an economist went duck hunting. When a duck flew by, the historian shot ten feet above it; the economist shot ten feet below it; and the statistician said, "Got him!"

The American social historians I will cite often use the term "mean" which has been defined as "sum of the observations divided by the number of observations." But often the mean does not reflect important evidence regarding a particular group. For instance, if a polygamist marries plural wives at the ages of 17, 18, 19, 22 and 65, the mean marriage age, 28.2, is skewed by the 65 outlier. Sometimes authors refer to "median," which selects the center age in the data group; this prevents outliers from skewing the results as much. Thus in the example I gave above, the median is 19. If the author provides standard deviation figures for a mean, it helps the reader understand the spread of the data better.

Often the historians I refer to provided only the mean—"mean age at first marriage" is a common phrase. Therefore, on the upper end, ages of women at 65 will be rare, and marriages in the early or mid 20s will be much more common. On the lower end, ages of women before 14 will

---

Smith, *Nauvoo Polygamy "...But We Called It Plural Marriage"* (Salt Lake City: Signature Books, 2008), 223–24, who counts 37.

be rare. So when authors refer to mean age at first marriage, we should remember that this is the spread of ages that we are talking about.

I will first give a broad overview of marriage age in history, in order to give a background for marriage age patterns that occur both in nineteenth-century America and in Mormon polygamy. Then I will look at marriage age in colonial America, to give the background for the nineteenth century, and to show that "very early marriage" was not common during that earlier era. After this I will examine marriage age in the nineteenth century in the New England and northeastern states, including data from the IPUMS census project for 1850. This is the heart of my paper and argument. Following this, I will then give a brief overview of marriage age in Utah in the 19th century, citing family historians such as Kathryn Daynes and Larry Logue, in order to compare Utah marriage age with marriage age in the east. The data cited will show that marriage age in Mormon polygamy was lower than in New England and northeastern states, and that polygamy was a cause of early marriage among women. I will also provide evidence that very early marriage—marriage of young women aged 14 and 15—was an accepted part of Mormon culture in the nineteenth century.[9]

Early Marriage in History

Before we focus on marriage age in America, it will be helpful to discuss factors that have affected marriage age throughout history.

Economics has always been an important factor affecting marriage age, as young people, especially in relatively modern Western Europe, have often delayed marriage until they achieved some financial stability. A bad economy at a certain time or place could cause marriages that were relatively late. Family historian Maris Vinovskis writes,

> In Western Europe in the sixteenth and seventeenth century, individuals usually did not marry unless they were economically able to create and maintain their own home. Under these circumstances, an early marriage was usually considered desirable as it signified relative independence from others and the start of one's own family (Stone, 1977). The requirement of being able to maintain an independent home

---

9. Obviously, any one of these sections of my paper could be expanded into a book. A detailed study of marriage age in Utah polygamy would be especially valuable.

forced many individuals to postpone their marriages or to remain single throughout their lives.¹⁰

This highlights a difference between elite and non-elite marriage, for elites, generally well-to-do, were financially able to marry earlier.

In the eighteenth-century Western world, family historian Beatrice Gottlieb concludes, people retreated from early marriage and late marriage. Society was edging toward a "perfect" marriage age—somewhere between 21 and 25, with women usually a year or two younger than men.¹¹

Family historians talk about a European pattern of marriage age, which can be summed up succinctly: Europeans married later than non-Europeans.¹² In the European pattern, on the average, men tended to marry in their late twenties (26–30) and women in their early or mid-twenties (24–27).

One specific cause of early marriage was a colonizing or pioneering situation, in which men greatly outnumbered the women or young women in a colony.¹³ Competition for wives naturally tends to drive down the marriage age of young women. However, after the imbalance of sexes ends in a colony, marriage age generally rises to normal levels in a generation or two. The classic example of low marriage age in a colony is the famous *Filles du Roi* in the mid-seventeenth-century colonial Quebec. Some 220 young women, many teens, were shipped to Canada because there was a great preponderance of men in the early colony. However, Gottlieb notes, "Only the first wave of French Canadian wives were so young."¹⁴

Another specific factor that has caused early marriage was the tendency for marriages to be used to create political or dynastic bonds. One

---

10. *An "Epidemic" of Adolescent Pregnancy? Some Historical and Policy Considerations* (NY: Oxford University Press, 1988), 7.

11. Beatrice Gottlieb, *The Family in the Western World from the Black Death to the Industrial Age* (NY: Oxford University Press, 1993), 60–61.

12. J. Hajnal, "European Marriage Patterns in Perspective," 101–43, in D. V. Glass and D. E. C. Eversley, *Population in History: Essays in Historical Demography* (Chicago: Aldine Publishing Company, 1965), 121. Hajnal's thesis pertains to Europe after the 16th century; before then, demographic evidence is lacking.

13. Gottlieb, *The Family in the Western World*, 60–61; Vinovskis, *An "Epidemic" of Adolescent Pregnancy?*, 8–9.

14. Gottlieb, *The Family in the Western World*, 60–61.

family historian, Stephanie Coontz, in her book *Marriage: A History: From Obedience to Intimacy or How Love Conquered Marriage*, has argued that it was not until the end of the 1700s that "marriage came to be seen as a private relationship between two individuals rather than one link in a larger system of political and economic alliances."[15] Classical Roman history is replete with examples of dynastic marriages. Often political marriages were arranged by parents, and were performed when their children were very young. Young women in elite families would simply expect that they would be married to further their families' best financial and political interests. Coontz entitles one chapter in her book "Playing the Bishop, Capturing the Queen: Aristocratic Marriages in Early Medieval Europe."[16] Marriage was part of the chess game of power politics.

In this, and in other ways, the marriage age among elites and lower classes differed. The lower classes had no need for political marriages, therefore non-elite young women were not married young for dynastic purposes.

When early marriage occurred to promote alliances among aristocrats and "urban patricians," sometimes these marriages were marriages on paper only, according to social historian, Beatrice Gottlieb.[17] They did not turn into actual marriages until the parties were older. Sometimes they never did turn into actual marriages.

So in European history, we have often had situations in which marriage age was high or low due to specific circumstances, a bad economy or a colonizing situation; however, when the abnormal circumstances ended, marriage age generally returned to its previous level.[18]

---

15. Stephanie Coontz, *Marriage: A History: From Obedience to Intimacy of How Love Conquered Marriage* (New York: Viking, 2005), 146.
16. Coontz, *Marriage: A History*, 88–103.
17. Gottlieb, *The Family in the Western World*, 60–61.
18. It is entirely true that in the ancient world, and in non-Western cultures, you can find many examples of early marriage. In India, in one province at a certain time, the *average* age at marriage was thirteen. Generally, Monahan states, these "very early marriages" were not consummated until the young women was sixteen or in her upper teens. Thomas Patrick Monahan, *The Pattern of Age at Marriage in the United States*, 2 vols. (Philadelphia : Printed by Stephenson-Brothers, 1951), 1:44, see also 43–47. Since older men sometimes married literal children, these children were often widowed at an early age. "In one province," writes marriage-age authority Monahan, "10% of the females under 5 years of age [are widows], and over 50% of those under 15 years of age are widows." Since there was a prohibition on widows remarrying, those girls and young women were prohibited from normal marriage in their later lives. "Early marriage" is not just a theoretical

Colonial New England

In the New England colonies, we find the same pattern that family historians have noted in colonial situations elsewhere. The early preponderance of men caused the marriage age of women to decrease, but as colonies became less "colonial," marriage age rose.

In addition, we have seen that advantageous economic situations caused marriage ages to lower somewhat. Therefore in America, where land was available, and you could build a log cabin and start a farm fairly easily (compared to England, for example), a young man would not have to put off marriage as long as in Europe. Therefore, logically enough, marriage ages were somewhat lower in America than in Europe. But a key question is, how much lower?

Early social historians of Colonial America, working from literary references, assumed that Americans married much younger than did the English. For example, Arthur Calhoun wrote, in 1960, "The early Puritans married young.... Girls often married at sixteen or under. Old maids were ridiculed or even despised. A woman became an 'antient maid' at twenty-five."[19] However, such statements have more recently been disputed. While these early social historians based their conclusions on assumption or on scattered literary references, a new generation of historians, John Demos, Philip Greven, and Kenneth Lockridge, used statistical evidence derived from town and church vital records, and produced an entirely different picture. Vinovskis writes, "They discovered (to everyone's surprise) that few New England girls had married as early as age fifteen or sixteen." Instead, the age of first marriage in colonial New England showed that women typically "married in their very early twenties and men married during their late twenties."[20] Monahan also discusses how many of these early social historians erred because they made generalizations not based on statistical evidence.[21]

---

issue in the world today; it is a common practice in many nations, and often has a negative impact on the lives of the persons involved. For a contrast, to show the modern European pattern, in Great Britain, at the end of the nineteenth century, 73% of women were single at age 20–24 and 42% were single at age 25–29. Hajnal, "European Marriage Patterns," 102.

19. Arthur Calhoun, *A Social History of the American Family* (New York, Barnes & Noble, 1960), 67.

20. Vinovskis, *An "Epidemic" of Adolescent Pregnancy?*, 8.

21. Monahan, *Pattern of Age at Marriage*, 1:104–5, 99–102.

Thus, in colonial New England (still long before the mid-nineteenth century, when LDS polygamy began), marriage age was fairly low, compared to the European pattern, but the age of marriage among women gradually increased as the colonies became less "colonial."[22]

In Demos' *A Little Commonwealth: Family Life in Plymouth Colony*, the key evidence is Table IV, "First Marriages in Plymouth Colony," in an appendix.[23] Mean age of women at time of first marriage was: "Born Before 1600": no data; "Born 1600–25": 20.6; "Born 1625–50": 20.2; "Born 1650–75": 21.3; and "Born 1675–1700": 22.3. This is still long before the 1830s and 40s, but it shows the gradual rise in marriage age as Plymouth became less of a colony. Demos writes, "The average age at marriage in this period was, in fact, much higher than has usually been imagined."[24]

Kenneth A. Lockridge studied colonial Dedham, Massachusetts, and commented on the general perception that American marriage age was much lower than in Europe. However, he noted that the average age at marriage in Europe "ranged around twenty-five years for women and twenty-seven years for men," but in Dedham the average age was "twenty-three for women and twenty-five for men."[25] This was lower, but not drastically lower.

Philip J. Greven studied marriages in four colonial generations in Andover, Massachusetts. In the fourth generation, he found that fourteen was the lowest age of marriage in his data, but unfortunately, he does not tell us how many fourteen-year-olds married. He does say that only "31.9 [percent of women] married before the age of 21."[26] In the first generation at Andover the mean age of marriage for women was 19.0, but in the fourth generation, it was 23.2.[27]

---

22. Vinovskis, *An "Epidemic" of Adolescent Pregnancy?*, 8.
23. John Demos, *A Little Commonwealth: Family Life in Plymouth Colony* (New York: Oxford University Press, 1970), 193.
24. Demos, *A Little Commonwealth*, 151.
25. Kenneth A. Lockridge, *A New England Town: the First Hundred Years, Dedham, Massachusetts, 1636–1736* (New York: Norton, 1970), 66.
26. Philip J. Greven, *Four Generations: Population, Land, and Family in Colonial Andover, Massachusetts* (Ithaca, NY: Cornell University Press, 1970), 209.
27. Vinovskis, *Fertility in Massachusetts*, Table 3.1, "Comparisons of the Mean Age at First Marriage in Colonial America," 44

Incidentally, marriage ages in the southern colonies were lower than in the New England colonies,[28] but the focus of this paper is on the New England and northeastern states.

Nineteenth-Century New England and Northeastern States

These are colonial data; our target time period is of course later, in the mid-nineteenth century. However, the colonial research has shown that as time went on, and America became less "colonial," women married later, and early marriage became increasingly rare. This progression would continue into the nineteenth century.

One historian who has dealt with the nineteenth century, Thomas Patrick Monahan, has made marriage age his specialty, authoring a two-volume work entitled *The Pattern of Age at Marriage in the United States*.[29] According to Monahan, the mean age of marriage in 1845 Massachusetts was 26.1 for males and 23.9 for females.[30] Just for comparison, in 1948, the mean age for men was 26.5, while for women it was 24.2.

In Massachusetts, in 1845, only 25.9 percent of women married for the first time were under 20. This figure does not tell us how many were 14, 15, 16, 17, 18, or 19, but it does tell us that about a quarter of the marriages were teen marriages.[31] In 1885, only 18.2 percent of married women were under 20, 72 percent were age 20–30, and 90.2 percent were under 30.[32]

Monahan has data for a number of northeastern states in the general period of Mormon polygamy. In New York State in 1855, 32.1 percent of women married for the first time were below 20[33]; in Rhode Island, in 1860, 28.9 percent of women married for the first time were below 20.[34]

---

28. Vinovskis, *An "Epidemic" of Adolescent Pregnancy?*, 8–9; David Hackett Fischer, *Albion's Seed: Four British Folkways in America* (New York: Oxford University Press, 1989), 76, 284–85.

29. Monahan, *The Pattern of Age at Marriage in the United States* (1951), see also his "One Hundred Years of Marriages in Massachusetts."

30. Monahan, "One Hundred Years of Marriages in Massachusetts," Table 1, 541. (The median age was 25 for males and 22.7 for females.)

31. Monahan, *The Pattern of Age at Marriage in the United States*, 1.160.

32. Ibid., 153. See also Michael R. Haines, "Long-term Marriage Patterns in the United States from Colonial Times to the Present," *History of the Family* 1.1 (1996): 15—39.

33. Monahan, *The Pattern of Age at Marriage in the United States*, 1.168.

34. Ibid., 173.

In Vermont, in 1858, 38.2 percent of women married for the first time were below 20. Thus women had a mean age at marriage of 22.6, median age 21.4.[35]

In most of these states, we cannot break down the pre-twenty age groups, as I mentioned. However, in New Jersey, Monahan gives detailed statistics on the pre-20 age groups. Figure 6.1 shows the data for 3,055 native-born women in first marriages in 1848–50[36].

Age	Percent	Age	Percent	Age	Percent
14	.1	22	11.0	30	1.1
15	.4	23	7.8	31	.4
16	1.4	24	5.6	32	.4
17	4.4	25	5.3	33	.2
18	13.4	26	2.8	34	.2
19	13.1	27	2.3	35-39	.8
20	15.1	28	1.9	40-44	.2
21	11.2	29	1.0	45&up	.1

Thus 32.8 percent of women were married in their teenage years, which is relatively high. However, we can see that the great majority of these were from the last two teenage years, 18 and 19. Marriages at age 14 were extremely rare, .1 of one percent. Marriage at age 15 was also less than one percent. Marriage at age 16 was not common; only 1.4 percent married at this age.

Again, as we have generally seen, age of marriage rises through time. For example, in 1947, in New Jersey, Figure 6.2 shows the marriage age percentages for women aged 14–20[37].

Age	Percent
14	
15	.2
16	1.0
17	2.6
18	7.4
19	10.7
20	12.7

---

35. Ibid., 175–76.
36. Ibid., 196.
37. Ibid.

Vinovskis observes that solid information on the nineteenth-century marriages is scarce, but does make some generalizations from census records. He states that the "mean age at first marriage in Massachusetts from 1845 to 1860 was about twenty-six for males and twenty-four for females.... Thus, at no time during the colonial or early national period did large numbers of very young adolescents regularly marry in New England."[38]

According to Monahan, very early marriages in nineteenth-century Massachusetts—females at the age of fifteen and under and males at seventeen years and under—"rarely exceeded 0.5 percent of all first marriages and more often amounted to less."[39] In the late eighteen hundreds in Massachusetts, very early marriages of females were at 0.3–0.4 percent.

Thus, Vinovskis writes:

> As the eighteenth century progressed and the sexual imbalance corrected itself, male colonists no longer had to take a young wife.... While some Americans had praised the virtues of very early marriages, few of them personally followed that advice. Indeed, in the nineteenth century many women increasingly felt that they should enjoy their youthful independence for as long as possible before settling down to the responsibilities of married life.[40]

Demographic historians Catherine Fitch and Steven Ruggles have estimated marriage age for the United States in 1850: the mean age of marriage for native-born whites was 26.6 for men and 22.9 for women (the median age was slightly lower, for men 25.3 and for women 21.3).[41] However, this includes southern states, so it is lower than it would be if Fitch and Ruggles had limited themselves to New England and northeastern states. According to Fitch and Ruggles, marriage age for women stayed stable until 1870 (though marriage age dropped for men after the

---

38. Vinovskis, *An "Epidemic" of Adolescent Pregnancy?*, 8–9.
39. Monahan, "One Hundred Years of Marriages in Massachusetts," 540.
40. Vinovskis, *An "Epidemic" of Adolescent Pregnancy?*, 8–9.
41. Catherine Fitch and Steven Ruggles, "Historical Trends in Marriage Formation," in Linda Waite, Christine Bachrach, Michelle Hindin, Elizabeth Thomson, and Arland Thornton, eds., *Ties that Bind: Perspectives on Marriage and Cohabitation* (Hawthorne, New York: Aldine de Gruyter, 2000), 59–88, 63. At age 17, 10% of native-born white women were married, while at age 21.3, 50% were married. See Table 4.1, 83. Unfortunately, such a chart as this does not give a breakdown on the ages before 17.

Civil War), and after this, median marriage age rose, until it was at 26 for men and 22 for women in 1890. They conclude that "In the nineteenth century, white Americans married fairly late, only slightly earlier than their counterparts in Western Europe."[42] Since Americans largely came from Western Europe, this is not surprising, unless one has made the assumption that Americans married at significantly lower ages than did Western Europeans.

IPUMS-USA Data on the 1850 and 1880 Censuses

IPUMS, "Integrated Public Use Microdata Series", is a "project dedicated to collecting and distributing United States census data." It states that it "consists of more than fifty high-precision samples of the American population drawn from fifteen federal censuses and from the American Community Surveys of 2000–2008.... These samples, which draw on every surviving census from 1850–2000, and the 2000–2008 ACS samples, collectively constitute our richest source of quantitative information on long-term changes in the American population."

IPUMS allows for online analysis of census data from 1850 to 2008, generally offering a 1% sample, selected at random, of the census data, though the 1880 census has a 10% sample. Such random sampling is a valid way to report and analyze data, and in fact is a basic aspect of modern statistical analysis.

According to the IPUMS User's Guide, for the 1850 census, including about 560,000 census pages, "The sample was drawn systematically from each microfilm reel, ordinarily at intervals of six pages. On each selected census page, one line [an individual] was randomly selected and designated as the sample point. Any valid sample unit [such as dwelling, household, family group] beginning at the sample point or within four subsequent lines was included in the sample, yielding a 1-in-100 sample with equal probabilities of inclusion for all individuals and households."[43]

The 1850 and 1880 censuses had a question asking if the respondent had been married in the previous year (in the 1850 census, "10. Married

---

42. Ibid., 82.
43. IPUMSUSA website, http://usa.ipums.org/usa/, at User's Guide, Chapter 2: Sample Designs, for 1850, (accessed January 10, 2010).

within the year."), which, combined with age, gives us a snapshot of age at marriage for 1849–1850. Since 1850 is fairly close in time to Mormon Nauvoo, the IPUMS 1850 census data—which allows us to look at individual states and regions—will be a valuable tool for comparison with Nauvoo and early Utah polygamy. The 1880 census will show age-range in northeastern America just before the demise of public Mormon polygamy.

While I think it is valid to look at the IPUMS database, there are some limitations to the census data. Michael Haines suggests that the "marriage during the previous year" question was underreported in nineteenth-century censuses.[44] This is obviously not an ideal situation, and it shows how human error enters into the quest for pure scientific data.

Nevertheless, if the "marriage during the previous year" question was underreported, it was presumably underreported for all age groups—which would still give us a valid overview of age-at-marriage distribution. But, someone might object, perhaps the under-16 new brides, or their husbands, were sensitive about their youth, and gave higher ages, which would presumably artificially inflate the 16 or 17 year old age groups. This is certainly possible, and would skew the report, from a strictly scientific point of view. On the other hand, it would be more evidence that marriage at 14 and 15 was not completely acceptable in the respondent's culture.

In addition, since we don't know when a respondent's birthday was, if a fifteen-year-old says he or she was married in the previous year, he or she might have been married either at age fourteen or fifteen. However, since this is entirely impossible to document, for the purposes of the discussion here I will assume that a respondent was married at the age when he or she answered the census question.

In addition, when invalid codes appeared in any of the key variables (age, sex, married within the last year), I did not use that response in its report. Unfortunately, this disallows a substantial amount of data,

---

44. Haines, "Long-term Marriage Patterns in the United States," 5. Haines thus believes that our records of marriage age are more precise as the century progressed. For the early nineteenth-century, "we are forced to rely on estimates and other scattered sources." However, he writes that "for the nineteenth century, censuses constitute the major source" for marriage demographics, with the federal census being the "main resource," 4.

1850
Entire USA

Cells contain:
- Column percent
- Confidence intervals (99 percent)
- N of cases

	1 Male	2 Female	Row Total		1 Male	2 Female	Row Total
13:13	.10 (0.00–0.35) 1	.10 (0.00–0.35) 1	.10 (0.00–0.28) 2	24:24	9.28 (6.93–11.63) 94	.25 (3.44–7.07) 53	7.27 (5.78–8.76) 147
14:14	.00 — 0	.30 (0.00–0.74) 3	.15 (0.00–0.37) 3	25:25	9.48 (7.10–11.85) 96	4.36 (2.70–6.02) 44	6.92 (5.47–8.38) 140
15:15	.10 (0.00–0.35) 1	1.19 (0.31–2.07) 12	.64 (0.18–1.10) 13	26:26	7.60 (5.45–9.75) 77	3.47 (1.98–4.96) 35	5.54 (4.23–6.85) 112
16:16	.20 (0.00–0.56) 2	3.07 (1.67–4.48) 31	1.63 (0.91–2.36) 33	27:27	4.54 (2.85–6.23) 46	1.98 (0.85–3.12) 20	3.26 (2.24–4.28) 66
17:17	.10 (0.00–0.35) 1	8.03 (5.82–10.24) 81	4.06 (2.92–5.19) 82	28:28	6.42 (4.43–8.40) 65	3.17 (1.75–4.60) 32	4.80 (3.57–6.02) 97
18:18	.69 (0.02–1.36) 7	11.30 (8.73–13.87) 114	5.98 (4.62–7.34) 121	29:29	3.16 (1.74–4.58) 32	.59 (0.00–1.22) 6	1.88 (1.10–2.66) 38
19:19	1.38 (0.43–2.33) 14	11.30 (8.73–13.87) 114	6.33 (4.93–7.73) 128	30:30	4.34 (2.69–6.00) 44	2.18 (0.99–3.37) 22	3.26 (2.24–4.28) 66
20:20	3.55 (2.05–5.06) 36	11.10 (8.55–13.65) 112	7.32 (5.83–8.81) 148	31:31	1.88 (0.78–2.98) 19	.40 (0.00–0.91) 4	1.14 (0.53–1.75) 23
21:21	7.40 (5.28–9.53) 75	8.62 (6.34–10.90) 87	8.01 (6.45–9.57) 162	32:32	2.96 (1.59–4.34) 30	.79 (0.07–1.51) 8	1.88 (1.10–2.66) 38
22:22	10.46 (7.98–12.95) 106	8.33 (6.08–10.57) 84	9.40 (7.72–11.07) 190	33:33	1.78 (0.71–2.85) 18	.30 (0.00–0.74) 3	1.04 (0.46–1.62) 21
23:23	10.07 (7.63–12.51) 102	6.84 (4.79–8.89) 69	8.46 (6.86–10.05) 171	34:34	1.28 (0.37–2.20) 13	.40 (0.00–0.91) 4	.84 (0.32–1.36) 17

FIGURE 6.3: IPUMS 1% census sample for 1850, valid cases, the entire U.S.A., showing age range for persons married within the previous year, with confidence intervals set at 99 percent.

1850
Entire USA

Cells contain:
- Column percent
- Confidence intervals (99 percent)
- N of cases

	1 Male	2 Female	Row Total		1 Male	2 Female	Row Total
35:35	1.18 (0.31–2.06) 12	.50 (0.00–1.07) 5	.84 (0.32–1.36) 17	46:46	.20 (0.00–0.56) 2	.20 (0.00–0.56) 2	.20 (0.00–0.45) 4
36:36	1.28 (0.37–2.20) 13	.30 (0.00–0.74) 3	.79 (0.28–1.30) 16	47:47	.49 (0.00–1.06) 5	.20 (0.00–0.56) 2	.35 (0.01–0.68) 7
37:37	.79 (0.07–1.51) 8	.59 (0.00–1.22) 6	.69 (0.22–1.17) 14	48:48	.20 (0.00–0.56) 2	.20 (0.00–0.56) 2	.20 (0.00–0.45) 4
38:38	.49 (0.00–1.06) 5	.50 (0.00–1.07) 5	.49 (0.09–0.90) 10	49:49	.39 (0.00–0.90) 4	.40 (0.00–0.91) 4	.40 (0.04–0.76) 8
39:39	.30 (0.00–0.74) 3	.30 (0.00–0.74) 3	.30 (0.00–0.61) 6	50:50	.39 (0.00–0.90) 4	.30 (0.00–0.74) 3	.35 (0.01–0.68) 7
40:40	1.28 (0.37–2.20) 13	.59 (0.00–1.22) 6	.94 (0.39–1.49) 19	51:51	.20 (0.00–0.56) 2	.40 (0.00–0.91) 4	.30 (0.00–0.61) 6
41:41	.30 (0.00–0.74) 3	.30 (0.00–0.74) 3	.30 (0.00–0.61) 6	52:52	.30 (0.00–0.74) 3	.00 — 0	.15 (0.00–0.37) 3
42:42	.59 (0.00–1.21) 6	.30 (0.00–0.74) 3	.45 (0.06–0.83) 9	53:53	.00 — 0	.20 (0.00–0.56) 2	.10 (0.00–0.28) 2
43:43	.39 (0.00–0.90) 4	.20 (0.00–0.56) 2	.30 (0.00–0.61) 6	54:54	.10 (0.00–0.35) 1	.30 (0.00–0.74) 3	.20 (0.00–0.45) 4
44:44	.49 (0.00–1.06) 5	.00 — 0	.25 (0.00–0.53) 5	55:55	.49 (0.00–1.06) 5	.10 (0.00–0.35) 1	.30 (0.00–0.61) 6
45:45	.99 (0.19–1.79) 10	.40 (0.00–0.91) 4	.69 (0.22–1.17) 14	56:56	.10 (0.00–0.35) 1	.00 — 0	.05 (0.00–0.18) 1

FIGURE 6.3 (cont.): IPUMS 1% census sample for 1850, valid cases, the entire U.S.A., showing age range for persons married within the previous year, with confidence intervals set at 99 percent.

1850

Entire USA

Cells contain: – Column percent
– Confidence intervals (99 percent)
– N of cases

	1 Male	2 Female	Row Total		1 Male	2 Female	Row Total
57: 57	.30 (0.00–0.74) 3	.00 — 0	.15 (0.00–0.37) 3	65: 65	.39 (0.00–0.90) 4	.00 — 0	.20 (0.00–0.45) 4
58: 58	.10 (0.00–0.35) 1	.10 (0.00–0.35) 1	.10 (0.00–0.28) 2	66: 66	.10 (0.00–0.35) 1	.10 (0.00–0.35) 1	.10 (0.00–0.28) 2
59: 59	.39 (0.00–0.90) 4	.10 (0.00–0.35) 1	.25 (0.00–0.53) 5	69: 69	.20 (0.00–0.56) 2	.10 (0.00–0.35) 1	.15 (0.00–0.37) 3
60: 60	.30 (0.00–0.74) 3	.00 — 0	.15 (0.00–0.37) 3	71: 71	.10 (0.00–0.35) 1	.00 — 0	.05 (0.00–0.18) 1
61: 61	.00 — 0	.20 (0.00–0.56) 2	.10 (0.00–0.28) 2	75: 75	.10 (0.00–0.35) 1	.00 — 0	.05 (0.00–0.18) 1
62: 62	.10 (0.00–0.35) 1	.00 — 0	.05 (0.00–0.18) 1	80: 80	.00 — 0	.10 (0.00–0.35) 1	.05 (0.00–0.18) 1
63: 63	.10 (0.00–0.35) 1	.00 — 0	.05 (0.00–0.18) 1	83: 83	.10 (0.00–0.35) 1	.00 — 0	.05 (0.00–0.18) 1
				COL. TOTAL	100.00 — 1,013	100.00 — 1,009	100.00 — 2,022

FIGURE 6.3 (cont.): IPUMS 1% census sample for 1850, valid cases, the entire U.S.A., showing age range for persons married within the previous year, with confidence intervals set at 99 percent.

but any error in a key variable would make the data useless under all circumstances.

With these caveats, I will look at the IPUMS data in 1850 and 1880 for four groups: the New England region (Connecticut, Maine, Massachusetts, New Hampshire, Rhode Island, Vermont); the Middle Atlantic region (New Jersey, New York, Pennsylvania), and the East North

Central region (Illinois, Indiana, Michigan, Ohio, and Wisconsin); and, just for interest, the totality of America at the time.[45]

I will start with the entire USA chart (see figure 6.3). For each age, we have the percentage from the sample first, then confidence interval, then the number of valid cases beneath it. The confidence intervals mean that, based on the 1% sample, there is a 99 percent certainty that the actual percentage is between the range given.

Thus, in the 1850 IPUMS 1% sample of valid responses, 2,022 people responded yes to the "married within the previous year" question—1,013 male and 1,009 female. In this group, one female was 13, three were 14, and twelve were 15—1.59 percent of the sample. This includes southern, northern and western states, as well as northeastern states—as we have noted previously, the southern and frontier states will have lower marriage rates than the northeastern states. Still, very early marriage, ages 13 to 15, is not a large group. There are substantial jumps up to 16 and from there to 17 (at 3.07 and 8.03 percent); 18, 19 and 20 are the largest groups.

Figure 6.4 shows the 1880 full USA IPUMS (including southern and western states), with a 10 percent sample. There were no marriages reported for girls at age 11 and 12; I deleted rows recording miniscule amounts for ages 0 to 10.

In 1880, marriage at age 13 is .12 percent, at age 14 is .45 percent; at age fifteen it is 1.52 percent; together, very early marriage is 2.09 percent.

New England predictably has a higher marriage age than this; in 1850 the largest groups range from 18 to 22, with 22 as the largest group, see figure 6.5. Thus, for the year 1850, 119 females responded that they had been married in the previous year, in the IPUMS 1% sample of valid cases. Of these, there were no marriages at ages 14 or 15, and only one at age 16. Seventeen was evidently the earliest that women generally were married in New England at this time.

---

45. See IPUMSUSA website, at http://usa.ipums.org/usa/ (accessed December 23, 2009). To reproduce my results, go to IPUMS-USA Online Data Analysis System, and select 1850. For Row, put age; for Column, sex; for Control, marrinyr(2); for Selection Filters, region(11) for New England, region(12) for Middle Atlantic, region(21) for East North Central; for Weight (none); for Decimals, 2; for Confidence level, 99 percent.

1880

Entire USA

Cells contain: —Column percent
—Confidence intervals (99 percent)
—N of cases

	1 Male	2 Female	Row Total		1 Male	2 Female	Row Total
13: 13	.01 (0.00–0.03) 1	.12 (0.04–0.21) 15	.07 (0.02–0.11) 16	24: 24	9.19 (8.50–9.88) 1,075	4.97 (4.46–5.48) 603	7.04 (6.61–7.47) 1,678
14: 14	.01 (0.00–0.03) 1	.45 (0.30–0.61) 55	.23 (0.15–0.32) 56	25: 25	8.91 (8.23–9.58) 1,042	3.99 (3.53–4.45) 484	6.40 (5.99–6.81) 1,526
15: 15	.02 (0.00–0.05) 2	1.52 (1.24–1.81) 185	.78 (0.64–0.93) 187	26: 26	6.32 (5.74–6.90) 739	3.05 (2.65–3.45) 370	4.65 (4.30–5.00) 1,109
16: 16	.05 (0.00–0.11) 6	3.86 (3.41–4.31) 468	1.99 (1.76–2.22) 474	27: 27	5.35 (4.81–5.89) 626	1.83 (1.52–2.14) 222	3.56 (3.25–3.87) 848
17: 17	.31 (0.18–0.44) 36	6.40 (5.82–6.97) 776	3.41 (3.10–3.71) 812	28: 28	5.00 (4.48–5.52) 585	1.90 (1.58–2.22) 231	3.42 (3.12–3.73) 816
18: 18	1.24 (0.98–1.50) 145	11.64 (10.89–12.39) 1,412	6.53 (6.12–6.95) 1,557	29: 29	3.19 (2.77–3.61) 373	1.01 (0.77–1.24) 122	2.08 (1.84–2.31) 495
19: 19	2.71 (2.32–3.10) 317	10.98 (10.25–11.71) 1,332	6.92 (6.50–7.34) 1,649	30: 30	3.88 (3.42–4.34) 454	1.66 (1.36–1.96) 201	2.75 (2.48–3.02) 655
20: 20	5.05 (4.53–5.57) 591	11.86 (11.10–12.62) 1,439	8.52 (8.05–8.98) 2,030	31: 31	1.92 (1.60–2.25) 225	.58 (0.40–0.75) 70	1.24 (1.05–1.42) 295
21: 21	8.97 (8.29–9.66) 1,050	8.99 (8.32–9.66) 1,091	8.98 (8.51–9.46) 2,141	32: 32	2.08 (1.74–2.42) 243	.64 (0.46–0.83) 78	1.35 (1.15–1.54) 321
22: 22	9.88 (9.17–10.59) 1,156	8.60 (7.95–9.26) 1,044	9.23 (8.75–9.71) 2,200	33: 33	1.32 (1.04–1.59) 154	.50 (0.34–0.67) 61	.90 (0.74–1.06) 215
23: 23	10.08 (9.36–10.79) 1,179	6.22 (5.66–6.79)	8.11 (7.66–8.57) 1,934	34: 34	.96 (0.73–1.19) 112	.41 (0.26–0.56) 50	.68 (0.54–0.82) 162

FIGURE 6.4: IPUMS 10% census sample for 1880, valid cases, the entire U.S.A., showing age range for persons married within the previous year, with confidence intervals set at 99 percent.

1880
Entire USA

Cells contain: −Column percent
−Confidence intervals (99 percent)
−N of cases

	1 Male	2 Female	Row Total		1 Male	2 Female	Row Total
35: 35	1.60 (1.30–1.90) 187	.90 (0.68–1.12) 109	1.24 (1.06–1.43) 296	46: 46	.34 (0.20–0.48) 40	.17 (0.08–0.27) 21	.26 (0.17–0.34) 61
36: 36	.82 (0.61–1.04) 96	.45 (0.29–0.60) 54	.63 (0.50–0.76) 150	47: 47	.27 (0.15–0.40) 32	.17 (0.08–0.27) 21	.22 (0.14–0.30) 53
37: 37	.88 (0.66–1.10) 103	.35 (0.22–0.49) 43	.61 (0.48–0.74) 146	48: 48	.30 (0.17–0.43) 35	.21 (0.10–0.31) 25	.25 (0.17–0.34) 60
38: 38	.86 (0.64–1.08) 101	.38 (0.24–0.52) 46	.62 (0.49–0.75) 147	49: 49	.24 (0.12–0.36) 28	.18 (0.08–0.28) 22	.21 (0.13–0.29) 50
39: 39	.50 (0.33–0.66) 58	.35 (0.22–0.49) 43	.42 (0.32–0.53) 101	50: 50	.55 (0.37–0.72) 64	.41 (0.26–0.56) 50	.48 (0.36–0.59) 114
40: 40	1.11 (0.86–1.36) 130	.56 (0.39–0.74) 68	.83 (0.68–0.98) 198	51: 51	.14 (0.05–0.22) 16	.12 (0.04–0.19) 14	.13 (0.07–0.19) 30
41: 41	.39 (0.24–0.54) 46	.20 (0.09–0.30) 24	.29 (0.20–0.38) 70	52: 52	.24 (0.12–0.36) 28	.16 (0.07–0.26) 20	.20 (0.13–0.28) 48
42: 42	.55 (0.37–0.72) 64	.33 (0.20–0.46) 40	.44 (0.33–0.55) 104	53: 53	.21 (0.10–0.32) 25	.15 (0.06–0.24) 18	.18 (0.11–0.25) 43
43: 43	.36 (0.22–0.50) 42	.19 (0.09–0.29) 23	.27 (0.19–0.36) 65	54: 54	.24 (0.12–0.36) 28	.08 (0.02–0.15) 10	.16 (0.09–0.23) 38
44: 44	.28 (0.16–0.41) 33	.25 (0.13–0.36) 30	.26 (0.18–0.35) 63	55: 55	.29 (0.16–0.42) 34	.23 (0.12–0.34) 28	.26 (0.18–0.35) 62
45: 45	.63 (0.44–0.82) 74	.35 (0.22–0.49) 43	.49 (0.37–0.61) 117	56: 56	.18 (0.08–0.28) 21	.11 (0.03–0.18) 13	.14 (0.08–0.21) 34

FIGURE 6.4 (cont.): IPUMS 10% census sample for 1880, valid cases, the entire U.S.A., showing age range for persons married within the previous year, with confidence intervals set at 99 percent.

1880
Entire USA

Cells contain: —Column percent
—Confidence intervals (99 percent)
—N of cases

	1 Male	2 Female	Row Total		1 Male	2 Female	Row Total
57: 57	.21 (0.10–0.32) 25	.10 (0.03–0.17) 12	.16 (0.09–0.22) 37	68: 68	.13 (0.04–0.21) 15	.12 (0.04–0.19) 14	.12 (0.06–0.18) 29
58: 58	.17 (0.07–0.27) 20	.13 (0.05–0.22) 16	.15 (0.09–0.22) 36	69: 69	.10 (0.03–0.18) 12	.04 (0.00–0.09) 5	.07 (0.03–0.12) 17
59: 59	.10 (0.03–0.18) 12	.08 (0.02–0.15) 10	.09 (0.04–0.14) 22	70: 70	.09 (0.02–0.16) 10	.19 (0.09–0.29) 23	.14 (0.08–0.20) 33
60: 60	.25 (0.13–0.37) 29	.34 (0.20–0.47) 41	.29 (0.20–0.38) 70	71: 71	.03 (0.00–0.08) 4	.02 (0.00–0.05) 2	.03 (0.00–0.05) 6
61: 61	.12 (0.04–0.20) 14	.12 (0.04–0.19) 14	.12 (0.06–0.17) 28	72: 72	.07 (0.01–0.13) 8	.10 (0.03–0.17) 12	.08 (0.04–0.13) 20
62: 62	.15 (0.05–0.24) 17	.07 (0.01–0.14) 9	.11 (0.05–0.16) 26	73: 73	.09 (0.02–0.16) 10	.02 (0.00–0.06) 3	.05 (0.02–0.09) 13
63: 63	.09 (0.02–0.16) 10	.08 (0.02–0.15) 10	.08 (0.04–0.13) 20	74: 74	.06 (0.00–0.12) 7	.07 (0.01–0.13) 8	.06 (0.02–0.10) 15
64: 64	.12 (0.04–0.20) 14	.09 (0.02–0.16) 11	.10 (0.05–0.16) 25	75: 75	.13 (0.04–0.21) 15	.11 (0.03–0.18) 13	.12 (0.06–0.17) 28
65: 65	.18 (0.08–0.28) 21	.21 (0.10–0.31) 25	.19 (0.12–0.27) 46	76: 76	.04 (0.00–0.09) 5	.04 (0.00–0.09) 5	.04 (0.01–0.08) 10
66: 66	.07 (0.01–0.13) 8	.08 (0.02–0.15) 10	.08 (0.03–0.12) 18	77: 77	.03 (0.00–0.08) 4	.02 (0.00–0.06) 3	.03 (0.00–0.06) 7
67: 67	.09 (0.02–0.17) 11	.09 (0.02–0.16) 11	.09 (0.04–0.14) 22	78: 78	.03 (0.00–0.06) 3	.05 (0.00–0.10) 6	.04 (0.01–0.07) 9

Figure 6.4 (cont.): IPUMS 10% census sample for 1880, valid cases, the entire U.S.A., showing age range for persons married within the previous year, with confidence intervals set at 99 percent.

1880
ENTIRE USA

Cells contain: —Column percent
—Confidence intervals (99 percent)
—N of cases

	1 Male	2 Female	Row Total		1 Male	2 Female	Row Total
79: 79	.05 (0.00–0.11) 6	.04 (0.00–0.09) 5	.05 (0.01–0.08) 11	87: 87	.00 — 0	.01 (0.00–0.03) 1	.00 (0.00–0.02) 1
80: 80	.06 (0.00–0.12) 7	.10 (0.03–0.17) 12	.08 (0.03–0.13) 19	88: 88	.01 (0.00–0.03) 1	.01 (0.00–0.03) 1	.01 (0.00–0.02) 2
81: 81	.01 (0.00–0.03) 1	.02 (0.00–0.05) 2	.01 (0.00–0.03) 3	90: 90	.03 (0.00–0.06) 3	.01 (0.00–0.03) 1	.02 (0.00–0.04) 4
82: 82	.01 (0.00–0.03) 1	.01 (0.00–0.03) 1	.01 (0.00–0.02) 2	94: 94	.00 — 0	.01 (0.00–0.03) 1	.00 (0.00–0.02) 1
83: 83	.00 — 0	.01 (0.00–0.03) 1	.00 (0.00–0.02) 1	96: 96	.01 (0.00–0.03) 1	.01 (0.00–0.03) 1	.01 (0.00–0.02) 2
84: 84	.01 (0.00–0.03) 1	.02 (0.00–0.05) 2	.01 (0.00–0.03) 3	99: 99	.00 — 0	.01 (0.00–0.03) 1	.00 (0.00–0.02) 1
85: 85	.00 — 0	.01 (0.00–0.03) 1	.00 (0.00–0.02) 1	106: 106	.00 — 0	.01 (0.00–0.03) 1	.00 (0.00–0.02) 1
86: 86	.01 (0.00–0.03) 1	.00 — 0	.00 (0.00–0.02) 1				
COL. TOTAL					100.00 — 11,700	100.00 — 12,134	100.00 — 23,834

FIGURE 6.4 (cont.): *IPUMS 10% census sample for 1880, valid cases, the entire U.S.A., showing age range for persons married within the previous year, with confidence intervals set at 99 percent.*

1850
New England States

Cells contain:
- Column percent
- Confidence intervals (99 percent)
- N of cases

	1 Male	2 Female	Row Total		1 Male	2 Female	Row Total
16: 16	.86 (0.00–3.12) 1	.84 (0.00–3.04) 1	.85 (0.00–2.41) 2	27: 27	7.76 (1.22–14.29) 9	4.20 (0.00–9.04) 5	5.96 (1.94–9.98) 14
17: 17	.86 (0.00–3.12) 1	5.88 (0.21–11.55) 7	3.40 (0.33–6.48) 8	28: 28	6.03 (0.22–11.85) 7	4.20 (0.00–9.04) 5	5.11 (1.37–8.84) 12
18: 18	.86 (0.00–3.12) 1	10.08 (2.83–17.34) 12	5.53 (1.65–9.41) 13	29: 29	4.31 (0.00–9.27) 5	2.52 (0.00–6.30) 3	3.40 (0.33–6.48) 8
19: 19	1.72 (0.00–4.90) 2	12.61 (4.61–20.60) 15	7.23 (2.84–11.63) 17	30: 30	5.17 (0.00–10.58) 6	2.52 (0.00–6.30) 3	3.83 (0.57–7.09) 9
20: 20	1.72 (0.00–4.90) 2	6.72 (0.69–12.76) 8	4.26 (0.83–7.68) 10	31: 31	2.59 (0.00–6.46) 3	.00 — 0	1.28 (0.00–3.18) 3
21: 21	3.45 (0.00–7.90) 4	9.24 (2.26–16.22) 11	6.38 (2.23–10.53) 15	32: 32	2.59 (0.00–6.46) 3	.00 — 0	1.28 (0.00–3.18) 3
22: 22	12.93 (4.74–21.13) 15	13.45 (5.22–21.67) 16	13.19 (7.45–18.94) 31	33: 33	1.72 (0.00–4.90) 2	.84 (0.00–3.04) 1	1.28 (0.00–3.18) 3
23: 23	10.34 (2.91–17.78) 12	5.88 (0.21–11.55) 7	8.09 (3.46–12.71) 19	35: 35	2.59 (0.00–6.46) 3	.84 (0.00–3.04) 1	1.70 (0.00–3.90) 4
24: 24	10.34 (2.91–17.78) 12	7.56 (1.19–13.94) 9	8.94 (4.09–13.78) 21	36: 36	.00 — 0	.84 (0.00–3.04) 1	.43 (0.00–1.53) 1
25: 25	11.21 (3.50–18.91) 13	6.72 (0.69–12.76) 8	8.94 (4.09–13.78) 21	37: 37	.86 (0.00–3.12) 1	.00 — 0	.43 (0.00–1.53) 1
26: 26	7.76 (1.22–14.29) 9	4.20 (0.00–9.04) 5	5.96 (1.94–9.98) 14	38: 38	.86 (0.00–3.12) 1	.00 — 0	.43 (0.00–1.53) 1

FIGURE 6.5: IPUMS 1% census sample for 1850, valid cases, New England division, showing age range for persons married within the previous year, with confidence intervals set at 99 percent.

1850

NEW ENGLAND STATES

Cells contain: −Column percent
−Confidence intervals (99 percent)
−N of cases

	1 Male	2 Female	Row Total		1 Male	2 Female	Row Total
40: 40	.86 (0.00–3.12) 1	.00 — 0	.43 (0.00–1.53) 1	51: 51	.00 — 0	.84 (0.00–3.04) 1	.43 (0.00–1.53) 1
44: 44	.86 (0.00–3.12) 1	.00 — 0	.43 (0.00–1.53) 1	54: 54	.86 (0.00–3.12) 1	.00 — 0	.43 (0.00–1.53) 1
49: 49	.86 (0.00–3.12) 1	.00 — 0	.43 (0.00–1.53) 1				
COL. TOTAL					100.00 — 116	100.00 — 119	100.00 — 235

FIGURE 6.5 (cont.): IPUMS 1% census sample for 1850, valid cases, New England division, showing age range for persons married within the previous year, with confidence intervals set at 99 percent.

The 1880 IPUMS report is slightly higher than the 1850 census, as illustrated in figure 6.6. Thus, in 1880 New England, .26 were married at age 14, and .78 were married at age 15—1.04 percent. Marriages at age 16 are not common, at 1.56 percent.

The 1850 marriage age data for the Middle Atlantic (New York, New Jersey and Pennsylvania) region are slightly lower than the 1850 marriage age data in New England, see figure 6.7. In the 283 females in this group, there are no examples of a 14-year-old who had been married in the previous year, but there are three 15-year-olds, about 1 percent. The most populous groups are ages 19 to 23.

In the 1880 table (figure 6.8), I removed one row for less than one year old. Thus, in 1880, marriages at age 13–15 account for about .70 percent.

In the East North Central Group (Illinois, Indiana, Michigan, Ohio, and Wisconsin) for 1850, the most popular marriage ages, for females, are 17–21, see figure 6.9.

1880

New England States

Cells contain: —Column percent
—Confidence intervals (99 percent)
—N of cases

	1 Male	2 Female	Row Total		1 Male	2 Female	Row Total
14:14	.13 (0.00–0.48) 1	.26 (0.00–0.73) 2	.20 (0.00–0.49) 3	25:25	7.87 (5.33–10.41) 59	4.42 (2.50–6.33) 34	6.12 (4.53–7.70) 93
15:15	.00 — 0	.78 (0.00–1.60) 6	.39 (0.00–0.81) 6	26:26	7.20 (4.76–9.64) 54	4.81 (2.81–6.80) 37	5.99 (4.42–7.56) 91
16:16	.13 (0.00–0.48) 1	1.56 (0.41–2.71) 12	.86 (0.25–1.46) 13	27:27	5.60 (3.43–7.77) 42	3.64 (1.89–5.38) 28	4.61 (3.22–5.99) 70
17:17	.00 — 0	3.64 (1.89–5.38) 28	1.84 (0.95–2.73) 28	28:28	3.87 (2.05–5.69) 29	4.16 (2.30–6.01) 32	4.01 (2.71–5.31) 61
18:18	.80 (0.00–1.64) 6	6.10 (3.87–8.33) 47	3.49 (2.27–4.70) 53	29:29	5.60 (3.43–7.77) 42	2.47 (1.02–3.91) 19	4.01 (2.71–5.31) 61
19:19	2.13 (0.77–3.50) 16	9.35 (6.64–12.06) 72	5.79 (4.24–7.33) 88	30:30	4.93 (2.89–6.98) 37	2.08 (0.75–3.41) 16	3.49 (2.27–4.70) 53
20:20	4.27 (2.36–6.17) 32	11.04 (8.12–13.96) 85	7.70 (5.93–9.46) 117	31:31	2.67 (1.15–4.19) 20	1.17 (0.17–2.17) 9	1.91 (1.00–2.81) 29
21:21	4.93 (2.89–6.98) 37	9.48 (6.75–12.21) 73	7.24 (5.52–8.95) 110	32:32	2.80 (1.24–4.36) 21	.65 (0.00–1.40) 5	1.71 (0.85–2.57) 26
22:22	8.80 (6.13–11.47) 66	8.70 (6.08–11.33) 67	8.75 (6.88–10.62) 133	33:33	1.20 (0.17–2.23) 9	.65 (0.00–1.40) 5	.92 (0.29–1.55) 14
23:23	10.13 (7.29–12.98) 76	6.88 (4.53–9.24) 53	8.49 (6.64–10.33) 129	34:34	.67 (0.00–1.43) 5	.52 (0.00–1.19) 4	.59 (0.08–1.10) 9
24:24	8.00 (5.44–10.56) 60	5.97 (3.77–8.18) 46	6.97 (5.29–8.66) 106	35:35	2.13 (0.77–3.50) 16	1.04 (0.09–1.98) 8	1.58 (0.75–2.40) 24

FIGURE 6.6: *IPUMS 10% census sample for 1880, valid cases, New England division, showing age range for persons married within the previous year, with confidence intervals set at 99 percent.*

1880
NEW ENGLAND STATES

Cells contain: −Column percent
−Confidence intervals (99 percent)
−N of cases

	1 Male	2 Female	Row Total		1 Male	2 Female	Row Total
36: 36	.80 (0.00–1.64) 6	.65 (0.00–1.40) 5	.72 (0.16–1.28) 11	47: 47	.27 (0.00–0.75) 2	.00 — 0	.13 (0.00–0.37) 2
37: 37	1.60 (0.42–2.78) 12	.39 (0.00–0.97) 3	.99 (0.33–1.64) 15	48: 48	.40 (0.00–1.00) 3	.39 (0.00–0.97) 3	.39 (0.00–0.81) 6
38: 38	1.07 (0.10–2.04) 8	.52 (0.00–1.19) 4	.79 (0.20–1.38) 12	49: 49	.13 (0.00–0.48) 1	.39 (0.00–0.97) 3	.26 (0.00–0.60) 4
39: 39	.80 (0.00–1.64) 6	.26 (0.00–0.73) 2	.53 (0.05–1.01) 8	50: 50	.80 (0.00–1.64) 6	.13 (0.00–0.47) 1	.46 (0.01–0.91) 7
40: 40	2.40 (0.96–3.84) 18	1.04 (0.09–1.98) 8	1.71 (0.85–2.57) 26	51: 51	.13 (0.00–0.48) 1	.13 (0.00–0.47) 1	.13 (0.00–0.37) 2
41: 41	.40 (0.00–1.00) 3	.39 (0.00–0.97) 3	.39 (0.00–0.81) 6	52: 52	.40 (0.00–1.00) 3	.39 (0.00–0.97) 3	.39 (0.00–0.81) 6
42: 42	.93 (0.03–1.84) 7	.39 (0.00–0.97) 3	.66 (0.12–1.19) 10	53: 53	.00 — 0	.13 (0.00–0.47) 1	.07 (0.00–0.24) 1
43: 43	.67 (0.00–1.43) 5	.26 (0.00–0.73) 2	.46 (0.01–0.91) 7	54: 54	.27 (0.00–0.75) 2	.13 (0.00–0.47) 1	.20 (0.00–0.49) 3
44: 44	.00 — 0	.39 (0.00–0.97) 3	.20 (0.00–0.49) 3	55: 55	.13 (0.00–0.48) 1	.26 (0.00–0.73) 2	.20 (0.00–0.49) 3
45: 45	.67 (0.00–1.43) 5	.26 (0.00–0.73) 2	.46 (0.01–0.91) 7	56: 56	.53 (0.00–1.22) 4	.00 — 0	.26 (0.00–0.60) 4
46: 46	.53 (0.00–1.22) 4	.65 (0.00–1.40) 5	.59 (0.08–1.10) 9	57: 57	.40 (0.00–1.00) 3	.26 (0.00–0.73) 2	.33 (0.00–0.71) 5

FIGURE 6.6 (cont.): IPUMS 10% census sample for 1880, valid cases, New England division, showing age range for persons married within the previous year, with confidence intervals set at 99 percent.

1880
NEW ENGLAND STATES

Cells contain: —Column percent
—Confidence intervals (99 percent)
—N of cases

	1 Male	2 Female	Row Total		1 Male	2 Female	Row Total
58: 58	.00 — 0	.26 (0.00–0.73) 2	.13 (0.00–0.37) 2	72: 72	.00 — 0	.13 (0.00–0.47) 1	.07 (0.00–0.24) 1
60: 60	.27 (0.00–0.75) 2	.26 (0.00–0.73) 2	.26 (0.00–0.60) 4	73: 73	.27 (0.00–0.75) 2	.13 (0.00–0.47) 1	.20 (0.00–0.49) 3
61: 61	.40 (0.00–1.00) 3	.13 (0.00–0.47) 1	.26 (0.00–0.60) 4	75: 75	.53 (0.00–1.22) 4	.13 (0.00–0.47) 1	.33 (0.00–0.71) 5
62: 62	.27 (0.00–0.75) 2	.00 — 0	.13 (0.00–0.37) 2	76: 76	.13 (0.00–0.48) 1	.13 (0.00–0.47) 1	.13 (0.00–0.37) 2
63: 63	.00 — 0	.13 (0.00–0.47) 1	.07 (0.00–0.24) 1	77: 77	.13 (0.00–0.48) 1	.00 — 0	.07 (0.00–0.24) 1
64: 64	.13 (0.00–0.48) 1	.13 (0.00–0.47) 1	.13 (0.00–0.37) 2	79: 79	.00 — 0	.13 (0.00–0.47) 1	.07 (0.00–0.24) 1
65: 65	.00 — 0	.52 (0.00–1.19) 4	.26 (0.00–0.60) 4	80: 80	.00 — 0	.26 (0.00–0.73) 2	.13 (0.00–0.37) 2
68: 68	.13 (0.00–0.48) 1	.13 (0.00–0.47) 1	.13 (0.00–0.37) 2	81: 81	.00 — 0	.13 (0.00–0.47) 1	.07 (0.00–0.24) 1
69: 69	.00 — 0	.13 (0.00–0.47) 1	.07 (0.00–0.24) 1	82: 82	.00 — 0	.13 (0.00–0.47) 1	.07 (0.00–0.24) 1
70: 70	.40 (0.00–1.00) 3	.13 (0.00–0.47) 1	.26 (0.00–0.60) 4	83: 83	.00 — 0	.13 (0.00–0.47) 1	.07 (0.00–0.24) 1
71: 71	.13 (0.00–0.48) 1	.00 — 0	.07 (0.00–0.24) 1	84: 84	.00 — 0	.13 (0.00–0.47) 1	.07 (0.00–0.24) 1
				COL. TOTAL	100.00 — 750	100.00 — 770	100.00 — 1,520

1850
MIDDLE ATLANTIC REGION

Cells contain:
- Column percent
- Confidence intervals (99 percent)
- N of cases

	1 Male	2 Female	Row Total		1 Male	2 Female	Row Total
15: 15	.00 — 0	1.06 (0.00–2.64) 3	.54 (0.00–1.33) 3	26: 26	11.91 (6.86–16.97) 33	4.59 (1.36–7.83) 13	8.21 (5.21–11.22) 46
16: 16	.00 — 0	2.12 (0.00–4.34) 6	1.07 (0.00–2.20) 6	27: 27	5.78 (2.13–9.42) 16	1.77 (0.00–3.80) 5	3.75 (1.67–5.83) 21
17: 17	.00 — 0	4.95 (1.60–8.30) 14	2.50 (0.79–4.21) 14	28: 28	6.86 (2.91–10.81) 19	3.89 (0.90–6.87) 11	5.36 (2.90–7.82) 30
18: 18	.00 — 0	6.36 (2.59–10.13) 18	3.21 (1.29–5.14) 18	29: 29	1.44 (0.00–3.31) 4	.35 (0.00–1.27) 1	.89 (0.00–1.92) 5
19: 19	.00 — 0	10.25 (5.56–14.93) 29	5.18 (2.76–7.60) 29	30: 30	5.78 (2.13–9.42) 16	2.83 (0.27–5.39) 8	4.29 (2.07–6.50) 24
20: 20	1.08 (0.00–2.70) 3	13.43 (8.16–18.69) 38	7.32 (4.47–10.17) 41	31: 31	1.44 (0.00–3.31) 4	.71 (0.00–2.00) 2	1.07 (0.00–2.20) 6
21: 21	5.42 (1.88–8.95) 15	11.66 (6.70–16.62) 33	8.57 (5.51–11.63) 48	32: 32	2.89 (0.27–5.50) 8	.35 (0.00–1.27) 1	1.61 (0.23–2.98) 9
22: 22	9.03 (4.55–13.50) 25	10.25 (5.56–14.93) 29	9.64 (6.42–12.87) 54	33: 33	1.81 (0.00–3.88) 5	.00 — 0	.89 (0.00–1.92) 5
23: 23	10.47 (5.69–15.25) 29	9.54 (5.00–14.08) 27	10.00 (6.72–13.28) 56	34: 34	1.44 (0.00–3.31) 4	.00 — 0	.71 (0.00–1.63) 4
24: 24	10.11 (5.40–14.81) 28	4.95 (1.60–8.30) 14	7.50 (4.62–10.38) 42	35: 35	.36 (0.00–1.30) 1	1.41 (0.00–3.24) 4	.89 (0.00–1.92) 5
25: 25	13.36 (8.05–18.67) 37	4.95 (1.60–8.30) 14	9.11 (5.96–12.25) 51	36: 36	1.44 (0.00–3.31) 4	.00 — 0	.71 (0.00–1.63) 4

FIGURE 6.7: IPUMS 1% census sample for 1850, valid cases, Middle Atlantic division, showing age range for persons married within the previous year, with confidence intervals set at 99 percent.

1850
MIDDLE ATLANTIC REGION

Cells contain: −Column percent
−Confidence intervals (99 percent)
−N of cases

	1 Male	2 Female	Row Total		1 Male	2 Female	Row Total
37: 37	.36 (0.00–1.30) 1	.71 (0.00–2.00) 2	.54 (0.00–1.33) 3	48: 48	.36 (0.00–1.30) 1	.35 (0.00–1.27) 1	.36 (0.00–1.01) 2
38: 38	.36 (0.00–1.30) 1	.35 (0.00–1.27) 1	.36 (0.00–1.01) 2	49: 49	.36 (0.00–1.30) 1	.35 (0.00–1.27) 1	.36 (0.00–1.01) 2
39: 39	.36 (0.00–1.30) 1	.00 — 0	.18 (0.00–0.64) 1	50: 50	.72 (0.00–2.04) 2	.00 — 0	.36 (0.00–1.01) 2
40: 40	.36 (0.00–1.30) 1	.35 (0.00–1.27) 1	.36 (0.00–1.01) 2	52: 52	.36 (0.00–1.30) 1	.00 — 0	.18 (0.00–0.64) 1
41: 41	.36 (0.00–1.30) 1	.35 (0.00–1.27) 1	.36 (0.00–1.01) 2	53: 53	.00 — 0	.35 (0.00–1.27) 1	.18 (0.00–0.64) 1
42: 42	2.17 (0.00–4.44) 6	.00 — 0	1.07 (0.00–2.20) 6	55: 55	.00 — 0	.35 (0.00–1.27) 1	.18 (0.00–0.64) 1
44: 44	.36 (0.00–1.30) 1	.00 — 0	.18 (0.00–0.64) 1	59: 59	.36 (0.00–1.30) 1	.35 (0.00–1.27) 1	.36 (0.00–1.01) 2
45: 45	2.17 (0.00–4.44) 6	.71 (0.00–2.00) 2	1.43 (0.13–2.73) 8	60: 60	.36 (0.00–1.30) 1	.00 — 0	.18 (0.00–0.64) 1
46: 46	.36 (0.00–1.30) 1	.35 (0.00–1.27) 1	.36 (0.00–1.01) 2				
				COL. TOTAL	100.00 277	100.00 283	100.00 560

FIGURE 6.7 (cont.): IPUMS 1% census sample for 1850, valid cases, Middle Atlantic division, showing age range for persons married within the previous year, with confidence intervals set at 99 percent.

1880
MIDDLE ATLANTIC REGION

Cells contain: – Column percent
– Confidence intervals (99 percent)
– N of cases

	1 Male	2 Female	Row Total		1 Male	2 Female	Row Total
13: 13	.00 — 0	.10 (0.00–0.28) 2	.05 (0.00–0.15) 2	24: 24	9.81 (8.04–11.59) 184	5.99 (4.62–7.36) 119	7.85 (6.73–8.96) 303
14: 14	.00 — 0	.25 (0.00–0.54) 5	.13 (0.00–0.28) 5	25: 25	8.37 (6.72–10.02) 157	5.23 (3.95–6.52) 104	6.76 (5.72–7.80) 261
15: 15	.00 — 0	.35 (0.01–0.70) 7	.18 (0.00–0.36) 7	26: 26	7.25 (5.71–8.80) 136	3.77 (2.67–4.88) 75	5.46 (4.52–6.41) 211
16: 16	.00 — 0	1.56 (0.84–2.28) 31	.80 (0.43–1.17) 31	27: 27	6.67 (5.18–8.15) 125	2.11 (1.28–2.95) 42	4.32 (3.48–5.17) 167
17: 17	.11 (0.00–0.30) 2	4.63 (3.41–5.85) 92	2.43 (1.79–3.07) 94	28: 28	6.08 (4.66–7.50) 114	2.16 (1.32–3.01) 43	4.07 (3.25–4.88) 157
18: 18	.64 (0.17–1.11) 12	8.30 (6.71–9.90) 165	4.58 (3.72–5.45) 177	29: 29	4.21 (3.02–5.41) 79	.91 (0.36–1.45) 18	2.51 (1.86–3.16) 97
19: 19	2.03 (1.19–2.87) 38	9.96 (8.23–11.70) 198	6.11 (5.12–7.10) 236	30: 30	4.21 (3.02–5.41) 79	2.32 (1.45–3.19) 46	3.24 (2.50–3.97) 125
20: 20	4.69 (3.43–5.95) 88	11.22 (9.40–13.05) 223	8.05 (6.92–9.18) 311	31: 31	1.92 (1.10–2.74) 36	.75 (0.25–1.26) 15	1.32 (0.85–1.79) 51
21: 21	7.63 (6.05–9.21) 143	10.82 (9.02–12.62) 215	9.27 (8.07–10.47) 358	32: 32	2.08 (1.23–2.93) 39	.60 (0.16–1.05) 12	1.32 (0.85–1.79) 51
22: 22	9.55 (7.80–11.30) 179	9.71 (8.00–11.43) 193	9.63 (8.41–10.86) 372	33: 33	1.44 (0.73–2.15) 27	.65 (0.19–1.12) 13	1.04 (0.62–1.46) 40
23: 23	9.81 (8.04–11.59) 184	8.86 (7.21–10.50) 176	9.32 (8.12–10.53) 360	34: 34	1.17 (0.53–1.81) 22	.25 (0.00–0.54) 5	.70 (0.35–1.04) 27

FIGURE 6.8: IPUMS 10% census sample for 1880, valid cases, Middle Atlantic division, showing age range for persons married within the previous year, with confidence intervals set at 99 percent.

1880
MIDDLE ATLANTIC REGION

Cells contain: —Column percent
—Confidence intervals (99 percent)
—N of cases

	1 Male	2 Female	Row Total
35: 35	1.23 (0.57–1.88) 23	.91 (0.36–1.45) 18	1.06 (0.64–1.49) 41
36: 36	1.17 (0.53–1.81) 22	.20 (0.00–0.46) 4	.67 (0.33–1.01) 26
37: 37	.48 (0.07–0.89) 9	.50 (0.09–0.91) 10	.49 (0.20–0.78) 19
38: 38	.69 (0.20–1.19) 13	.55 (0.12–0.98) 11	.62 (0.30–0.95) 24
39: 39	.48 (0.07–0.89) 9	.60 (0.16–1.05) 12	.54 (0.24–0.85) 21
40: 40	1.01 (0.42–1.61) 19	.40 (0.04–0.77) 8	.70 (0.35–1.04) 27
41: 41	.48 (0.07–0.89) 9	.25 (0.00–0.54) 5	.36 (0.11–0.61) 14
42: 42	.53 (0.10–0.97) 10	.40 (0.04–0.77) 8	.47 (0.18–0.75) 18
43: 43	.32 (0.00–0.66) 6	.25 (0.00–0.54) 5	.28 (0.06–0.51) 11
44: 44	.48 (0.07–0.89) 9	.10 (0.00–0.28) 2	.28 (0.06–0.51) 11
45: 45	.64 (0.17–1.11) 12	.40 (0.04–0.77) 8	.52 (0.22–0.82) 20
46: 46	.21 (0.00–0.49) 4	.10 (0.00–0.28) 2	.16 (0.00–0.32) 6
47: 47	.16 (0.00–0.40) 3	.15 (0.00–0.38) 3	.16 (0.00–0.32) 6
48: 48	.27 (0.00–0.57) 5	.15 (0.00–0.38) 3	.21 (0.02–0.40) 8
49: 49	.16 (0.00–0.40) 3	.35 (0.01–0.70) 7	.26 (0.05–0.47) 10
50: 50	.37 (0.01–0.74) 7	.25 (0.00–0.54) 5	.31 (0.08–0.54) 12
51: 51	.16 (0.00–0.40) 3	.25 (0.00–0.54) 5	.21 (0.02–0.40) 8
52: 52	.21 (0.00–0.49) 4	.20 (0.00–0.46) 4	.21 (0.02–0.40) 8
53: 53	.16 (0.00–0.40) 3	.05 (0.00–0.18) 1	.10 (0.00–0.24) 4
54: 54	.11 (0.00–0.30) 2	.05 (0.00–0.18) 1	.08 (0.00–0.19) 3
55: 55	.43 (0.04–0.81) 8	.20 (0.00–0.46) 4	.31 (0.08–0.54) 12
56: 56	.00 — 0	.15 (0.00–0.38) 3	.08 (0.00–0.19) 3

FIGURE 6.8 (cont.): IPUMS 10% census sample for 1880, valid cases, Middle Atlantic division, showing age range for persons married within the previous year, with confidence intervals set at 99 percent.

1880
MIDDLE ATLANTIC REGION

Cells contain: – Column percent
– Confidence intervals (99 percent)
– N of cases

	1 Male	2 Female	Row Total		1 Male	2 Female	Row Total
57:57	.37 (0.01–0.74) 7	.25 (0.00–0.54) 5	.31 (0.08–0.54) 12	68:68	.11 (0.00–0.30) 2	.15 (0.00–0.38) 3	.13 (0.00–0.28) 5
58:58	.16 (0.00–0.40) 3	.10 (0.00–0.28) 2	.13 (0.00–0.28) 5	69:69	.05 (0.00–0.19) 1	.05 (0.00–0.18) 1	.05 (0.00–0.15) 2
59:59	.11 (0.00–0.30) 2	.10 (0.00–0.28) 2	.10 (0.00–0.24) 4	70:70	.11 (0.00–0.30) 2	.15 (0.00–0.38) 3	.13 (0.00–0.28) 5
60:60	.21 (0.00–0.49) 4	.30 (0.00–0.62) 6	.26 (0.05–0.47) 10	71:71	.05 (0.00–0.19) 1	.00 — 0	.03 (0.00–0.09) 1
61:61	.11 (0.00–0.30) 2	.05 (0.00–0.18) 1	.08 (0.00–0.19) 3	72:72	.00 — 0	.25 (0.00–0.54) 5	.13 (0.00–0.28) 5
62:62	.11 (0.00–0.30) 2	.15 (0.00–0.38) 3	.13 (0.00–0.28) 5	73:73	.11 (0.00–0.30) 2	.05 (0.00–0.18) 1	.08 (0.00–0.19) 3
63:63	.05 (0.00–0.19) 1	.15 (0.00–0.38) 3	.10 (0.00–0.24) 4	74:74	.05 (0.00–0.19) 1	.05 (0.00–0.18) 1	.05 (0.00–0.15) 2
64:64	.16 (0.00–0.40) 3	.15 (0.00–0.38) 3	.16 (0.00–0.32) 6	75:75	.16 (0.00–0.40) 3	.20 (0.00–0.46) 4	.18 (0.00–0.36) 7
65:65	.21 (0.00–0.49) 4	.20 (0.00–0.46) 4	.21 (0.02–0.40) 8	77:77	.05 (0.00–0.19) 1	.00 — 0	.03 (0.00–0.09) 1
66:66	.05 (0.00–0.19) 1	.15 (0.00–0.38) 3	.10 (0.00–0.24) 4	78:78	.00 — 0	.05 (0.00–0.18) 1	.03 (0.00–0.09) 1
67:67	.05 (0.00–0.19) 1	.15 (0.00–0.38) 3	.10 (0.00–0.24) 4	79:79	.11 (0.00–0.30) 2	.00 — 0	.05 (0.00–0.15) 2

FIGURE 6.8 (cont.): IPUMS 10% census sample for 1880, valid cases, Middle Atlantic division, showing age range for persons married within the previous year, with confidence intervals set at 99 percent.

1880

MIDDLE ATLANTIC REGION

Cells contain: —Column percent
—Confidence intervals (99 percent)
—N of cases

	1 Male	2 Female	Row Total		1 Male	2 Female	Row Total
80: 80	.00 — 0	.10 (0.00–0.28) 2	.05 (0.00–0.15) 2	86: 86	.05 (0.00–0.19) 1	.00 — 0	.03 (0.00–0.09) 1
81: 81	.05 (0.00–0.19) 1	.00 — 0	.03 (0.00–0.09) 1	88: 88	.00 — 0	.05 (0.00–0.18) 1	.03 (0.00–0.09) 1
COL. TOTAL					100.00 — 1,875	100.00 — 1,987	100.00 — 3,862

FIGURE 6.8 (cont.): IPUMS 10% census sample for 1880, valid cases, Middle Atlantic division, showing age range for persons married within the previous year, with confidence intervals set at 99 percent.

Here there are two examples in the 14–15 year old category, less than one percent.

In 1880, once again, I deleted the row for less than one year old, see figure 6.10. Here, .92 percent are in the age category 13–15. So we come to the conclusion that very early marriages of young women with marriage age 14 or 15, from 1850 to 1880, did take place, but were not very common, in the New England and northeastern states. By the reports of the IPUMS database for the 1850 census, the 13 to 15 age bracket combined: 0% in New England, 1.06% in the Middle Atlantic division, and .88% in the East North Central division. For the 1880 census, with its ten percent sample: the 13–15 age bracket combined accounted for 1.04 percent in the New England states, .70 in the Middle Atlantic division, and .92 in the East North Central division.

Early Marriage in Polygamous Nauvoo and Utah

Joseph Smith practiced polygamy especially in Nauvoo from 1841 to 1844 (when he married 31 of his 33 plural wives, by my counting). He introduced the practice to a number of his followers before his death in 1844, and polygamy began to be widely practiced before Mormons left Illinois for Utah in 1846. Polygamy was openly practiced in Utah starting

1850
East North Central Region

Cells contain: – Column percent
– Confidence intervals (99 percent)
– N of cases

	1 Male	2 Female	Row Total		1 Male	2 Female	Row Total
14:14	.00 — 0	.44 (0.00–1.58) 1	.22 (0.00–0.78) 1	25:25	8.15 (3.49–12.82) 19	3.08 (0.10–6.07) 7	5.65 (2.86–8.44) 26
15:15	.00 — 0	.44 (0.00–1.58) 1	.22 (0.00–0.78) 1	26:26	5.15 (1.38–8.92) 12	3.08 (0.10–6.07) 7	4.13 (1.73–6.53) 19
16:16	.43 (0.00–1.54) 1	2.64 (0.00–5.42) 6	1.52 (0.04–3.00) 7	27:27	3.43 (0.33–6.54) 8	3.08 (0.10–6.07) 7	3.26 (1.12–5.41) 15
17:17	.00 — 0	10.57 (5.26–15.89) 24	5.22 (2.53–7.90) 24	28:28	6.01 (1.96–10.06) 14	2.64 (0.00–5.42) 6	4.35 (1.89–6.81) 20
18:18	.86 (0.00–2.43) 2	14.54 (8.45–20.63) 33	7.61 (4.41–10.81) 35	29:29	5.58 (1.67–9.49) 13	.00 — 0	2.83 (0.83–4.83) 13
19:19	.00 — 0	6.61 (2.32–10.90) 15	3.26 (1.12–5.41) 15	30:30	3.00 (0.09–5.92) 7	.88 (0.00–2.50) 2	1.96 (0.28–3.63) 9
20:20	6.01 (1.96–10.06) 14	12.33 (6.65–18.02) 28	9.13 (5.65–12.61) 42	31:31	1.29 (0.00–3.21) 3	.44 (0.00–1.58) 1	.87 (0.00–1.99) 4
21:21	9.44 (4.46–14.43) 22	9.69 (4.58–14.80) 22	9.57 (6.01–13.12) 44	32:32	3.43 (0.33–6.54) 8	1.76 (0.00–4.04) 4	2.61 (0.68–4.53) 12
22:22	9.01 (4.13–13.90) 21	6.61 (2.32–10.90) 15	7.83 (4.58–11.07) 36	33:33	2.15 (0.00–4.62) 5	.00 — 0	1.09 (0.00–2.34) 5
23:23	10.30 (5.12–15.48) 24	7.49 (2.94–12.04) 17	8.91 (5.47–12.35) 41	34:34	1.72 (0.00–3.93) 4	.88 (0.00–2.50) 2	1.30 (0.00–2.67) 6
24:24	10.73 (5.45–16.01) 25	4.41 (0.86–7.95) 10	7.61 (4.41–10.81) 35	35:35	1.29 (0.00–3.21) 3	.00 — 0	.65 (0.00–1.62) 3

FIGURE 6.9: *IPUMS 1% census sample for 1850, valid cases, East North Central division, showing age range for persons married within the previous year, with confidence intervals set at 99 percent.*

1850
East North Central Region

Cells contain: −Column percent
−Confidence intervals (99 percent)
−N of cases

	1 Male	2 Female	Row Total		1 Male	2 Female	Row Total
36: 36	2.15 (0.00−4.62) 5	.44 (0.00−1.58) 1	1.30 (0.00−2.67) 6	50: 50	.43 (0.00−1.54) 1	.88 (0.00−2.50) 2	.65 (0.00−1.62) 3
38: 38	.86 (0.00−2.43) 2	.00 − 0	.43 (0.00−1.23) 2	51: 51	.00 − 0	.88 (0.00−2.50) 2	.43 (0.00−1.23) 2
39: 39	.00 − 0	.88 (0.00−2.50) 2	.43 (0.00−1.23) 2	53: 53	.00 − 0	.44 (0.00−1.58) 1	.22 (0.00−0.78) 1
40: 40	1.72 (0.00−3.93) 4	.88 (0.00−2.50) 2	1.30 (0.00−2.67) 6	55: 55	.86 (0.00−2.43) 2	.00 − 0	.43 (0.00−1.23) 2
41: 41	.43 (0.00−1.54) 1	.88 (0.00−2.50) 2	.65 (0.00−1.62) 3	56: 56	.43 (0.00−1.54) 1	.00 − 0	.22 (0.00−0.78) 1
43: 43	.43 (0.00−1.54) 1	.44 (0.00−1.58) 1	.43 (0.00−1.23) 2	59: 59	.43 (0.00−1.54) 1	.00 − 0	.22 (0.00−0.78) 1
45: 45	.00 − 0	.44 (0.00−1.58) 1	.22 (0.00−0.78) 1	60: 60	.43 (0.00−1.54) 1	.00 − 0	.22 (0.00−0.78) 1
46: 46	.00 − 0	.44 (0.00−1.58) 1	.22 (0.00−0.78) 1	61: 61	.00 − 0	.44 (0.00−1.58) 1	.22 (0.00−0.78) 1
47: 47	.86 (0.00−2.43) 2	.00 − 0	.43 (0.00−1.23) 2	63: 63	.43 (0.00−1.54) 1	.00 − 0	.22 (0.00−0.78) 1
48: 48	.43 (0.00−1.54) 1	.00 − 0	.22 (0.00−0.78) 1	66: 66	.43 (0.00−1.54) 1	.00 − 0	.22 (0.00−0.78) 1
49: 49	.43 (0.00−1.54) 1	.88 (0.00−2.50) 2	.65 (0.00−1.62) 3	69: 69	.43 (0.00−1.54) 1	.44 (0.00−1.58) 1	.43 (0.00−1.23) 2

FIGURE 6.9 (cont.): *IPUMS 1% census sample for 1850, valid cases, East North Central division, showing age range for persons married within the previous year, with confidence intervals set at 99 percent.*

1850

East North Central Region

Cells contain: —Column percent
—Confidence intervals (99 percent)
—N of cases

	1 Male	2 Female	Row Total		1 Male	2 Female	Row Total
75: 75	.43 (0.00–1.54) 1	.00 – 0	.22 (0.00–0.78) 1	83: 83	.43 (0.00–1.54) 1	.00 – 0	.22 (0.00–0.78) 1
				COL. TOTAL	100.00 – 233	100.00 – 227	100.00 – 460

FIGURE 6.9 (cont.): IPUMS 1% census sample for 1850, valid cases, East North Central division, showing age range for persons married within the previous year, with confidence intervals set at 99 percent.

in 1847, and was publicly announced in 1852. During the "Reformation," in 1856–1858, LDS church leaders visited congregations in Utah trying to renew the Saints' commitment to the Mormon faith, and challenging them to keep all the commandments exactly, including the commandment to enter plural marriage. This caused an uptick in plural marriages during that era.[46]

The history of Mormonism and Mormon polygamy has many examples of early marriage, which became an accepted part of nineteenth-century Mormon culture. Statistics, as well as common sense, have shown that polygamy tended to cause early marriage.

BYU family historian Kathryn M. Daynes, who studied marriage patterns in the small town of Manti, Utah, in the nineteenth century in her excellent book *More Wives Than One: Transformation of the Mormon Marriage System 1840–1910*, provides statistical evidence indicating that the mean age of marriage in Utah was much lower than in New England.[47] She divides her data sample into three groups, or cohorts: born

---

46. Paul H. Peterson, "The Mormon Reformation of 1856—1857: The Rhetoric and the Reality", *Journal of Mormon History* 15 (1989): 59—88. For polygamy encouraged during the Reformation, see pages 71–72, 80. (There were a rash of divorces after the Reformation, because some had entered plural marriages in haste).

47. Kathryn M. Daynes, *More Wives Than One: Transformation of the Mormon Marriage System 1840–1910* (Urbana: University of Illinois Press, 2001), 94–96. I disagree with some of Daynes' arguments, but this is nevertheless an superb book.

1880
East North Central Region

Cells contain: —Column percent
—Confidence intervals (99 percent)
—N of cases

	1 Male	2 Female	Row Total		1 Male	2 Female	Row Total
13: 13	.00 — 0	.08 (0.00–0.21) 2	.04 (0.00–0.11) 2	24: 24	9.95 (8.42–11.47) 255	5.86 (4.68–7.05) 154	7.88 (6.92–8.85) 409
14: 14	.00 — 0	.23 (0.00–0.47) 6	.12 (0.00–0.24) 6	25: 25	10.81 (9.23–12.39) 277	4.30 (3.28–5.32) 113	7.52 (6.57–8.46) 390
15: 15	.00 — 0	.61 (0.22–1.00) 16	.31 (0.11–0.51) 16	26: 26	6.71 (5.44–7.99) 172	3.39 (2.48–4.30) 89	5.03 (4.25–5.81) 261
16: 16	.00 — 0	2.51 (1.73–3.30) 66	1.27 (0.87–1.67) 66	27: 27	6.28 (5.05–7.52) 161	1.94 (1.25–2.64) 51	4.09 (3.38–4.79) 212
17: 17	.20 (0.00–0.42) 5	5.56 (4.41–6.71) 146	2.91 (2.31–3.51) 151	28: 28	5.74 (4.55–6.92) 147	2.06 (1.34–2.77) 54	3.87 (3.18–4.56) 201
18: 18	.47 (0.12–0.82) 12	10.02 (8.50–11.53) 263	5.30 (4.50–6.10) 275	29: 29	3.39 (2.47–4.32) 87	1.29 (0.73–1.86) 34	2.33 (1.79–2.87) 121
19: 19	1.99 (1.28–2.70) 51	11.31 (9.72–12.90) 297	6.71 (5.81–7.60) 348	30: 30	3.63 (2.68–4.58) 93	1.29 (0.73–1.86) 34	2.45 (1.89–3.00) 127
20: 20	2.85 (2.00–3.70) 73	12.15 (10.50–13.79) 319	7.55 (6.61–8.50) 392	31: 31	2.30 (1.54–3.07) 59	.65 (0.24–1.05) 17	1.46 (1.03–1.89) 76
21: 21	7.57 (6.22–8.92) 194	10.47 (8.93–12.01) 275	9.04 (8.01–10.06) 469	32: 32	2.38 (1.60–3.16) 61	.69 (0.27–1.10) 18	1.52 (1.08–1.96) 79
22: 22	9.36 (7.88–10.85) 240	10.24 (8.72–11.77) 269	9.81 (8.75–10.87) 509	33: 33	1.17 (0.62–1.72) 30	.23 (0.00–0.47) 6	.69 (0.40–0.99) 36
23: 23	10.73 (9.15–12.31) 275	6.66 (5.41–7.92)	8.67 (7.67–9.68) 450	34: 34	1.17 (0.62–1.72) 30	.46 (0.12–0.80) 12	.81 (0.49–1.13) 42

FIGURE 6.10: *IPUMS 10% census sample for 1880, valid cases, East North Central division, showing age range for persons married within the previous year, with confidence intervals set at 99 percent.*

1880
East North Central Region

Cells contain: —Column percent
—Confidence intervals (99 percent)
—N of cases

	1 Male	2 Female	Row Total		1 Male	2 Female	Row Total
35: 35	1.83 (1.15–2.52) 47	.53 (0.17–0.90) 14	1.18 (0.79–1.56) 61	46: 46	.39 (0.07–0.71) 10	.08 (0.00–0.21) 2	.23 (0.06–0.40) 12
36: 36	.59 (0.20–0.97) 15	.53 (0.17–0.90) 14	.56 (0.29–0.83) 29	47: 47	.31 (0.03–0.60) 8	.11 (0.00–0.28) 3	.21 (0.05–0.38) 11
37: 37	.74 (0.30–1.18) 19	.42 (0.09–0.74) 11	.58 (0.31–0.85) 30	48: 48	.55 (0.17–0.92) 14	.19 (0.00–0.41) 5	.37 (0.15–0.58) 19
38: 38	.78 (0.33–1.23) 20	.53 (0.17–0.90) 14	.66 (0.37–0.94) 34	49: 49	.20 (0.00–0.42) 5	.08 (0.00–0.21) 2	.13 (0.00–0.27) 7
39: 39	.55 (0.17–0.92) 14	.19 (0.00–0.41) 5	.37 (0.15–0.58) 19	50: 50	.47 (0.12–0.82) 12	.34 (0.05–0.64) 9	.40 (0.18–0.63) 21
40: 40	.78 (0.33–1.23) 20	.30 (0.03–0.58) 8	.54 (0.28–0.80) 28	51: 51	.20 (0.00–0.42) 5	.15 (0.00–0.35) 4	.17 (0.02–0.32) 9
41: 41	.35 (0.05–0.65) 9	.08 (0.00–0.21) 2	.21 (0.05–0.38) 11	52: 52	.39 (0.07–0.71) 10	.15 (0.00–0.35) 4	.27 (0.08–0.46) 14
42: 42	.59 (0.20–0.97) 15	.34 (0.05–0.64) 9	.46 (0.22–0.71) 24	53: 53	.27 (0.01–0.54) 7	.42 (0.09–0.74) 11	.35 (0.14–0.56) 18
43: 43	.43 (0.10–0.76) 11	.19 (0.00–0.41) 5	.31 (0.11–0.51) 16	54: 54	.27 (0.01–0.54) 7	.08 (0.00–0.21) 2	.17 (0.02–0.32) 9
44: 44	.43 (0.10–0.76) 11	.38 (0.07–0.69) 10	.40 (0.18–0.63) 21	55: 55	.35 (0.05–0.65) 9	.15 (0.00–0.35) 4	.25 (0.07–0.43) 13
45: 45	.39 (0.07–0.71) 10	.27 (0.01–0.53) 7	.33 (0.12–0.53) 17	56: 56	.27 (0.01–0.54) 7	.11 (0.00–0.28) 3	.19 (0.04–0.35) 10

FIGURE 6.10 (cont.): IPUMS 10% census sample for 1880, valid cases, East North Central division, showing age range for persons married within the previous year, with confidence intervals set at 99 percent.

1880
East North Central Region

Cells contain:
- Column percent
- Confidence intervals (99 percent)
- N of cases

	1 Male	2 Female	Row Total		1 Male	2 Female	Row Total
57: 57	.16 (0.00–0.36) 4	.08 (0.00–0.21) 2	.12 (0.00–0.24) 6	68: 68	.23 (0.00–0.48) 6	.04 (0.00–0.14) 1	.13 (0.00–0.27) 7
58: 58	.04 (0.00–0.14) 1	.11 (0.00–0.28) 3	.08 (0.00–0.18) 4	69: 69	.12 (0.00–0.29) 3	.04 (0.00–0.14) 1	.08 (0.00–0.18) 4
59: 59	.00 — 0	.08 (0.00–0.21) 2	.04 (0.00–0.11) 2	70: 70	.00 — 0	.23 (0.00–0.47) 6	.12 (0.00–0.24) 6
60: 60	.08 (0.00–0.22) 2	.23 (0.00–0.47) 6	.15 (0.01–0.29) 8	71: 71	.00 — 0	.04 (0.00–0.14) 1	.02 (0.00–0.07) 1
61: 61	.12 (0.00–0.29) 3	.15 (0.00–0.35) 4	.13 (0.00–0.27) 7	72: 72	.08 (0.00–0.22) 2	.04 (0.00–0.14) 1	.06 (0.00–0.14) 3
62: 62	.08 (0.00–0.22) 2	.08 (0.00–0.21) 2	.08 (0.00–0.18) 4	73: 73	.08 (0.00–0.22) 2	.00 — 0	.04 (0.00–0.11) 2
63: 63	.04 (0.00–0.14) 1	.00 — 0	.02 (0.00–0.07) 1	74: 74	.12 (0.00–0.29) 3	.11 (0.00–0.28) 3	.12 (0.00–0.24) 6
64: 64	.12 (0.00–0.29) 3	.11 (0.00–0.28) 3	.12 (0.00–0.24) 6	75: 75	.12 (0.00–0.29) 3	.04 (0.00–0.14) 1	.08 (0.00–0.18) 4
65: 65	.23 (0.00–0.48) 6	.15 (0.00–0.35) 4	.19 (0.04–0.35) 10	76: 76	.12 (0.00–0.29) 3	.08 (0.00–0.21) 2	.10 (0.00–0.21) 5
66: 66	.12 (0.00–0.29) 3	.15 (0.00–0.35) 4	.13 (0.00–0.27) 7	77: 77	.04 (0.00–0.14) 1	.04 (0.00–0.14) 1	.04 (0.00–0.11) 2
67: 67	.08 (0.00–0.22) 2	.19 (0.00–0.41) 5	.13 (0.00–0.27) 7	78: 78	.04 (0.00–0.14) 1	.04 (0.00–0.14) 1	.04 (0.00–0.11) 2

FIGURE 6.10 (cont.): IPUMS 10% census sample for 1880, valid cases, East North Central division, showing age range for persons married within the previous year, with confidence intervals set at 99 percent.

1880
East North Central Region

Cells contain:
- Column percent
- Confidence intervals (99 percent)
- N of cases

	1 Male	2 Female	Row Total		1 Male	2 Female	Row Total
79: 79	.04 (0.00–0.14) 1	.08 (0.00–0.21) 2	.06 (0.00–0.14) 3	84: 84	.04 (0.00–0.14) 1	.04 (0.00–0.14) 1	.04 (0.00–0.11) 2
80: 80	.04 (0.00–0.14) 1	.11 (0.00–0.28) 3	.08 (0.00–0.18) 4	96: 96	.00 — 0	.04 (0.00–0.14) 1	.02 (0.00–0.07) 1
82: 82	.04 (0.00–0.14) 1	.00 — 0	.02 (0.00–0.07) 1	99: 99	.00 — 0	.04 (0.00–0.14) 1	.02 (0.00–0.07) 1
COL. TOTAL					100.00 — 2,563	100.00 — 2,626	100.00 — 5,189

FIGURE 6.10 (cont.): IPUMS 10% census sample for 1880, valid cases, East North Central division, showing age range for persons married within the previous year, with confidence intervals set at 99 percent.

before 1852 (many of these people entered polygamy during the Reformation), born between 1852 and 1869, and born between 1870 and 1890.

The overall mean age of marriage for non-immigrants, people born in Utah, in the first cohort in Manti, was 18.07. One would assume, since men generally married women a year or two younger than they were, that the mean age for non-immigrant women was 16 to 17. (Immigrants married on the average at age 25.12.) In the second cohort the mean age at first marriage for non-immigrants was 20.46, so the mean for non-immigrant women was probably about 18 or 19.[48] In the third period immigrants were not a significant factor.

Daynes states that this mean age for entering marriage, which she derived from Manti records, was typical of Utah, and she cites studies by Mineau, Bean and Skolnick; Mineau, Bean and Anderton; and by Larry Logue (for St. George), to support this generalization.[49]

---

48. Daynes, *More Wives Than One*, 96, table 1.
49. Daynes, *More Wives Than One*, 96. Geraldine P. Mineau, L. L. Bean and M. Skolnick, "Mormon Demographic History II: The Family Life Cycle and Natural Fertility," *Population*

For example, Geraldine P. Mineau, L. L. Bean and M. Skolnick write, "In our first (1800–1809) birth cohort, fewer than one-third had married by age 20 (31 percent), but more than half of the 1850s birth cohort (55.8 percent) were married before the age of 20."[50] (Mineau, Bean and Skolnick deliberately exclude polygamous families "to eliminate the confounding effect of polygyny,"[51] yet the polygynous effect will nevertheless be there, because polygamy will always cause increased competition for women, which will drive down the marriage age in both monogamous and polygamous LDS marriages.[52])

Larry Logue, in his book *A Sermon in the Deseret: Belief and Behavior in Early St. George*, shows that the median age of women at first marriage in nineteenth-century St. George was 18.9; in Philadelphia at the same time, the median age was 25.[53] One might ask: was this age at marriage simply typical of frontier culture? Logue says no: while frontier marriage ages were younger than eastern ages, the marriages of the residents of St. George "were even younger than among the [analogous] western couples..., without the circumstances that apparently encouraged youthful marriages on the frontier."[54]

To return to Daynes. In her first cohort, at age sixteen, a remarkable 27 percent of the women were married. This undoubtedly included a number of young women married at ages 14 and 15. At age 20, 83 percent were married, and at age 24, only 3 percent were single. This apparently includes immigrants.[55]

In the second cohort, this percentage has decreased; 6 percent of women were married by age 16, and 57 percent had married by age 20. For a contrast, in 1880 in the IPUMS report of the Middle Atlantic

---

Studies 33 (November 1979): 429–46, 439; Geraldine P. Mineau, L. L. Bean and Douglas L. Anderton, "Migration and Fertility: Behavioral Change on the American Frontier," *Journal of Family History* 14 (January 1989): 43–61; Larry M. Logue, *A Sermon in the Deseret: Belief and Behavior in Early St. George, Utah* (Urbana: University of Illinois Press, 1988), 56.

50. Mineau, Bean and Skolnick, "Mormon Demographic History II," 438.
51. Ibid., 431.
52. To me, this appears to be a flaw in their argument.
53. Logue, Table 6, in *A Sermon in the Deseret*, 56.
54. Logue, *A Sermon in the Deseret*, 62, see also 63–64. The circumstances that would encourage early marriage on the frontier, as I understand Logue's argument, were economic opportunities (plentiful land, good jobs), and a significant shortage of women who had migrated to the frontier.
55. Daynes, *More Wives Than One*, 95.

(New York, New Jersey and Pennsylvania) region, 2.26 percent of young women had married by age 16, and 36.37 percent of young women had married by age 20.

Thus, in nineteenth-century Utah, early marriage, including very early marriage, marriage at age 14 or 15, was common. There were fewer early marriages in Utah as time went on, but they were always more frequent than in the eastern American states.[56]

Causes of Early Marriage in Polygamous Utah

The analyses of Vinovskis and Gottleib offer one important possible factor for early marriages in Utah—there tends to be an imbalance of more men than women in pioneering situations, on the frontier, in colonies in their early stages. Much of nineteenth-century Utah settlement might qualify as a frontier situation—and as Mormons settled in southern Utah, Idaho, Arizona, Mexico, Wyoming, Colorado, and Canada, the frontier environment continued while central Utah became more settled.

In spite of this, there was not as much imbalance of men and women in pioneering situations among Mormons as in other cultures.[57] We do not have the severe imbalance of men found in the kinds of colonizing Gottleib and Vinovskis discuss.

However, polygyny—in which men marry multiple women—by definition causes an imbalance of the sexes. If a small group of men marry multiple wives in a certain community, there are obviously fewer women available as a result, and the competition for marriageable women or young women will be all the more intense. This would serve to drive down the age of marriage for girls and women. Daynes writes, "The scarcity of marriageable women resulting from so many polygamous marriages in the 1850s meant that men then sought wives among increasingly younger women."[58] In 1857, during the Reformation, apostle Wilford Woodruff wrote to apostle George A. Smith, "nearly all are try-

---

56. Daynes, *More Wives Than One*, 97.
57. See Logue, *Sermon in the Deseret*, 64. In some colonizing situations throughout history, men formed the great majority of early settlers. This was not the case in Utah. Though the very first company to reach Salt Lake was all male (with the exception of three or four wives of the highest leaders), after that women formed an important part of pioneer companies.
58. Daynes, *More Wives Than One*, 114.

ing to get wives, until there is hardly a girl fourteen years old in Utah, but what is married, or just going to be."[59] Daynes' statistics show that Woodruff was not exaggerating.

She writes, "The demand for plural wives continued to create a scarcity of marriageable women until the 1880s, thus depressing the age at marriage for Utah women."[60] It was specifically polygamy that was an important factor causing early marriage. Thus, in Manti, in 1860, just after the Reformation in the 1850s, when a number of polygamous marriages were entered into, a remarkable 55% of the women between 14 and 20 were married, and of these, about 41% married into polygamy. In the decades before and after the 1850s, the numbers were not as high, but still about 29% of women between 14 and 20 were married in those decades (but with a much lower percentage of women entering into polygamy, about 3 or 4 percent).[61]

One example from church history shows the impact of polygamy on marriage age. Charles Rich, later a member of the Quorum of the Twelve Apostles, married fourteen-year-old Harriet Sargent on March 28, 1847. Rich's biographer wrote that she was "a beautiful young woman, fully matured" and that she was "much sought after, both by married and by single men."[62] This shows a culture in which there was intense competi-

---

59. Woodruff to George A. Smith, April 1, 1857, in Journal History on that date; discussion in Thomas G. Alexander, *Things in Heaven and Earth: The Life and Times of Wilford Woodruff, a Mormon Prophet* (SLC: Signature Books, 1991), 187.

60. Daynes, *More Wives Than One*, 110.

61. Daynes, *More Wives Than One*, 109, Figure 6. In 1880, only about 13 percent of women were married between 14 and 20. Daynes concludes her discussion of marriage age in polygamy: "That women were scarce worked to improve women's position in Mormon society." *More Wives Than One*, 115. Since polygamy by definition caused marriage age to decrease, especially among young women, Daynes apparently sees no adverse effects from early marriage. Many family historians, however, have identified significant problems in early marriage: younger wives often have more limited educational opportunities; having children at an early age presents significant health risks; there is increased chance of divorce; in addition, young women in early marriage relationships are often brought into marriages that they did not choose. R. Jenson and R. Thornton, "Early Female Marriage in the Developing World," *Gender and Development* 11.2 (July 2003): 9–19; Susheela Singh and Renee Samara, "Early Marriage Among Women in Developing Countries," *International Family Planning Perspectives* 22.4 (December, 1996): 148–175.

62. John Henry Evans, *Charles Coulson Rich: Pioneer Builder of the West* (New York: MacMillan, 1936), 96–97; Smith, *Nauvoo Polygamy*, 377. Rich's five plural wives were aged 33, 15, 20, 14 and 14, and he was aged 35–37 when he married them. This is clearly not the pattern of the bishop taking care of older widows by marrying them that some Latter-day Saint historians have emphasized. This sometimes happened, but it is just one of several motivations for plural marriage.

tion for marriageable women, which lowered the typical marriage age for young women.

If these principles apply to the culture of the FLDS church, it would indicate that one of the reasons for the young women marrying so early is the probable intense competition for women in a "closed" isolated society in which there are no obvious biological imbalances of male and female, but in which polygyny would create the artificial imbalance of more men than women available for marriage. Apparently, this has caused competition for marriage partners, and thus has driven down the marriage age among young women. Arranged very early marriage as a cultural institution—despite its legal dangers—has resulted.

Altman and Ginat, in their book on modern polygamists in two communities, *Polygamist Families in Contemporary Society*, state that 54.9 percent of the 51 women in the demographic group they studied married at age 15–19.[63] This is a remarkably high figure for early marriage, compared to non-Mormon family patterns, in the European family pattern and in the New England and the northeastern states.

One of the dysfunctional aspects of such a culture is it would leave many single young men without wives, if many of the fifteen or sixteen-year-old girls are marrying older men who already have plural families. In 1860 Manti, there were three unmarried males for every unmarried female.[64] In nineteenth-century Mormonism, the mission field served as a place where men could find wives, including plural wives. FLDS young men would not have this option in the same way, and we find the phenomenon of "lost boys" in the FLDS enclave of Colorado City/Hildale, in which young men are reportedly pressured to leave the community.[65]

---

63. Irwin Altman and Joseph Ginat, *Polygamist Families in Contemporary Society* (Cambridge: Cambridge University Press, 1996), 468, tables 6 and 7. Of the 51 wives, 0 were age 14, 3 were age 15 (5.88%), 2 were age 16 (3.92%), 7 were 17 (13.93%), 8 were 18 (15.69%), and 8 were 19 (15.69%).
64. Haynes, *More Wives Than One*, 110.
65. Angie Wagner, "Boys Seek Salvation Outside Church," *Los Angeles Times*, September 5, 2004, http://articles.latimes.com/2004/sep/05/news/admn-lostboys5 (accessed January 11, 2010); Erik Eckholm, "Boys Cast Out by Polygamists Find Help," New York Times, September 9, 2007, http://www.nytimes.com/2007/09/09/us/09polygamy.html?_r=1. (accessed on January 13, 2010). See also Altman and Ginat, *Polygamist Families in Contemporary Society*, 463, who conclude that in a polygamist community, nearly all women become plural wives, but only a limited percentage of men are able to become polygamists.

Another example of early marriage (for the wife) comes from southern Utah. James Bleak, author of the irreplaceable history of Dixie, "Annals of the Southern Utah Mission," was called to help settle St. George in late 1861, when he was thirty-two. In addition to this call, according to a recent article on Bleak, Brigham Young "instructed Bleak to marry fifteen-year-old Jane Thompson" as Bleak's third wife. Both Jane and James were reluctant to marry, but Jane talked with Brigham, "and learned from him the wisdom of his advice." They were sealed on October 26, 1861.[66]

Dynastic alliance was also an important cause of early marriage in Mormon culture. We have seen Joseph Smith marrying teen-age Helen Mar Kimball in a dynastic marriage.[67] Marriages of alliance for church leaders continued in Utah, and they would also contribute to early marriage. Because polygamy was especially encouraged among Mormonism's elite—the higher a man rose in the hierarchy, the more he was expected to live the law of plurality—there would be a natural tendency for the elite to marry among each other by means of plural marriages.[68]

For example, apostle Wilford Woodruff offered his fourteen-year-old daughter to president Brigham Young in 1857, during the Reformation, but Young said he was not marrying younger women at the time.[69] On March 4, 1859, Phebe Amelia, a seventeen-year-old daughter of Woodruff, married another apostle, Lorenzo Snow.[70]

When men married very young wives, sometimes they delayed consummation until years later. For example, on November 11, 1843, Woodruff, forty-six at the time, married fifteen-year-old Emma Smith. However, she had no children until seven months after she turned nineteen. Woodruff's biographer, Thomas Alexander, reasonably concludes, "He probably refrained from sexual relations with Emma until she became older."[71]

---

66. Brandon J. Metcalf, "James G. Bleak: From London to Dixie," *Journal of Mormon History* 35.1 (Winter 2009): 117–56, 151–52. This is an example of a high church leader prescribing marriage partners for church members. For another example, see Kimball, *Heber C. Kimball*, 95.

67. I do not use the term "dynastic marriage" to mean that Joseph Smith was literally trying to create a dynasty; I simply mean that elite Mormons were seeking to create a bond—sometimes a spiritual bond, with eschatological dimensions—through marriage.

68. Many non-elite men and women also entered into plural marriage.

69. Alexander, *Things in Heaven and Earth*, 187.

70. Ibid., 213; Wilford Woodruff diary, April 4, 1859 (Kenney, 5:323, cf. 5:22, 5:278).

71. Alexander, *Things in Heaven and Earth*, 167–68.

Another well-known example is John D. Lee's marriage to twelve- or fourteen-year-old Mary Ann Williams during the Reformation in 1856, with the understanding that he would not have sexual relations with her until she was older. As it turned out, she put off having relations with him, and she and one of Lee's sons fell in love, and Lee released her from the marriage to him and allowed her to marry his son.[72]

As we have seen, in world history, often early marriages in dynastic situations were not consummated at first.

Thus, we can conclude that marriage age in polygamous Mormon culture was lower than marriage age in the New England and northeastern states. Early marriage and very early marriage were an accepted part of Mormon culture, and polygamy was an important factor that contributed to marriage at lower ages. Dynastic marriage was also a factor causing early marriage in Mormon polygamy.

Conclusions

We have seen that marriage age in history fluctuates depending on a number of factors: economic, geographic, religious, and social. Economic downturns can cause marriage age to go up (because young people often delay marriage until they have the prospect of economic security or owning land), and wars can cause marriage age to drop as couples marry before the man leaves for military service. In addition, dynastic marriage often required arranged marriages of boys and girls at young ages, though these often did not turn into real marriages until much later. Male-female imbalances due to historical circumstances can cause marriage age to dip—for example, in colonies, in which there is a preponderance of men, marriage age of women generally lowers, due to intense competition for fewer women. In American history, marriage age of women on the frontier has been generally lower than in the east, for this reason.

---

72. Juanita Brooks, *John Doyle Lee: Zealot, Pioneer Builder, Scapegoat* (Logan, UT: Utah State University Press, 1992), 233, 239–40, *Emma Lee* (Logan: Utah State University Press, 1978), 8, 11; Smith, *Nauvoo Polygamy*, 604. See also chapter 17 of Lorraine (Richardson) Manderscheid, cp., *Some Descendants of John Doyle Lee*, at http://wadhome.org/lee/chapter_17.html (accessed December 24, 2009). The twelve year age is dependent on genealogical records; a census record would make her fourteen at the date of marriage. However, age in census records is often imprecise, so I believe the genealogical evidence is more reliable.

Mormon communities did have imbalances in which there were more males than marriageable females, but this did not occur simply because they were on the frontier, as Mormon men and women tended to migrate together. Instead, it is well documented that polygamy caused more males than marriageable female in Mormon communities. This is certainly logical—if a number of men have plural wives in a community, this would limit the availability of women for other men, both polygamists and monogamists. A competition for marriageable women resulted, which caused the marriage age to lower, and early marriage (young women marrying in their teens) and very early marriage (young women marrying at ages 14 and 15) became an acceptable part of Mormon polygamous culture.

In addition, as polygamy was emphasized and often required among the Mormon elite, dynastic marriage sometimes took place, and this often involved early marriage for young women.

Mormon cultural acceptance of very early marriage presents a contrast to the New England and northeastern states' patterns of marriage in the nineteenth century, in which very early marriage was rare. The New England and northeastern states' typical statistics for mean age at marriage were much higher than Utah's in the nineteenth century.

Thus, I do not find the arguments of some Mormon historians that very early marriage was common in the past convincing, as they seem too general and imprecise. There are many exotic examples of early marriage in various cultures and countries, but the society we should be looking at is the New England and northeastern states culture that was the background for early Mormonism. The work of social historians allows us to conclude, with some precision, that very early marriage was rare in that environment. In mid-nineteenth century New Jersey, for example, only 1.9 percent of young women were married at age 14–16, and most of that group, 1.4 percent, were married at the age 16. The percentage married at age 14 (.1) was almost negligible. The incidence of very early marriage in Joseph Smith's plural family, and in later Mormonism, was much higher than that. The IPUMS data I cite show that in the New England and Northeastern states, both in 1850 and 1880, marriage age at 13 to 15 was usually less than or about one percent.

A much more convincing path for Mormon historians to follow, when they are trying to put Joseph Smith's marriage to fourteen-year-old Helen Mar Kimball into context, would be to emphasize that it was a dynastic marriage, a marriage arranged by elite Mormon leaders, Joseph Smith and an apostle, Heber C. Kimball. Joseph Smith's plural marriages sometimes represented dynastic marriages that linked him to other Mormon leaders, such as apostles Brigham Young, Heber C. Kimball or Willard Richards and prominent Mormons such as Newel K. Whitney and Cornelius Lott. Since historical reality and the human soul are complex, this doesn't rule out parallel motivations for marriage—one may want to marry someone for five or six good reasons. But the dynastic motivation was present in a number of LDS elite plural marriages. This dynasticism would be heightened by LDS theological perspectives—for instance, you may have wanted to be linked to Joseph Smith, not just because he was the most elite marriage partner in your culture, per se, but because the marriage link would have eschatological significance both for you and your family, would increase your chances for the highest exaltation.[73]

As I have written elsewhere, there is no explicit evidence for or against sexuality in the Joseph Smith-Helen Mar Kimball marriage; despite this lack of explicit evidence, my judgment is that it is unlikely that the marriage was consummated.[74] We can draw the valid parallel from American and European history of elite early marriages that were not consummated until the marriage participants were much older. This pattern, as we have seen, can also be found in Utah Mormonism.

In conclusion, the cultural legacy of early and very early marriage in nineteenth-century Mormon polygamy is a troubling one. One conservative historian of LDS polygamy, Gregory Smith, has justifiably criticized historical "presentism" in looking at Nauvoo and Utah polygamy—expecting people in the past to adhere to our modern culture

---

73. See Helen Mar Whitney's memoir of her marriage to Joseph Smith, Jeni Broberg Holzapfel and Richard Neitzel Holzapfel, eds., *A Woman's View: Helen Mar Whitney's Reminiscences of Early Church History* (Provo, UT: Religious Studies Center, BYU, 1997), 481–88.

74. Thus I disagree with Timothy Egan, see above, and others who take it as certain that Helen Mar and Joseph Smith consummated their marriage; it is not just not certain, it is unlikely, in my judgment. I also agree with Craig Foster that Jon Krakauer is wrong on this issue, see Foster, "Doing Violence to Journalistic Integrity," at n. 78. However, I find dynastic marriages of teenage girls problematic, even if sexual consummation is delayed.

in unreasonable ways.[75] And journalists such as Jon Krakauer, Timothy Egan and Lawrence O'Donnell have undoubtedly gone to extremes in their rhetoric and arguments dealing with early Mormon polygamy.[76] However, Gregory Smith, after arguing that we must make allowances for culturally accepted racist attitudes held by early U.S. political leaders, also states, "A caution against presentism is not to claim that no moral judgments are possible about historical events, or that it does not matter whether we are racists or not." Finding the correct balance here is difficult. If we bend over backwards to justify racist attitudes held by George Washington, for example, we run the risk of appearing to justify racism.

Therefore, when early Mormon leaders such as Joseph Smith or Brigham Young participated in marriage with very young women, or authorized very young women to be married, finding the correct balance in avoiding presentism, yet not condoning very early marriage for young women, may be difficult. Gregory Smith gives a political example; but in a religious situation, this difficulty might be heightened, as Joseph Smith and Brigham Young are viewed as prophets in direct contact with God, and many modern Latter-day Saints try to follow their examples as thoroughly as possible. These historical examples from nineteenth-century Mormonism undoubtedly have had an impact on modern polygamists.

---

75. Gregory L. Smith, "Polygamy book/Age of wives."
76. See nn. 2–3 above.

Joseph Smith Jr., the Question of Polygamous Offspring, and DNA Analysis

BY UGO A. PEREGO

Introduction

During the last decade, DNA testing has contributed to the improvement of a broad range of disciplines. It transformed paternity testing from rudimentary eye color and blood type assessments to precise and accurate affirmations of biological relationship, to the resolution of 99.99%. It created a new niche within the fields of archaeology and anthropology (termed archaeogenetics)[1] where the histories, identities, migrations, and relationships of ancient people and civilizations can now be studied from a molecular point of view.[2] Other areas which have greatly benefited from the introduction of genetic analysis are forensic

---

1. Antonio Amorim, "Archaeogenetics," *Journal of Iberian Archaeology* 1 (1999): 15–25.
2. See for example Alessandro Achilli and others, "Mitochondrial DNA variation of modern Tuscans supports the near eastern origin of Etruscans," *American Journal of Human Genetics* 80 (2007): 759–768.

investigation and the study of historical events, where other methods may have proven insufficient for providing conclusive answers in the past.³ With even greater pertinence to the current topic, DNA testing has provided invaluable assistance to family historians, who are able to corroborate traditional genealogical documentation by adding genetic evidence to resolve previously ambiguous family connections.⁴ Included in such instances are several cases of disputed biological paternities involving Joseph Smith Jr., founder of the Mormon movement. Although somewhat disputed in the past, there is now a great abundance of evidence to support that, as a religious leader, Joseph Smith introduced the practice of polygamy, even if it is still not completely clear to what extent he practiced it.⁵

That being said, how confidently can DNA testing be applied to genealogical questions? While DNA is not a panacea that completely replaces traditional genealogical research, it can provide an added level of understanding and an increased degree of confidence to traditional research findings. It is estimated that more than one million people have used some form of DNA testing to learn something about their ancestry.⁶ DNA testing applied to resolving dubious paternities has application to the study of polygamy. Many such relationships in the early years of the Mormon Church were surreptitious in nature thus leaving room for speculation regarding the extent to which polygamy was practiced. Obviously, the existence and identification of offspring would provide unquestionable evidence about the former-day parties involved. Joseph Smith spoke often of a numerous and eternal posterity as one of the explanations for introducing polygamy.⁷ Joseph himself had several documented biological children from his first recorded wife, Emma Hale

---

3. Ugo A. Perego, Jayne E. Ekins, and Scott R. Woodward, "Mountain Meadows Survivor? A Mitochondrial DNA Examination," *Journal of Mormon History* 32 (2006): 45–53.

4. See for example Ugo A. Perego, Kaisa Bailey, Pekka Hellemaa, "'Anchoring' Family History through DNA," *Family Chronicle* (2009): 42–44; J. Michael Hunter and Ugo A. Perego, "DNA and Genealogy: A Case Study," *Family Chronicle* (2009): 29–31.

5. Richard P. Howard, "The Changing RLDS Response to Mormon Polygamy: A Preliminary Analysis," *The John Whitmer Historical Association Journal* 3 (1983): 14–28.

6. Howard Wolinsky, "Genetic Genealogy Goes Global," *EMBO Reports* 7, no. 11 (2006): 1072–1074. Also see Blaine Bettinger, "The Genetic Genealogist: How Big Is the Genetic Genealogy Market?", http://www.thegeneticgenealogist.com/2007/11/06/how-big-is-the-genetic-genealogy-market (accessed June 17, 2010).

7. Doctrine and Covenants (LDS) 132:30–34.

Smith, but no other children have been confirmed as being born from any of his alleged polygamous relationships. However, different sources suggest that a few individuals are possible candidates for biological children of Joseph Smith considering facts such as time of birth (from the date of sealing and within eight or nine months of his death in June 1844), known opportunities for cohabitation, family accounts, or even physiognomy.[8] A partial list and corresponding references of alleged children attributed to Joseph Smith through relationships other than with his first wife Emma is provided in figure 7.1.

The History of DNA and the Joseph Smith Family

In the early phases of the developing niche of molecular genealogy, the Joseph Smith Sr. family was identified as a test case for reconstructing ancestral DNA profiles and using this information to investigate questions of progeny, as well as further ancestry. The number of living descendants of Hyrum Smith alone exceeds 15,000, and additionally a number of genealogical situations exist within the family that are ideal applications of the new science of molecular genealogy.[9]

The basics of molecular genealogy

Within the nucleus of the cells, each person carries genetic material called DNA, which is organized in structures called chromosomes: 23 inherited from their mother and 23 from their father. DNA is the blueprint of life, providing the cell with the instructions to perform all the necessary biological functions. Moreover, information stored in our DNA can provide valuable information about one's past, although the ancestral signal can be quite difficult to isolate and trace due to the reshuffling and loss of one parent or the other's genetic material that occur at each subsequent generation. Two exceptions are found in the paternally inherited Y chromosome (Ycs) and the maternally inherited mitochondrial DNA (mtDNA). These uniparental markers don't recombine with nuclear DNA, but remain mostly intact generation after genera-

---

8. Fawn M. Brodie, *No Man Knows My History: The Life of Joseph Smith, the Mormon Prophet*, 2d ed. rev. (New York: Alfred A. Knopf, 1971), 297–298, 460–462.

9. Ugo A. Perego, Ann Turner, Jayne E. Ekins, and Scott R. Woodward, "The Science of Molecular Genealogy," *National Genealogical Society Quarterly* 93 (2005): 245–259.

Child	Mother	Source
Oliver Norman Buell	Presendia Huntington	A
John Reed Hancock	Clarissa Reed	A
Moroni Llewellyn Pratt	Mary Ann Frost	A
Orson Washington Hyde	Nancy Marinda Johnson	A
Frank Henry Hyde	Nancy Marinda Johnson	A
Josephine Rosetta Lyon (Fisher)	Sylvia Sessions	A, B, C
Josephine Henry (King)	Margaret Creighton	D
Mosiah Lyman Hancock	Clarissa Reed	E
Zebulon Williams Jacobs	Zina Diantha Huntington	C
Carolyn Delight	Lulu Vermillion	E
Alleged son or daughter	Hannah Dubois	C
Alleged son or daughter	Fanny Alger	B
George Algernon Lightner	Mary Rollins Lightner	A, C
Sarah Elizabeth Holmes	Marietta Carter	E

FIGURE 7.1: *Provisional list of alleged children recorded as being born through the union of Joseph Smith Jr. and women other than Emma Hale, his first documented wife.*
SOURCES: A – Fawn M. Brodie, *No Man Knows My History*; B – Todd Compton, *In Sacred Loneliness*; C – Richard S. Van Wagoner, *Mormon Polygamy*; D – Larry R. King, *The Kings of the Kingdom*; E – Personal communication in possession of the author.

tion. Population geneticists and molecular genealogists have employed Ycs and mtDNA extensively in reconstructing strict and unbroken paternal and maternal lineages, respectively. The majority of our DNA is found in the remaining chromosomes, termed autosomes. Autsomal DNA may also contain a surviving genetic legacy of any of our ancestors, while Ycs and mtDNA are limited to progenitors found on the two outermost branches of our family tree (figure 7.2).

The analysis of Ycs proved to be particularly useful in resolving a number of questions surrounding the ancestry and posterity of Joseph Smith Jr. (hereafter referred to only as Joseph Smith). In addition large sections of autosomal DNA have also been reconstructed for the Smith

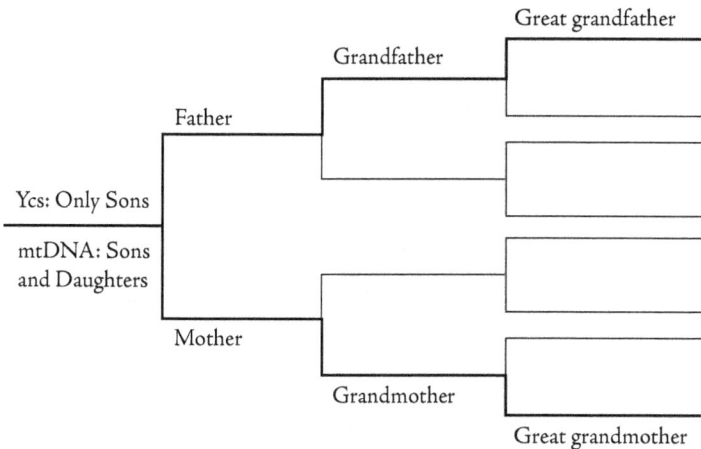

FIGURE 7.2 – *Pedigree representing Y chromosome (Ycs) and mitochondrial DNA (mtDNA) paternal and maternal inheritance patterns respectively.*

family for future case studies. With regard to Joseph Smith's ancestry, genetic analysis had already been considered in the 1990s as a means to assist in locating the exact birth place of Joseph Smith's paternal third-great-grand father, a Robert Smith of Boxford, Massachusetts, who emigrated from Lincolnshire, England, in the earlier part of the seventeenth century.[10] To test this hypothesis, we initially reconstructed the Ycs profile (haplotype) of the Smith family with the optimistic anticipation of someday finding Smith individuals in the UK carrying a similar genetic signature. Since the Ycs is found only in males and since it follows the surname line of the pedigree chart, we were able to successfully and accurately establish a Ycs profile for the Smith family by identifying a number of living descendants sharing Asael Smith (Joseph Smith's grandfather) as the most recent common ancestor (MRCA) and carrying the Smith surname (figure 7.3).[11]

---

10. Elaine C. Nichols, "Corrections to Joseph Smith's English Ancestry: The Parentage of Robert Smith of Boxford, Massachusetts," *Utah Genealogical Journal* 19 (1991): 138–143.

11. Mark A. Jobling, "In the Name of the Father: Surnames and Genetics," *Trends in Genetics* 17 (2001): 353–357. Materials and methods regarding the reconstruction of the Smith Ycs profile have been described in Ugo A. Perego, Natalie M. Myres, and Scott R. Woodward, "Reconstructing the Y-Chromosome of Joseph Smith: Genealogical Applications" *Journal of Mormon History* 31 (Fall 2005): 42–60.

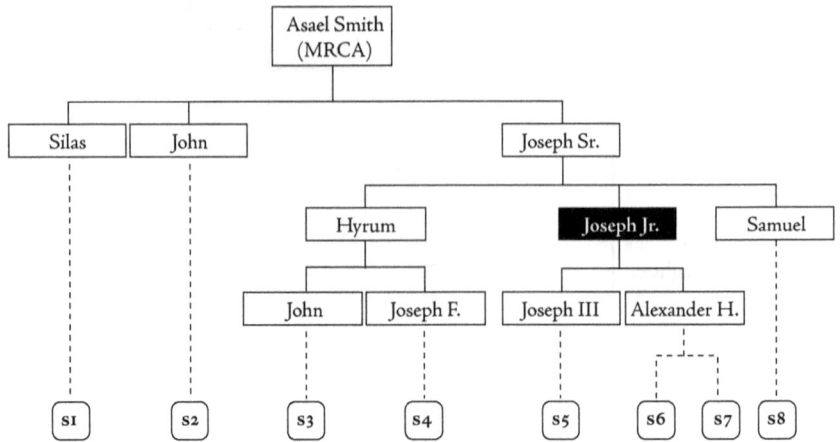

FIGURE 7.3 – *Schematic pedigree representing male lines of the Smith family sharing Asael Smith as their most recent common ancestor (MRCA). Individuals S1 – S8 contributed DNA samples that were utilized to reconstruct an accurate Y chromosome profile for Joseph Smith Jr. (see figure 7.4).*

Although any male descendant of the Joseph Smith family line would carry their paternal ancestor's Ycs haplotype, in order to test cases involving alleged biological offspring in subsequent generations, two aspects must be taken into consideration. First, to exclude possible non-paternity events (NPEs), it is mandatory to obtain genetic data from multiple documented male descendants whose MRCA is the man suspected to be the biological father of the alleged posterity. In this case, direct male descendants of Joseph Smith needed to be tested in order to confidently reconstruct Joseph Smith's exact Ycs profile. This presents a challenge in that Joseph Smith had eleven children with Emma (two adopted),[12] but only four biological sons that grew to adulthood, and only two of them — Joseph Smith III and Alexander Hale Smith — are survived by a living biological posterity. The next consideration is the gender of the alleged child. Because Ycs is paternally inherited, only cases involving suspected sons could be tested using this uniparental marker. Any potential biological daughter of Joseph Smith born through one of his several polygamous relationships would not carry the father's Ycs, thus

---

12. Michael Kennedy, "Joseph and Emma's Family," *Ensign* (February 2008): 39–41.

leaving the more complex deciphering of autosomal DNA as the only alternative.[13]

Fortunately, a few direct male descendants of both Joseph Smith III and Alexander Hale Smith were identified and willingly donated a DNA sample to this project. Additionally, other descendants from Joseph Smith's brothers (Samuel and Hyrum), as well as others descending from Joseph Smith's uncles also contributed a biological specimen from which DNA was extracted and Ycs data obtained. Over time, with the intent of examining autosomal DNA questions, more than one hundred individuals — males and females — sharing Asael Smith as their MRCA donated DNA and genealogical data to Sorenson Molecular Genealogy Foundation (SMGF).

Testing Smith paternal lines with Asael Smith as the MRCA in addition to direct male descendants of Joseph Smith excluded any chances of NPEs, and also confirmed the value of two ambiguous markers (alleles). Ycs data for the Smith family is summarized in figure 7.4, which include the individuals reported on the schematic pedigree in figure 7.3. At first twenty-four and then eventually a total of forty-three short tandem repeat (STR) markers were confidently reconstructed for the Joseph Smith Ycs profile. Although only two descendants may be sufficient to reconstruct a MRCA Ycs profile, additional paternal lines needed to be tested to increase confidence of each allele value. In particular markers DYS439 and DYS449 (12 and 30 respectively) required further testing from related Smith males to confidently infer their allelic values.[14] These findings were confirmed in a 2009 study published in the prestigious *American Journal of Human Genetics*, where the Joseph Smith Ycs was inferred by mining data from public genetic databases containing DNA information of Hyrum Smith's descendants.[15]

---

13. Mitochondrial DNA testing is not helpful in confirming father-daughter biological relationships as it is inherited exclusively from the girl's mother. See also Perego and Woodward, "Mountain Meadows Survivor? A Mitochondrial DNA Examination," 53–61.

14. DYS is an acronym for *DNA Y-Chromosome Segment*. Few differences at the same DYS markers (loci) can be occasionally observed even in individuals sharing a documented biological relationship. These changes are the result of random mutations occurring along the radiating paternal lineages.

15. Jane Gitschier, "Inferential Genotyping of Y Chromosomes in Latter-Day Saints Founders and comparison to Utah Samples in the HapMap Project," *American Journal of Human Genetics* 84 (2009): 251–258.

Locus	S1 descendent of Silas Smith	S2 descendent of John Smith	S3 descendent of Hyrum through John	S4 descendent of Hyrum through Joseph F.	S5 descendent of Joseph Jr. through Joseph III	S6 descendent of Joseph Jr. through Alexander	S7 descendent of Joseph Jr. through Alexander	S8 descendent of Samuel Smith	Joseph Smith Jr. Inferred Y-s Haplotype
DYS19	14	14	14	14	14	14	14	14	14
DYS385a	11	11	11	11	11	11	11	11	11
DYS385b	13	13	13	13	13	13	13	13	13
DYS388	12	12	12	12	12	12	12	12	12
DYS389I	14	14	14	14	14	14	14	14	14
DYS389II	30	30	30	30	30	30	30	30	30
DYS390	(25)	24	24	24	24	24	24	24	24
DYS391	11	11	11	11	11	11	11	11	11
DYS392	14	14	14	14	14	14	14	14	14
DYS393	13	13	13	13	13	13	13	13	13
DYS426	12	12	12	12	12	12	12	12	12
DYS437	15	(14)	15	15	15	15	15	15	15
DYS438	12	12	12	12	12	12	12	12	12
DYS439	12	12	12	12	12	(11)	12	12	12
DYS441	14	14	14	14	14	14	14	14	14
DYS442	17	17	17	17	17	17	17	17	17
DYS444	12	12	12	12	12	12	12	12	12
DYS445	12	12	12	12	12	12	12	12	12
DYS446	13	13	13	13	13	13	13	13	13
DYS447	25	25	25	25	25	25	25	25	25
DYS448	18	18	18	18	18	18	18	18	18
DYS449	30	30	30	30	(31)	30	30	30	30
DYS452	30	30	30	30	30	30	30	30	30
DYS454	11	11	11	11	11	11	11	11	11
DYS455	11	11	11	11	11	11	11	11	11
DYS456	17	17	17	17	17	17	17	17	17
DYS458	17	17	17	17	17	17	17	17	17

FIGURE 7.4: *Y chromosome profiles (haplotypes) from male descendants of different Smith lines sharing Asael Smith (Joseph Smith Jr.'s grandfather) as their most recent common ancestor (see figure 7.3). This information was used to reconstruct Joseph Smith Jr.'s Y chromosome signature. Mutated values from Joseph Smith Jr.'s inferred haplotype are circled. (Figure continued on next page.)*

Locus	S1 descendent of Silas Smith	S2 descendent of John Smith	S3 descendent of Hyrum through John	S4 descendent of Hyrum through Joseph F.	S5 descendent of Joseph Jr. through Joseph III	S6 descendent of Joseph Jr. through Alexander	S7 descendent of Joseph Jr. through Alexander	S8 descendent of Samuel Smith	Joseph Smith Jr. Inferred Ycs Haplotype
DYS459a	9	9	9	9	9	9	9	9	9
DYS459b	10	10	10	10	10	10	10	10	10
DYS460	11	11	11	11	11	11	11	11	11
DYS461	12	12	12	12	12	12	12	12	12
DYS462	11	11	11	11	11	11	11	11	11
DYS463	24	24	24	24	24	24	24	24	24
DYS464a	15	15	15	15	15	15	15	15	15
DYS464b	16	16	16	16	16	16	16	16	16
DYS464c	16	16	16	16	16	16	16	16	16
DYS464d	17	17	17	17	17	17	17	17	17
GGAAT1B07	10	10	10	10	10	10	10	10	10
YCAIIa	19	19	19	19	19	19	19	19	19
YCAIIb	23	23	23	23	23	23	23	23	23
YGATAA10	15	15	15	15	15	15	15	15	15
YGATAC4	23	23	23	23	23	23	23	23	23
YGATAH4.1	12	12	12	12	12	12	12	12	12

FIGURE 7.4 (continued)

By testing additional male lines and with findings confirmed by a second independent study, we approach total confidence that the Ycs data obtained can be correctly assigned to Joseph Smith and his paternal relatives. If a cheek swab could be acquired from Joseph Smith himself, the DNA would not be any different from the profile we reconstructed from his living descendants. However there is no need to exhume bodies and test bones. The inferences obtained using this technology are highly accurate.

The Posterity of Joseph Smith

With the Ycs profile of Joseph Smith in hand, questions about the progeny of Joseph Smith can also be addressed. It is essential to note that any direct paternal descendent of Joseph Smith, no matter who the mother is, will have the same Ycs profile as has been established for Joseph Smith via his documented sons Joseph Smith III and Alexander Hale Smith, and reinforced by descendants of Hyrum and Samuel Smith. Reviewed here are five cases of proposed paternity. Each is unique in its history and background but represents a possible direct paternal connection to Joseph Smith, and therefore can be directly assessed using the Ycs approach. While each case uses this same technology, it is evaluated in a slightly different way, demonstrating that while there are some limitations, a wide range of possible scenarios can be addressed with DNA testing.

Following these five cases is the case of Josephine Lyon, a question of paternity which is currently being addressed through the emerging science of autosomal DNA testing.

Case #1: Moroni Llewellyn Pratt — The Ideal Situation

In her book *No Man Knows My History*, author Fawn Brodie speculates that Moroni Llewellyn Pratt was Joseph Smith's son, based on a number of assumptions.[16] Moroni Pratt was born on December 7, 1844, and his recorded father is Parley P. Pratt. However, Moroni's mother, Mary Ann Frost, has been recorded as being both the wife of Parley and later of Joseph Smith. Children born from Parley's and Mary Ann's union in the years following the death of Joseph Smith in 1844 were still sealed to the prophet, as was the custom in those days.[17] Having the predetermined Ycs profile of Joseph Smith available, the remaining requirement for investigating Moroni's biological paternity is his own Ycs profile for purposes of comparison. This was obtained by collecting DNA samples from two male individuals who shared Moroni as their paternal MRCA.

---

16. Brodie, *No Man Knows My History*, 345, 484. See also, Todd Compton, *In Sacred Loneliness: The Plural Wives of Joseph Smith* (Salt Lake City: Signature Books, 1997), 763 note V.

17. Thomas Milton Tinney, *The Royal Family of the Prophet Joseph Smith, Junior; First President of the Church of Jesus Christ of Latter-day Saints* (N.p.: Tinney-Green[e] Family Organization Publishing Company, 1973), 12, L. Tom Perry Special Collections, Lee Library, Brigham Young University, Provo, Utah, records this proxy sealing information: "GS# 183, 374—Res. Page 513-514 Proxy Sealings, # 3660—Joseph Smith, Junior. Sealing Date: Feb. 6, 1846 at 1:30 P.M. solemnized by H.C. Kimball; Witnesses &: [meaning more than one witness] Wm. Redfield F.D. Richards—No. 19, page 3. M.S. #1 Mary Ann Frost, #3164, born Jan. 14, 1809 at Groton, Caledonia, Vermont; #2 Parley P. Pratt, #3163, Proxy for time."

As stated earlier, it is important to have at least two representatives in order to exclude any possible cases of undocumented NPEs.

The two individuals who contributed DNA samples to be used to reconstruct Moroni's Ycs haplotypes were descendants of two of Moroni's sons: Irving and Lester. Their Ycs profiles were an exact match, so consequently Moroni's Ycs haplotype is inferred with great confidence. By directly comparing each genetic marker for Joseph Smith's Ycs alongside those of Moroni, it was possible to conclusively answer a genealogical question that has been the subject of speculation for more than one hundred and fifty years.[18] As observed in figure 7.5, the two haplotypes have several differences between them. Based on the established Ycs mutation rate, the time to the MRCA between these two paternal lineages predates the birth year of Moroni by more than two-thousand years.[19] Therefore, the DNA test performed conclusively determines that Moroni Pratt is not the biological offspring of Joseph Smith.

However the question remains, if Joseph Smith was not the father of Moroni, can we say with certainty that it was Parley? To test this hypothesis, two descendents of Parley P. Pratt through two other sons were tested. The profile of these individuals matched each other, thus allowing inference of Parley's own Ycs profile. The exact matches between Parley and all of his sons' lineages tested, including Moroni, confirmed that the latter was indeed Parley's, and not Joseph's, biological son. This case demonstrates an ideal situation in which Ycs data for all the interested lines can be reconstructed from living descendants in order to assess paternity questions from the past. Unfortunately, the availability of such conclusive data is not always the case.

---

18. Additional figures and tables are found in Perego, "Reconstructing the Y-Chromosome of Joseph Smith."

19. Bruce Walsh, "Estimating the Time to Most Recent Common Ancestor for the Y Chromosome or Mitochondrial DNA for a Pair of Individuals," *Genetics* 158 (2001): 897–912; Manfred Kayser and others, "Characteristics and Frequency of Germline Mutations at Microsatellite Loci from the Human Y Chromosome, as Revealed by Direct Observation in Father/Son Pairs," *American Journal of Human Genetics* 66 (2000): 1580–1588.

Case #2: *Zebulon Jacobs — Testing Brothers*

Zebulon Jacobs was considered a possible son of Joseph Smith, as stated by Richard Van Wagoner in *Mormon Polygamy*.[20] His brother, Henry C. Jacobs, was born in 1846, two years after the martyrdom of Joseph Smith, and therefore excluded as a possible Joseph Smith descendant. DNA samples were collected and analyzed for descendants of both Zebulon and Henry, and the two Ycs haplotypes were a perfect match (figure 7.5).[21] This indicates that they share the same biological father – recorded as Henry Bailey Jacobs — although additional paternal lines could not be tested to ensure it. However, the Jacobs' profile differs from that of Joseph Smith at nine locations, removing Joseph Smith from the pool of candidate biological fathers.

Case #3: *Orrison Smith — Direct Testing*

Fanny Alger has been recorded as the possible first plural companion of Joseph Smith, although evidence about this union is quite inconsistent. Purportedly, in 1836 Fanny was pregnant, but no additional information is available about the birth of the child and the name of the father.[22] Several years ago, a man surfaced who claimed to be a descendant of an Orrison Smith, son of Joseph Smith and Fanny Alger. The only supporting information available about this Orrison Smith was the approximate year of birth (1834) and the location of his birth (somewhere in Ohio). As of today, the public genealogical database FamilySearch.org still lists him as a son of Joseph Smith and Fanny Alger.[23] While the previous two case studies presented strong genetic evidence in excluding Joseph Smith as the biological father of the two alleged sons, this case presented the specific challenges of dealing with a single descendant with a poorly documented genealogy. All that could be done at that time was to run the DNA of the individual that contacted us (he himself being a Smith and claiming a direct paternal ancestry to Orrison) and compare his DNA with Joseph Smith's inferred Ycs haplotype. The com-

---

20. Richard S. Van Wagoner, *Mormon Polygamy: A History* (Salt Lake City: Signature Books, 1989), 48–49.
21. Perego, "Reconstructing the Y-Chromosome of Joseph Smith."
22. Compton, *In Sacred Loneliness*, 35–36. See also Brodie, *No Man Knows My History*, 345.
23. http://www.familysearch.org (accessed June 19, 2010).

JOSEPH SMITH AND DNA   245

Locus	Moroni L. Pratt	Zebulon Jacobs	Orrison Smith	Oliver N. Buell	Mosiah L. Hancock	Joseph Smith Jr.
DYS19/394	14	14	14	14	(13)	14
DYS385a	11	11	11	–	(17)	11
DYS385b	(12)	(14)	(14)	16	(19)	13
DYS388	12	12	12	(13)	12	12
DYS389I	(13)	(13)	(13)	(13)	14	14
DYS389II	(29)	(28)	(29)	30	(31)	30
DYS390	(23)	(22)	(25)	(23)	24	24
DYS391	11	11	(12)	(10)	11	11
DYS392	(13)	(13)	(13)	(12)	(11)	14
DYS393	13	13	(13)	(14)	(14)	13
DYS426	12	12	12	(11)	(11)	12
DYS437	15	15	(14)	(14)	–	15
DYS438	12	12	12	(10)	–	12
DYS439	12	(11)	12	(11)	(11)	12
DYS441	–	–	–	14	–	14
DYS442	–	–	–	17	–	17
DYS444	–	–	–	–	–	12
DYS445	–	–	–	(10)	–	12
DYS446	–	–	–	(10)	–	13
DYS447	25	25	(24)	25	–	25
DYS448	–	–	–	(20)	–	18
DYS449	–	–	–	30	–	30
DYS452	–	–	–	(29)	–	30
DYS454	11	11	11	11	–	11
DYS455	11	11	11	11	–	11
DYS456	–	–	–	(14)	–	17
DYS458	–	–	–	(16)	–	17
DYS459a	–	–	–	(8)	–	9

FIGURE 7.5: Inferred Y chromosome haplotypes for the five case study candidates compared to the inferred haplotype for Joseph Smith Jr. Circled numerals indicate the differences between haplotypes clearly demonstrating that they each belong to a separate paternal line. "–" indicates data that is not available for that particular marker. Allele values are reported following the currently approved standards proposed by the National Institute of Standard Technology (NIST).

Locus	Moroni L. Pratt	Zebulon Jacobs	Orrison Smith	Oliver N. Buell	Mosiah L. Hancock	Joseph Smith Jr.
DYS459b	–	–	–	–	–	10
DYS460	11	11	11	11	–	11
DYS461	12	12	12	12	–	12
DYS462	11	11	11	(12)	–	11
DYS463	–	–	–	(23)	–	24
DYS464a	–	–	–	(11)	–	15
DYS464b	–	–	–	(14)	–	16
DYS464c	–	–	–	(14)	–	16
DYS464d	–	–	–	(15)	–	17
GGAAT1B07	10	(9)	10	10	–	10
YCAIIa	19	19	19	(20)	–	19
YCAIIb	23	(24)	23	(21)	–	23
YGATAA10	15	15	15	(14)	–	15
YGATAC4	23	23	(24)	23	–	23
YGATAH4.1	(11)	(13)	12	(11)	–	12

FIGURE 7.5 *(continued)*

parison resulted in nine differences between haplotypes, which are too many to indicate a possible biological relationship within Joseph Smith's lifetime (figure 7.5). Notwithstanding its poor documentation, until an additional paternal descendant of Orrison can be identified and tested, we cannot completely rule out the alleged connection since we cannot rule out NPEs in the generations separating Orrison Smith from the individual tested.

Case #4: Oliver Norman Buell — The Added Value of Online Databases

Another paternity case mentioned in Fawn Brodie's book is that of Oliver Norman Buell, the son of Presendia Huntington and her recorded husband Norman Buell. Oliver was born in Clay County, Missouri, in 1840 during a time when Norman was no longer affiliated with the Mormon Church. Among other things, the cited evidence for paternity comes from an uncanny resemblance between Oliver Norman Buell and his proposed half brother, Joseph Smith III.²⁴

Unfortunately, two individuals sharing Oliver Buell as their MRCA could not be located. In absence of this preferable scenario, two descendants of Oliver's grandson, Owen F. Buell born in 1894, were tested. Their Ycs profiles matched exactly, allowing the inference of Owen's Ycs profile.²⁵ Although this haplotype could likely represent Oliver Buell's true profile, it is not possible to exclude the possibility of an NPE — such as an undocumented adoption or illegitimacy — that may have occurred in the two intervening generations between Oliver and his grandson. If that was the case, conclusions drawn from the Owen Buell haplotype could not be correctly extended to Oliver Buell. To circumvent this difficulty, a novel approach was considered to more conclusively determine the paternity of Oliver N. Buell, with the goal to increase the likelihood that the genetic profile we had for Owen is also representative of his grandfather Oliver, Joseph Smith's alleged son.

The SMGF houses a correlated genetic and genealogical database that includes a large Ycs component. Using the Ycs profile for Owen Buell, we queried the database for possible matches. A single match was obtained with the surname Buell, sharing 40 of the 43 Ycs haplotype obtained from Owen's two grandsons. Through traditional genealogical investigation it was discovered that the anonymous Buell donor in the SMGF database shared a common paternal ancestor with the Oliver Buell's line in the person of Samuel W. Buell, born in 1641. Based on the Ycs molecular clock, an interval of 400 years is enough time for the three differences observed between the two paternal haplotypes to have occurred. With the confirmation of relationship between the two Buell lines, it is also possible to conclude with a high degree of certainty that at least 40 STRs could be accurately inferred to Oliver's Ycs haplotype.

Using the 40 marker inferred haplotype of Oliver Buell, a direct comparison was made to Joseph Smith's Ycs profile. This analysis showed that out of 40 markers there were too many differences between haplotypes to entertain the possibility of Joseph Smith being the biological father of

---

24. Brodie, *No Man Knows My History*, portrait facing 299, 301–02, 345–46, 460–62.

25. Ugo A. Perego, Jayne E. Ekins, and Scott R. Woodward, "Resolving the Paternities of Oliver N. Buell and Mosiah L. Hancock through DNA," *The John Whitmer Historical Association Journal* 27 (2008): 128–136.

Oliver Buell (figure 7.5). Moreover, due to the fact that a strong link was already determined between the two descendants of Owen Buell and the individual in the SMGF database, we already knew that Oliver is indeed a Buell and not a Smith.

Case #5: Mosiah Lyman Hancock — Little Sometimes Is Enough

There is a journal entry stating that at the onset of her son's illness, Clarissa Reed said to Joseph Smith, "Our Mosiah is dying."[26] There are several individuals, including LDS historians and family members, who have taken this phrase to infer Joseph Smith's biological paternity of this child, though Clarissa could have been indicating her husband, Levi Hancock. Mosiah Lyman Hancock was born in Kirtland, Ohio, on April 9, 1834.

At the onset of this investigation, a descendant of Mosiah surfaced already having in hand a 12 marker Ycs profile. Although more markers are needed to confidently confirm or refute relationship between individuals, some preliminary assessments can be made. A haplotype of only 12 markers is not usually enough to determine with great confidence if two individuals truly share a common paternal ancestor (identical-by-descent, or IBD) or if they coincidentally share a similar genetic profile (referred to as identical-by-state, or IBS). Basically, if too few markers are compared a false positive outcome could result. Further, with only one descendant of Mosiah it is not possible to rule out possible NPEs in the intervening generations.

However, using the 12-marker haplotype to query the SMGF Ycs database produced six exact matches sharing the Hancock surname. Genealogical examination of the pedigrees associated with each one of the SMGF matches revealed a common paternal ancestor with the Hancock lineage of interest, coalescing to Mosiah's grandfather.[27] All of these considerations combine to give fair confidence that the 12-marker profile represents a true biological Hancock line to which Mosiah also belonged. Additionally, when compared to the same 12 markers from Jo-

---

26. Emily Hancock (Mosiah's daughter) recorded such affirmation in her voice journal. Personal correspondence dated May 9, 2007, from Emily's grandson in possession of the author.
27. Perego, "Resolving the Paternities."

seph Smith Ycs profile (figure 7.5), too many differences are observed to allow the possibility of Joseph Smith as the father, thus suggesting Levi Hancock as the true biological father of Mosiah Hancock.

These five cases provide a glimpse of the range of possible situations that can be addressed by combining genealogical data with Ycs haplotypes. However, as explained earlier, only cases involving alleged sons on strictly unbroken paternal lines can be considered with this approach. If the biological relationship to test involved a possible daughter of Joseph Smith, neither Ycs nor mtDNA testing could be of assistance. X chromosome (the female counterpart of the Ycs) or autosomal DNA analysis would be the only two genetic systems that could be utilized in such cases, although interpreting the results of these tests is not as straightforward as with Ycs and mtDNA. Additionally, any hypothesis of alleged children of Joseph Smith that do not have living descendants in the present day also pose serious difficulty to this type of genetic analysis. Therefore, it is highly unlikely that all the proposed cases of paternities involving Joseph Smith will ever be addressed and resolved by this methodology. However, new technological advancement in the field of autosomal DNA testing may allow for further investigations that previously would not have been touched by Ycs or mtDNA testing.

This technology is currently being employed in resolving the paternity of Josephine Rosetta Lyon Fisher.

Case #6: Josephine Rosetta Lyon Fisher — An Autosomal DNA Approach

Josephine was born on February 8, 1844, in Nauvoo, Illinois. Her recorded parents are Sylvia Porter Session and Windsor Palmer Lyon, who were married in Far West, Missouri, in 1838. The case of Josephine is interesting in that it is possibly the strongest case of an alleged biological child born of Joseph Smith through a polygamous union, but the well-developed sciences of Ycs and mtDNA testing cannot address their relationship at all. Josephine's disputed paternity is based on an affidavit containing her mother's confession on her dead bed:

> Just prior to my mothers death in 1882 she called me to her bedside and told me that her days on earth were about numbered and before she passed away from mortality she desired to tell me something which she had kept as an en-

tire secret from me and from all others but which she now desired to communicate to me. She then told me that I was the daughter of the Prophet Joseph Smith, she having been sealed to the Prophet at the time that her husband Mr. Lyon was out of fellowship with the Church.[28]

Significant weight has been given to this affidavit as it relates to Josephine's paternity. Considering that there is documented evidence about Sylvia's union to Joseph Smith and that Windsor had physically relocated outside of their home at the time of Josephine's conception and birth,[29] it is plausible that such declaration has reference to an actual biological association between Josephine and Joseph Smith. The very name of Josephine seems to imply a connection to the Mormon Prophet. However, as demonstrated in the previous cases, situational accounts that historically have been accepted as evidence, proved to be speculative.

Despite the interpretation of Sylvia Sessions' statement, the greatest challenge from a genetic testing perspective is the incompatibility of Josephine's gender with well established genetic testing techniques. Being a woman, she did not inherit the male-characteristic Ycs from her father and her mtDNA is not applicable in this situation as the mother's identity is not in question. A different avenue of testing was in order for this particular question.

Starting in 2000, a considerable number of DNA samples from individuals — both males and females — descending from six of Josephine's ten children were collected through the assistance of the Sessions family group. To date, more than 120 people sharing Josephine Rosetta Lyon as their MRCA and removed from her by as few as three generations have contributed a DNA sample together with their pedigree chart to assist in this case study. It was obvious that the issue of Josephine's paternity was more than just an historical question, as hundreds of her descendants wanted to discover if the biological connection to Joseph Smith was real. All were hopeful that autosomal DNA could provide some answers.

After just a short decade, technological advances in the field of genetics make it possible to generate data from hundreds of thousands of single nucleotide polymorphisms (SNPs) from the autosomal genome.

---

28. Compton, *In Sacred Loneliness*, 183.
29. Brian C. Hales, "The Joseph Smith — Sylvia Sessions Plural Sealing: Polyandry or Polygyny?" *Mormon Historical Studies* 9 (Spring 2008): 41–57.

The large amount of data produced through this method is phenomenal and was unthinkable just few years ago. Providing a meaningful analysis of it requires powerful computers and algorithms capable of interpreting the data in light of the hypotheses that are being tested. Rather than an unambiguous and clear genetic signal obtained from the analysis of uniparental markers, the large quantity of SNPs produced cannot be linked in a straightforward way to specific branches of the family tree. However, ancestral legacy can be measured using genetic scores, percentages, and probabilities that must be carefully taken in consideration within the familial context being tested.

Using the recently developed Affymetrix 6.0 GeneChip®,[30] nearly one million SNPs were generated from a small number of carefully selected individuals belonging to both the Lyon and Smith families. DNA samples were run on a GeneChip® Scanner 3000 7G and analysis of the data was conducted in collaboration with scientists at the University of Utah.

Based on the inheritance properties of DNA and considering factors such as the random loss of part of the genetic signal at each subsequent generation (a feature known as genetic drift), a measurable genetic contribution of Smith DNA among Lyon's descendants would be somewhat expected if Joseph Smith was the actual father of Josephine. However, considerable discrepancy was observed in the results obtained. Such incongruity could be linked to genetic drift or to other contributing factors: more "Smith DNA" could have survived in some individuals but not in others, or Joseph Smith may or may not have been Josephine's father and alternative reasons could explain the genetic discrepancy observed. In order to address this issue, we evaluated the possibility of genetic contribution from other common ancestors in addition to the alleged ancestry linked to the union between Joseph Smith and Sylvia Sessions. This assessment was performed using empirical genealogical data.

Family trees were provided by participants at the time of the contribution of the biological specimen to the Josephine Lyon case study. These records were extended and verified using primary sources and online databases by the genealogical team at SMGF. Common ancestors

---

30. http://affymetrix.com (accessed June 19, 2010).

and corresponding degrees of relationships were carefully analyzed to determine the amount of DNA that would be expected to be shared between closely related individuals. This line of investigation was poised on the fact that descendants from the Smith and Lyon/Fisher families are part of the same pioneer stock that participated in the first colonization of the Great Salt Lake Valley nearly 150 years ago, and could have potentially had many overlapping ancestors. A considerable number of additional ancestral relationships between the descendants tested for the Smith and Lyon families were catalogued in this genealogical exercise.

Although the presented assessment of the data is preliminary, the finding of additional common ancestors existing among the individuals tested proved to be significant and cannot be ignored in light of the genetic scores (GS) obtained. In fact, it appears that Josephine's descendants with the highest genetic affinity to the Smith family gene pool were also closely related to Smith's descendants through common ancestors besides the purported Joseph Smith ancestry. Likewise, individuals with the lowest scores were more distantly related. Figures 7.6A–F show such examples from the dataset analyzed. Each figure contains one set of individuals — one from the Smith and the other from the Lyon's families — that were tested for autosomal SNPs and whose DNA was compared in order to obtain a GS. The additional information in each figure includes genealogical data describing all the ancestors they have in common and the degrees of relationship derived by such genealogical connections. Most likely, as in the comparison reported in figure 7.6A, the higher genetic score observed could be linked to the fact that the two individuals are also second cousins once removed through a common ancestor that was born in 1862. Likewise, the lowest genetic score, as reported in figure 7.6F, could be explained by the more distant familiar relationship shared by Josephine's descendant with the member of the Smith family tested (an occurrence of fourth degree cousinship and one as a third cousin once removed).

In summary, as this work progresses and analysis is performed in light of the multiple familial relationships shared by both Josephine Lyon's and Joseph Smith's descendants, it is clear that a lot of "genealogical noise" is also present. This complicates any attempt to identify a clear and straightforward genetic signal from Joseph Smith in Josephine's descen-

FIGURE 7.6A — Genetic Score 185.98
Smith (S-623328) and Lyon (S-693396)*

Common Ancestors and Birthdates	Generations	Relationship
Mon (Mans) Monson (22 July 1862)	7	$2C_1R$
Thomas Scott (1594)	24	$10C_2R$

FIGURE 7.6B — Genetic Score 179.74
Smith (S-623328) and Lyon (S-681833)*

Common Ancestors and Birthdates	Generations	Relationship
Mon (Mans) Monson (22 July 1862)	7	$2C_1R$
Thomas Scott (1594)	24	$10C_2R$

FIGURE 7.6C — Genetic Score 127.47
Smith (S-633895) and Lyon (S-693359)

Common Ancestors and Birthdates	Generations	Relationship
Joel Hills Johnson (23 Mar. 1802)	8	$3C$
Anthony Johnson Stratton (11 Jan. 1824)	9	$3C_1R$
William Sabin (11 Oct. 1609)	21	$9C_1R$
Edward Griswold (1607)	23	$10C_1R$
John Emery Sr. (29 Sept. 1598)	23	$10C_1R$
Thomas Scott (1594)	24	$10C_2R$

FIGURES 7.6A–F (continued on following page): Six examples of autosomal DNA comparison between members of the Smith and Lyon's families. The genetic score for each pair of individuals is reported in the corresponding table together with information about their common ancestors, number of generations separating them, and their biological relationships (i.e. 4C = 4th cousin, 9C2R = 9th cousin twice removed, 11C1R = 11th cousin once removed, etc.). Genetic scores indicate the amount of DNA shared between each pair of individuals. The higher the value reported, the larger the amount of the DNA shared.

* S-681833 and S-693396 are siblings and they were both included in the study for calibration purposes. The similar genetic scores in figures 7.6A and 7.6B is in agreement with the ancestry both individuals share.

Figure 7.6D — Genetic Score 77.83
Smith (S–633895) and Lyon (S–693351)

Common Ancestors and Birthdates	Generations	Relationship
Joel Hills Johnson (23 Mar. 1802)	9	3C1R
Anthony Johnson Stratton (11 Jan. 1824)	10	4C
William Sabin (11 Oct. 1609)	22	9C2R
Edward Griswold (1607)	24	11C
John Emery Sr. (29 Sept. 1598)	24	11C
Thomas Scott (1594)	25	11C1R

Figure 7.6E — Genetic Score 58.88
Smith (S–633895) and Lyon (S–693375)

Common Ancestors and Birthdates	Generations	Relationship
Sanford Porter (7 Mar. 1790)	7	4C
Thomas Scott (1594)	24	10C2R

Figure 7.6F — Genetic Score 56.21
Smith (S–682958) and Lyon (S–693347)

Common Ancestors and Birthdates	Generations	Relationship
Samuel Carter (1 Sept. 1836)	9	3C1R
Thomas Scott (1594)	10	4C

Figures 7.6A–F (continued from previous page).

dants. In other words, the challenge that researchers face is to be able to distinguish the genetic contribution by Joseph Smith in the purported paternity of Josephine, from all the other related Smiths who married ancestors of Josephine's descendants before and after Joseph Smith's time. It is possible that this paternity case may never be fully resolved by means of genetic testing, although it appears that the analysis obtained to date shows a strong genetic association of Josephine's descendants to the multiple documented genealogical relationships observed, independent of the claim that Joseph Smith was Josephine's biological father.

Conclusions

The analysis of alleged paternities involving Joseph Smith, the Mormon Prophet, through the use of DNA could further the understanding of the extent and nature of his involvement with the practice of polygamy. If one of the explanations of introducing polygamy as part of one of the fundamental doctrines in this dispensation was to have a numerous posterity, it is at least puzzling considering that as of today no biological children of Joseph Smith have been identified besides those born with his wife, Emma Hale. The Ycs cases reviewed and summarized in this essay provide strong evidence against Joseph Smith being the father of the five boys recorded as his from the different historical sources examined, and such results should be taken into consideration in future publications dealing with Joseph Smith's polygamous unions and the corresponding alleged paternities. However, it is likely that not all the cases of children linked to the founder of Mormonism will ever be resolved through DNA testing due to limitations such as the gender of the child or the lack of living progeny. Ancient DNA analysis using remains from Joseph Smith and some of his other purported children could be an option for additional case studies and any data retrieved with this approach could be more easily interpreted, but the bureaucracy involved with exhumation permits, accurately identifying burial sites, and obtaining high-quality DNA samples adds to the complexity of this alternative methodology.

DNA has inarguably added a new and powerful level of comprehension with regard to ancient and recent historical events. Genetic evidence may offer a valuable complement when other sources of information to investigate the past are not sufficient to provide conclusive answers. Genetic analysis has the capacity to impact the study of time periods spanning from our species' origins hundreds of thousands of years ago to the identification of previously unknown details in the life of historical figures that lived just few decades ago.[31] DNA may contribute significantly to deciphering the ancient and recent history of people as long as suitable biological specimens are attainable, testable hypotheses formulated, and

---

31. Alessandro Achilli and Ugo Perego, "Mitochondrial DNA: A Female Perspective in Recent Human Origins and Evolution," in Paola Spinozzi and Alessandro Zironi, eds., *Origins as a Paradigm in the Sciences and in the Humanities* (Goettingen: V&R Unipress, 2010), 41–58.

appropriate methodologies applied. However, it must be remembered that genetic analysis alone does not replace other methods traditionally employed in historical and genealogical research. It enhances conventional means and becomes more relevant when analyzed within a specific context and in combination with other sources of information.

RLDS Church Reaction to the LDS Doctrine and Covenants' Section 132: Conflicting Responses and Changing Perceptions[1]

by Newell G. Bringhurst

The reaction of the Reorganized Church of Jesus Christ of Latter Day Saints (now known as the Community of Christ) to an 1843 Revelation "relating to the new and everlasting covenant" attributed to Joseph Smith, has evoked conflict and indeed changed as the Reorganization itself evolved from its inception during the early 1850s down to the present.

The "New Organization" which emerged in the early 1850s, as the precursor to the Reorganized Church of Jesus Christ of Latter Day Saints, made clear its strong opposition to the practice of plural marriage, with one of its early prominent spokesmen, Zenas H. Gurley, declaring

---

1. The author wishes to thank Richard P. Howard, Mark A. Scherer, William D. Russell, John C. Hamer, Lawrence Foster, and Marjory Keith-Riggs for their insights and information. Special thanks to Barbara Bernauer and the staff of the Community of Christ Library-Archives for their help locating documents.

it "an abomination in the sight of the Lord God..."[2] But at the same time "many of the earliest Reorganization leaders accepted as fact that Joseph Smith had been responsible for the introduction of polygamy."[3] In particular, two early RLDS spokesmen, William Marks and Isaac Sheen, both of whom personally knew and interacted with the Mormon leader conceded that Joseph Smith "was somehow involved in the inception of the spiritual wife doctrine which led to polygamy at Nauvoo."[4] Specifically, William Marks recalled Smith's acknowledgment of polygamy's existence, with the Mormon leader proclaiming it a "cursed doctrine" that would "eventually prove the overthrow of the Church" stating that "there must be every exertion made to put it down." According to Marks, Smith indicated his intention to "go before the congregation" of the church "and proclaim against" it and "prefer charges against those in transgression." But Smith was killed before he could act.[5]

More specific in linking Smith to the practice, was Isaac Sheen, editor of the RLDS Church's official newspaper, the *True Latter Day Saint Herald*, stating that the Mormon leader "repented of his connection with this doctrine, and said it was of the devil." Apparently seeking to atone himself, Smith in the words of Sheen "resigned himself into the arms of his enemies, he said he was going to Carthage to die. At that time he also said, if it had not been for that accursed spiritual wife doctrine, he would not have come to that. By his conduct at that time [Smith] proved the sincerity of his repentance, and of his profession as a prophet."[6]

Joseph Smith III, by contrast, sought to completely disassociate his father's involvement with polygamy. Immediately after becoming RLDS President in April 1860, Joseph III expressed "utter abhorrence" at the practice. He then stated:

---

2. As quoted in *The History of the Reorganized Church of Jesus Christ of Latter Day Saints*, 8 volumes (Independence, MO: Herald Publishing House, 1951), 3:215.

3. This according to Alma R. Blair citing sources contemporary to Joseph Smith's lifetime. See Blair's, "RLDS Views of Polygamy: Some Historiographical Notes," *John Whitmer Historical Association Journal* 5 (1985), 19.

4. As quoted in Richard P. Howard, "The Changing RLDS Response to Mormon Polygamy: A Preliminary Analysis," *John Whitmer Historical Association Journal* 3 (1983).

5. Letter from William Marks to Isaac Sheen, October 23, 1859, as published in the *True Latter Day Saints Herald*, January 1860, 22–23.

6. Ibid., *True Latter Day Saints Herald*, January 1860, 24.

I have been told that my father taught such doctrines. I have never believed it and never can believe it. If such things were done, than I believe they never were done by divine authority. I believe my father was a good man, and a good man never could have promulgated such doctrines.[7]

Some six years later, the RLDS leader stated emphatically that "Joseph Smith was not a POLYGAMIST in 1843 and 1844, as I have every reason to believe, from every proof that I have been able to gather." The younger Smith then rejected "the allegation that a Revelation was given in 1843 contradicting the Book of Mormon and Doctrine and Covenants." Dismissing its authenticity, he proclaimed it a Utah Mormon invention. The document in question "was not laid before any part of the church for SANCTION and was only told to a part for their *acquiescence*, Brigham Young having had it 'in his desk' under a 'patent lock.'"[8] In 1883 Joseph III once more denounced this "purported revelation" attributing its origins to "Brigham Young, alone." It did not appear "until eight long years after Joseph Smith was dead…No one else has testified to the genuineness of it…" with Young producing it only "after the long practice of the doctrine [of plural marriage] could not be further concealed or denied…"[9]

Directly contradicting Joseph III, was Isaac Sheen, who as early as 1860 affirmed that Joseph Smith Jr. produced a revelation in connection with "this [spiritual wife] doctrine." Ultimately the Mormon leader renounced the practice ordering "the revelation on that subject to be burned."[10] Seven years later the RLDS Church First Presidency and Twelve further acknowledged the existence of a revelation in considering the following: "Resolved, that we do not believe that the revelation, alleged to have come through Joseph Smith, the Martyr, authorizing polygamy, or spiritual wifery, came from God, neither do we believe that J. Smith was in any wise the author or excuser of these doctrines." The proposed resolution was, however, tabled when it failed to receive unani-

---

7. *True Latter Day Saints Herald*, May 1860, 103. The definitive work on Joseph Smith III, including an extensive discussion of the RLDS leader's vigorous efforts to disassociate his father from Mormon polygamy, is Roger D. Launius, *Joseph Smith III: Pragmatic Prophet* (Urbana and Chicago: University of Illinois Press, 1988). See especially, Chapter 9, "The Legacy of Plural Marriage," 190–246.

8. *True Latter Day Saints Herald*, August 15, 1866, 63.

9. *The Saints' Advocate*, July 1883, 348.

10. *True Latter Day Saints Herald*, January 1860, 24.

mous support. This was followed by a statement by Church President Joseph Smith III that its passage "would do more injury than good."[11]

Debate over the extent of Joseph Smith's involvement with plural marriage, including the question of a revelation, continued to divide RLDS leaders and spokesmen over the following decade. On one side was Joseph Smith III who waged a sustained campaign from the late 1870s on "to establish his father's innocence."[12] On the other was Zenas H. Gurley Jr., a member of the RLDS Council of Twelve, who openly criticized Smith's efforts, directly telling the RLDS leader that he, Gurley was "sore and chagrined at the attempts [being] made...to establish the innocence of your father touching polygamy, as though the work of God depended in any sense upon his innocence or guilt" concluding: "I believe firmly in your father's guilt and think it susceptible of proof, and have for years."[13] Joseph Smith III in response reaffirmed his contention that Joseph Jr. "was not the human author of that polygamic revelation, nor of Utah polygamy."[14]

Joseph III's efforts to disassociate his father from plural marriage were aided by his mother, Emma Smith Bidamon, who on two separate occasions declared that "her husband had not taught or practiced polygamy and that she had never seen a revelation revealing it."[15] On the first, in 1867, she was questioned by RLDS Church Apostle Jason Briggs, who asked: "Did you ever see any document...purporting to be a revelation to authorize polygamy?" She answered, "No, I never did." In response to a second question: "Did Joseph Smith ever teach you the principles of polygamy, as being revealed to him, or as a correct and righteous principle? She replied, "He never did."[16]

---

11. Minutes of the Council of Twelve, RLDS Church, April 9, 1867, Book A, 34 as quoted in Howard, "The Changing RLDS Response to Mormon Polygamy," 16.

12. Howard, "The Changing RLDS Response to Mormon Polygamy," 17.

13. Letter, Z. H. Gurley [Jr.] to Joseph Smith III, March 23, 1879, Community of Christ Archive, Independence, Missouri, as quoted in Howard, The Changing RLDS Response to Mormon Polygamy," 17.

14. Letter, Joseph Smith III to Z. H. Gurley, April 2, 1879, Community of Christ Archives, Independence, Missouri, as quoted in Howard, "The Changing RLDS Response to Mormon Polygamy," 18.

15. These words of Alma Blair in "RLDS Views of Polygamy," 20.

16. *The Messenger*, 1:23, as quoted in *The History of the Reorganized Church of Jesus Christ of Latter Day Saints*, 3:352. The definitive study of Emma Smith is Linda King Newell and Va-

Emma returned to the issue, once more, in 1879, shortly before her death. She was again asked: "What about the revelation on polygamy? Did Joseph Smith have anything like it? What of spiritual wifery?" Her response was both more detailed and nuanced. "There was no revelation on either polygamy or spiritual wives." She then added:

> There were some rumors of something of the sort, of which I asked my husband. He assured me that all there was of it was, that, in a chat about plural wives, he had said: "Well, such a system might possibly be, if everybody was agreed to it, and would behave as they should; but they would not; and, besides, it was contrary to the will of heaven."

But then she stated in more definite terms: "No such thing as polygamy, or spiritual wifery, was taught, publically or privately, before my husband's death, that I have now, or ever had any knowledge of." She then, however, added the following:

> At one time my husband came to me and asked me if I had heard certain rumors about spiritual marriages, or anything of the kind; and assured me that if I had, that they were without foundation; that there was no such doctrine, and never should be with his knowledge or consent.

She concluded, "I know that he had no other wife or wives than myself, in any sense, either spiritual or otherwise."[17]

Also affirming Joseph Smith's non-involvement with polygamy was a second family member, younger brother William, who responded to the direct question: "Did Joseph, the Seer, teach that polygamy was essential to salvation and a fullness of glory?" The younger Smith answered: "Joseph taught no polygamy—not to my knowledge."[18] And on a second occasion William Smith recalled, "We would as well cut off our right hand as to have taught that there was any legitimacy in polygamy, in the early days of the church."[19]

---

leen Tippetts Avery, *Mormon Enigma: Emma Hale Smith, Prophet's Wife, "Elect Lady," Polygamy's Foe—1804–1879* (Garden City, New York: Doubleday, 1984).

17. *The Saints' Herald*, 26: 289–90.

18. *The Saints' Advocate*, 1:61 as quoted in *The History of the Reorganized Church of Jesus Christ of Latter Day Saints*, 3:360.

19. William Smith, "An 13 April 1883 Statement in the Kirtland Temple," as quoted in *The History of the Reorganized Church of Jesus Christ of Latter Day Saints*, 3:360. William Smith's statements of denial must be characterized as both dishonest and disingenuous given his over- enthu-

A third member of Joseph Smith Jr.'s family, his sister, Katharine Smith Salisbury provided "testimony" concerning allegations of the Mormon prophet's involvement with "spiritual wives." She stated that she had "never heard him at any time mention such a thing as the plural wife system or order" adding that "I heard noting of such a doctrine existing until a year after his death." Concluding she stated "I certify that I know my brother had no wife except his lawful wife, Emma. He neither had any other wives nor did he advocate such a doctrine."[20]

As for the origins of polygamy, Joseph Smith III and others within the Reorganization "gave the honor to Brigham Young and his associates in the Twelve."[21] In support of this contention, RLDS spokesmen referred to an interview that Young had with Senator Lyman Trumbull of Illinois, as published in *Alta California*, a San Francisco newspaper, wherein the Utah Mormon leader allegedly stated that "polygamy, which you object to, was not originally a part of our system, but was adopted by us as a necessity, *after we came here* [to the Great Basin]."[22] The evolving RLDS position was "that polygamy was foisted on the Latter Day Saint movement as official doctrine" in 1852 when Utah Mormon leaders published Smith's alleged revelation on the topic.[23]

Critiquing both the veracity and contents of the "purported 1843 Revelation" were two important RLDS spokesmen, namely, Alexander H. Smith, the younger brother of Joseph III, and Jason Briggs, a member of the RLDS Quorum of Twelve. Alexander Smith in a nine page pamphlet entitled "Polygamy: Was It an Original Tenet of the Church of Jesus Christ of Latter Day Saints?" flatly stated "I do not believe that [Joseph Smith Jr.] ever received a revelation from God on the matter… It is evident that a supposed copy of a revelation" Smith continued "has

---

siastic embrace of the practice both during Joseph Smith's lifetime and following his death. For a good discussion of William Smith's active acceptance of polygamy, see: Kyle Walker, "William Smith's Quest for Ecclesiastical Station: A Schismatic Odyssey, 1844–93," in Newell Bringhurst and John Hamer, ed., *Scattering of the Saints: Schism with Mormonism* (Independence, MO: John Whitmer Books, 2007), 92–114.

20. *Saints' Herald*, April 13, 1893, 40:275 as reprinted in *The History of the Reorganized Church of Jesus Christ of Latter Day Saints*, 5: 207.

21. These, the words of Alma Blair in "RLDS Views of Polygamy: Some Historiograhical Notes," 21.

22. *Alta California* [n.d.] as reprinted in *True Latter Day Saints Herald*, 16:158.

23. As noted by Alma Blair in "RLDS Views of Polygamy: Some Historiograhical Notes," 21.

been palmed off upon the people [ie Utah Mormons] by a designing set of men, who have certainly lost the priesthood they once held and have made money and women their only pleasure, that they might gratify to the fullest extent lustful desires and wicked pleasures." He further dismissed the document in question as "a contradiction of the gospel plan of salvation, in as much as it purports to be a new and everlasting covenant..."[24]

Jason Briggs analyzed the revelation through a series of newspaper essays entitled "The Basis of Polygamy" published in *The Messenger*, an RLDS publication which he edited.[25] Briggs claimed to have "disposed of the authenticity of that document" as he termed it through a verse-by-verse critique of its contents. He then enquired "after its genuineness" stating that:

> It purports to have been given through Joseph Smith; which if true, our conclusions respecting its character would make him either the victim, or the instrument of deception and fraud. It must be remembered that its appearance, other than in some dark corner, if indeed there, was not until August 1852, over eight years after the death of Joseph Smith.[26]

In conclusion, Briggs labeled Mormon polygamy, itself "a 'cursed doctrine'; a fraud in its origin; false in principle; ruinous in practice; and founded in selfishness and lust; and only maintained by degradation on the one hand, and violence and despotism on the other..."[27]

RLDS efforts to undermine the veracity of the so-called polygamy revelation while at the same time disassociating Mormonism's founder from all aspects of polygamy, manifested itself in officially sanctioned church publications. Most prominent was the masthead of *The Saints'*

---

24. Alexander H. Smith, "Polygamy: Was it an Original Tenet of the Church of Jesus Christ of Latter Day Saints?" (Plano, Illinois: Reorganized Church of Jesus Christ of Latter Day Saints, 1871)

25. Jason Briggs, "The Basis of Polygamy: Examination of the So-called Revelation of July 12, 1843, *The Messenger of the Reorganized Church of Jesus Christ of Latter Day Saints* (Salt Lake City, UT), February 1875, 13–14; March 1875, 17–18; April 1875; June 1875. Shortly thereafter, the four newspaper articles were combined into an eight page pamphlet published under the title *The Basis of Polygamy: A Criticism upon the (so-called) Revelation of July 12th, 1843* (Plano, Illinois: The Herald Office, 1875)

26. Jason W. Briggs, "The Basis of Polygamy," *The Messenger*, April 1875.

27. Jason W. Briggs, "The Basis of Polygamy," *The Messenger*, June 1875.

Herald which carried two scriptural citations affirming monogamy while condemning polygamy and/or concubinage. The first verse drawn from the Book of Mormon proclaimed: "Harken to the word of the Lord: For there shall not any man among you have save it be one wife and concubines he shall have none."[28] The second, from the Doctrine and Covenants, stated "We Believe that one man should have one wife, and one woman but one husband. Except in case of death, when either is at liberty to marry again."[29] These two verses appeared on *The Saints' Herald* masthead from January 1860 until September 1927.[30]

Also the RLDS Church exonerated Joseph Smith Jr. from the practice through its official *History of the Reorganized Church of Jesus Christ of Latter Day Saints* authored by RLDS Church President Joseph Smith III and Apostle Heman C. Smith and brought forth in multiple volumes beginning in the late 1890s. The authors dismissed the July 1843 document "purporting to be a revelation given through Joseph Smith, which not only justified" plural marriage but also mandated obedience "under the pain of damnation…What is more astounding" is that these same Utah Mormons confessed to "practicing this doctrine at the time they denied it, thus convicting themselves of hypocrisy, lying and deceit." Given these circumstances, the Reorganization "questioned the genuineness and authenticity of this purported revelation, and has demanded the proof, contending that the statements of these self convicted witnesses are not sufficient to establish their affirmation."[31] Also dismissive of the revelation was Inez Davis Smith, a daughter of Heman C. Smith who in her one volume *The Story of the Church* stated that "Both Hyrum Smith and Joseph Smith gave their testimonies and both denied and branded as a lie that a revelation had been received by the latter providing for polygamy."[32]

Not surprisingly, leaders and spokesmen for the Reorganized Church manifested a sense of vindication following the 1890 Manifesto, whereby

---

28. Book of Mormon, Jacob, 2:36, Community of Christ Edition. In the Utah LDS edition of the Book of Mormon, Jacob, 2:27.

29. Doctrine and Covenants, 111:4b, Community of Christ, edition. This particular section was a part of the original Doctrine and Covenants, published in 1835, but removed by the Utah LDS Church in its 1876 edition, when Section 132 was added.

30. *The History of the Reorganized Church*, 5: 67.

31. *The History of the Reorganized Church*, 3:348.

32. Inez Smith Davis, *The Story of the Church* (Independence, MO: Herald House, 1934), 488.

Utah Latter-day Saint leaders declared their opposition to further plural marriages. Joseph Smith III through the pages of *The Saints' Herald* proclaimed the Manifesto "a remarkable event in the history of the Mormon people of Utah [that] demands more than a passing notice from us."[33] "We rejoice that" Utah Mormon President Wilford Woodruff "and the late conference over which he presided had the good sense to publicly and officially abandon polygamy" carefully adding that "we do not exult over their humiliation. On the contrary we shall be glad to see them and the people they represent return fully to" what Smith termed "the old paths, which is the good way, and find rest in their souls." Although the RLDS leader pointedly noted that "we have never doubted that the Utah Mormons would officially repudiate and put away polygamy, for the reason that it can not endure criticism in the light of the sacred books of the Mormons up to 1876, nor the authentic history of the church over which Joseph Smith the Seer presided up to the time of his death." The offensive practice, Smith further noted "stole 'privately' in among the Saints prior to August 29th, 1852 when it was forced upon the Utah Mormons by Brigham Young and his fellows..."[34] "The history of events" leading up to the Manifesto, itself "has shown that Pres. [Brigham] Young made a mistake in his 1852 declaration" that "a paper...was a revelation from God through Joseph Smith...authorizing and commanding the practice of plural marriage."[35]

Some four years later, RLDS leaders and spokesmen considered their position further validated in the wake of an initial favorable ruling in the Temple Lot Suit—a case which pitted that denomination against the Church of Christ (Hedrickite) for possession of the Temple Lot in Independence, Missouri. U.S. Circuit Court Judge, John F. Phillips made direct reference to the issue of polygamy and the LDS Church, even though the latter denomination was not a party in the Temple Lot Suit, itself. Specifically, Phillips' ruling stated that polygamy's "first appearance as a dogma of the church appeared in the Utah church in 1852." He concluded:

---

33. *The Saints' Herald*, October 11, 1890.
34. "Mormons Will Obey," *The Saints' Herald*, October 18, 1890.
35. "That Manifesto," *The Saints' Herald*, November 1, 1890.

The claim is made by the Utah Church that this doctrine is predicated on a revelation made to Joseph Smith in July, 1843. No such revelation was ever made public during the life of Joseph Smith, and under the law of the church it could not become an article of faith, until submitted to and adopted by the church. This was never done.[36]

The decision is an important one in that it holds that the doctrine of polygamy as practiced by the Utah branch was not sanctioned by the original church, and that the followers of Brigham Young have wandered away after false dogmas and doctrines asserted the *Kansas City Times*, concluding that "it was quite conclusively proven that the doctrine of polygamy had no existence until after the death of Joseph Smith."[37]

Nine years later, in 1903, Joseph Smith III publicly urged leaders of the Utah-based Latter-day Saint Church to expunge "the so-called revelation on plural marriage" from their Doctrine and Covenants. The RLDS leader provided a list of fifteen reasons why it should be removed, concluding with the assertion that:

> The document…never was sufficiently identified or certified. The connection of Joseph Smith with it has never been satisfactorily accounted for. We object further to its continuing in the book for the reason that as a whole it is out of character with the teaching of the Church during the time of Joseph and Hyrum Smith and the revelations received and acknowledged by the Church up to the time of their death.[38]

---

36. "Decision in the Temple Lot Case in the Circuit Court of the United States for the Western Division of the Western District of Missouri, Lamoni, Iowa," 49, as quoted in *The History of the Reorganized Church of Jesus Christ of Latter Day Saints*, 5:238.

37. *Kansas City Times*, March 4, 1894; as quoted in *The History of the Reorganized Church of Jesus Christ of Latter Day Saints*, 5:239–40.

38. Joseph Smith III, "Editorial: Why It Should Be Expunged," *The Saints' Herald*, December 9, 1903. Spokesmen for the LDS Church in rejecting this RLDS suggestion and defending the 1843 Revelation, avoided references to plural marriage in stating: "The assurance and expectation that the holy wedlock of the new and everlasting covenant with its sacred ties and family endearments, shall survive the tomb, exist beyond the grave, and form the beginning of a kingdom and a dominion in celestial glory that shall never end, are among the grandest beliefs and anticipations of the true Latter Day Saints, and they are embodied in the revelations that our would-be critics desire us to expunge from the book that contains some of the sublimest manifestations of the mind and will and purpose of God ever made known to man. We are not compelled to bow to such dictum, and people with ordinary sense will perceive the reason why," *Deseret Evening News*, May 16, 1903.

Concurrently, RLDS officials sought to further delegitimize polygamy in recommending the enactment of a U. S. Constitutional amendment prohibiting the practice of polygamy in all American states and territories. This was done through a resolution adopted by the RLDS General Conference in April 1902, and reiterated by that same body the following year. The resolution directed against what it termed "unlawful cohabitation" stated, "This repudiates the practice of living with more than one woman as wives at the same time."[39] Such RLDS actions were undoubtedly inspired, at least in part, by ongoing controversy relative to the Congressional hearings debating the seating of Utah Mormon Apostle Reed Smoot, recently elected to the United States Senate.[40] As for seating him, Joseph Smith III, in his role as *Saints' Herald* editor found no good reason to keep the Mormon Apostle from entering the Senate, given that "he is not a polygamist" with the RLDS leader stating that "To oppose Senator Smoot simply because he is a 'Mormon' smacks strongly of disregard of religious liberty."[41]

But at the same time, the *Saints Herald* used the occasion to restate its negative position relative to polygamy, itself, noting that:

> The advocates and practicers [sic] of plural marriage are in this senatorial examination being brought prominently before the American public and are being put on record…It is well enough for us of the Reorganized Church who have long been antagonizing the dogma of plural marriage and its practice by those advocating it in living, cohabiting with, and holding out to the communities in which they live their plural wives as wives…[42]

Joseph Smith III also availed himself of the opportunity to lambast "the so-called revelation on plural marriage" reiterating the arguments used in the past by various RLDS spokesmen affirming the document's spurious nature.[43]

---

39. *The History of the Reorganized Church*, 5: 579; *General Conference Minutes*, 1903: 616–17 as quoted in *The History of the Reorganized Church*, 6: 53.
40. For a definitive treatment of the Reed Smoot Case see: Kathleen Flake, *The Politics of American Religious Identity: The Seating of Senator Reed Smoot, Mormon Apostle* (Chapel Hill: University of North Carolina Press, 2004).
41. "Editorial Items," *Saints' Herald*, 25 February 2003, 1174.
42. *Saints' Herald*, 51:243 as quoted in *The History of the Reorganized Church*, 6:108.
43. "Editorial: Inconsistent Teaching—or Practice—Which?" *Saints' Herald*, March 30, 1904.

Some thirty years later, RLDS First Presidency Counselor, Elbert A. Smith, took leaders of the Utah Mormon Church to task in responding to a June 1933 LDS Church First Presidency statement also known as "the Final Manifesto"—a document condemning those Utah Mormons perpetuating the practice of plural marriage. Specifically, Smith characterized the statement as defending "the institution of plural marriage as of divine origin" for asserting that "its present practice [is] being prevented by human legislation and the pledge given when Utah was admitted as a State." Smith further added that RLDS Church spokesmen had "refrained from any extended discussion of this subject [plural marriage] for many years past, trusting that it might fade into oblivion and be forgotten, but it seems not to fade" noting that "individual members" of the LDS Church "persistently continue the practice." He then went on to lambast "the so-called revelation" or "section 132 of the Utah Book of the *Doctrine and Covenants* [sic] discounting, once more "its authenticity" with the long list of arguments used in the past.[44]

Meanwhile, debate and discussion continued among RLDS leaders and spokesmen over the precise date of polygamy's origins, including Joseph Smith's role in producing a revelation. Heman C. Smith, in a 1900 article was willing to entertain the possibility of a somewhat earlier date for the introduction of plural marriage, stating "polygamy and spiritual wifery were confined for at least three years after the death of Joseph Smith...inculcated [by] the Quorum of Twelve over which Brigham Young presided."[45] Also questioning Joseph Smith's complete innocence were others associated with the RLDS Church who expressed stronger doubts concerning the "official" church position. One-time RLDS Church stalwart, Jason Briggs, provided an 1888 recollection, completely at odds with his earlier position, frankly stating:

> I was at Nauvoo in 1843 the year it was found necessary to legalize polygamy by a revelation. No, I have no doubt as to the authorship of that revelation of July 12, 1843. It has all the ear marks necessary

---

44. Elbert A. Smith, "Utah Mormon Polygamy: Its Origin and Present Status," *Saints' Herald*, September 5, 1933. Italics in the original.

45. Heman C. Smith, "The Factions of Polygamy and Spiritual Wifery" (February 21, 1900), 9 as quoted in Alma Blair, "RLDS Views of Polygamy: Some Historiograhical Notes," 21.

to identify it as the production of the mouth piece of those days [i.e., Joseph Smith]!⁴⁶

A second RLDS member, James Whitehead recalled Smith's role in producing a revelation, specifically "a short document permitting couples already married to be sealed to each other to be sealed for eternity." The statement in question, Whitehead, carefully added, "had nothing to do with marriage in this life…it was this revelation Emma burned, not the Utah perversion."⁴⁷

Such debate and discussion continued into the twentieth century, pervading the highest councils of RLDS Church leadership. In 1934 RLDS Quorum of the Twelve President Paul M. Hanson brought to the attention of then-Church President Frederick M. Smith and his younger brother Israel A. Smith the fact of Joseph Smith Jr.'s probable involvement with polygamy as reflected in recently discovered documents contained in the RLDS archives, specifically the *Nauvoo Expositor*, the *Nauvoo Neighbor*, and three letters written by William Marks "relating to his conversations about polygamy with Joseph the Seer just before his death."⁴⁸ Disclosure of this information, sparked "serious debate among RLDS leaders" carried on, unbeknownst to the larger Church membership.⁴⁹ Hanson expressed concern that such "ideas" as he termed them "will be picked up by the press, or some other publication and the church with its 'extreme position' held by nearly all of its representatives, the church would in my opinion, 'come out on the short end of the horn.' What to do in the matter is a very difficult thing to know, considering all of the circumstances." He then concluded: "No one is benefited by evading the truth, however. The question is—what is truth?"⁵⁰ Hanson pushed his fellow apostles within the Quorum of the Twelve "to formu-

---

46. Jason W. Briggs to J. T. Clark, 13 February 1888. Printed in *The Return* 4:21 (December 1, 1895), 3.

47. These the words of Alma Blair in "RLDS Views of Polygamy," 21. Blair in a footnote states that "earlier, James Whitehead had told W. W. Blair that "Joseph Smith, Jr. had taught and practiced polygamy" giving as a reference remarks given to W. W. Blair and contained in W. W. Blair Journal, June 17, 1874, 13, Community of Christ Archives.

48. As quoted in Norma Derry Hiles, *Gentle Monarch: The Presidency of Israel A. Smith* (Independence, MO: Herald House, 1991), 86.

49. David J. Howlett, "Remembering Polygamy: The RLDS Church and American Spiritual Transformation in the Late Twentieth Century," *John Whitmer Historical Association Journal*, 24, 2004, 152; Hales, *Gentle Monarch*, 85–9.

50. As quoted in Hiles, *Gentle Monarch*, 87.

late a policy for the church to adopt in response to the issue of polygamy, which remained a contentious issue out in the field."⁵¹

All of this, notwithstanding, RLDS leaders chose to uphold the church's long-standing position affirming the "innocence" of Joseph Smith vis-à-vis plural marriage. Particularly vigorous in this regard was Israel Smith, a grandson of Joseph Smith and lawyer by training, destined to become RLDS President in 1946. In a 1941 interview with the *San Diego Union*, the RLDS leader stated unequivocally, "Joseph Smith never sanctioned polygamy and never practiced it."⁵² As noted by one scholar, Israel Smith "like his father, Joseph Smith III tied the truthfulness of the Restoration message to the veracity and integrity of its founder." For Israel, "polygamy was unthinkably evil and, therefore, could not ever be connected to God's anointed, faithful prophet Joseph Smith, Jr."⁵³

In the mid-1940s Israel Smith vigorously asserted Joseph Smith Jr.'s noninvolvement with polygamy in a series of articles entitled "The Origin of 'Mormon' Polygamy" published in the *Saints' Herald*. Smith revisited many of the arguments made by earlier RLDS leaders and spokesmen. In his first article published in August 1945, Smith argued that "Brigham Young and [his] associates" did not "began the practice of polygamy" until "after the death of Joseph Smith" and only then "without semblance of church authorization of assent." The RLDS leader went on to characterize the revelation attributed to his grandfather a spurious document "conceived in a dark corner" to justify a practice "practiced in breathless secrecy, apologized for by leaders" of the Utah Mormon Church "whose statements are not only in conflict with themselves but misrepresentations of facts…"⁵⁴ In his second article published the following month, Israel Smith refuted Utah Mormon claims that "Joseph Smith received the alleged revelation on polygamy" the RLDS leader basing his assertion on statements that Joseph and Hyrum Smith made "in their own defense" before the Nauvoo City Council in June 1844 concluding that

---

51. As quoted by Hiles, *Gentle Monarch*, 103.
52. *The San Diego Union*, August 23, 1941 as quoted in Hiles, *Gentle Monarch*, 100.
53. Quoting David J. Howlett in "Remembering Polygamy," 152–53.
54. Israel A. Smith, "The Origin of 'Mormon' Polygamy," Part I, *Saints Herald*, August 25, 1945, 12–13.

"if he [Joseph Smith] spoke the truth upon [that] occasion...than the Mormons in Utah have grossly and foully misrepresented him."[55]

Later that same year RLDS leaders faced new questions concerning Joseph Smith's involvement in plural marriage in the wake of controversial author Fawn M. Brodie's *No Man Knows My History: The Life of Joseph Smith* published in November 1945. In researching her biography, Brodie had received significant help, specifically access to documents in the RLDS archives, such openness sanctioned by then-Church President, Frederick M. Smith, and his younger brother Israel Smith.[56] But these same RLDS leaders came to regret the help they provided, upon receiving a copy of the pre-publication galleys of Brodie's biography in September 1945, specifically objecting to the author's documentation of Joseph Smith's direct involvement in polygamy. Israel Smith scornfully dismissed her arguments stating that: "Brodie works hard to prove that there were bastard children born to Joseph...." Smith, sought to hold up the book's publication threatening legal action against both the author and publisher, Alfred A. Knopf. Drawing on his own legal background Smith suggested a "libel of the dead suit" asserting that Brodie's biography was "full of error and will greatly damage not only the Latter Day Saint organization, but also the family and descendants of Joseph Smith." [57]

Although Israel Smith did not pursue legal action, he took the lead in attacking the book in a series of three published articles. The first in the December 1, 1945, *Saints' Herald*, dismissed Brodie's biography as "another vicious attack on the church, its founder, and the Restoration...made by a renegade Mormon."[58] The second appeared one week later, in the same publication under the title "The Brodie 'Atrocity.'" It characterized the author as "entirely controlled by her deadly animosity against the church and its founder" labeling the biography "a very un-

---

55. Israel A. Smith, "The Origin of 'Mormon' Polygamy," Part II, *Saints Herald*, September 22, 1945, 12, 14.

56. For discussion of the whole Brodie episode as it involved the Reorganized Church, see: Newell G. Bringhurst, "'The Renegade' and the 'Reorganites': Fawn M. Brodie and her Varied Encounters with the Reorganized Church of Jesus Christ of Latter Day Saints," *John Whitmer Historical Association Journal* 12 (1992), 16–30.

57. Ibid., 22–24.

58. Israel Smith, "Apostates and Joseph Smith," *Saints Herald*, December 1, 1945.

worthy book."⁵⁹ Smith's third article, was actually a "letter to the editor" of *Time* magazine, which appeared some two months later in response to an earlier positive book review of the Brodie biography. Smith asserted that the Reorganized Church was "the only faction of the Latter Day Saints which retains the original doctrines" taught by founder Joseph Smith asserting that Mormonism's Founder "was not responsible for 'Mormon polygamy" and was not [himself] a polygamist." But then Israel Smith concluded his letter on a curiously ambiguous note:

> While it is true that I am interested in maintaining that [Joseph Smith] was an inspired prophet, yet I can and do say that If he was a polygamist, if he was responsible for the alleged document on polygamy…which we do not believe and which we emphatically deny; then he broke both the law of God and the laws of the land, and to that extent was a "fallen prophet."⁶⁰

In the wake of the controversy surrounding Brodie's *No Man Knows My History* and after Israel Smith became RLDS Church President in 1946, the new leader decreed that all "indefensible papers and letters," i.e., those asserting Joseph Smith's involvement with polygamy and contained in the church archives be "unavailable for researchers and historians."⁶¹ Concurrently, various RLDS Church spokesmen both echoed and affirmed the arguments of Israel Smith, RLDS Church Historian, Even Fry asserted that "Joseph Smith, the martyr, did not author or practice polygamy."⁶² Particularly emphatic in its arguments was a 1965 RLDS tract, authored by church spokesman, Aleah Koury, who stated:

---

59. Israel Smith, "The Brodie 'Atrocity,'" *Saints Herald*, December 8, 1945.
60. Israel Smith, Letter to the Editor," *Time*, February 25, 1946.
61. Hiles, *Gentle Monarch*, 140–41. There is however some disagreement concerning the access to such documents. According to David J. Howlett, "Once he became president of the RLDS Church [Israel Smith] locked away all controversial papers in a gigantic vault in the green-domed Auditorium." Whereas Norma Hiles states: "I never found any official policy which had been adopted concerning records and papers being withheld for study or research that were in the archives. However, it was an 'iron clad" rule for many years that papers and letters perceived to be too controversial were never available to church appointees, church officials, or researchers. They were literally locked away." Hiles, *Gentle Monarch*, 157, ff. 4.
62. These words of Alma Blair in "RLDS Views on Polygamy," 22.

The alleged doctrine and document on the plurality of wives presented by Brigham Young in 1852 contradicted the strict laws of morality revealed to the church through Joseph [Smith]. Joseph could not honestly sign a document bearing a doctrine that he had pronounced to be 'false and corrupt,' and contrary to the moral and constitutional law of the land, the church, and the teachings of the Lord, Jesus Christ.[63]

However, by this time, other scholars within the RLDS community began to view Joseph Smith relative to his involvement with polygamy in a more open light, inspired, at least in part, by emergence of the so-called "New Mormon History."[64] Significant in this regard was RLDS Church Historian, Charles A. Davies, who in two articles published in the *Saints' Herald* in 1962, reassessed Joseph Smith's role relative to plural marriage, albeit in a cautious fashion. In the first, Davies conceded that the plural marriage system in Nauvoo emerged "naturally out of the Saints' speculations about what the hereafter would be like." As for Joseph Smith's role it "seems evident" that the Mormon leader "had countenanced some concepts of 'sealing for eternity'...but this definitely was not plural marriage or itself." Davies then added: "All of this speculation about marriage in eternity was in error...those who believe this doctrine were wrong. If Joseph Smith was one of those he made an error. But it was not criminal."[65] In his second article, Davies focused specifically on Smith and the question of a revelation on polygamy. Davies did acknowledge that the Mormon leader "did indeed, have a revelation in 1843–44" but one limited to permitting already married couples to be sealed for eternity. Smith's revelation, had nothing to do with plural marriage, with Davies asserting that: "History does not impeach Joseph Smith in the matter of a document sponsoring polygamy...Human he was, but that he produced the document presented by Young in 1852 is unproved." As for that document presented by Utah Mormons as Joseph Smith's 1843 Revelation, Davies dismissed it with unvarnished scorn to be an "unau-

---

63. Aleah G. Koury, *The Truth and the Evidence* (Independence, MO: Herald Publishing House, 1965) 50.

64. For an overview of such scholarship identified with the "New Mormon History" as it evolved during this period see: Newell G. Bringhurst and Lavina Fielding Anderson, *Excavating Mormon Pasts: The New Historiography of the Last Half Century* (Salt Lake City, UT: Greg Kofford Books, 2004).

65. Charles A. Davies, "Spiritual Marriage," *Saints' Herald*, May 1, 1962.

thentic document" and/or "deliberately doctored publication" which if proved genuine would make "Joseph Smith a liar of the deepest hue." In general, Davies fell back on the long-held RLDS position that Brigham Young and not Joseph Smith was "the originator of polygamy."[66]

Some two years later, Robert B. Flanders, a professor of history at Graceland College, an RLDS institution, in his carefully researched *Nauvoo: Kingdom on the Mississippi* both implicated Joseph Smith in the origins of celestial marriage and discussed the 1843 Revelation attributed to him. Specifically Flanders stated that: "During the spring and summer of 1843 the doctrine and practice of celestial marriage was formally woven into the fabric of sacred observances" with Smith "publically [alluding] to the new rite several times in the period."[67] Flanders then discussed what he labeled "the document of July, 1843, on celestial marriage." While not directly linking its authorship to Joseph Smith, Flanders provided a detailed overview of its "unusual history" specifically that "it was not made public during the lifetime of the Prophet" with "its contents...known only in a limited circle" and not published until 1852. Flanders further stated:

> Since then there has been controversy between Utah Mormons and the antipolygamy Saints, notably the Reorganized Church over the veracity of the document. Until recently the popular and quasi-official view of the latter group has been that the document was authored in Utah and was a forgery, and that the abundant testimony to the contrary was part of a conspiracy to conceal the truth. Whether the manuscript was altered or not before its publication can probably never be known from documentary sources, if possibly biased testimony be excluded.[68]

In general given "polygamy's alleged revelatory origins" Flanders "carefully explained its circumstances but left room for those who denied its existence. Rather than arbitrarily placing the blame for polygamy on any

---

66. Charles A. Davies, "Section 132, Utah D.&C.: A New Look at That Document on Polygamy," *Saints' Herald*, June 15, 1962.
67. Robert B. Flanders, *Nauvoo: Kingdom on the Mississippi* (Urbana, Ill: University of Illinois Press, 1965), 272.
68. Ibid., 275.

one individual, Flanders addressed plural marriage as emerging from a secretive atmosphere of temple ritual starting with celestial marriage."[69]

The response to Flanders' book among the RLDS faithful was mixed. Flanders was informally approached by Graceland College President, Harvey Grice, in response to an RLDS First Presidency request that he, Grice "talk to" the author—a move coming in response to rumors that Flanders had "gone over to the Mormons." An "official response" came from a President of the RLDS Quorum of the Seventy who "impeached the book" with the pointed rhetorical question: "Now what are we supposed to tell our men out in Mormon country?" On the other side was an equally pointed comment from an elderly RLDS women, who told Flanders: "Thank God someone finally told the truth about Nauvoo!" adding "My grandfather was there, and he knew. They always said he was lying, but they were the liars!"[70] Although Flanders' book in the words of one scholar "did not represent the official position of the [RLDS Church]," noting that "many" church members "did not read it," but "those who did began to find the contours of the known land stranger. They began to raise questions that needed answers."[71]

Exerting an even more profound impact in breaking down the so-called "polemical wall on polygamy built by RLDS Apologists for over a century" was Lawrence Foster, a non-RLDS historian out of a Methodist tradition, whose scholarship culminating in his seminal book, *Religion and Sexuality*, convincingly linked Joseph Smith both to the origins of plural marriage and authorship of the 1843 Revelation.[72] Foster discussed Smith's bringing forth of plural marriage within the context of what he described as "Five revelations—and four other statements accepted as revelation by the Utah Church…given between January 19, 1841, and July 12, 1843. These provided the doctrinal basis for a new

---

69. These the words of Mark A. Scherer in evaluating Flanders' work in "'Answering Questions No Longer Asked': Nauvoo, Its Meaning and Interpretation in the RLDS/ Community of Christ Church," *John Whitmer Historical Association, 2002 Nauvoo Conference, Special Edition*, 76.

70. Such reactions recalled by Robert B. Flanders in "Nauvoo on my Mind," *John Whitmer Historical Association, 2002 Nauvoo Conference Special Edition*, 2.

71. David J. Howlett, "Remembering Polygamy," 155.

72. Ibid., 157.

worldview that made possible the introduction of plural marriage."[73] He directly linked the July 12, 1843, revelation to a number of important emerging doctrinal concepts, among the most essential being "eternal family relationships."[74]

But what most disturbed RLDS leaders and laypersons was Foster's disclosure of Smith's involvement in polygamy at Kirtland during the 1830s—a fact brought forth in a paper presented at the 1977 Meeting of the Mormon History Association. In attendance was RLDS Apostle, Bill Higdon, who, following that gathering, met with members of the RLDS First Presidency, and other church officers to discuss an appropriate response, specifically "to help RLDS members deal with what was felt might be a strong negative reaction to the implications of Foster's" findings.[75] Shortly, thereafter, the RLDS First Presidency, under the leadership of recently installed President Wallace B. Smith asked Church Historian, Richard P. Howard "to investigate the topic of polygamy in Nauvoo and report his findings."[76] Howard undertook careful, thorough research, which proceeded slowly, taking the better part of five years. Finally, in late November 1982 Howard presented his "carefully researched conclusions" to President Wallace B. Smith, whose response was mixed. Specifically the RLDS leader considered a section entitled, "The common sense argument about Joseph Smith's involvement in polygamy," to be "a little abrasive." The following month Howard's paper was further reviewed by the church's Joint Council—an eighteen member group consisting of the RLDS First Presidency, the Quorum of the Twelve, and the Presiding Bishopric. A second body "The Commission of History" composed largely of professional historians affiliated with the RLDS Church also reviewed the manuscript. In the wake of several additional meetings, these with members of the RLDS First Presidency in January, 1983, Howard acted on their recommendations and further revised his paper.[77] In retrospect, Howard characterized the final revi-

---

73. Lawrence Foster, *Religion and Sexuality: The Shakers, the Mormons, and the Oneida Community* (New York: Oxford University Press, 1981), 143–44.
74. Ibid., 142–46.
75. As quoted in Howlett, "Remembering Polygamy," 157.
76. Ibid., 158.
77. Ibid., 60–61.

sion, variously, as "heavily edited," "watered down," and "a painful compromise."[78]

As for the most appropriate venue for Howard to present his findings, there was also much discussion. Upon the recommendation of the RLDS First Presidency, it was decided that the best place would be the September 1983 meeting of the John Whitmer Association with concurrent publication of the essay in the *John Whitmer Historical Association Journal* under the title, "The Changing RLDS Response to Mormon Polygamy: A Preliminary Analysis."[79] Howard acknowledged that "Polygamy began at Nauvoo as a consequence of Mormon history filled with eclectic, speculative theological ferment." "It its first expression" Howard continued, "Mormon polygamy was meant for celestial life" but in time it "was seen by some" as justified as a "practice in this life also." Thus "some of the top Mormon leaders [began] to contract polygamous marriages in this life" as well.[80] Concerning the role of Joseph Smith, himself, Howard assigned him "direct responsibility for the eternal marriage covenant (celestial marriage—marriage for eternity), and for its logical consequence, celestial polygamy." But at the same time "only an indirect responsibility, for earthly Nauvoo polygamy in the 1843-44 period can be documented as attributable to Joseph Smith Jr."[81]

Not addressed by Howard's formal John Whitmer presentation or published essay was the so-called "Foster thesis" asserting the beginnings of polygamy at Kirtland in 1835, specifically Joseph Smith's involvement with Fanny Alger. Howard, when asked directly about their relationship *vis-à-vis* the beginnings of Mormon polygamy, dismissed it as "just an adulterous affair."[82]

As for official RLDS response, the Church First Presidency issued a press statement "distancing itself" from Howard's presentation asserting that "the *John Whitmer Historical Association Journal* was not an official publication of the church, and its authors do not reflect official church

---

78. As stated by Richard Howard in e-mail communication to Newell G. Bringhust, July 3, 2010; and by Howard in e-mail to William D. Russell, dated August 24, 2002. The latter quote is in William D. Russell, "A Brief History of the John Whitmer Historical Association," *John Whitmer Historical Association 2002 Nauvoo Conference Special Edition*, 151.
79. Howlett, "Remembering polygamy," 161.
80. Richard P. Howard, "The Changing RLDS Response to Mormon Polygamy," 24.
81. Ibid., 25.
82. As quoted in Howlett, "Remembering Polygamy," 162.

positions."[83] Specifically the RLDS press release stated "The Church Historian, Richard P. Howard is recognized as a reputable and qualified Historian. As such his writings stand on their own merits."[84] Such official disclaimers, notwithstanding, Howard's article in the words of one scholar represented "the first public admission by any RLDS official of Joseph Smith's complicity in polygamy."[85] A second characterized it as "an important incident in the history of the RLDS Church" in that it "acknowledged the fact that the RLDS cannot excuse Joseph Smith, Jr. from involvement in polygamy. They can't blame it on Brigham [Young] anymore, after a century of accusations."[86]

Also reacting to Howard's article was Richard Price, an RLDS member and highly vocal dissident. Price, opposed to what he perceived as the Reorganized Church's excessive departure from traditional beliefs and practices, emerged as a principal spokesmen for the "Restorationist" or "fundamentalist" movement that split from the Reorganized Church.[87] Price vigorously rejected Richard Howard's assertion of Joseph Smith's involvement with polygamy presenting his views through a full-page advertisement in the *Independent Examiner* in October 1983 under the title "Polygamy: How the Latter Day Saints were Betrayed by Men Nearest the Prophet." Price did concede the existence of polygamy at Nauvoo, but asserted that it was not introduced by Joseph Smith, whom Price proclaimed "innocent" of all involvement. Rather it was introduced by other Latter Day Saint leaders who in Price's words "used" Joseph Smith's "name to cover their own sins." Those most responsible for the practice included John C. Bennett, along with certain individuals in the LDS Quorum of the Twelve, most especially Brigham Young.[88]

---

83. As quoted in Russell, "A Brief History of the John Whitmer Historical Association," 152.

84. *Independence Examiner*, October 8, 1983, 6c, as quoted in Howlett, "Remembering Polygamy,"

85. Quoting David Howlett, "Remembering Polygamy." 163.

86. Quoting William D. Russell, "A Brief History of the John Whitmer Historical Association," 152.

87. For an overview of Price and his career, see: William D. Russell, "Richard Price: Leading Publicist of the Reorganized Church's Schismatics" in Roger Launius and Linda Thatcher, eds. *Differing Visions: Dissenters in Mormon History* (Urbana Illinois: University of Illinois Press, 1994), 319–42.

88. Richard Price, "Polygamy: How the Latter Day Saints Were Betrayed by the Men Nearest the Prophet," *Independence Examiner*, October 22, 1983.

As for the so-called "Document of July 1843," Price acknowledged the existence of what he dubbed "a revelation on marriage" produced by Joseph Smith. However, following Smith's death "Utah Mormon authorities took the original or a copy of it, to Salt Lake—and later destroyed it." The reason for its destruction was because "it did not teach polygamy or celestial marriage! If it had taught either one, it would have been the most highly prized document in Utah today." In its place, a spurious document was produced and passed off as Joseph Smith's revelation mandating plural marriage, first revealed by Brigham Young to his Utah Mormon followers in August 1852.[89]

Some two years later, RLDS scholar Alma R. Blair, a professor of history at Graceland College, brought forth his own analysis, "RLDS Views of Polygamy: Some Historiographical Notes." Blair praised Howard for his "historical contribution" and "excellent narrative."[90] But then he suggested that Howard had not given "more credit to the possibility that Joseph Smith, Jr. was also, for a time, the supporter of earthly polygamy." Blair further asserted that in light of statements made by certain individuals who knew the Mormon leader, including William and Jane Law, William Marks, and Austin Cowles, "it would seem more might be made of [Joseph] Smith's involvement" in its practice and promotion. Blair then posed a rhetorical question: "Can we be certain Joseph Smith, Jr., did not have some second thoughts about continuing polygamy, if not for theological reasons perhaps for political advantage?" He concluded, "The roots and time of polygamy's appearance are not yet fully defined—nor is its character."[91]

Also reflective of a greater openness in discussing polygamy and Joseph Smith's involvement with it in the early church were two RLDS scholars who produced histories published under "official" church auspices during the decade of the 1990s. Paul M. Edwards, a direct descendent of Joseph Smith, and one-time director of the RLDS Temple School, in

---

89. Ibid. Price's newspaper article was reprinted in a pamphlet entitled *The Polygamy Conspiracies: How the Latter Day Saints Were Betrayed by Men Nearest the Prophet* (Independence, Mo.: Cumorah Books, 1984). A later elaboration of his arguments is contained in Richard and Pamela Price, *Joseph Smith Fought Polygamy*, Volume I, (Independence MO: Price Publishing Co., 2000).
90. Blair, "RLDS Views of Polygamy," 24.
91. Ibid, 25, 26.

Our Legacy of Faith asserted that "polygamy originated in the Nauvoo Church, 1840–44."[92] "The doctrine was kept as secret as possible, and what was known of Joseph's involvement caused considerable unrest" with Edwards concluding: "There can be little doubt that Joseph Smith, Jr., was aware of the existence and practice in Nauvoo."[93] Richard Howard in *The Church Through the Years* said that "Polygamy appears largely to have grown out of Nauvoo Mormonism's esoteric rituals designed to bind families together for eternity." He further stated that "The reality of secret polygamy in the upper levels of church leadership became public knowledge by early 1844."[94] Howard, however, avoided implicating Joseph Smith directly in its involvement and/or implementation, except in quoting and/or paraphrasing those individuals who knew and interacted with the Mormon leader during his lifetime, specifically William Marks, Issac Sheen, William Law, and Jacob Scott.[95]

More recently, both leaders and historians within the Community of Christ have manifested an even greater willingness to openly discuss Joseph Smith's involvement with polygamy, in all of its aspects. Particularly striking is W. Grant McMurray, President of the Community of Christ from 1996 to 2004, who in a lecture presented at the 2006 annual meeting of the John Whitmer Historical Association addressed this issue in a frank, forthright fashion. In presenting his remarks, the one-time Community of Christ leader called upon his fellow parishioners to free themselves from certain "mistaken ideas" concerning past history of the Reorganization. He then proclaimed that Joseph Smith did, in fact, engage in polygamy. McMurray conceded: "I don't think we will ever fully know the extent of Joseph Smith's involvement in the introduction and practice of polygamy. However, no credible historian is arguing today that he had no involvement whatsoever." Such denial in the past, McMurray lamented:

> became one of the two foundational issues from which the Reorganization shaped its identity. It was a part of the evolving theological

---

92. Paul M. Edwards, *Our Legacy of Faith: A Brief History of the Reorganized Church of Jesus Christ of Latter Day Saints* (Independence, MO: Herald Publishing House), 107.
93. Ibid., 109–110.
94. Richard P. Howard, *The Church Through the Years*, two volumes, (Independence, MO: Herald Publishing House, 1992), 1:192–93.
95. Ibid.

and cultural milieu of early Mormonism. We don't need to prove or disprove it, or to concoct revisionist theories like "serial adultery" or "ministerial abuse." We need only to say the Reorganization has never accepted it and waste not one further word in defense of our position.[96]

Also addressing the issue, albeit in a more oblique fashion is current Community of Christ President, Stephen M. Veazey in a 2008 presentation entitled "Perspectives on Church History." He frankly stated that: "Truth has nothing to fear from scrutiny" adding that "The 'apologetic' approach to church history—presenting our story in as favorable a light as possible—is not sufficient for the journey ahead. That approach does not evidence the integrity that must be fundamental to our witness and ministry." Seeming to allude to Joseph Smith, without mentioning him by name, Veazey confessed:

> Our history also includes human leaders who said and did things that can be shocking to us from our current perspective and culture. Historians try not to judge—instead they try to understand by learning as much as possible about the context and meaning of those words and actions at the time. The result is empathy instead of judgement. Our scriptures are consistent in pointing out that God, through grace, uses important people for needed ministry and leadership.[97]

Reflective of a greater willingness to confront the question of Joseph Smith's involvement in plural marriage is a recent book written by three historians associated with the Community of Christ, entitled *Community of Christ: An Illustrated History*. As authored by David J. Howlett, Barbara B. Walden, and John C. Hamer, this work frankly states that Joseph Smith "began to redefine marriage and family, itself" through the "practice [of] a form of polygamy, known as celestial or plural marriage."[98]

---

96. W. Grant McMurray, "'Something Lost, Something Gained': Restoration History and Culture Seen from 'Both Sides Now,'" *John Whitmer Historical Association Journal*, (2007), 27:53. Italics in original.

97. Stephen M. Veazey, "Perspectives on Church History," October 1, 2008 http:www.cofchrist.org/ourfaith/history.asp?pr=yes (accessed Sept. 1, 2010).

98. David J. Howlett, Barbara B. Walden, and John C. Hamer, *Community of Christ: An Illustrated History* (Independence, MO.: Herald Publishing House, 2010), 13.

Also dealing with the issue in a forthright manner is Community of Christ World Historian Mark A. Scherer who acknowledges Joseph Smith's active involvement in both practicing and promoting plural marriage. Scherer, places polygamy's origins in the 1830s, occurring in Kirtland, Ohio, and rooted in what he labels the Mormon leader's "indiscretion" with Fanny Alger and extending to other women, all this constituting what Scherer labels "ministerial abuse."[99] This, in turn, evolved toward "sacralization" of the practice by the early 1840s following the Mormon migration to Nauvoo.[100]

Concerning Joseph Smith's authorship of a revelation on the topic, Scherer states that "On July 12, 1843 the prophet allegedly pronounced a secret revelatory statement authorizing polygamy that admonished Emma to be faithful and true to her husband, and threatened her salvation." Thus Scherer acknowledges Smith's authorship, specifically that "Joseph wrote out the ten-page statement" and in quoting Smith's secretary William Clayton: "After it [the revelation] was wrote [sic] Presidents Joseph And Hyrum presented it and read it to [Emma] who said she did not believe a word of it and appeared very rebellious." In the end, Emma reluctantly went along with "the polygamous celestial marriage system" consenting to her husband's marriages to Emily and Eliza Partridge. In return "Emma was sealed to Joseph for time and eternity."[101]

In general, Scherer views plural marriage in a less-than-positive light, noting that it "was the only doctrine that [Emma] opposed." The polygamy issue, he asserts "took its toll on the Mormon movement" ultimately prompting Joseph Smith's "rejection of it once he saw the long-term damage it was wreaking on the movement." In conclusion Scherer states: "Because of this aberrant marital practice the Latter Day Saint tradition would carry these events of the Restoration Era as their burden of history."[102]

---

99. This term first used to describe Smith's actions in Mark A. Scherer, "As Neither Apologist nor Cynic: Filling in the Gap and Keeping the Theologians Honest," *Journal of the John Whitmer Historical Association*, 25 (2005), 8–9.

100. Comments contained in e-mail from Mark A. Scherer to Newell G. Bringhurst, July 14, 2010.

101. Ibid.

102. Ibid.

In conclusion, there is a clear irony in the current position assumed by the Community of Christ as contrasted with that of the LDS Church relative to Joseph Smith's involvement with polygamy including his bringing forth of the 1843 revelation on the "New and Everlasting Covenant." Specifically this involves a contemporary willingness on the part of spokesmen within the Community of Christ to assert a direct link between polygamy and celestial marriage, akin to that of nineteenth century LDS defenders of Mormon polygamy. Whereas current spokesmen within the LDS Church in discussing Smith's seminal revelation vigorously assert celestial marriage as a separate and distinct concept from plural marriage—a position analogous to that assumed by various spokesmen within the Reorganization throughout the late nineteenth century and into the twentieth.

Afterword

BY JESSIE L. EMBRY

IN 1976 I started conducting interviews with children of LDS Church sanctioned polygamous families for the Charles Redd Center for Western Studies, a research center at Brigham Young University. During the next decade the Redd Center conducted over two hundred interviews with these elderly people who grew up in Mormon polygamous homes. In 1987 I published *Mormon Polygamous Families: Life in the Principle* based on those interviews.[1] At the time, I believed I was writing the final word on Mormon polygamy. But I was wrong. Richard S. Van Wagoner's book *Mormon Polygamy* came out the year before mine.[2] And that was only the beginning of a flood of books on the Mormon mar-

---

1. Jessie L. Embry, *Mormon Polygamous Families: Life in the Principle* (Salt Lake City: University of Utah, 1987). The book was reprinted in 2009. Jessie L. Embry, *Mormon Polygamous Families: Life in the Principle* (Salt Lake City: UT: Greg Kofford, 2009).
2. Richard Van Wagoner, *Mormon Polygamy* (Salt Lake City: Signature Books, 1986).

riage practice that continues with this volume.³ Several other studies in process will continue to ask questions about Mormon polygamy.

This volume is the first in a series about Mormon plural marriage from Joseph Smith Jr. to the twentieth-first century. The articles tackle some of the most difficult questions regarding plural marriage: When did Smith marry his first plural wife and who was it? How old were polygamous wives in the nineteenth century? When and how did Smith receive the revelation about plural marriage? How did various Restorationist churches that trace their beginnings to Smith react to the revelation on plural marriage, known as Section 132 of the LDS Church Doctrine and Covenants? How did the revelation change Mormons' views of the family? Did any of Smith's plural wives have his children? Did the Mormons only practice polygyny (a man having more than one wife) or was there also polyandry (a woman having more than one husband)?

Do the articles in this book resolve the questions? Just as my book was not the final word on Mormon plural marriage, these articles do not provide complete answers. But they do provide alternative solutions. The essays in this volume reinforce my view that it will be impossible to completely understand early Mormon polygamy since it was practiced in secret from when it started to 1852 when the Latter-day Saints safely ensconced in Utah, made a public announcement. A decade later federal legislation made it against the law in the United States. From then until LDS Church President Wilford Woodruff issued the Manifesto in 1890, polygamy was practiced "on the underground" to avoid U.S. marshals. Plural marriage did not end immediately in the LDS Church. Mormon Church President Joseph F. Smith's 1904 Second Manifesto excommunicated members who continued the practice. The third volume in this series tells of those who continued to practice plural marriage, even though not sanctioned by the Church of Jesus Christ of Latter-day Saints. With this history of secrecy, Mormons did not establish rules of behavior like other cultures that have practiced plural marriage for generations. The authors demonstrate the problems in answering questions because there will always be disputes over what sources to trust.

---

3. Patricia Lyn Scott published a bibliography of Mormon polygamy in 1993. Patricia Lyn Scott, "Mormon Polygamy: A Bibliography, 1977–91, *Journal of Mormon History* 19:1(Spring 1993):133–55.

Even if these articles are not the final word, they do provide valuable insights. Don Bradley tackles the initial question of who was Joseph Smith's first plural wife. For years many scholars have assumed it was Fanny Alger. Bradley accepts that conclusion, but also shows how Smith's relationship with Alger might be considered an extramarital affair and not marriage. There are basically three positions that scholars can take regarding this issue: Smith had no relationship with Alger, he was married to her, he was only having an affair. Bradley completely rules out the first possibility, but some scholars still affirm there was no relationship. With Bradley's explanation of existing sources and conversations with others aware of the sources, I am more convinced that unless there is some totally unused document, scholars will not be able to answer the question of the first wife. Finding contemporary, reliable sources is very difficult.

According to Joseph Smith, God commanded him to marry plural wives. But what are the origins of the July 1843 Revelation affirming "The New and Everlasting Covenant"? And what has been its impact? Newell Bringhurst approaches these questions from both an LDS and RLDS point of view. Scholars have suggested that Smith wrote the final version when his brother Hyrum suggested that Joseph's wife Emma might accept the doctrine if presented with a revelation. Bringhurst summarizes these stories. He then outlines how the LDS Church used the revelation to focus on plural marriage and then switched the focus to eternal marriage. His essay on the RLDS/Community of Christ's views of Section 132 gives the same information from the Smith family's point of view. These two essays provide a new perception of LDS views of polygamy from a twentieth and twenty-first century point of view.

Whatever the circumstances surrounding the July 1843 Revelation, scholars have often explored how Mormons reacted to the thought of marrying more than one wife and the concept of eternal marriage. Craig Foster's article examines that question. According to Foster, early Mormons, especially those who had lost loved ones, rejoiced in the idea of family relationships continuing in the next life. Section 132 provided that hope. But Section 132 is also about plural marriage, and historian Lawrence Foster argues that polygamy moved the focus from the individual family to the community. It also strengthened kinship relations as Mormon leaders married members of other leaders' families. While Craig Foster makes an important argument about the role of eternal marriages and the developing Latter-day Saint understanding of family relationships, he ignores other possible underlying reasons for polygamy. On the other hand, he does deal with what people said and not the assumptions that Lawrence Foster makes.[4]

Mormon polygamy is especially troublesome because on the surface one can see events, but there are not sources to understand the motivations. The evidence seems to point, for example, that Joseph Smith married other men's wives and proposed to even more. So did Smith practice polyandry? The answer seems to be yes. Brian Hales outlines all of the possible polyandrous relationships. The "why" is almost impossible to solve. For example, was Smith only testing Heber C. Kimball's faith when Smith proposed to Vilate Kimball? That is what Smith said afterwards, but maybe he was serious and withdrew his plan when he saw Heber's and Vilate's reactions.

Craig Foster, Greg Smith, and David Keller's and Todd Compton's articles deal with another age old question. How old were Joseph Smith's wives? Clearly some of them were underage by twenty-first century standards. But were they the norm for the times? These two essays show that statistics are never the final word. Numbers may not lie, but how the scholar picks the numbers can. Foster, Smith and Keller argue that early marriage on the frontier was not unusual. Compton uses numbers from more settled areas to show that "early marriages" and "very early marriages" were not the norm. When I was researching Mormon polygamous families, a historian commented about all the underaged marriages. My unscientific sample did not reveal many fourteen-year-olds marrying in polygamy. Compton says that historian Kathryn Daynes found more, but he ignores that Daynes used a cohort of 14–20 years of age, a very long span in young girls' lives. While Daynes does mention there was a shortage of women of marriageable age, her figures show an average age

---

4. Lawrence Foster, *Religion and Sexuality: The Shakers, the Mormons, and the Oneida Community* (New York: Oxford University Press, 1981), 136, 139–40, 176, 198. Foster argues that polygamy was to control families (136), "strengthen kinship relations and social solidarity" (139–40), reinforce men's roles (176), and provide temporal support for families (198). In some ways Lawrence Foster agrees with Craig Foster when he writes, "Mormon religion really was about the family; earthly and heavenly family ideals were seen as identical" (239).

for monogamous marriages in Utah as 16.49 in 1857 and of plural marriages as 16.42 in 1860.[5] Daynes and Lowell (Ben) Bennion are looking for more numbers to answer the types of questions like ages of wives in Utah. But regardless of what they find there will still always be questions because there are cases where Mormon men married very young brides as plural wives.

Another persistent question is: Did Joseph Smith have children with his plural wives? While there are secondhand stories, there are no direct examples. Ugo A. Perego uses DNA samples to show there is no direct connection. But since having children shows sexual relations, many of those interested in Mormon polygamy will still have the question and hope for a descendant or two.

The essays in this book deal with a number of important questions. But where does the study of polygamy go from here? As I read through these essays, I wondered if scholars need to come up with new questions. Maybe there are questions other than when Joseph Smith married his first plural wife? How many wives did he have? How old were they? And how did people react? Some of those questions might be related to determining the basic motivation for the practice as attempted by Lawrence Foster in his path-breaking study. Another would be to compare Mormon polygamy to societies where men married more than one wife or had non-Victorian marriage practices. That comparison should include other communal groups similar to what Lawrence Foster did in examining the Shakers and the Oneida communities.

Those questions could be expanded to look at issues beyond plural marriage. How does Mormonism fit into the larger communal studies movement? For example, after the French Revolution many people focused on secular individualism. Communal groups like the Mormons, the Shakers, and the Oneida community saw greater strength in groups working together. According to Lawrence Foster, "The Mormons were considerably closer to the family ideals" in the United States than the Shakers and the Oneida community."[6] How did Mormons compare to other nineteenth century groups? Historian Mark C. Carnes feels that

---

5. Kathryn M. Daynes, *More Wives than One: Transformation of the Mormon Marriage System, 1840–1910* (Urbana: University of Illinois Press, 2001), 106–08.
6. Foster, 239.

Victorian males looked for ways to restore their position after the Industrial Revolution.[7] Did that idea impact Joseph Smith's introduction of plural marriage? While the sources do not readily answer these questions, rhetorical theories might be used to better understand what people were saying.

While I recognize the need for new questions, I am caught in the old trap. In *Mormon Polygamous Families* I asked the same questions that sociologist Kimball Young did in *Isn't One Wife Enough?*[8] But I believe that scholars will continue to just rehash the same information unless someone comes up with new questions. Then Mormon history could be "researched" and "reinvestigated" and not just "retold," defended, or attacked as Jan Shipps suggests.[9] Her idea was not new though. Historian Roger D. Launius has suggested that Fawn M. Brodie's controversial *No Man Knows My History* retarded the study of Mormon history because scholars either supported or refuted her claims about Joseph Smith.[10] In the same way, I believe that the study of Mormon polygamy needs to ask new questions. I should not have remade *Isn't One Wife Enough?* I should have come up with a new storyline.

I fear though that even if scholars come up with new questions, the old questions will continue to dominate, because as historian Thomas G. Alexander has pointed out, people are interested in sex and violence.[11] As a result, there will always be an interest and a market for books on Mormon polygamy. Volumes like this show the variety of opinions. There is no one easy answer.

---

7. Roger D. Launius, "From Old to New Mormon History: Fawn Brodie and the Legacy of Scholarly Anaylsis of Mormonism," *Reconsidering No Man Knows My History: Fawn M. Brodie and Joseph Smith in Restropect*, Newell G. Bringhurst, ed. (Logan, Utah: Utah State University Press, 1996), 214.
8. Kimball Young, *Isn't One Wife Enough?* (New York: Holt, 1954).
9. Jan Shipps, "Richard L. Bushman, the Story of Joseph Smith and Mormonism, and the New Mormon History," *Journal of American History* 94:2(September 2007), 516.
10. Launius, 195.
11. This quote from numerous personal conversations with Thomas G. Alexander over the years.

Appendix:
Joseph Smith's Plural Wives: Total Number, Reasons for, and Methods of Selection

THE TOTAL NUMBER of women to whom Joseph Smith was married has been hotly debated among various writers and historians, with extreme disagreement over the precise number. LDS Assistant Church Historian Andrew Jenson tallied twenty seven, whereas Smith biographer, Fawn M. Brodie, added twenty-one to Jenson's list for a total of forty-eight plural wives.[1] A significantly higher number was given by Mormon writer, Stanley S. Ivins asserting that Smith was married to some eighty-four women![2] Much more conservative was scholar Danel Bachman who identified just thirty-one spouses for the Mormon leader.[3] Similarly conservative, is Todd Compton, the foremost expert on the topic, who in his seminal study of Joseph Smith's wives, settled on just thirty-three women—a figure which we accept as most convincing.[4]

---

1. Special thanks to Suzanne L. Foster and Brian C. Hales for their help and advice in compiling this Appendix.
   Fawn McKay Brodie, *No Man Knows My History: The Life of Joseph Smith, the Mormon Prophet* (New York: Vintage Books, 1995), 457. On Brodie's handling of the plural marriage evidence, see Todd Compton, "Fawn Brodie on Joseph Smith's Plural Wives and Polygamy: A Critical View," in *Reconsidering No Man Knows My History: Fawn M. Brodie and Joseph Smith in Retrospect*, ed. Newell G. Bringhurst (Logan, Utah: Utah State University Press, 1996), 154–94.
2. Stanley S. Ivins collection, Utah State Historical Society, Box 12, Fd. Ivins list was reproduced in Jerald and Sandra Tanner, *Joseph Smith and Polygamy* (Salt Lake City: Modern Microfilm, n.d.), 41–41.
3. Danel W. Bachman, "A Study of the Mormon Practice of Polygamy before the Death of Joseph Smith," (Master's thesis, Purdue University, 1975), 112–116:
4. Todd M. Compton, *In Sacred Loneliness* (Salt Lake City: Signature Books, 1997). Differing with Compton are D. Michael Quinn, who in *The Mormon Hierarchy: Origins of Power* (Salt Lake City, UT.: Signature Books, 1994), 587–88, assigned a total of 47 wives to the Mormon leader; and George D. Smith, in his *Nauvoo Polygamy "...but we called it celestial marriage"* (Salt Lake City, UT: Signature Books, 2008), 621–22, was more conservative in his estimate of 38 women married to Joseph Smith. And Brian Hales in his own forthcoming study has calculated a list of some 34 women married to the Mormon leader which he divided into three categories:

Also puzzling historians are the reasons and methods used by Joseph Smith in selecting his plural wives. As with so many other aspects of his life, Smith's plural marriages produce more questions than answers. Nevertheless, one point that is clear about polygyny, as well as other aspects of early Latter-day Saint doctrine and lifestyle, is that Joseph Smith and the "early Mormons were not just Bible readers, they were living the Bible."[5] Smith and his followers literally viewed themselves and their lives in modern-day Biblical terms.

Perplexing are Joseph Smith's reasons and methods of selecting his plural wives. Did Joseph Smith follow Biblical practices in selecting his plural wives? Like the ancient patriarchs of the Old Testament, some of Smith's wives were related, being distant cousins, like Helen Mar Kimball, fourth cousins, twice removed; or Emily and Eliza Partridge, fourth cousins, twice removed; or Rhoda Richards, who was a fourth cousin; and Fanny Young Murray, who was a sixth cousin.[6] The blood connections, however, were much further than discussed in the Bible and probably had very little to do with the actual selection process.

That is not to say family connections, or at least the potential thereof, had nothing to do with selecting plural wives. These marriages appear to have been a conscientious effort to unite Smith to the families of certain individuals he loved and respected. In other words, some of Joseph Smith's marriages served "as a means of strengthening kinship relations" among selected followers.[7]

One way of describing these marriages would be as "dynastic" marriages. Among the more noteworthy dynastic marriages were Smith's marriages to the daughter of Heber C. Kimball, fourteen year-old Helen Mar Kimball, as well as to the older sisters of two other Mormon apostles, Willard Richards and Brigham Young, specifically, Rhoda Richards and Fanny Young Murray.[8]

Other important Latter Day Saints were linked to Joseph Smith through marriage. Specifically, Presiding Mormon Bishop, Newel K.

"time only" 3 women; "time and eternity" 18 women; and "eternity only" 13 women. Chart provided by Hales to the authors, September 5, 2010.

5. Compton, *In Sacred Loneliness: The Plural Wives of Joseph Smith*, 75.
6. Quinn, *The Mormon Hierarchy: Origins of Power*, 588 and Ancestral File.
7. Lawrence Foster, *Religion and Sexuality: The Shakers, the Mormons, and the Oneida Community* (New York: Oxford University Press, 1981), 139–40.
8. Compton, *In Sacred Loneliness*, 487, 497, 558, 609.

Whitney, whose daughter, Sarah Ann Whitney was married to the Mormon leader in 1842. William Huntington, a councilor in the Nauvoo High Council saw two of his daughters betrothed to Smith. Todd Compton also classified three additional marriages as dynastic: These included that of Smith to Flora Ann Woodworth, daughter of Lucian Woodworth, a close friend, architect, and construction foreman of the Nauvoo House; his marriage to Desdemona Fullmer, daughter of David Fullmer, a prominent church leader; and finally, the Mormon leader's liaison to Melissa Lott, daughter of Cornellius Lott—a leader of the Smith body guard and manager of his farm. All three took place in 1843.[9]

Unfortunately, Compton never adequately defined the term dynastic and his interpretation is rather nebulous. He is not alone. Other historians have used the term dynastic without adequately explaining the meaning. A common theme with those using this term was the desire of Joseph Smith's plural wives and their families to seal themselves to him in order to ensure their own eternal salvation and, in the process, achieving Smith's exaltation. Rex Eugene Cooper wrote, "The women sealed to Joseph Smith believed that by virtue of that sealing they would participate in his salvation in the celestial kingdom."[10]

But could there have been another reason for desiring to link themselves and their families to the prophet of the restoration? Could the decision also have been influenced by an intense love and admiration for their prophet? Could there have also been, given the new understanding of the eternal family or what Cooper calls a "kinship-based covenant system,"[11] a desire to unite themselves eternally in familial bonds with the man they loved and honored as a prophet of God?

The key definition of dynastic is "a sequence of rulers from the same family, stock, or group."[12] Rather than using this strict definition of "rul-

---

9. Ibid., 388–89. It has also been suggested that two other of Smith's marriages were also dynastic in nature, specifically, those to Emily Dow Partridge and her older sister Eliza Maria Partridge, given that they were the daughters of Edward Partridge, first bishop of the church, who served in that capacity until his death in 1840. Compton, *In Sacred Loneliness*, 396–456, discusses their lives and place in Mormon history.

10. Rex Eugene Cooper, *Promises Made to the Fathers: Mormon Covenant Organization* (Salt Lake City: University of Utah Press, 1990), 140.

11. Ibid., 108.

12. As found at Dictionary.com, http://dictionary.reference.com/browse/dynastic (accessed Sept. 12, 2010).

ers," perhaps Joseph Smith's dynastic marriages could have been the people with whom he was particularly associated because of ecclesiastical or community positions and, of course, the bonds of special friendship. These characteristics would be more in line with the actual meaning of the term "dynastic."

But there were obviously other reasons for Joseph Smith's selecting these women to be his plural wives. To believing members of the LDS and other restoration churches that accept Smith's plural marriage as a divine commandment, the obvious reason is he was divinely inspired to select these women to be his eternal wives. These reasons included, among other things, friendship, proximity, and assistance.

With that in mind, we have prepared a list of the plural wives of Joseph Smith and have suggested possible reasons for selecting these women to be his wives. While the women involved had varied and differing reasons for agreeing to marry the Mormon Prophet, there appear to be four primary reasons for entering plural marriage. These are as follows:

1. Assistance—Some women Joseph married were either widows or never had been married. While assistance was probably more spiritual than financial or material in nature, there were, nevertheless, some who needed such a marital connection to the prophet. A few women, for instance, were married to non-members[13] and they would have certainly been in need of spiritual assistance by being sealed to a priesthood holder.

2. Dynastic—Some marriages would be considered dynastic based on the official definition but with a twist as explained above. In order to be considered a dynastic marriage, the woman's family needs to have met at least two of three criteria. The woman's family would had to have been long-term friends of Joseph Smith and his family; the father, brother, or husband of the woman would had to have held an ecclesiastical position; or, the father, brother, or husband of the woman would had to have held a position (elected or appointed, actual or de facto) of prominence in the community.

---

13. See Brian C. Hales, "The Puzzlement of Polyandry" in this volume.

3. Friendship—There was a long-term friendship between the woman's family and Joseph Smith and his family but the family did not meet the other two criteria of dynastic marriages.

4. Proximity—A number of Joseph Smith's plural wives lived in or near the residence of the Mormon leader. Specifically a number lived in his home as maids or performing other types of service. There were also a few wives that resided in homes in which he stayed while traveling. These women, therefore, were in close proximity to the prophet.

Obviously, the selection process was not that simplistic and Joseph Smith's reasons for choosing the women in question were probably more complex and due to more than a single reason. With this in mind, more than one category may appear with the initial of the main reason or category capitalized and the initial of the lesser reasons or categories being small letters.

Wife's Name	Year Married	A	D	F	P	Comments
1. Fanny Alger	1834–35		D		P	Her uncle, Levi Hancock, became one of the Seven Presidents of Seventy.[1]
2. Lucinda Pendleton Morgan Harris	1838?				P	Joseph & Emma lived for a time in her house.[2]
3. Louisa Beaman	1841		D	f		Her brother-in-law, Joseph Bates Noble, was bishop of the Nauvoo 5th Ward.[3]

1. Quinn, 550, and "Fanny Alger," *Joseph Smith's Polygamy*, http://www.josephsmithspolygamy.com/JSWives/FannyAlger.html (accessed August 29, 2010).
2. Compton, 48, and Bachman, "A Study of the Mormon Practice of Plural Marriage Before the Death of Joseph Smith," 113, 333.
3. "Joseph Bates Noble," 2, http://www.xmission.com/~jatwood/JBN-1810/Noble,%20Joseph%20Bates-1810.pdf (accessed August 28, 2010).

Wife's Name	Year Married	A	D	F	P	Comments
4. Zina Diantha Huntington Jacobs	1841			f	P	She lived for a time in the Smith household and her brother, Dimick, was a close friend of Joseph Smith's.[4]
5. Presendia Lathrop Huntington Buell	1841	A		F		Her husband, Norman Buell, was "bitterly opposed to Mormonism."[5]
6. Agnes Moulton Coolbrith Smith	1842	A				As Don Carlos Smith's widow, this was a Levirate marriage.[6]
7. Sylvia Porter Sessions Lyon	1842			F	p	The Sessions family first met Joseph Smith in Kirtland.[7]
8. Mary Elizabeth Rollins Lightner	1842	a		F		Married to non-Mormon Adam Lightner, her family had known Joseph Smith since 1831.[8]
9. Patty Bartlett Sessions	1842			F	p	The Sessions family first met Joseph Smith in Kirtland.[9]
10. Marinda Nancy Johnson Hyde	1842		D	f		She was the wife of apostle Orson Hyde and had known Joseph Smith since 1831.[10]
11. Elizbaeth Davis G. B. Durfee	1842			F		She was an early friend of the Smith family and was used as an intermediary and confidant of potential plural wives.[11]
12. Sarah Kingsley Cleveland	1842	A			p	While John Cleveland, Sarah's husband was not a member, he was friendly toward the church. They lived in a house not far from the Mansion House.[12]

4. George D. Smith, *Nauvoo Polygamy: "...but we called it celestial marriage,"* 34.
5. Compton, 122–23.
6. Ibid., 145.
7. Smith, 32.
8. Compton, 207, and Smith, 36.
9. Smith, 32.
10. Compton, 228–29.
11. Ibid., 260–263.
12. Ibid., 271, 281.

Wife's Name	Year Married	A	D	F	P	Comments
13. Delcena Diadamia Johnson Sherman	1842	A	D	F		The widow of Lyman R. Sherman, one of the Seven Presidents of Seventy, she was also a sister of Joseph's close friend, Benjamin F. Johnson.[13]
14. Eliza Roxcy Snow	1842			F	P	Twice she resided in the Smith home and was, from Kirtland a friend of the Smith family. Her brother, Lorenzo Snow, who was called as an apostle in 1849, was also a close friend of Joseph Smith's.[14]
15. Sarah Ann Whitney	1842		D	f	p	Her father, Newel K. Whitney, was a general (later presiding) bishop, and her family were early friends of the Smith family.[15]
16. Martha McBride Knight	1842	A	D	f		She was the widow of Vinson Knight, a presiding bishop. The Knight and Smith families were early friends.[16]
17. Ruth Daggett Vose Sayers	1843	A		f		They were friends of Joseph Smith, although Edward Sayers appears to have not been a member. Both Edward and Ruth asked for her to be sealed to Joseph Smith.[17]
18. Flora Ann Woodworth	1843		D	F	p	Her father, Lucien Woodworth, temple architect, was a close friend of Joseph's and apostle Lyman Wight. He also acted as LDS ambassador to Sam Houston in the Republic of Texas.[18]

13. Ibid., 294–95, and Quinn, 580.
14. Compton, 309, 312–14.
15. Ibid., 342, and Quinn, 601.
16. Compton, 365, and Quinn 559.
17. Compton, 382–83, and Church of Jesus Christ of latter-day Saints, Church History Library, MS 17956, Andrew Jenson Papers [ca. 1871–1942], Box 49, Folder 16. Special thanks to Brian C. Hales for providing this information.
18. Compton, 389, and Melvin C. Johnson, *Polygamy on the Pedernales: Lyman Wight's Mormon Villages in Antebellum Texas, 1845 to 1858* (Logan, Utah: Utah State University Press, 2006), 4.

APPENDIX

Wife's Name	Year Married	A	D	F	P	Comments
19. Emily Dow Partridge	1843		D		p	A daughter of the late Edward Partridge, first bishop of the church.[19]
20. Eliza Maria Partridge	1843		D		p	A daughter of the late Edward Partridge, first bishop of the church.[20]
21. Almera Johnson Woodward	1843			F	p	Almera lived with her brother, Benjamin F. Johnson, with whom Joseph often stayed when traveling to Macedonia, Illinois southeast of Nauvoo.[21]
22. Lucy Walker	1843			f	P	Family members had worked for Joseph Smith and she lived in his household.[22]
23. Sarah Lawrence	1843				P	Both she and her sister lived in the Smith home.[23]
24. Maria Lawrence	1843				P	Both she and her sister lived in the Smith home.[24]
25. Helen Mar Kimball	1843		D		p	Daughter of apostle Heber C. Kimball.[25]
26. Hannah S. Ells	1843			f	P	She resided with the Benbow family and was good friends with the Woodruff family.[26]
27. Elvira Annie Cowles Holmes	1843			f	P	Her father, Austin Cowles, was a member of the stake high council but left the church over plural marriage. Her husband, Jonathan Holmes, was a bodyguard of the prophet.[27]

19. Compton, 396–97.
20. Ibid.
21. Ibid., 295–298.
22. Ibid., 461–63.
23. Ibid., 473–76.
24. Ibid.
25. Ibid., 486–87, and Quinn, 557.
26. Compton, 536–37.
27. Ibid, 543–51, and Smith 203–04.

Wife's Name	Year Married	A	D	F	P	Comments
28. Rhoda Richards	1843	a	D		p	A sister of apostle Willard Richards, she lived in Joseph Smith's Red Brick Store.[28]
29. Desdemona Wadsworth Fullmer	1843				P	She resided in the Smith household for a time.[29]
30. Olive Grey Frost	1843		D		P	A sister-in-law of Parley P. Pratt and close friends of the Sessions, she was in close proximity to Joseph Smith.[30]
31. Melissa Lott	1843			f	P	Her father managed Joseph Smith's farm outside of Nauvoo and she lived for a time in Smith's Nauvoo home.[31]
32. Nancy Maria Winchester	1843?			f	P	The Winchesters and Smiths were friends from the Kirtland period and she was one of the youngest members of the Nauvoo Relief Society.[32]
33. Fanny Young Carr Murray	1843	A	D			The older sister of apostle Brigham Young and twice a widow.[33]

28. Compton, 558 and Quinn, 575.
29. Compton, 580.
30. Ibid., 590–91.
31. Ibid., 597–98.
32. Ibid., 606–07; Smith, 209–10; and "Nancy Maria Winchester," *Joseph Smith's Polygamy*, http://www.josephsmithspolygamy.com/JSWives/NancyWinchester.html (accessed August 30, 2010).
33. Compton, 616–17.

About the Contributors

DON BRADLEY, currently a graduate student, is pursuing a degree in history and religious studies under the direction of Professor Phillip L. Barlow at Utah State University. He has written and researched extensively on Joseph Smith and polygamy, having articles published in various scholarly journals, including *Sunstone*.

NEWELL G. BRINGHURST, an emeritus professor of history and Political Science at the College of Sequoias in Visalia, California, is the author/editor of nine previously published books. The most recent was *the Mormon Quest for the Presidency* (2008) which he co-authored with Craig L. Foster. Bringhurst has served as president of both the Mormon History Association (1999–2000) and the John Whitmer Historical Association (2005–06).

TODD COMPTON, who holds a Ph.D. in classics from UCLA, is the author of *In Sacred Loneliness: The Plural Wives of Joseph Smith* (1997) and the co-editor of *A Widows Tale: The 1884–1896 Diary of Helen Mar Whitney* (2003). He also wrote *Victim of the Muses: Poet as Scapegoat, Warrior and Hero* (2006). He is presently writing a biography of Mormon Indian Missionary and explorer, Jacob Hamblin.

JESSIE L. EMBRY is the Associate Director of the Charles Redd Center for Western Studies at Brigham Young University. She is the author of ten books and over one-hundred articles on Utah and Mormon history topics. Among her relevant works are *Mormon Polygamous Families: Life in the Principle* (1987) and *Mormons & Polygamy: Setting the Record Straight* (2007).

CRAIG L. FOSTER, a research specialist in the LDS Church Family History Library, is the author of *Penny Tracts and Polemics: A Critical Analysis of Anti-Mormon Pamphleteering in Great Britain, 1837–1860* (2002), co-author of *The Mormon Quest for the Presidency* (2008), and author of *A Different God?: Mitt Romney's Presidential Campaign, the Religious Right, and the Mormon Question* (2008). Foster served as co-executive secretary of the Mormon History Association from 1995 to 2001.

BRIAN C. HALES, an anesthesiologist at Davis Hospital and Medical Center in Layton, Utah, has researched and written extensively on the topic of Mormon polygamy. Along with numerous articles, his two books include *Mormon Polygamy and Mormon Fundamentalism: The Generations After the Manifesto* (2006) and *Mormon Fundamentalism: Setting the Record Straight* (2008). He is currently completing a two volume work entitled *Joseph Smith's Polygamy: History*, and *Joseph Smith's Polygamy: Theology*.

DAVID KELLER, a faculty member at Utah Valley University in Orem, Utah, teaches computer engineering courses. He has been a regular contributor to the Bloggernacle since 2006, writing on the subjects of early Christianity, plural marriage, and other controversial aspects of Mormon history. As a hobby genealogist, he became interested in nineteenth century marriage statistics after discovering a possible thirteen-year old bride on his non-Mormon Keller line.

LINDA KING NEWELL, a writer, editor, and independent historian, has written extensively on the topic of nineteenth century Mormon polygamy. Most noteworthy is her seminal *Mormon Enigma: Emma Hale Smith, Prophet's Wife, 'Elect Lady,' Polygamy's Foe* (1985) which she co-authored with Valeen Tippetts Avery. She served as editor of *Dialogue: A Journal of Mormon Thought*, and Director of Special Projects at Deep Springs College in Deep Springs, California. She served as president of both the Mormon History Association (1996–97) and the John Whitmer Historical Association (1987–88).

UGO PEREGO, a senior researcher and director of operations for the non-profit Sorenson Molecular Genealogy Foundation in Salt Lake City, Utah, is also an adjunct faculty member of the Biology Department at Salt Lake City Community College. He holds a Ph.D. in Human Genetics from the University of Pavia, Italy. He has presented and published extensively on the application of DNA pertaining to population migrations and expansions, genealogy and ancestry, and historical events, including LDS history.

GREGORY SMITH studied research physiology and English at the University of Alberta, ultimately entering medical school, where he earned his M.D. degree. After completing his residency in family medicine at St. Mary's Hospital in Montreal, Quebec, he returned to Alberta, where he practices family medicine. His research interests focus on LDS plural marriage and on DNA and the Book of Mormon with the results of his research published in the *FARMS Review*.

Index

A

Abanes, Richard, 104
Adultery, 17, 25–36, 56, 57, 65, 66, 119, 122
Alexander, Nancy Smith, 41, 42
Alger, Clarissa Hancock, 18, 19, 23, 53, 244
Alger, Fanny, 4, 5, 14–57, 133, 154, 236, 277, 294
Alger, John, 44
Anderson, Robert D., 6
Anti-Polygamy Standard, 28
Arrowsmith, William, 106
Avery, Valeen Tippetts, 2, 62, 63

B

Bachman, Danel, 59, 62, 63, 64, 104, 122, 155, 290
Bailey, Calvin, 116
Bailey, Lydia, 147
Bartlett, Patty, 100, 108, 129, 138, 148, 150, 151, 154, 295
Beaman, Louisa, 5, 16, 17, 154, 294
Bennett, John C., 51, 278
Bergera, Gary, 25, 128
Blair, Alma R., 279
Bleak, James, 228
Bond, Charlotte, 30, 41
Bond, Lewis and Ezra, 30, 33, 34
Book of Mormon, 3
Bowes, John, 106
Braden, Clark, 27, 29, 30, 34, 40, 41, 51
Bradley, Don, 145
Bradley, Martha Sonntag, 103
Brewer, Fanny, 26, 30, 33
Briggs, Jason, 260, 262, 263, 268
Brimhall, George H., 112
Brodie, Fawn M., 2, 6, 60, 72, 102, 124, 153, 242, 246, 271, 272, 290
Brooke, John L., 9
Browitt, Martha, 140
Brunson, Seymour, 92
Buell, Norman, 107, 108, 110, 133, 151
Buell, Oliver Norman, 236, 245, 246, 247, 248
Buell, Presendia Huntington, *See* Huntington, Presendia Lathrop
Bullock, Thomas, 139
Bushman, Richard L., 2, 10, 61, 68, 95, 106

C

Cannon, George Q., 78
Carter, Marietta, 236
Charles, Melodie Moench, 65, 69
Christofferson, Todd, 185
Clark, J. Reuben, 84, 85
Clayton, William, 62, 73, 79, 128
Cleveland, John, 107, 109, 110, 151
Cleveland, Sarah Kingsley, *See* Kingsley, Sarah
Community of Christ, *See* RLDS Church
Compton, Todd, 2, 25, 26, 100, 101, 103, 106, 110, 114, 122, 126, 130, 131, 140, 143, 144, 147, 148, 149, 155, 156, 157, 180, 290, 292
Coolbrith, Agnes Smith, 154, 295
Cooper, Rex Eugene, 292
Cowdrey, Oliver, 14, 16, 17, 19, 20, 22, 23, 26, 27, 28, 30, 31, 32, 36, 42, 43, 50, 52, 53, 54, 57, 92
Cowles, Austin A., 73, 74, 76, 279

Cowles, Elvira Annie, 100 109, 141, 151, 154, 297
Creighton, Margaret, 236
Custer, Solomon, 15, 24, 26, 35

D

Davies, Charles, 273, 274
Davis, Elizabeth, 100, 109, 142, 150, 151, 154, 295
Davis, George T. M., 124
Daynes, Kathryn M., 8, 100, 219, 224
Delight, Carolyn, 236
Deming, Arthur B., 40, 51
Devoto, Bernard, 124
Dibble, Hannah Ann Dubois Smith, *See* Dubois, Hannah
Doctrine and Covenants Section 132, *See* Polygamy, Family, and RLDS Church
Dowen, J. C., 40, 50
Dubois, Hannah, 106, 236
Durfee, Elizabeth Davis, *See* Davis, Elizabeth
Durfee, Jabez, 107, 109, 110, 142, 151
Dutcher, Esther, 130, 136, 146, 151

E

Edwards, Paul M., 279, 280
Egan, Timothy, 184, 232
Ehat, Andrew, 101
Elders' Journal, 42, 52
Ellingson, Janet, 25, 26, 35
Ells, Hannah, 154, 297
Embry, Jessie, 65
Evans, John Henry, 83, 85

F

Family, concept of, 87–98
Ferris, Mrs. B. G., 124
Fischer, David Hackett, 88
Flanders, Robert B., 274, 275
Foster, Craig L., 134, 185, 186

Foster, Lawrence, 2, 6, 7, 67, 73, 100, 275, 276
Frost, Mary Ann, 236, 242
Frost, Olive, 154, 298
Fry, Even, 272
Fullmer, David, 292
Fullmer, Desdemona, 154, 292, 298
Fundamentalist Mormons, 84, 86, 227

G

Gordon, Sarah Barringer, 65, 71
Grant, Heber J., 84
Grant, Jedediah M., 99
Groesbeck, Jess, 7
Gurley, Zenas H., 257, 260

H

Hales, Brian C., 22, 25, 34, 70
Hall, William, 106
Hamer, John C., 281
Hancock, John Reed, 236
Hancock, Levi, 18, 19, 20, 26, 248, 249
Hancock, Mosiah, 18, 19, 20, 45, 53
Hancock, Mosiah Lyman, 236, 245, 246, 248, 249
Hansen, Klaus J., 8, 9
Hanson, Paul M., 269
Hardy, Carmon, 71
Harris, George, 107, 109, 110, 143, 151
Harris, Lucinda Pendleton Morgan, *See* Lucinda Pendleton
Hawley, John, 44
Higbee, Francis, 75
Hill, Donna, 2
Hill, Fanny, 29
Hill, Miss, 28, 29, 33, 54
Hitchens, Christopher, 156
Holbrook, Alfred, 41, 42
Holmes, Elvira Annie Cowles, *See* Cowles, Elvira Annie
Holmes, Jonathan, 107, 109, 110, 141, 149, 151

Holmes, Sarah Elizabeth, 236
Howard, Richard P., 276, 277, 278, 279, 280
Howlett, David J., 281
Huntington, Dimick, 121, 128, 137
Huntington, Presendia Lathrop, 100, 103, 105, 108, 121, 136, 151, 154, 236, 246, 295
Huntington, William, 292
Huntington, Zina Diantha, 100, 104, 105, 106, 108, 121, 129, 137, 150, 151, 154, 236, 295
Hyde, Frank Henry, 236
Hyde, John, 106
Hyde, Marinda Nancy Johnson, *See* Johnson, Marinda Nancy
Hyde, Orson, 107, 110, 124, 139, 140, 140, 149, 151
Hyde, Orson Washington, 236

I

Ivins, Stanley, 153, 290

J

Jacob, Udney Hay, 7
Jacobs, Henry B., 107, 108, 110, 137, 149, 151
Jacobs, Zebulon Williams, 236, 244, 245, 246
Jacobs, Zina Huntington, *See* Huntington, Zina Diantha
Jensen, Marlin K., 185
Jenson, Andrew, 15, 23, 114, 129, 145, 153, 290
Johnson, Almera, 154, 297
Johnson, Benjamin F., 20, 40, 44, 51, 55, 133
Johnson, Delcena, 154
Johnson, Marinda Nancy , 4, 100, 103, 106, 108, 138, 140, 141, 149, 150, 151, 154, 236, 295

K

Kelley, E. L., 29
Khoury, Aleah, 272
Kimball, Heber C., 231
Kimball, Helen Mar, 154, 231, 291, 297
Kimball, Sarah, 144
Kimball, Stanley, 116
Kingsbury, Joseph C., 109, 110, 130, 131, 132, 147, 149, 151, 180, 181
Kingsbury, Sarah Ann Whitney, *See* Whitney, Sarah Ann
Kingsley, Sarah, 100, 109, 133, 136, 151, 154, 295
Kirtland Temple, 14, 57, 91
Knight, Lydia Goldthwaite, 49, 116
Knight, Martha McBride, *See* McBride, Martha
Knight, Newel , 49, 116
Knight, Vinson, 146
Krakauer, Jon, 153, 155, 157, 232

L

Law, Jane, 74, 279
Law, William, 73, 74, 76, 279, 280
Law, Wilson, 73
Lawrence, Maria, 154, 297
Lawrence, Sarah, 154, 297
Lee, Ann, 8
Lee, John D., 139, 146, 229
Lightner, Adam, 107, 108, 110, 151
Lightner, George Algernon, 236
Lightner, Mary Elizabeth Rollins, *See* Rollins, Mary Elizabeth
Logue, Larry, 224
Lott, Cornelius, 142, 231, 292
Lott, Malissa, 127, 145, 154, 292, 298
Lyman, Amasa, 128
Lyon, Josephine Rosetta, 111, 112, 113, 114, 115, 117, 118, 236, 249, 250, 251, 252, 253, 255
Lyon, Sylvia Sessions, *See* Sessions, Sylvia

Lyon, Windsor, 107, 108, 113, 114, 115, 115, 117, 118, 131, 151, 249, 250

M

Marks, William, 73, 115, 258, 269, 279, 280
Marquardt, Michael, 131
Marriage,, age patterns, general, 158–162, 167–172, 174–175, 188–190, age patterns, Illinois area, 179–181, age patterns, Mormon conformance to , 175–179, age patterns, New England and Northeastern states, 191–196, early marriage in Nauvoo and Utah, 216–229, economic and cultural factors, 166–167, 172–174, legal tradition, 162–166
McBride, Martha, 146, 154, 296
McLellin, William E., 27, 28, 29, 33, 34, 45, 54
McMurray, W. Grant, 280
Millennial Star, 60, 120
Millett, Robert L., 95
Morain, William, 6
Moreton, Mr., 27, 33, 34
Morgan, Edmund, 88
Morgan, William, 5
Morse, Justus, 128

N

Nauvoo Expositor, 74, 75, 76
Nauvoo High Council, 73, 74, 117
Newell, Linda King, 2, 62, 63
Noble, Joseph B., 16, 17, 19, 128
Noyes, John Humphrey, 8

O

O'Donnell, Lawrence, 153, 156, 232
Old Testament, 4, 64, 121, 291
Olney, Oliver, 38, 39, 51
Oneida Community, 8

P

Partridge, Eliza, 35, 154, 291, 297
Partridge, Emily, 35, 127, 142, 154, 291, 297
Pearl of Great Price, 60–61, 79, 80
Pelton, G. S., 40, 51
Pendleton, Lucinda, 5, 16, 43, 44, 105, 143, 151, 154, 294, 100, 105, 109, 150
Penrose, Charles W., 120
Phelps, William W., 39, 124
Polygamy, 1890 Manifesto, 2, 80, 81, 85, 265, ages of plural wives, 152–154, Article on Marriage, 20, 21, 22, 37, 39, 47, 48, 49, 50, 55, celestial marriage, 67, 78, 85, 96, DNA analysis, 233–256, Doctrine and Covenants Section 132, 10, 59–98, 125, 257–285, dynastic marriage, 9, 228, 228, 231, 291, 292, 293, eternal marriage, 95, 98, eternity only sealings, 127–132, 135, 136, final manifesto, 84, 268, New and Everlasting Covenant, 77, 95, 98, 126–127, 283, number of wives, 290–298, offspring, 10, 232–256, patriarchal order of marriage, 7, 78, phases, 1, polyandry, 99–151, public disclosure of in 1852, 10, 77, reasons for entering, 8, 293–294, reasons for implementing, 5–10, second manifesto, 81, teenage brides, 152–183
Pratt, Moroni Llewellyn, 236, 242, 243, 245, 246
Pratt, Orson, 60, 78, 96, 119, 124
Pratt, Parley P., 124, 134, 242, 243
Pratt, Sarah, 105, 120
Price, Richard, 278, 279

Q

Quinn, D. Michael, 103, 126

R

Reed, Clarissa, 18, 236, 248
Reynolds v. U.S., 80

Rich, Charles, 226
Richards, Rhoda, 154, 291, 298
Richards, Willard, 128, 139, 231, 291
Rigdon, Nancy, 139
Rigdon, Sidney, 26, 39, 48, 76, 124
RLDS Church, 257–285
Roberts, Brigham H., 83
Robinson, Ebenezer, 21, 22, 38, 39, 43, 44, 51, 53
Rollins, Mary Elizabeth, 40, 51, 100, 103, 104, 108, 130, 133, 135, 136, 136, 143, 145, 151, 154, 236, 295

S

Salisbury, Katherine Smith, 262
Sargent, Harriet, 226
Sayers, Edward, 107, 109, 110, 129, 151
Sayers, Ruth Vose, *See* Vose, Ruth
Scherer, Mark, 281, 282
Scott, Jacob, 280
Sessions, David, 107, 108, 110, 138, 151
Sessions, Patty Bartlett, *See* Bartlett, Patty
Sessions, Sylvia, 100, 10, 108, 111, 112, 113, 114, 115, 116, 117, 118, 130, 132, 136, 147, 149, 150, 151, 154, 236, 249, 250, 295
Shakers, 8
Sheen, Isaac, 258, 259, 280
Sherman, Delcena Johnson, 146, 296
Sherman, Lyman R., 40, 51
Sherman, Royal Lyman, 146
Sjodahl, J. M., 83
Smith, Albert, 151
Smith, Alexander Hale, 238, 239, 262
Smith, Elbert, 268
Smith, Emma Hale, 4, 15, 17, 19, 20, 24, 25, 27, 28, 29, 34, 35, 47, 62, 63, 64, 73, 234, 238, 255, 260, 261, 262
Smith, Frederick M., 269, 271
Smith, George A., 119
Smith, George D., 2, 25, 72, 102, 103, 155, 156, 157
Smith, Gregory, 231, 232

Smith, Heman, 264, 268
Smith, Hyrum, 73, 74, 76, 77, 97, 116, 235, 239, 270
Smith, Israel, 270, 271
Smith, Joseph, *See* Polygamy
Smith, Joseph F., 81, 120
Smith, Joseph Fielding, 83
Smith, Joseph III, 27, 28, 29, 238, 258, 259, 260, 262, 264, 265, 266, 267, 270
Smith, Orrison, 244, 245, 246
Smith, Samuel, 239
Smith, Wallace B., 276
Smith, William, 261
Snow, Eliza R., 23, 24, 35, 46, 47, 54, 125, 154, 296
Snow, Erastus, 78
Snow, Lorenzo, 10, 228
Soby, Leonard, 73

T

Talmage, James, 82, 83, 84, 85
Taylor, John, 78, 97, 131
Thompson, Jane, 228
Toscano, Paul and Margaret, 69

V

Van Wagoner, Richard S., 20, 25, 106, 244, 285
Veazey, Stephen M., 281
Vermillion, Lulu, 236
Vogel, Dan, 121, 122
Vose, Ruth, 100, 103, 109, 129, 130, 132, 136, 146, 148, 149, 151, 154, 296

W

Walden, Barbara B., 281
Walker, Lucy, 144, 154, 297
Warsaw Message, 75
Warsaw Signal, 38
Webb, Chauncey, 15, 45, 46, 54
Webb, Eliza, 15, 19, 20, 30, 44, 45, 54
Wells, Daniel H., 130

Whitehead, James, 269
Whitmer, John, 39, 51, 52
Whitney, Newel, 128, 231, 292
Whitney, Sarah Ann, 100, 103, 109, 127, 130, 131, 136, 151, 154, 180, 181, 292, 296
Winchester, Benjamin, 23
Winchester, Nancy, 154, 298
Winters, Elizabeth, 4
Woodruff, Phebe Amelia, 228
Woodruff, Wilford, 78, 79, 85, 93, 97, 228, 265
Woodward, Almera Johnson, *See* Johnson, Almera
Woodward, Mary Brown Firmage, 103
Woodworth, Flora Ann, 145, 154, 292, 296
Woodworth, Lucian, 292
Woolley, John, 84
Woolley, Lorin C., 84
Wright, William, 141
Wyl, Wilhelm, 104

Y

Young, Ann Eliza Webb, 104, 139
Young, Brigham, 55, 77, 78, 93, 97–98, 119, 124, 125, 128, 138, 143, 147, 228, 231, 232, 258, 262, 265, 266, 270, 273, 278, 279, 291
Young, Fanny, 143, 144, 154, 291, 298

www.ingramcontent.com/pod-product-compliance
Lightning Source LLC
Chambersburg PA
CBHW070531160426
43199CB00014B/2241